TRIUMPH AND TRAGEDY

JOURNEYING THROUGH 1000 YEARS OF JEWISH LIFE

IN POLAND

JEWISH JOURNEYS CONNECTING GENERATIONS

WRITTEN AND COMPILED BY
JOEL PADOWITZ

EDITED BY
NAFTALI SCHIFF & TZVI SPERBER

3rd Revised Edition from 2012

© 2013 by JRoots.

All rights reserved

ISBN-10: 1937887065   ISBN-13: 978-1-937887-06-3

Compiled by Joel Padowitz

Email: info@jroots.org.uk

Tel: +44 (0) 20 8457 2121

Fax: +44 (0) 20 8457 2127

Web: Jroots.org.uk

Printed in Israel

This book is dedicated to

PEARL LAZARUS

a true eshet chayil
on the occasion of her 85th birthday

with love and dedication
by her husband and soul mate Bernhard,
together with their appreciative children;

and in memory of our family members
and all the other innocent victims of the Shoah.

"Remembrance leads to salvation, forgetfulness to exile."
—Baal Shem Tov

Dedicated to the memory of

Helen Lee (neé Richman) ע"ה

by her loving husband, children and grandchildren

Maras Kayla bas Avraham Abba

מרת קילא בת ר׳אברהם אבא ע"ה

Proud of her Polish roots and imbued with
a love of tradition and Yiddishkeit.

Forward looking and understanding the importance
of instilling these values in future generations.

May her memory be a blessing and source of
inspiration to all who knew her.

In tribute to the Rajchman Family הי"ד
Koprzywnica, Poland
Murdered Treblinka, October 1942.

ת.נ.צ.ב.ה

JROOTS MAP OF POLAND

POLAND

☆ Jewish centres of note

◎ Other major cities

☠ Nazi death camps

卐 Nazi concentration camps

⋰⋱ Poland's pre-WWII borders

0 mi   50 mi   100 mi

0 km   100 km

Baltic Sea

LITHUANIA

Kaliningrad   **RUSSIA**

Gydnia

Gdansk☆

Chelmno☠   Jedwabne☆

Lomza☆   ☆Tykocin

☆Bialystok

☆Aleksandrow

☠Treblinka

Berlin   ☆Plock   ☆Belz

Buk☆ ☆Poznan

WARSAW☆   ☆Siedlce

POLAND   ☆Gora Kalwaria

Lodz☆   Kock☆   Wlodowa☆

Piotrokow☆   Radom☆   ☠Sobibor

Kaziemierz Dolny☆   ☆Leczna

Majdanek卐☆Lublin   ☆Chelm

Wroclaw☆   ☆Krasnik ☆Izbica

Czestochowa☆   ☆Kielce ☆Opatow

Sandomirez☆ Szczebrzeszyn☆☆Zamosc

Pinczow☆   ☠Belzec

☆Bedzin ☆Dzialoszyce   Tarnograd☆

Dubrowa Tarnovska☆   ☆Lezajsk

Prague◎   Krakow☆卐Plaszow Rzeszow☆☆Lancut

Auscwitz-Birkenau☠卐   ☆Tarnow

CZECH   ☆L'vov

REPUBLIC   ☆Bobowa ☆Przemysl

Nowy Sacz☆

SLOVAKIA

AUSTRIA ◎Vienna ◎Bratislava

HUNGARY

SIR MARTIN GILBERT, C.B.E, D.LITT.

9 LYSANDER GROVE
LONDON N19 3QY

TO WHOM IT MAY CONCERN

Dear Sir,

It has become a truism to say that Jewish education is central to the maintenance of Jewish identity and the perpetuation of the Jewish people. But it is a truism that is both important and urgent. There is now limited time and opportunity for today's generation to be able to visit the sites of pre-war Jewish European life - and the places of destruction, resistance and survival – in the company of Holocaust survivors.

I am familiar with the work being done by Naftali Schiff and Zvi Sperber, who have joined together to launch an ambitious scheme to ensure that the torch of testimony is passed to the next generation. They are dedicated leaders with a wealth of experience.

For some time, JRoots has been organizing the "Journey to Poland: Past, Present and Future" trips that enable young British and American Jews to discover their roots, and to gain a greater understanding of Jewish life, fate and continuity. This has been done in a way that ensures maximum benefit. It is a remarkable feat of organization and planning, part of a sustained effort by JRoots to further Jewish education among young people.

I give this project my full support, am glad to be associated with it, and very much hope that it will be successful.

Yours sincerely

Martin Gilbert

---

office of the
CHIEF RABBI

It gives me great pleasure to associate myself with the work of JRoots. Their purpose is to educate and empower young Jews through meaningful travel experience and in the process allow them to enjoy and explore their Jewish culture, identity and heritage.

At present the emphasis of JRoots is in passing on the torch of Jewish memory and consciousness to the younger generation by way of journeys to Poland, often accompanied by Survivors. The JRoot's experience has proved to be a very powerful one that encompasses the past, present and future and challenges each participant to connect with their own sense of Jewish identity.

I wish JRoots continued success in their most important work.

With blessings and all good wishes

Chief Rabbi Lord Sacks
26 July 2010/15 Av 5770

Table of Contents

Dear Fellow Traveler,

Poland boasts one of the most fascinating and enlightening histories of the Jewish Diaspora. It also bears witness to the worst suffering, degradation and destruction humanity has ever wrought upon its own species. There will be moments during your travels when you experience soaring inspiration and pride. However, there will be other times when you visit scars painfully etched onto our collective memory that have never healed.

Your journey will pose challenges: some demanding intellectual integrity, others requiring emotional courage. There may well be tears. Yet, you may also be surprised to discover reservoirs of personal strength, trust and aspiration that you never knew existed—both in yourself and in others. Today, Jews everywhere struggle with their identity. Why be Jewish? What does it mean to "be" Jewish? How could such suffering ever have happened? Why the Jews? What would have been my response had I been there—as a Jew, or as a Gentile? What is the role of Israel? What is the future of world Jewry? What is my place in it?

To appreciate what it means to be a Jew requires an exploration that delves into our past, examines our present and visualizes our future. We are not here to judge; neither the past, nor the present—and certainly not each other. There are myriad feelings that may arise. Feelings are never right or wrong. They are simply yours—yours to keep to yourself or to share. As a disparate group of Jews coming from a wide range of religious backgrounds and cultural commitments, we will be reminded that as a People we are only as strong as our mutual respect allows. That which unites us on this journey is our common desire to understand our past. And perhaps, after having touched some of the richest, yet most bloodstained parts of our still unfolding historic tapestry, each of us will be that much more sensitive and aware of the choices we must make in order to weave our own future.

RABBI NAFTALI SCHIFF
EXECUTIVE DIRECTOR, JROOTS
NAFTALI@JROOTS.ORG.UK

RABBI JOEL PADOWITZ
GUIDEBOOK'S AUTHOR
JOEL@JROOTS.ORG.UK

TZVI SPERBER
DIRECTOR, JROOTS
TZVI@JROOTS.ORG.UK

Introduction to Triumph and Tragedy

Poland is Much More than a Graveyard

Jews today tend to associate Poland exclusively with the horrors of the Holocaust. Poland has been called "the world's biggest graveyard," because on its soil was where most of the systematic murder of our people during World War II took place. However, it is very shortsighted to view Poland as little more than the darkest corner of Europe into which the Nazis concentrated the Jews before exterminating them.

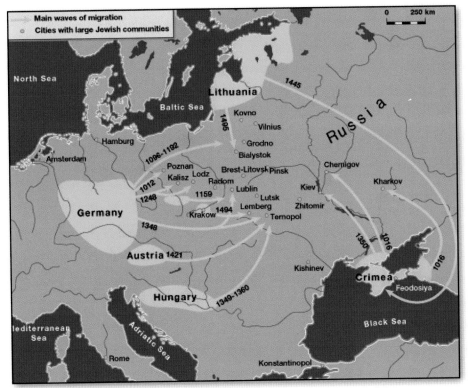

Map depicting the waves of immigration to Poland throughout the Middle Ages

Jews have lived in Poland for over a thousand years. In fact, for centuries, Poland was the most Jew-friendly state in Europe. Countless thousands of persecuted Jews throughout Christian Europe found refuge in Poland. For hundreds of years, Poland was the largest, most significant, most intellectually vibrant Jewish community in all of Europe. In fact, at its peak in the 17th century, the majority of the world's Jews lived in Poland, a land referred to in Latin as, paradisus Iudaeorum: Jewish paradise.[1]

Poland became a distinct political entity in 966 CE, and rapidly became a formidable kingdom in Eastern Europe. Interestingly, in the same year, the oldest known extensive account of Poland was written by a Jew named Abraham Ben Jacob. He was an international tradesman and diplomat on a journey from his native Toledo in Moslem Spain to the Holy Roman Empire and Slavic countries.

The first Jews to arrive in Poland were probably members of an international network of Jewish merchants known as Rahdanites who traded between the Christian and Islamic worlds during the early Middle Ages, traversing much of Europe, North Africa, the Middle East, Central Asia and parts of India and China.

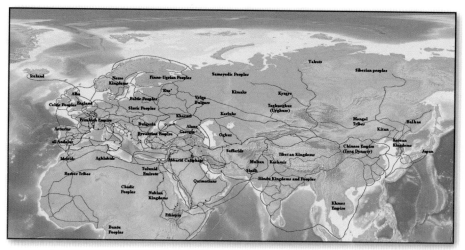

Map of the civilized world, circa 870 CE by Brian Gotts. Trade routes of the Radhanite Jewish merchants are shown in blue. Other major trade routes shown in purple.

Przemysl: The First Permanent Jewish Community in Poland

Though few records from the time remain, a Jewish source from the early 11th century mentions the town of Przemysl as a site along the trade route of international Jewish merchants. These were quite possibly the very first Jews to arrive in Poland. Since then, Jews have maintained an almost continuous presence in Przemysl for 900 years until the onset of World War II. When the Germans entered Przemysl, the Jewish population stood at around 24,000, some 30% of the city.

There was nothing outstanding about the Jewish community of Przemysl throughout the ages. Even serious students of the Holocaust may not recognize her name. Her story is like so many hundreds of others in the region; yet there is something extraordinary that we can extract from the life story of this otherwise ordinary town: She was there when it all began, and she was there at the bitterest end. Her story provides us with a sweeping overview of Jewish life in Poland. If we just lend an ear, we will hear a "firsthand" account of the life of Polish Jewry from the cradle to the grave.

Timeline Of Przemysl: A typical Jewish community of Poland whose story provides an overview to all of Jewish history in Poland. [2]

1050

A colony of Jewish merchants settles in Przemysl.

1332

Economic and legal rights are extended to Jews of the region.

1419

Official mention of "Jewish street" (Platea Iudaeorum) in Przemysl.

1542

Census lists 18 Jewish families living in Przemysl; 7 own houses.

Przemysl in the 16th century

1559

First legal regulation of the Jewish community in Przemysl. This ruling stipulated that whereas "Jews had been living on the Jewish street in Przemysl for a long time" but "they had not yet been granted a privilege which would allow them to settle permanently, nor guarantee them peace and security," they would now be granted the privilege of settling permanently in Przemysl.

1561

Przemysl synagogue is attacked by Polish burghers (members of the mercantile class) who resented Jewish economic competition.

1571

King Sigismund Augustus appeals to the municipal authorities and the residents of Przemysl to uphold the rights granted to Jews. A penalty of 6,000 Polish *zlotys* is to be imposed for violation of such rights.

1576

Privilege "ad bonum ordinum" by King Stefan Batory, grants Jews the right to elect their own religious and lay leaders and awards them full autonomy.

1592 Construction of a stone synagogue building begins in Przemysl, to replace the wooden structure.

1608 Economic decline of the city. Competition between Jewish and Christian merchants intensifies. A complaint is brought before the Przemysl municipality against the Jews, alleging that "by their subtlety and slyness" they constitute an economic threat to the burgher merchants.

1628 Attack on the "Jewish street." Private houses are demolished. The Jewish hospital and stores are plundered.

1630 A Christian woman, tortured to the point that she ultimately died, alleges Jews persuaded her to steal a consecrated host (bread used in a Christian rite known as the Eucharist). As a result, Moses (Moszko) Szmuklerz is imprisoned by municipal authorities, tortured and burnt at the stake.

1637 The "Jewish street" in Przemysl is almost completely destroyed by fire; however, the synagogue is spared.

1638 King Wladyslaw IV issues a privilege asserting the Przemysl Jewish community's right to rebuild after the fire. The king expresses his concern that Jewish rights are not being respected and that the royal treasury might suffer if the Jews are not able to rebuild. The privilege grants the Przemysl *kahal* (semi-autonomous Jewish governing body) hegemony over the surrounding Jewish orphaned communities. This allows the city *kahal* to raise money through tax collection.

1644

Jews own about 40 houses in Przemysl.

1645

The long-lasting economic conflict between the Polish and Jewish communities is normalized after years of disputes and prolonged litigation. A historic contract is achieved, regulating the boundaries within which Jewish merchants and artisans were to "ply their vocations." This agreement was in effect until the first partition of Poland in 1772.

1648 - 1649

The Chmielnicki revolt. Przemysl is rescued by Karol Korniakt, a nobleman from the neighbouring town of Zurawica. Korniakt helps the besieged town by mobilizing thousands of men. Jews participate in the defence of the city. The Chmielnicki troops retreat.

1656

King Jan Kasimir appeals to the Polish military to "have mercy upon the Jews and not oppress or harm them in any way." Apparently, Polish troops tended to "be a nuisance," particularly to the Jews.

1661

Desperate economic times for the Przemysl Jewish community. A king's decree allows the Jewish community to use the synagogue as collateral against which to borrow money.

LATE 1600S

The town's economic situation declines. The Jewish community is forced to borrow money from Polish nobility, which tries to recover their money using all available means. Jews are assaulted at market places, their merchandise is looted, and the Jewish quarter is destroyed by fire. Jews are subsequently relieved of much of their tax burden so the community can rebuild.

1681

King Jan III Sobieski extends debt repayment until 1692. The king further extends repayment dates to prevent wide-scale emigration.

1700s   The economic situation of the city declines further. Many Jews leave the city seeking relief from debt and severe taxation.

1746   Jesuit students plunder the Jewish quarter, looting Jewish homes. They break into the synagogue and demolish its interior. The Holy Ark and the Torah scrolls are destroyed. The synagogue archive, which includes important documents from the *wojewoda's* (governor of the province's) court, is also destroyed.

1752   Prince August Czartoryski, the Przemysl *wojewoda*, issues a decree for Jews to return to the city or face severe penalties.

1757   Przemysl magistrate allows Jews to settle and trade outside of the Jewish quarter.

1759   Trial in Przemysl of seven Jews from neighbouring Stupnica for the alleged ritual murder of a three-year-old child. The defendants are subjected to torture. Six are sentenced to death. Although one woman's life is spared, she is sent to city prison. Jewish population in the greater Przemysl area, including 33 neighbouring Jewish communities (*kahals*): 25,724.

1765   There are 2,418 Jews in Przemysl.

1772   First partition of Poland. Przemysl is incorporated into Austria as part of Galicia.

1867   Jews are granted equal rights to those of other residents of the Austro-Hungarian Empire.

1890	Przemysl population is 35,209 including 10,998 Jews. A Reform "Temple" is established.
1908	Przemysl has electricity.
1914	The city is besieged by the Russians in October.
1915	Przemysl surrenders in March. Much of the Przemysl fortress is destroyed. Soon after Przemysl's surrender, Jews are expelled from the city.
1916	Austro-Hungarian and German armies take over Przemysl.
1918	In October, the city proclaims independence. In November, Ukrainians capture part of the city on the right bank of the San River, soon to be taken over by the Poles.
1919	Przemysl becomes part of independent Poland.
1921	Przemysl population is 47,958, including 18,360 Jews.
1939	14 September: Przemysl falls to the Germans. 16-19 September: First arrests and executions of 102 Jews, mostly political activists and members of the Jewish intelligentsia.

This is a photograph of the interior of the main Synagogue of Przemysl, taken around the year 1900 when there were about 12,000 Jews living there

A memorial plaque was recently unveiled at the cemetery listing the 102 names.

21 September: The Germans leave the territory on the east bank of the San river and burn down the Old Synagogue and the Temple.

28 September: According to the Ribbentrop-Molotov Pact, the Soviet Army takes over the city. The state border is set along the San river, with the left bank under German and the right bank under Soviet control.

1940

April-May: Approximately 7,000 Jews are deported from Soviet occupied Przemysl to Eastern Russia.

1941

20 June: Przemysl's total population is 65,790, of which 16,500 are Jews (25% of total population).

22 June: Germany attacks the Soviet Union, breaking their Pact.

28 June: The entire city of Przemysl falls to the Germans. A week later, Germans demand that a Judenrat be established.

1942

20 June: Approximately 1,000 Jewish men are transported to the Janowska camp in Lvov.

16 July: Przemysl ghetto is closed off. Death penalty is imposed for Jews who illegally leave the ghetto and for non-Jews who try to help them.

27 July: First *Aktion* starts. The disabled, sick, elderly and children

1942 Con't

are taken to the nearby woods in Grochowce, where they are killed. Approximately 6,500 Jews are sent to the death camp in Belzec. On 31 July and 3 August another 6,000 are transported.

18 November: Second *Aktion.* 3,500 are transported to Belzec. The ghetto is downsized and divided into Ghetto A (for 800 workers) and Ghetto B (for 4,000 non-workers).

31 December: Total Przemysl population is 50,738, of which 3,030 are Jews.

1943

2-3 September: Approximately 3,500 Jews, who had avoided Nazi census figures by hiding in bunkers, are transported to Auschwitz. About 600 people from Ghetto A are sent to the labour camp in Szebnie.

11 September: 1,580 Jews are murdered in the courtyard of the Piramowicza school. Their bodies burn for five days. Two hundred and fifty people are kept alive to clean the area.

28 November: Some of the 250 "cleaners" are transported to Szebnie, and the rest are transported to Stalowa Wola or Auschwitz by the end of February 1944.

1944

27 July: Soviet Army re-enters the city.

We know precious little of how the first Jew in Przemysl lived. But we do know exactly how the last Jew of Przemysl to be killed in the Holocaust died. Based on the testimony of Yosef Buzhminsky at the Eichmann trial, noted historian Martin Gilbert retells the story:

...shortly before the Red Army entered Przemy'l, Yosef Buzhminsky saw, in a courtyard, "a little girl about six years old playing there. Gestapo and SS men arrived, surrounded the courtyard. It was a Polish family consisting of eight people. They began whipping the girl, and then they executed all of them right there in the courtyard." The Polish family had hidden the Jewish girl. It was for that "crime" that they and the girl were shot.[3]

This was the last synagogue built in Przemysl. It was completed in 1918. During the War, the German Army used it as a stable. Today, this is all that is left of the Jewish community of Przemysl. The building is now a public library.

Relating to National Tragedy

As is well known and documented, the Nazis and their collaborators murdered approximately six million Jews. Judaism teaches that each of these person's lives was of infinite value. The loss of just one life is tantamount to losing an entire world. Imagine for a moment the significance of losing one person you love. Now, multiply that by six million. The magnitude of the tragedy, the horror and the pain is simply unimaginable.

Nine Polish Jews who perished: Who would they have become?

While the many catastrophes that have befallen our people are undeniably upsetting—and so they should be—in most cases, it is a mistake to focus excessively on the evil that was perpetrated against us. Not because we should be forgiving, or even accepting of it—there is no excuse for hatred, let alone murder—but because there is relatively little to be gained on our part from harbouring resentment.

> "RESENTMENT IS LIKE DRINKING POISON AND WAITING FOR IT TO KILL YOUR ENEMY."
> – NELSON MANDELA

We should endeavour, rather, to appreciate the significance of our own loss, and to understand what we have to gain by uncovering our past. Therefore, before we explore the years of death in Poland, we will focus on the life that once was.

It would be both foolish and inhuman to attempt to estimate the "value" of the loss of Polish Jewry in terms of what they could have achieved for themselves or what they could have contributed to humanity. Again, every life is of infinite value, and each one that was cut short is an immeasurable loss. Nevertheless, in order to get an intuitive feel for what was lost to humanity as a whole, consider the following simplistic point: Three million of the Holocaust victims were Jews from Poland, about 90% of Polish Jewry of the time. In the fifty years following World War II (1946–1995), there were 165 Nobel prizes awarded. Polish-born Jews who survived the war, and who represent perhaps 1/10,000th of the world population, won nine of them!

Nine Polish Jews who survived: Look who they became.

Roald Hoffmann — Andrzej Viktor Schally — Georges Charpak — Shimon Peres — Menachem Begin — Joseph Rotblat — Isaac Bashevis Singer — Tadeus Reichstein — Shmuel Yosef Agnon

Roald Hoffmann	(b. 1937)	Winner of Nobel Prize in Chemistry	1981
Andrzej Viktor Schally	(b. 1926)	Winner of Nobel Prize in Medicine	1997
Georges Charpak	(b. 1924)	Winner of Nobel Prize in Physics	1992
Shimon Peres	(b. 1923)	Winner of Nobel Prize in Peace	1994
Menachem Begin	(1913–1992)	Winner of Nobel Prize in Peace	1978
Joseph Rotblat	(1908-2005)	Winner of Nobel Prize in Peace	1995
Isaac Bashevis Singer	(1902–1991)	Winner of Nobel Prize in Literature	1978
Tadeus Reichstein	(1897–1996)	Winner of Nobel Prize in Chemistry	1950
Shmuel Yosef Agnon	(1888–1970)	Winner of Nobel Prize in Literature	1966

Just imagine what the other 90% of Polish Jewry who did not survive the war could have contributed to humanity. The collective creative genius that was Polish Jewry achieved much that has shaped who we are today. Some 80% of Ashkenazi Jewry, or about two-thirds of all the Jews alive today, can trace their ancestry back to greater Poland. So now, let us turn back to the opening chapters of the story of Polish Jewry and see what we can learn about our past and about ourselves.

PART 1:
POLAND — ONE THOUSAND YEARS OF HISTORY

Jewish Origins in Poland (966–1347)

Perspective on Anti-Semitism

Before we can understand the significance of Poland to medieval Jewry, why Poland became the country of choice for so many and the reason for the vicissitudes of Jewish fortunes in Poland and the rest of Europe, we must understand the tenor of the times.

1st Century

In recent decades, Holocaust education has become a cornerstone of Jewish education. However, if we are to understand our Jewish heritage from a historical perspective, we must view it in the proper context. Trying to understand Jewish history—the longest running history of any people on the planet—through the perspective of a single event, no matter how significant, is a bit like trying to tell time by watching a clock's second hand.

11th Century

Although we don't like to admit it, at almost all times and in almost all places of our long history, anti-Semitism has been part and parcel of Jewish life. In fact, anti-Semitism is virtually as old as Judaism itself. It has been pointed out that the oldest written reference to the Jews as an independent people is when the Egyptian Pharaoh promulgated a decree to oppress them. The Talmud—the sprawling, 1500-year-old codification of collective Jewish consciousness—makes a similarly unoptimistic point regarding the inseparability of anti-Semitism and the Jewish experience. It suggests that Sinai—a name given to the mountain at which the Jewish nation was born—is etymologically related to the Hebrew word *sinah*, which means hatred. Not only was Judaism born at the foot of Sinai, but so too was anti-Semitism.

> "IN EACH AND EVERY GENERATION THEY RISE UP AGAINST US TO ANNIHILATE US."
> –PASSOVER HAGGADAH

The Holocaust may be unique in terms of its horrific magnitude and cold-blooded methodical approach; at no other time were millions of Jews systematically killed in the space of a few years. However, calamities in which enormous Jewish populations were massacred for political, religious or ideological reasons have, unfortunately, been all too common.

Year	Jews Killed (approx.)	Event	Location
70	1,100,000	Destruction of Jerusalem by the Romans	Israel
132-135	500,000+	Quashing of the "Bar Kochba" rebellion	Israel
1096	+/- 18,000	First Crusade destroys one-third of Jewish population	W. Europe
1146-48	100,000+	Almohad (Moslem) massacres	Morocco/Spain
1348-9	10,000 +	Poisoned-well libels lead to butchering of 350+ communities	W. Europe
1648-56	100,000+	Chmielnicki massacres	E. Europe
1932-38	100,000+	Stalin purges Jews in Reign of Terror	USSR (Russia)
1939-45	6,000,000	Nazi regime's systematic genocide	Europe

Sampling of Major Atrocities in Jewish History

In the first century, immediately before the birth of Christianity, there were about eight million Jews comprising approximately 10% of the Roman Empire. Projecting from those figures, one would expect the worldwide Jewish population today to be around 200 million. Instead, we find the current figure is somewhere between 13 and 14 million.[7] By the middle of the second century, the Jewish population, slaughtered by the Roman sword, had been halved to around four million. One thousand years later, because of relentless persecution, this number was quartered again to around one million Jews.[9]

In the five centuries from 1000 to 1500, during which the world's total Jewish population may never have exceeded one million, it is estimated that some 380,000 Jews were killed in anti-Jewish massacres, mostly at the hands of Christians. In percentage terms, the persecutions of the Middle Ages were comparable to the Holocaust, though they were spread out over 500 torturous years, rather than five unimaginable ones.

It is remarkable to consider the dedication of the millions of Jews over the millennia who sacrificed everything to hold on to their Judaism when they could have easily forsaken it and been "saved" by converting to the dominant religion.

Anti-Semitism in Europe During the Middle Ages

Simply put, it was not easy to be a Jew in Christian Europe during the Middle Ages. Under the auspices of the Church, local clergy throughout the region continuously spewed anti-Semitic rhetoric, seeking to incite hatred for Jews amongst their parishioners. Unfortunately, they were disturbingly successful.

Burning of Jews in Medieval Germany

The Crusades

The most ancient rationale for anti-Jewish defamation was the accusation of deicide—that Jews were collectively responsible for the death of the Christian god himself. It was from the deep resentment arising from the absurd but enduring condemnation of so-called Christ killers, that the persecution of Jews in Christian Europe emerged.

It was only a matter of time before the continual vilification of the Jews would prompt a violent outburst. The first major eruption of anti-Jewish activity in Europe occurred during the Crusades—armed pilgrimages intended to liberate the Holy Land from Muslim rule.

Pope Urban II preaches the First Crusade at the Council of Clermont

The First Crusade, which occurred in 1099, was preached by Pope Urban II who promised forgiveness for one's sins in the form of "indulgences" to any Christian who took the Crusader vow and set off for Jerusalem.

Pope Urban II advocated the necessity of violence against infidels in order to maintain the "Peace of God." Though he did not preach violence specifically

> "...THE SWARM OF DEICIDES, THE LAWLESS PEOPLE THE JEWS.... BUT GIVE THEM, LORD, THEIR RETRIBUTION BECAUSE THEY PLOTTED AGAINST YOU IN VAIN."[10]
> (TAKEN FROM THE EASTERN ORTHODOX / BYZANTINE CATHOLIC GREAT THURSDAY LITURGY.)

against the Jews, he assured abundant reward from heaven for all those who took up arms against heretics, and expiation from sin for all who died in the religious struggle. The Church's rhetoric and promises fomented a religious fervour that swept through Europe, mobilizing tens of thousands from all levels of society.

The Church's vitriol against the infidel, though primarily focused on Muslims, inspired outbreaks of vicious, bloody anti-Semitism. Many "good Christians" wondered why they should travel thousands of miles to fight Muslim non-believers in the Holy Land without first eliminating the Jewish non-believers closer to home.

The extent of the anti-Jewish sentiment amongst the Crusaders is apparent in the oath of Godfrey of Bouillon, a medieval knight and the leader of an army of the First Crusade, who swore "... to go on this journey only after avenging the blood of the crucified one by shedding Jewish blood and completely eradicating any trace of those bearing the name 'Jew.'"[11]

Though Godfrey was bribed by the Jews to refrain from violence, other crusaders were steadfast in their determination to eradicate the Jews. The murderous rampages that ensued in the German Rhineland have been called "the first Holocaust" by some historians. Perhaps a full third of the Jewish communities in the "Holy Roman Empire," the major centre of Jewish life in Christian Europe at the time, were massacred.

13th century depiction of Crusader atrocities

32

Blood Libels

Aside from deicide, the most common anti-Jewish canard of the time was the allegation that Jews used human blood, typically that of kidnapped Christian children, in their religious ceremonies. These false accusations of ritual murder have come to be referred to as "blood libels."

Although the oldest recorded blood libel is found in the writings of Apion, an early 1st century pagan Greco-Egyptian, no further incidents are recorded until the 12th century, when blood libels began to proliferate in Christian Europe. All together, there have been about 150 recorded distinct regional outbreaks of blood libels (not to mention thousands of rumours). Most of these reports of libel occurred in the Middle Ages, and in almost every case, Jews were ultimately

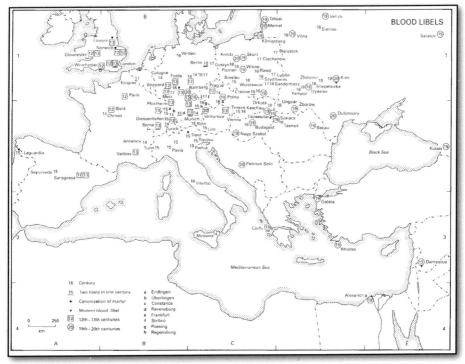

Map of historic blood libels

murdered, sometimes by mobs, sometimes following torture and a trial.

It is noteworthy that anti-Semitic blood libels still emerge to this very day. As recently as August 2009, Sweden's largest daily newspaper, the Aftonbladet, devoted a double-page spread in its cultural section to an article entitled, "They Plunder the Organs of our Sons," claiming that Israeli soldiers are abducting Palestinians to steal their organs! Similarly, libellous accusations in the 21st century have been promulgated in the Russian, Syrian, Iranian, French and Lebanese media.

A picture from Hartmann Schedel's "World Chronicle" from 1493 depicting the supposed kidnap and murder of two-year-old Simon of Trent. In 1475, his father alleged that he had been kidnapped and murdered by the local Jewish community. Fifteen local Jews were sentenced to death and burned. Simon was regarded as a saint, and was canonized by Pope Sixtus V in 1588. His status as a saint was removed in 1965 by Pope Paul VI.

Desecration of the Host

Another common calumny that circulated in the Middle Ages, which prompted widespread massacres of Jews and ultimately migration towards Poland, was known as the "Desecration of the Host."

The Catholic, Orthodox and Anglican Churches all believe that during the celebration called the Eucharist, the offerings of bread and wine (the "host") literally change into the body and blood of Jesus. Jews were accused of stealing consecrated bread and wine and desecrating them to re-enact the crucifixion of Jesus by stabbing or burning the host, or by otherwise abusing it.

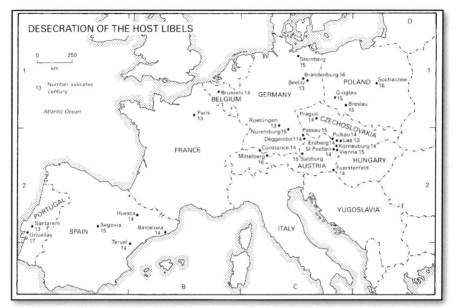

Map of locations of Desecration of the Host libels

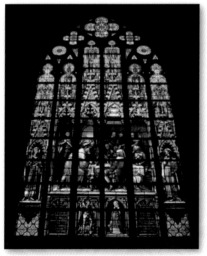

Cathedral Saint-Michel-and-Gudule of Brussels. One of the stained glasses with scene of the profanation of the alleged Hosts by Jews in 1370

Jews depicted torturing the Host, on a Belgian tapestry

Ostracism, Pogroms, Massacres

Virtually wherever Jews lived, they were ostracized, and local communities made it clear that they were undesirable and unwelcome.

A Brief List of Legal Actions Taken Against Jews in Europe During the Early Middle Ages

1181	England	Property confiscation
1195	France	Property confiscation
1215	Rome	Lateran Council of Rome decrees that Jews must wear the "badge of shame" in all Christian countries. Jews are denied all public sector employment and are burdened with extra taxes.
1215	Toulouse (France)	Mass arrests
1218	England	Jews forced to wear badges
1240	France	Talmud confiscated
1242	Paris	Talmud burned
1267	Vienna	Jews forced to wear horned hats

14th century requisite red hat for Jews of Rome

German Jewish hats on the Naumburger Lettner in the Naumburg cathedral, 13th century

Jewish knob-pointed hat, England, 13th century

36

From the 14th to 16th centuries, German Jews were required to wear a yellow badge of shame, often with the inscription "Der Juden Zeichen / Welches Sie ihren Kleidern zu tragen schuldig" ("The Jewish badge which they must wear on their clothing".)

Expulsions from cities and principalities were common. Sometimes the Jews were allowed to return after a few years. In other cases the expulsions were final. The Jews were expelled from England in 1290, France in 1306 and 1394 and Spain in 1492, as well as from many of the German principalities.

In response to the various accusations of ritual murder and Host desecrations, a wave of massacres began in 1298. Often collectively referred to by the name "Rindfleisch Massacre," these killings spread through 146 communities throughout the region, leaving some 5,000 dead. (The Crusades had already cost the lives of some 18,000 Jews, or about one-third of the entire population in the region.)

Pogroms were not limited to countries in Western Europe. From the Iberian Peninsula to the Holy Land, pogroms were a horrid fact of life for Jews whenever they found themselves under Christian rule.

Abbreviated List of Significant Pogroms

1096	Germany	First Crusade massacres
1099	Jerusalem	Jews burned alive by crusaders
1146–1147	France & Germany	Massacres of the Second Crusade
1189–1190	England	Mob attacks against Jews culminating in the Massacre of York, 16 March 1190
1236	France	Forced conversion/massacre
1263–1266	England	Jewish communities sacked by insurgents in the Baron's War
1298	Germany	The Rindfleisch Massacres: After the libel of Host desecration is perpetrated against the Jews of Germany, approximately 150 Jewish communities, are murdered by violent mobs
1320	France and Spain	The Shepherds' Crusade: 120 communities massacred
1336–1339	Germany	Armleder Massacres: violent gangs ravaged the Jewish communities of Franconia, Alsace and Bohemia
1348–1350	Europe	Throughout Europe, Jews were massacred in the wake of the Black Plague
1391	Spain	Mob riots lead to the murder of one third of the Jews of Spain and the forced conversion of another third

Poland was certainly not untouched by anti-Semitism. For example, in 1267 the Church Council of Wroclaw (Breslau) outlined a policy of isolation and segregation of the Jews. However, these discriminatory acts were mild in comparison to the violence Jews faced in other European countries.

Poland International Safe Haven

For some 700 years, with few (albeit heinous) exceptions, Jews enjoyed relative peace and prosperity in Poland. From the founding of the first Kingdom of Poland in 1025, Poland was one of the most liberal countries in Europe. It was in this atmosphere of tolerance that so many Jews would come to find sanctuary.

As a matter of general policy, even though the Church pushed for the persecution of Jews, the rulers in Poland usually protected them. Christianity had reached Poland scarcely a hundred years prior, in the year 966, and the Christian anti-Semitism, which would come to characterize the general European attitude toward Jews, had not yet taken as deep a root in the Polish national psyche. Thus, many Jews seeking asylum from France and Germany fled east, where Poland's more flexible rulers permitted them to settle throughout the entire country without restriction.

The first Jewish migration from Western Europe to Poland occurred at the very end of the 11th century. Among the earliest Jews to arrive in Poland were those fleeing from Prague's first pogrom in 1096. Jews from Bohemia (modern-day Czech Republic) as well as from Germany settled primarily in the Polish region known as Silesia, in and around its capital Wroclaw (Breslau). These Jewish immigrants usually engaged in trade, though some owned landed estates.

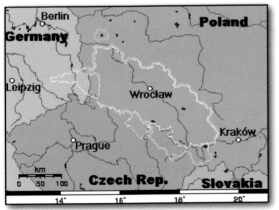

Historic Silesia outlined in light blue

Boleslaw III (1086–1138)

Migrations to Poland continued through the efforts of Poland's king, Boleslaw III, who assumed the throne at the age of sixteen and ruled from 1102–1138. Boleslaw III encouraged Jews to settle throughout Poland. He recognized the utility of the Jews in the development of the commercial interests of the state. Jews formed a middle class where the general population consisted of landlords and peasants and were instrumental in promoting the commercial interests of the nascent country. Jews quickly came to form the backbone of the Polish economy and were even employed in the 12th century by various princes and kings to work in the Royal Mint as engravers and as technical supervisors. Jewish integration developed to such an extent that certain coins minted in the region bore Hebrew markings.

This coin, minted during the reign of Mieszko III (1173-1202), bears an inscription written in Hebrew characters saying, "משקאקרל" meaning "Mieszko the King," in a medieval language known as Knaanic (or *Lashon Kenaan*). This language was a Hebraicized Slavic language, which had a relationship to 12th century Polish, similar to the relationship between Yiddish and German. Knaanic disappeared in the 16th century, supplanted by Yiddish. It is unclear whether a heavy influx of Jewish immigrants from German-speaking lands in the 15th century turned Yiddish into the primary language of Polish Jewry, or whether Knaanic is actually the direct predecessor of Yiddish which turned into Yiddish with the large influx of German-speaking Jews.

The General Charter of Jewish Liberties

During the 13th century, the Kingdom of Poland fragmented internally into a number of smaller provinces. The "core" province was known as Wielkopolska (translated as "Greater Poland," but which actually comprised only a single province in the larger Kingdom of Poland.)

In 1264, Boleslaw the Pious, Duke of Wielkopolska, issued a General Charter of Jewish Liberties known as the "Statute of Kalisz," which established a liberal legal position for Jewish autonomy and freedom in the province. The charter guaranteed protection under the law, including safety and personal liberties for Jews such as freedom of religion, trade and travel. The statute specifically granted Jews the right to conduct money-lending operations. It imposed heavy penalties for any vandalism to their cemeteries or synagogues. The act enabled a virtually autonomous Jewish nation to exist within Poland, including courts based on Halacha (Jewish Law) which had exclusive jurisdiction over Jewish legal matters.

Map of modern day Poland, and its provincial borders. Wielkopolska is marked in dark green.

Soon after the Wielkopolska charter, Silesia—the region of greatest Jewish settlement—followed suit so as not to lose their Jewish population. Prince Henry IV of Breslau, the capital city of Silesia, went even further, imposing heavy penalties upon those who accused Jews of ritual murder.

Unfortunately, the political rights extended to the Jews prompted the Catholic clergy to react with hostility. In 1267, the Council of Breslau created segregated Jewish quarters in Silesian towns with substantial Jewish populations and ordered Jews to wear a special emblem. Jews were banned from holding offices where Christians would be subordinate to them and were forbidden to build more than one synagogue in each town. These clergy-backed resolutions, however, were generally not enforced by the temporal leadership, thanks to the profits that the Jews' economic activity yielded for the princes.

Kasimir III The Great

In 1333, an adept diplomat and administrator, Kasimir (Casimir) III, assumed the throne and succeeded in reuniting Poland and expanding its power. For these achievements, he is known as Kasimir the Great.

Kasimir was great in another, entirely different capacity as well: He was a great friend of the Jews. The vast majority of Ashkenazic Jewry can trace their ancestry to Poland, thanks to his beneficence.[17] Legend has it that Kasimir's fondness of

Jews extended to the point that he took for himself a Jewish mistress named Esterka[18] (a Polish version of the Hebrew name, Esther).

Although nowadays we are outraged by any country that formally treats Jews as second-class citizens, it was virtually unheard of in Christian Europe before the 19th century to afford Jews equality under the law; however, Kasimir did just that. He ensured that the Jewish population had all the rights accorded to other citizens. Jews were welcome to settle throughout Poland in great numbers, and Kasimir vowed to protect them as people of the king.

Kasimir III, the Great (1310-1370), by Jan Matejko

Whether a Jewish mistress was the impetus behind Kasimir's largesse to the Jews remains the subject of conjecture. Either way, though Jews had lived relatively well in Poland before his rise to power, Kasimir's reign marks an era of significant Jewish prosperity. He extended Wielkopolska's Charter of Jewish Liberties to all of Poland and increased its concessions. Under pain of death, Kasimir prohibited the kidnapping of Jewish children for the purpose of enforced Christian baptism, and he inflicted heavy punishments for the desecration of Jewish cemeteries. He also founded the city of Kazimierz, which later came to be known as "the Jewish City." In response to Kasimir's magnanimity, streams of Jewish immigrants headed east to Poland.

Fear and Hatred (1347–1500)

Anti-Semitism Creeps into Poland

While for the greater part of Kasimir's reign the Jews of Poland enjoyed tranquillity, toward its close, heavy German immigration to Poland provoked increased anti-Jewish sentiment. The economic success of the Jews incited jealousy and friction between them and their Christian counterparts. Persecution gradually increased, especially as the clergy pushed for less tolerance of Jews. Polish traders and artisans, fearing Jewish rivalry, supported the harassment.

The Black Death

Anti-Jewish activity reached its climax in reaction to one of the worst pandemics the world has ever known. Starting in 1348, the Black Death took the lives of some 25-50 million Europeans—between a quarter and a half of the continent's entire population.[20]

Illustration of the Black Death from the Toggenburg Bible (1411)

Because 14th century healers were at a loss to explain the source of the epidemic, Europeans convinced themselves that the Plague was the result of a Jewish conspiracy to poison the wells. In quixotic retaliation, Jewish communities throughout Europe were massacred.

In February 1349, violent mobs murdered 2,000 Jews in Strasbourg (France). Throughout German lands, Jewish communities such as those in Nuremberg, Mainz and Cologne, were totally wiped out. By 1351, 60 major and 150 smaller Jewish communities had been murdered en masse. In many locales, Jews who survived the massacres were expelled. Unfortunately, the Jews of Poland were not spared this carnage.

According to a contemporary non-Jewish source, almost all the Jews of Poland were slaughtered.[21]

In revenge for allegedly being responsible for the Black Plague, Jews identified by a yellow badge are burned at the stake (Luzerner Schilling, 1515).

The Plague Ends, but Anti-Semitism Persists

Ultimately, the spread of the Black Death came to an end, and Europe began to rebuild itself, but distrust and disdain of Jews remained, even in Poland. In the 14th and 15th centuries, many Polish Jews worked as intermediaries in international trade. Their extensive experience in trade finance and links with far-flung Jewish communities endowed Jewish merchants with an advantage over local merchants.

Manuscript from ca. 1470 depicting Giovanni (John) da Capistrano (1386 -1456)

In the 1450s, anti-Jewish riots flared up in Breslau (Poland) and in other Silesian cities. They were inspired by the Franciscan friar John (Giovanni) of Capistrano, a papal envoy who carried out a ruthless campaign against the Jews. Inspired by his fiery sermons, many southern German regions expelled their entire Jewish populations. At Breslau, Jews were burned at the stake. Jews were banished from Warsaw and all of Lower Silesia. For a period of two years, the ancient privileges of the Jews that had been granted under the Charter of Jewish Liberties were abolished "as contrary to divine right and the law of the land." In reward for his efforts, "Saint" John was canonized at least once—perhaps twice[23] —and to this day the Roman Catholic church has an annual feast day dedicated to him!

The Golden Age of Polish Jewry (1492 - 1648)

Migration of Populations

Due to relentless persecution, as the 15th century drew to a close, the world's total Jewish population stood roughly where it had been five centuries before: around the one million mark. Of these, a mere 24,000 Jews lived in Poland and Lithuania, dispersed among some 85 towns. Everything, however, was about to change.

Although European Jews had been subject to ongoing expulsions throughout the Middle Ages, the late 1400s was a time of massive upheaval. At the hands of the Christians, Jews were driven from Austria, Bohemia, the various states that would become Germany, Provence (part of Modern France), Savoy (SE of Modern

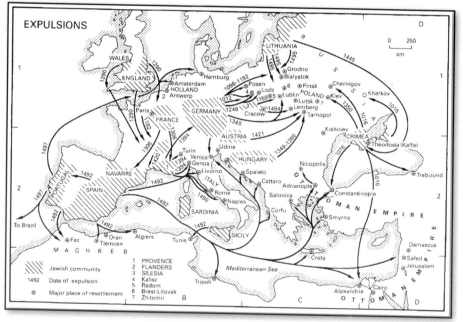

Map of Jewish expulsions in Europe

France/NW of Modern Italy), most of the Italian Peninsula (including Lombardy, Tuscany, Piedmont, Sardinia, Sicily), Geneva (Switzerland), Lithuania and Kiev (modern Ukraine).

Taken individually, each of these expulsions was tragic. Together, they were catastrophic. However, even this collective calamity was totally eclipsed by the expulsion of Jews from Spain in 1492. In that year, Jewry faced a cataclysm the magnitude of which had not been suffered since Roman times. Scholars disagree regarding the number of Jews that Catholic monarchs Ferdinand and Isabella

19th century depiction of the Wandering Jew

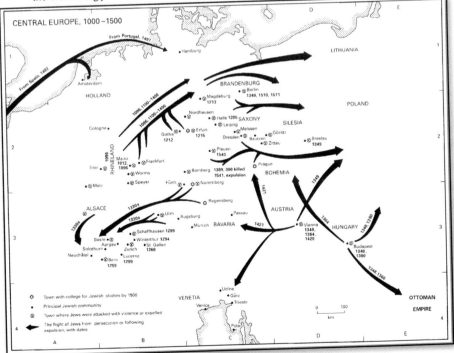

Map of Jewish migrations in Europe 1000–1500

forced to convert or flee from Spain. Estimates range from as few as 200,000 to as many as 800,000. Noted historian Paul Johnson gives the figure 341,000.[24] In other words, somewhere between a quarter and a third of world Jewry had lived in the Iberian Peninsula and was forced to abandon their religion or their homes. Many, perhaps most, initially fled to Portugal, where they eluded persecution— but only for five years, before facing a similar fate. In both Spain and Portugal, before and after 1492, converted Jews suffered terribly at the hands of the Inquisition for secretly adhering to the faith of their fathers.

All told, perhaps the majority of European Jewry was forced to relocate around the year 1500. Most of the Iberian refugees eventually found safe haven in the Ottoman Empire: modern Turkey and Greece. Poland became the recognised sanctuary for exiles from Germany, Bohemia, Hungary and Lower Silesia and soon rose in prominence to be the cultural and spiritual centre of Ashkenazic Jewry.

Jewish Life During the Golden Age

At the commencement of the 16th century, life in Poland for the Jews may have been better than elsewhere, but it certainly was not free from strife.

Jewish Poland and Lithuania in the 16th and 17th centuries

48

In 1495, the Jews had been forcibly relocated from the city of Krakow to the "Jewish town" of Kazimierz across the Vistula River. In the same year they were expelled from Lithuania. At that time Polish Jewry was forced to remain overtly distinct. Polish Jews were required to wear distinctive Jewish clothes. Jews living in the various cities and towns throughout Poland were typically concentrated in the Ulica Zydowska (the "Jewish Street"). Their houses were typically made of wood, as opposed to the more permanent brick or stone used by their Christian neighbours.

Despite these initial hurdles for the Jewish community, their quality of life steadily improved throughout the 1500s. By the second half of the century, the reunited Poland-Lithuanian Commonwealth was home to the most influential, most comfortable, most autonomous Jewish community in the world. In 1503, in response to the massive influx of Jews, the Polish monarchy established a Chief Rabbinate and appointed Jacob Pollack as the Chief Rabbi. In the same year Jews were readmitted to the Grand Duchy of Lithuania.

Sigismund I the Old
(ruled 1506–1548)

The tide turned in full-force with the ascension of Sigismund I to the throne in 1506. For more than 40 years, he protected the Jews of his realm who created their own world within a world. They spoke their own language, Yiddish. They had their own sections of town, at the centre of which was their synagogue. In a number of cities such as Krakow, the synagogue served as a fortress of sorts to protect from any would-be uprisings. By 1534, Jews had become accepted as legitimate members of Polish society, and the law requiring Jews to wear special clothes was repealed.

Krakow's fortress-like "Old Synagogue." Originally built in the 15th century and rebuilt in 1570, this is the oldest standing synagogue in Poland. This picture was taken during WWII.

49

Sigismund's successor, Sigismund II Augustus, who ruled from 1548-1572, followed in the tolerant ways of his father. It was during his reign that Polish Jewry entered the height of its Golden Age. In 1551, Sigismund II formally confirmed Jewish autonomy in the region by reaffirming their right to elect a board of commissioners (known as a *kahal*) to direct communal affairs. King Sigismund II also granted the Jews permission to choose their own Chief Rabbi.

Sigismund II Augustus
(ruled 1548-1572)

The Chief Rabbinate held power over law and finance, appointing judges and other officials. The Polish government permitted the Chief Rabbinate to grow in power, largely for their own purposes of efficient tax collection. Only thirty percent of the money raised by the Rabbinate served Jewish causes. The rest went to the Crown to "protect" the Jews.

Another major development in 16th century Poland was that the Jews were allowed to have their own governing body called the Va'ad Arba Artzot (the Council of the Four Lands.) The Council was composed of various rabbis from the four major Polish provinces (Greater Poland, Lesser Poland, Volhynia and Podolia) who oversaw the affairs of the Jews in Eastern Europe.

In 1569, the Kingdom of Poland united with the Grand Duchy of Lithuania to form the Polish-Lithuanian Commonwealth (which also included modern-day Belarus and Ukraine). At the time, this was the largest state in Eastern Europe. About ten percent of its population of seven million were Jews. This means that between half and three-quarters of world Jewry were now in Poland. The Golden Age of Polish Jewry was in full swing: Poles allowed Jewish life to develop and scholarship flourished.

Religious Life and the Golden Age

Until now, we have focused almost exclusively on Jewish relations with gentile hosts, political rights and demographics; however, we have given little consideration to Jewish culture. It is vital to understand that Jewish culture throughout the ages revolved primarily around Torah law and the study of it. Because so much of the Jewish life in Poland was predicated on Torah study, it is important to understand what exactly Torah study is all about and Polish Jewry's relationship to it.

Background

For centuries, Jews have been called the "People of the Book" because of the legendary devotion, inordinate resources and countless hours that they have invested in the pursuit of Torah knowledge. Consider that in 1424, more than 200 years after its founding in 1209, Cambridge University had in its possession a total of 122 books, each worth the value of a farm.[27] Now consider that in 1242, at the behest of the French Crown and Pope, the Talmud was "put on trial" after which some 10,000 Jewish volumes were found in the personal libraries of local Jewry and were burned in Paris.[28] For thousands of Jewish men in every generation, Torah study has been a lifelong occupation and the highest mark of achievement. Even before the advent of the printing press, literacy amongst Jewish men stood above 95%, while illiteracy amongst non-Jewish men stood at a similar level.[29]

As difficult as it is to overstate the importance of Torah study, it is even harder to exaggerate the esteem in which the Torah itself was held. Throughout the millennia, the Torah has been venerated as the mandate of the nation and quite literally the marriage contract between G-d and the Jewish people. More than that, Torah has been seen as the greatest expression of G-d's love: His

Torat Chaim, instructions for living. Since time immemorial, Jews have considered the Torah as nothing less than the basis and objective of all existence. The Zohar, the premier book of Jewish mysticism, expresses it thus, "G-d looked into the Torah, and created the world; the Jew looks into the Torah and sustains it."[30]

According to Jewish tradition, G-d revealed Himself to the entire Jewish nation at Mount Sinai 3,300 years ago. There, He conveyed the Torah: a comprehensive set of principles regarding how to get the most out of this world while simultaneously achieving a transcendence that will carry one into the next. From that time, these principles were transmitted exclusively by word of mouth from generation to generation. For this reason, they are often referred to as the Oral Law. Traditional Judaism maintains that this Oral Law has been conveyed in an unbroken chain of tradition from teacher to student through the generations, from Moses until today.

For a total of approximately 1500 years (c. 1250 BCE-250 CE) following the death of Moses, the hub of the Torah tradition was in the Land of Israel. The first 1000 of these years, starting with the generation of Joshua in the 13th century BCE and continuing until that of Ezra in the 4th century BCE, is known as the time of the Prophets, during which another 19 prophetic works were written. When added to the Five Books of Moses, these comprise the 24 books of the Bible (called Tanach in Hebrew and the Old Testament by Christians).

During the Roman Period, enduring hardships endangered the fidelity of the oral transmission, so the Torah leadership of the time, led by Rabbi Yehudah HaNasi (the Prince), felt compelled to codify an outline of the Oral Law. This outline is called the Mishna, meaning "restatement," because it was a restatement of the principles taught at Sinai. Almost immediately thereafter, ongoing Roman persecution made life in Israel impossible, and most of Jewry migrated east, to Babylonia (modern-day Iraq). By the 3rd century, the epicentre of the Torah tradition moved to Babylonia, where it would remain for almost 800 years (roughly 250-1000 CE).

Over the centuries, disputes arose regarding the implications of various sections of the Mishna, and ultimately a more detailed formulation of the Oral Law had to be articulated. Near the end of the 5th century this was accomplished as the Babylonian Talmud—an enormous work that spans some 20,000 large pages in English translation!

Early in the 11th century, social and economic conditions forced the Torah centres to move west from Babylon to Europe. At this time, the Jewish world split into three main regions, which during the Middle Ages (c. 1000-1500) would become distinct cultures. The first remained in the Moslem world, in the Middle East, Asia and North Africa. Their descendants are called today *Edot haMizrach*, the communities of the East. The second illustrious Jewish community arose in Spain. In Hebrew, Spain is called Sepharad; hence these Jews have come to be known

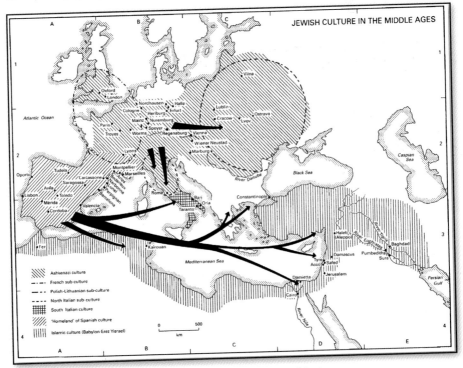

Map of Jewish culture during the Middle Ages

as Sephardic. A third broad group of Jews settled in Germany and France. The Hebrew name for Germany is Ashkenaz, so Jews descendant from this region are called Ashkenazi.

At the end of the 11th century, only about 3% of the total Jewish population was Ashkenazi. However, the tide slowly turned, particularly during the migrations to Poland during the Golden Age, and by the eve of the Holocaust, Ashkenazi Jews had accounted for 92% of the total Jewish population.[32]

With the above background in mind, we can now appreciate the events and personalities that shaped Polish Jewry for centuries.

Poland as the Religious Centre of World Jewry

At the turn of the 16th century, the Jews who moved from Bohemia to Poland established a community of their own in Krakow. Rabbi Yaakov Pollack (1460-1541), who had been a rabbi in Prague, officiated as rabbi of Krakow and then as the first Chief Rabbi of Poland. His arrival in Poland was a watershed for the community. Pollack organised the first school for the study of the Talmud (known as a yeshiva) in Poland. The institution trained young men to introduce the study of the Talmud into other Polish communities.

Over the course of the next 350 years, Poland would become an ever-strengthening centre of Torah scholarship. Within two generations, by the mid-1500s, Poland was the undisputed capital of Torah learning.

The "Talmud Torah" in Lodz

Rabbi Pollack's most famous student was Rabbi Shalom Shachna, who in 1515 established the yeshiva in Lublin. At the time, Lublin was the third largest Jewish community in Poland, and Shachna drew students from all over Europe. The academy at Lublin became so prestigious that in 1567 the king granted the Rosh Yeshiva (head of the yeshiva) the title of rector and rights equal to those of rectors in Polish universities. This, as well as the great scholarship of those who studied there, has led some to refer to Lublin as the "Jewish Oxford."

Out of Schachna's yeshiva emerged the most important rabbinic figure in Polish history: Rabbi Moshe Isserles (the Rema). A fuller treatment of the Rema, his life and significance, can be found at the beginning of Part 4 of this book.

Jewish education became a central focus and preoccupation in Poland. The custom was for Jewish boys aged three to ten to be educated at a *cheder* (literally "a room") where they would learn to read and study the written Torah, Prophets and some Mishna. Some would continue studying and until the age of thirteen, attending communal classes or studying with a private tutor, during which time Talmud was introduced. From the age of Bar Mitzvah, the overwhelming majority of Jewish youth joined the local labour force, apprenticing with artisans and tradesmen. A small minority continued their Torah study until their mid-teens, by which time they would be Talmudic scholars, since that had been their sole occupation from their earliest days. Only rare scholars continued full-time studies past the age of sixteen or seventeen. Until that point in their education, they would have been studying in the local synagogue with the local rabbi. However, if an aspiring scholar was indeed exceptional, he would probably need to journey from his hometown to another city nearby where a more accomplished rabbi would be able to continue to provide worthwhile tutelage. Small congregations of students would assemble around the various famous rabbis scattered throughout Poland and its environs. Out of these informal Torah centres would emerge the next generation of rabbinic leadership for Eastern European Jewry.[33]

Death, Deceit and Disillusion (1648–1734)

The Chmielnicki Massacres

Jews from the western provinces of Poland moved to the Ukraine because of the economic opportunities created when Poland expanded into the region. Polish Jewry was finally experiencing relative peace. The Polish government recognised the worthwhile niche Jews filled for them. Many Jews served as middle men, collecting taxes for the aristocracy from the peasantry amongst which were the Ukrainian Cossacks. Jews also contributed to the wealth of Poland and its general economy through the taxes they paid, as well as by increasing local commerce. Although the church applied pressure on the Polish lords to

Map depicting principal sites of Chmielnicki massacres

persecute the Jews and limit their influence, the Polish lords did not heed them and supported the status quo by granting autonomy and freedom to the Jews. The Jews retained religious freedom and prospered financially and spiritually.

This arrangement, though comfortable for the Jews and worthwhile for the wealthy Poles, caused dissent and jealousy among the peasantry. At the same time, the nationalistic Cossacks wanted to free the Ukraine from Polish domination. The Jews were the most accessible link in the economic chain upon which they could project their anger. It was a pogrom waiting to happen.

The year 1635 saw the first explosion of Ukrainian violence against Poles and Jews. An attempt was made for revolution, but the Cossacks were crushed. They would return with renewed vigour 13 years later.

The spark to ignite the tinderbox was Bogdan Chmielnicki. He was a young cavalryman who had fought with the Cossacks and the Poles against the Turks, who now began instigating the Cossacks to rise up against the Jews. He successfully spread a rumour that the Poles had sold the Cossacks as slaves "into the hands of the accursed Jews." Chmielnicki had charisma, and his fury and hatred fanned the rage of the Cossacks. He enjoyed several initial successes in battle and was soon seen as the fledgling saviour of the oppressed Cossacks and Ukrainian peasantry.

Rage spread like wildfire. The Ukranian peasantry united with the Cossacks who sought to free the Ukraine from Polish domination. Together, these two oppressed groups annihilated Polish Jewry in a series of vicious massacres.

Here is one description from Lithuanian Rabbi Shabbetai ben Meir HaCohen (1621-1662), also known as the Shach, who survived the period.

On the same day, 1,500 people were killed in the city of Human in Russia on the Sabbath. The nobles [Cossacks], with whom the wicked mob had again made an alliance, chased all the Jews from the city into the fields and vineyards where the villains surrounded them in a circle, stripped them to their skin, and ordered them to lie on the ground. The villains spoke to the

Jews with friendly and consoling words: "Why do you want to be killed, strangled, and slaughtered like an offering to your G-d Who poured out His anger upon you without mercy? Would it not be safer for you to worship our gods, our images and crosses, and we would form one people which would unite together?" But the holy and faithful people who so often allowed themselves to be murdered for the sake of the Lord, raised their voices together to the Almighty in Heaven and cried: "Hear O Israel the Lord our G-d, the Lord is one..."

In 1648 and 1649, Cossack hordes led by Chmielnicki massacred between 100,000 and 200,000 Jews in Poland in the most horrendous ways. Violence against the Jews was renewed in 1654–1655 during the war between Russia and Poland which was incited by Chmielnicki. The communities of Lithuania, which had been spared in 1648–1649, fell victim to this second wave of massacres. Eyewitness accounts of the atrocities that took place are as frightful as any from the Nazi era, and it is clear that the Nazis had ample precedent from which they could learn their heinous craft.

The Shabbetai Zvi Debacle

Note: The foregoing historical section until the end of Part 1 is a direct adaptation of the historical writings of historian Ken Spiro.

Jewish mysticism, more popularly known as Kabbalah (literally, "that which was received"), is an interpretation of the Torah that focuses on the deepest, esoteric teachings of Judaism. According to Jewish tradition, this level of understanding of the Torah was revealed at Mount Sinai, but because of its subtlety and complexity, was reserved for only an initiated few. The key work of Kabbalah is the Zohar, the "Book of Splendour." The contents of this book were first revealed by Rabbi Shimon bar Yochai in approximately 100 CE while he lived in a cave, hiding from the Romans. The Spanish Rabbi Moses de Leon (1240-1305) was the first to bring the Zohar into the public forum. From that point on, interest in the Kabbalistic tradition began to permeate the general Jewish population. Within a few centuries, the secret interpretation became more widely known and was finally published, and disseminated generally. Few, however, could understand it; and many egregiously misunderstood it.

Mysticism, because it often attempts to explain the deeper meaning behind the events of history, is often associated with Messianic expectation. But Messianic expectation, which is a basic tenet of Judaism unrelated to mysticism, per se, can sometimes be misplaced and lead to crises in the Jewish world.

Shabbetai Zvi (1626-1676), sketched in Smyrna, 1665

Such a crisis occurred in the late 1600s. Jewish suffering of the previous 150 years—the expulsions, the Inquisition and most recently, the atrocious Chmielnicki massacres—set the scene. Jewish morale was low. It seemed that things could simply not get any worse. Surely, the time had arrived for Messianic salvation.

At this time, a mystic named Shabbetai Zvi rose to

prominence. Born in 1626 in Smyrna, Turkey, he was by all accounts a brilliant, charismatic, albeit emotionally volatile man. By the age of 20, he had been given the title of Chacham, "wise man," by the members of his community. However, soon thereafter, his behaviour grew erratic, and people came to realise that though brilliant, he was mentally unstable; so, he was exiled.

Depiction of Zvi crowned as the Messiah, Amsterdam, 1666

Shabbetai Zvi wandered the Middle East, and in 1665 found himself in Gaza. There he met another so-called mystic by the name of Nathan, who became his tireless promoter. Nathan convinced Shabbetai Zvi that he was the Messiah and started sending letters to Jewish communities throughout the world announcing the Messiah's arrival in Israel.

One account of what happened next comes from a primary source, a Jewish woman living in Germany named "Gluckel of Hameln," whose memoirs give us insight into the life of European Jewry in the 17th century.

> Our joy when the letters arrived [from Smyrna] is not to be told. Most of them were addressed to Sephardim, who, as fast as they came, took them to their synagogue and read them aloud. Young and old, the Germans too hastened to the Sephardic synagogue...
>
> Many sold their houses and lands and all their possessions, for any day they hoped to be redeemed. My good father-in-law left his home in Hameln, abandoned his house and lands and all his goodly furniture... 34

It must be noted, however, that although Shabbetai Zvi had a huge following in the Jewish world (much more than Jesus ever had), the majority of the European rabbis, who saw how Shabbetai Zvi was changing and deviating from or violating Jewish law, were not fooled and warned against him.

When the Ottoman authorities caught wind of his Messianic claims, Shabbetai Zvi was brought before the Sultan and given the choice of converting to Islam or death. Shabbetai promptly converted, donned a turban and took the name, Aziz Mehmed Efendi. For his cooperation, he was even given a royal title, "Keeper of the Sultan's Gate." He continued to claim that he was the Messiah, and the Sultan eventually exiled him.

The Shabbatean debacle had come to a surprisingly abrupt end. News of Shabbetai's conversion spread throughout the Jewish world, leaving his followers in a state of shock. The countless believers who had had such high hopes for imminent redemption were crushed.

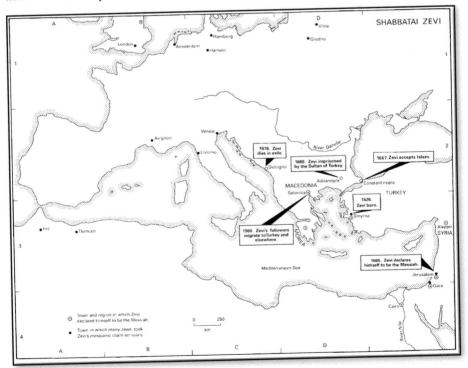

Map of key locations in the Shabbetai Zvi debacle

Polish Jewry had recently been devastated by Chmielnicki and his murderous men. Those who were lucky enough to survive the massacres had been crushed by the economic and political turmoil that embroiled all of Poland. Whatever psychological capital remained, they wagered on the coming redemption. With their hopes dashed, the people were now deeply in need of comfort.

What the Jews of Poland needed was an inspirational leader who could lift their spirits and light up their lives. It would take some 60 years, but that man, the Ba'al Shem Tov (the Man of the Good Name) would eventually come, and he brought with him a new-found joie de vivre.

The Rise of the Hassidic Movement (1734-1795)

The Ba'al Shem Tov

Israel ben Eliezer, known as the Ba'al Shem Tov (literally, "Master of the Good Name"), is regarded as the founder of the Hassidic movement. He was born in Okup, (modern-day Ukraine) and was orphaned at a young age. He was probably cared for by the local community and received a standard education. Although he was not an outstanding student, he was known to have an especially intense emotional connection to G-d, which he developed as he wandered alone in the fields and forests, talking to his Creator.

Despite his humble beginnings, the Ba'al Shem Tov grew up to study with a secret society of Jewish mystics, the *Nistarim* (hidden ones), and eventually became a revered rabbi. He worked as an assistant school-master, labourer and *shochet* (ritual slaughterer) , maintaining the appearance of a peasant to conceal his wisdom and piety.

Israel ben Eliezer, the Ba'al Shem Tov (1698-1760)

In 1734, when the Ba'al Shem Tov was 36, he revealed himself as a wise and holy man. His magnetism attracted many disciples. Great scholars, as well as common-folk, were drawn by stories replete with mystical lore and wordless hymns called "*niggunim*," which revived and uplifted the soul. He laid the foundation for Hassidic thought, stressing the importance of *devekut* (cleaving to G-d) and feeling the presence of G-d in all aspects of one's life.

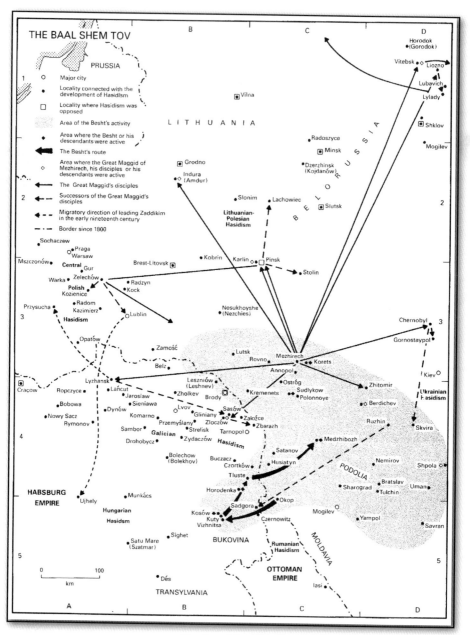

The rise of Hassidism

Hassidic Thought

Although Judaism has always maintained that joy and an active relationship with G-d are basic requirements of a "good Jew," it is Torah study that had historically been emphasised as the primary means to those ends.

In 18th century Poland, the Jewish social elite were the Torah scholars. Although almost all Jewish men were literate at that time, few had the time, resources and intellectual capabilities required to become serious Torah scholars. For many who were scholars, strenuous study often supplanted other efforts to develop an emotional relationship with G-d.

A major component of Hassidic culture, which addressed the needs of the unlearned Jew, was the telling of stories. These stories are of a distinctive style: seemingly simple, they are in truth parables with layers of metaphoric lessons. The following Hassidic tale describes the way the early Hassidic masters diagnosed the spiritual ailment of the Jews at that time:

An apprentice blacksmith, having learned his trade from the master, made a list for himself of how he must go about his craft: how he should pump the bellows, secure the anvil and wield the hammer. He omitted nothing. When he went to work at the king's palace, however, he discovered to his dismay that he could not perform his duties, and was dismissed. He had forgotten to note one thing — perhaps because it was so obvious — that first he must ignite a spark to kindle the fire. He had to return to the master, who reminded him of the first principle which he had forgotten.[36]

The Ba'al Shem Tov initiated a new movement known as Hassidism (or "Chassidus" as a Chassid would pronounce it) that emphasized bringing G-d into all aspects of one's life, particularly through intense prayer and joyous singing. The Ba'al Shem Tov taught that even the deeds of the simplest Jew, if performed with pure intentions, were equal to those of the greatest scholars.

The Ba'al Shem Tov taught that erudite Torah learning was not the only way to draw close to G-d. He preached personal piety, good deeds and happiness, even during difficult circumstances, as alternative legitimate ways to forge a connection with G-d. Any Jew, however humble, could aspire to great spirituality.

When the Ba'al Shem Tov died in 1760, Rabbi Dov Ber (1704-1772), known as the Maggid of Mezritch, assumed the mantle of leadership of the Hassidic movement. He further developed many of the movement's philosophies. Interestingly, the famed psychologist Carl G. Jung said that all of his advances in psychology were pre-empted by Rabbi Dov Ber. This gives one an idea of the magnitude of the Maggid's insight into human nature.[37]

The Maggid's disciples went off to develop particular streams within the Hassidic movement and to found their own dynasties. Amongst them were:

- Rebbe Elimelech of Lizhensk (see his profile in Part 4)

- Rabbi Shneur Zalman of Liadi, the author of the famous work, the Tanya, and founder of the Lubavitch sect of Hassidism

- Rabbi Nachman of Breslov (1772-1811) a great-grandson of the Ba'al Shem Tov, who is perhaps best known for his allegorical stories of beggars and princes through which he tried to teach deep truths to simple people

Today, there are probably close to half a million Hassidic Jews worldwide. Each of the various Hassidic sects have names—Kotzk, Sanz, Belz, Lubavitch, Skver— that refer to cities in Poland, Lithuania and Ukraine. When these Hassidic communities moved, they took the names with them.

Mitnagdim — The Opposition

The leading personality opposed to the Hassidic movement was Rabbi Eliyahu ben Shlomo Zalman, known as the Vilna Gaon ("Genius of Vilna"). The Gaon was a brilliant scholar who made an enormous impact on Jewish learning. A person of wide-ranging interests and author of some 70 books on various subjects, the Vilna Gaon excelled in every aspect of scholarship. He was what we might call the "intellectual king" of the Jews.

Rabbi Eliyahu of Vilna (1720-1797)

Perhaps the Vilna Gaon's most serious concern with Hassidim was the de-intellectualization of Torah. The Hassidic movement was largely a movement of simple, uneducated Jews, and he feared that Jewish scholarship might be replaced by singing and dancing. He also vehemently objected to the Hassidic concept that G-d is "in all things" fearing it may lead to a pagan theology of pantheism. Similarly, he was wary of the Hassidic emphasis on attaching oneself to a spiritual mentor known as a *rebbe*. The Gaon was opposed to this practice, out of concern that it would ultimately lead disciples to believe one's *rebbe* was their conduit to G-d, which Judaism holds to be an idolatrous notion. He also foresaw the possibility that Hassidic culture was conducive for producing another false messiah. Finally, the Gaon, along with many other rabbis, strongly objected to changing the formal text of the Jewish prayer services.

The Vilna Gaon was so strongly opposed to the Hassidic movement that he and others like him came to be called Mitnagdim, which means "those who are against." In 1772, the Mitnagdim excommunicated the Hassidim. The following is an excerpt from the excommunication order (April 1772):

Our brethren, sons of Israel..., as you know, new people have appeared, unimagined by our forefathers...and they associate amongst themselves and their ways are different from other Children of Israel in their liturgy.... They behave in a crazed manner and say that their thoughts wander in all worlds...and they belittle the study of the Torah, and repeatedly claim that one should not study much, nor deeply regret one's transgressions.... Therefore, we have come to inform our brethren, Children of Israel, from near and far...and to sound to them the voice of excommunication and banishment...until they themselves repent completely....[38]

While the creation of the Hassidic movement did initially cause a serious split in the Jewish world, it did not create a permanent separation. Today there are Hassidic sects who are very scholarly, maintaining their own yeshivot where they study the Talmud intensely. In hindsight, the Hassidic movement contributed significantly to the revitalization of Eastern European Jewry. It kept many Jews connected to Judaism who may well have been lost because they didn't have the time or ability to study.

As a result of the Hassidic contribution, Judaism became stronger and more ready to face the two-pronged assault that would face them in the upcoming century: that of the Russians against their freedoms, and of the Haskalah (Jewish "Enlightenment" movement) against their beliefs.

Life Under the Russians (1795 - 1918)

The Jews of Poland Become the Jews of Russia

In 1770, the Poland-Lithuanian Commonwealth was one of the largest nations in Europe. With a population of well over a million Jews, it was also home to the majority of European Jewry. Russia, Poland's neighbour to the east, had always been loath to absorb Jews, so in 1770 there were only about 100,000 Jews in all of Russia.

In 1772, Russian, Prussian and Austrian troops simultaneously invaded the Polish-Lithuanian Commonwealth and occupied pre-agreed provinces in an event known as the First Partition of Poland. Russia's annexation added 600,000 Jews

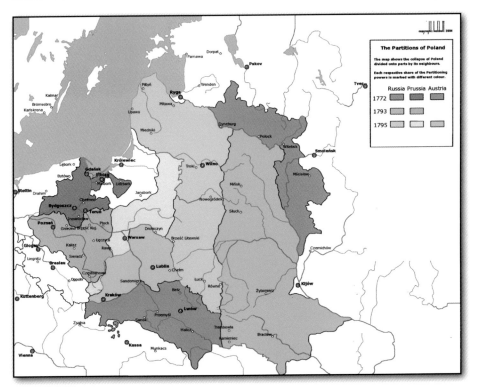

to her population. In 1793, Poland's imperialistic neighbours further carved up Poland. Included in Russia's slice of the Polish pie were another 400,000 Jews. After the Third Partition in 1795, in which Russia inherited 250,000 more Jews, the independent Polish state was no more, and Russia became home to more Jews than any other nation.

After the Napoleonic wars and the subsequent territorial divisions, another 100,000 Jews came under the rule of the Russian Czar, bringing the total Russian Jewish population to about 1.5 million (30-40% of world Jewry).

Czar Alexander I deeply distrusted the Jews, considering them traitors and a national burden. He sought a solution to the "Jewish problem" and concluded that a policy of confinement was necessary to minimize the Jewish threat to his reign. Beginning in 1795, Jews were forbidden to reside or travel outside the area known as the Pale of Settlement, the borders of which were finalised in 1812.

The Pale of Settlement

The word "pale" derives from the Latin word *palus*, meaning "stake" as in to "stake out one's territory," and refers to the region of western Russia to which Jewish settlement was restricted. The Russian Pale was first created by Catherine the Great in 1791 after several failed attempts by her predecessors to remove Jews from Russia entirely unless they converted to Russian Orthodoxy.

The reasons for its creation were primarily economic and nationalist. While Russian society had traditionally been divided into nobles, serfs and clergy, industrial progress led to the emergence of a middle class. This demographic segment was rapidly being filled by Jews who did not previously belong to any class. By limiting the areas of Jewish residence, the imperial powers attempted to ensure the growth of a non-Jewish middle class in the rest of the country.

At its peak, the Pale, which included previously Polish and Lithuanian territories, had a Jewish population of over five million, which represented the largest concentration (40%) of world Jewry at that time.

From the Baltic to the Black Sea, the Pale stretched across 25 provinces and included most of eastern Poland, Lithuania, White Russia, the Ukraine, the Crimea and Bessarabia.

The policy of confinement was ultimately not sufficient to satisfy Czar Alexander I. In 1804, he imposed further limits on Jewish residence and economic activity even within the Pale. The sale of liquor to locals, and employment and residence in integrated villages were privileges granted to non-Jews alone. The new policy had a devastating effect on the nearly one-third of the Jews who had previously supported themselves through the liquor trade.

The Jews of Russia were specifically expelled from Moscow and St. Petersburg, and forced into the Pale. Later, they were also expelled from rural areas within the Pale, and forced to live only in *shtetls* (small towns with large Jewish populations).

Despite the oppression, *tzedakah* (Jewish charity) thrived as Jews helped each other. Martin Gilbert writes in his A*tlas of Jewish History* that no province in the Pale had less than 14% of Jews on relief, and Lithuanian and Ukrainian Jews supported as much as 22% of their poor populations:

"Among the charitable societies organised by Jews, were those to supply poor students with clothes, soldiers with kosher food, the poor with free medical treatment, poor brides with dowries and orphans with technical education."

This was an incredibly sophisticated social welfare system. In times of great hardship, no Jew was abandoned.

A Jewish water carrier in the Pale where most cities had no other form of water distribution

Forced Conscription

Nicholas I, emperor and autocrat of all the Russians and king of Poland (ruled 1825-1855)

Alexander I's successor, Czar Nicholas I, came to be known as the Iron Czar. He was a brutal, dispassionate ruler who reserved much of his wrath for the Jews. He is best (worst) remembered for his strict enforcement of the cruel Statutes on Conscription which came to be known as the "Cantonist Decrees." (The name came from the word "canton," meaning "military camp.")

Under the Statute, Jewish boys as young as seven or eight were sent to local cantons (military schools) where they were prepared for entry into the Russian army. Cantonists, as these young conscripts were called, were then forced to remain in military service for 25 years! Loneliness, beatings, malnutrition and disease were the lot of these unfortunates, only half of whom ever saw their families again.

As far as the Jewish community was concerned, conscription was a death sentence. Some Jewish parents were so desperate that they would actually cut off one of their son's fingers so he would be unable to hold a gun, hoping thereby to avert his conscription.

Tragically, the cantonist system had an even more sinister outcome. Jewish communal leaders were responsible for filling the Czar's quotas. Inevitably, wealthier Jews bought freedom from the Russian army for their sons, while poor families had no similar recourse. The fear of being kidnapped and handed over to a Russian military school haunted the Jewish poor, the orphaned and other weak segments of the Jewish population. Tragically, in response to the Czar's decree, some Jews engaged in kidnapping, eager as they were to deliver up young boys for a fee. In this way, the Czar succeeded in depleting Jewish numbers and inflicting untold suffering on individuals and families, while simultaneously undermining the cohesiveness of Jewish communities.

The Birth of the Modern Yeshiva

In 1803, the Jewish world witnessed a revolution with the establishment of the first modern yeshiva, or institute of higher Jewish education. The opening of the Yeshiva in Volozhin (modern-day Belarus) was a direct response to the social and political

The Volozhin Yeshiva

turmoil of the times, and it resulted in renewed interest in rigorous Torah study. Today, the Yeshiva of Volozhin can be credited with preserving and revitalizing Torah education at a critical moment in Jewish history, as well as with raising the level of respect shown to the Torah and its scholars.

Prior to 1803, Jewish education throughout Europe was almost entirely informal. In the latter half of the 18th century, war, economic upheaval and the partition of Poland conspired to unravel the centuries-old ad hoc approach to Jewish education. As the Haskalah (Enlightenment) gained momentum throughout Europe, the vitality of the traditional educational system was further compromised, damaging the respect accorded to Torah study and scholars and threatening Jewish learning everywhere.

Rabbi Chaim Itzkowitz, known simply as Rabbi Chaim of Volozhin, the foremost disciple of the Vilna Gaon, opened the Yeshiva of Volozhin in response to the need for a more systematic and structured approach to Jewish higher education. His approach to Torah learning emphasized constant devotion to an intense, rigorous analysis of the Talmudic text.

Rabbi Chaim sent a letter to communities throughout Poland and Lithuania stating his goals and plans for the Yeshiva and encouraging them to send their strongest students (and financial support). The appeal sparked excitement in the Jewish world, and the finest students vied for spots in Volozhin. The students who were privileged to gain entry became the next generation's community leaders, teachers and synagogue rabbis.

The Yeshiva flourished, both under the leadership of Rabbi Chaim Volozhiner and his successors. In 1880, Rabbi Chaim HaLevi Soloveitchik (Rabbi Chaim Brisker) joined Rabbi Naftali Tzvi Yehudah Berlin (the "Netziv" — see his profile in Part 4) in leading the Yeshiva to even greater heights. Rabbi Chaim Brisker revolutionized the Torah-learning methodology of the Yeshiva, and his methodology is still the basis of study in yeshivot today.

Throughout the 1800s, the Russian government tried to weaken Jewish institutions throughout its empire. These attempts culminated in 1891 when the government issued a host of restrictive laws that were intended to undermine the goals and purpose of the Yeshiva. Soon thereafter, the Netziv refused to accept the demands of the authorities, and, seeing no other option, reluctantly closed the Yeshiva. Though it reopened a few years later, it never regained its former prominence.

The Yeshiva's closing marked the end of a brilliant era. As painful as it was, however, the closing of the Volozhin Yeshiva triggered a period of expansion and growth. When the Yeshiva disbanded, its outstanding teachers and students were dispersed throughout Europe, where they flowered into a new network of yeshivas and communities.

Following the Holocaust, many of these yeshivas were relocated to America, England, and Israel and they followed the model established by Rabbi Chaim. The impact of the Yeshiva of Volozhin is deeply felt even today, as Rabbi Chaim's systematic, highly-structured approach to learning remains the primary method of education in the Jewish world.

Haskalah and Secularization

In the late 18th century, the Enlightenment swept Western Europe. As a result, western European nations granted Jews a host of new legal freedoms and the opportunity to advance politically, socially and economically. In the early 19th century, many Jews joined the Enlightenment movement with a style all their own, creating a phenomenon known as the "Haskalah" in the Jewish world. Those Jews who subscribed to the Haskalah's secular ideologies were known as "Maskilim." The Maskilim believed that only by casting off the shackles of old-fashioned Jewish life and adopting the culture and lifestyles of their neighbours, would they be accepted by European societies. Instead of remaining "a people apart," as Jews had always been, they would become equal to all other peoples.

In Jewish circles, non-traditional Biblical scholarship and criticism quickly developed, creating a new genre of literature known as the Haskalah of Chochmas Yisrael (the Science of Judaism). The attitudes and aims of these books vastly differed from those of Orthodox scholarship. These new works explained classical Jewish texts, practices and history in order to record Jewish culture for posterity, rather than to promote traditional Judaism as a viable, meaningful way of life for the contemporary Jew.

The Jews in Eastern Europe had little desire to be accepted by the Poles or Russians whom they saw as culturally boorish. Thus, the Haskalah in Eastern Europe developed differently than in the Western states. The Eastern Maskilim did not aim to assimilate into Polish or Russian society. They only wanted to be perceived as less "foreign" in order to gain equal political rights. They hoped that anti-Semitism would decrease as the gentiles began to regard "enlightened" Jews—who did not practice the unfamiliar rituals and customs of the Orthodox—as less threatening.

Instead of adopting local culture and language to facilitate assimilation into mainstream society as was done in Western Europe, the Eastern European Maskilim tried to open the minds of Jews to secular ideas by writing in Hebrew and in "*mama loshen*" (Yiddish). Hebrew was revived as a cultural medium. For centuries, Hebrew had only been used for prayer and the writing and study of holy texts. Now, it was used by the most influential secular authors of the day.

While the Haskalah movement abandoned many of the traditional Jewish ways, it did not offer a viable alternate form of culture to continuing Jewish life. Many young people became involved in political movements such as Bundism, Socialism and Communism, which promoted the Jewish values of social justice and equality without the trappings of Judaism. Zionism was the movement commited to establishing a homeland for the Jewish people, but this was a national movement, not a religious one. Never before had there been such a generation gap in Jewish society. The young saw it as progress, while many of the older generation viewed these social developments as inimical to Jewish cultural survival.

Protocols of The Elders of Zion

Around the turn of the 20th century, the Russian secret police began to circulate a forgery which became the most famous anti-Semitic document in history—The Protocols of the Elders of Zion (first published in 1903). These protocols purported to be the minutes of a secret meeting of world Jewish leaders, which supposedly took place once every hundred years for the purpose of plotting how to continue to control the world.

As ridiculous as this might sound to us today, the Protocols were seized upon as "proof" that the world was dominated by Jews who were responsible for all of the world's problems.

Front page illustration from 1911 edition of a book that contained The Protocols of the Elders of Zion. The captions read: "Thus we shall win," "Mark of antichrist," "Unlawfulness," "Tarot," "INRI," "Great mystery"

Fans and proponents of the Protocols have included such anti-Semites as: Henry Ford, the founder of Ford Motor Company; Adolf Hitler; Egyptian President Gamal Abdel Nasser; and King Faisal of Saudi Arabia, among others.

Despite the fact that the Protocols are a proven forgery whose allegations are completely ridiculous and an expression of the worst kind of anti-Semitism, the Protocols continue to sell briskly today and are carried by huge bookstore chains such as Barnes and Noble and amazon.com in the name of freedom of speech.

Pogroms

Throughout the Pale of Settlement, the level of government-sponsored anti-Semitism under the Czars was incomparably worse than it had been when Poland was independent. There were so many pogroms against the Jews that it is impossible to even list them all. Between 1903 and 1907 alone there were 284 pogroms with over 50,000 casualties.

These pogroms were seldom spontaneous. Incitement by Christian clergy around the Christian holidays could occasionally drive the masses into a frenzy. In Czarist Russia, most of the pogroms were government organised. Why would the Czarist government organise mobs to target Jews? Jews were the classic scapegoats for the economic problems of Russia (and many other countries in history).

Of course, the problems of Russia had nothing to do with the Jews. The problems of Russia had to do with its totally backward, feudal and highly corrupt regime. One of the ways of diverting attention from the corruption was to blame the Jews and to allow the masses to blow off steam by taking it out on the Jews.

The government of the new Czar, Alexander III, organised one pogrom after another from 1881 to 1894 to keep the anger of the masses focused on the Jews.

In addition to the pogroms, Alexander III promulgated a series of laws against the Jews. These laws were called the May Laws and they included such prohibitions as:

1   It is henceforth forbidden for Jews to settle outside the cities and townships.

2   The registration of property and mortgages in the names of Jews is to be halted temporarily. Jews are also prohibited from administering such properties.

3   It is forbidden for Jews to engage in commerce on Sundays and Christian holidays.

Berel Wein writes of the reign of Alexander III:

> *"Expulsions, deportations, arrests and beatings became the daily lot of the Jews, not only of their lower class, but even of the middle class and the Jewish intelligentsia. The government of Alexander III waged a campaign of war against its Jewish inhabitants.... The Jews were driven and hounded, and emigration appeared to be the only escape from the terrible tyranny of the Romanovs."* [40]

When Alexander III died, he was succeeded by Nicholas II, the last of the

Jewish children, victims of a 1905 pogrom in Yekaterinoslav (today's Dnepropetrovsk)

Romanovs, whose incompetence and inflexibility helped bring about the Russian Revolution. The new Czar had to cope with the mess left behind by his father, and he did so badly. During his reign, one of the most famous pogroms took place in Kishinev, on Easter, 6-7 April, 1903.

The Kishinev pogrom occurred during a period of tension in Russia (two years before the first, unsuccessful revolution). Wanting to dispel the tension, the Czarist government once again organised a pogrom against the Jews. Unlike previous pogroms, however, the Kishinev pogrom received substantial international attention.

To follow is an excerpt from a description of the pogrom printed in the New York Times:

It is impossible to account the amount of goods destroyed in a few hours. The hurrahs of the rioting. The pitiful cries of the victims filled the air. Wherever a Jew was met he was savagely beaten into insensibility. One Jew was dragged from a streetcar and beaten until the mob thought he was dead. The air was filled with feathers and torn bedding. Every Jewish household was broken into and the unfortunate Jews in their terror endeavoured to hide in cellars and under roofs. The mob entered the synagogue, desecrated the biggest house of worship and defiled the Scrolls of the Law.

The conduct of the intelligent Christians was disgraceful. They made no attempt to check the rioting. They simply walked around enjoying the frightful sport. On Tuesday, the third day, when it became known that the troops had received orders to shoot, the rioters ceased.

The 12,000 Russian soldiers in the city did nothing to halt the violence. Two days later, 118 Jewish men, women, and children had been murdered, 1,200 were wounded, and 4,000 families were left homeless and destitute.

After Kishinev, pogroms became standard government policy. The violence reached its climax in October 1905 and continued throughout 1906 when pogroms were virtually a daily Russian occurrence. The police and army openly supported the rioters and protected them against Jewish efforts of self-defence.

By the end of the 19th century Jews were desperate for change. Some adopted the Zionist movement's solution that the only possible respite for the persecuted Jews would be in a land of their own. Others felt seeking asylum in the desert of Palestine was an escapist's pipedream. Instead, they joined every alternative, extreme, and/or radical political faction they could find. Some became anarchists, others communist, socialist or Bundists. They would do anything for change — and it was about to come with the advent of the Russian Revolution and World War I after which Poland once again found itself on the map.

The Interwar Period (1918–1939)

Poland was a primary battle ground of World War I. Though the fighting ravaged the country, shortly after the armistice with Germany in November 1918, Poland regained its independence from Russia as the Second Polish Republic. It reaffirmed its independence after a series of military conflicts, the most notable being the Polish-Soviet War (1919–1921) when Poland inflicted a crushing defeat on the Red Army.

The Republic of Poland was now reborn as the sixth largest country in Europe with a rapidly growing population. By the 1930s, more than 32 million people called Poland "home." Of these, Jews numbered around 3.5 million people, or about 10% of the total Polish population. Poland was once again the largest Jewish centre in all of Europe.

Though the numbers suggest that Jews held a significant place in Polish society, the reality of Jewish life in the Second Republic was somewhat less than desirable. The various ethnicities residing in Poland (65% ethnic Poles, 16% Ukrainians, 10% Jews) may have lived side by side, but they certainly did not live together. Factors preventing the three groups from intermixing included insurmountable differences in language, religion and customs. One of the few things many Poles and Ukrainians could agree on was their anti-Semitic sentiment.

Economic upheaval during the interwar period made life difficult for all, but those most affected by the turmoil were small business owners, merchants and craftsmen, two-thirds of whom were Jewish. Polish Jews held 50% of Poland's clothing and leather industries, as well as 70% of all retail establishments throughout the country. Yet, despite these impressive figures, Jewish enterprises were not often successful, and most Jews lived in dire poverty.

Political figures made liberal use of Jew-hatred when outlining party platforms during the rebuilding of the Polish state. In the 1930s, anti-Jewish attitudes were reinforced by government policies such as boycotts against the Jews and a 1936 statute that placed restrictions on ritual slaughter. Actions perpetrated against

Parliamentary election poster for the National Unity Camp, 1938, calling on Poles to isolate the Jews so they might be expelled from Poland

the Jewish business sector left hundreds of thousands of Jewish families without the means to earn a livelihood.

Polish Jews looked to education as the way out of the cycle of poverty and as a chance for a better life. Because Poland permitted Jewish doctors and lawyers to pursue private practices, medical and legal studies were, in particular, very popular among Polish Jewish youth. Jews maintained an astonishing professional presence in Poland, accounting for 56% of all doctors, 43% of all teachers, 22% of all journalists and 33% of all lawyers.[44]

The nation grew openly anti-Semitic. Many academic as well as business associations introduced exclusionary bylaws. Formal boycotts were applied to Jewish stalls in the public markets, while guards were posted at the entry to Jewish shops in order to stave off Christian customers.

Universities were scenes of anti-Semitic incidents directed and produced by students connected to nationalistic movements. The students placed pressure on university administrators to introduce the so-called "ghetto benches," or

Students at the Lvov Polytechnic demand the introduction of the "ghetto bench" 1937

separate benches for Jewish students. It was these nationalistic students who had clamoured for and succeeded in having the universities introduce the numerus clausus, or Jewish student quotas.

In this climate of anti-Semitic propaganda and provocation, there was an ever-growing wave of violence against Jewish Poles. In the second half of the 1930s, a wave of pogroms spread throughout Poland in Przytyk,

Czestochowa, Lublin, Bialystok and Grodno. In addition to the horror of these pogroms, in which 79 Jews were killed and 500 injured, government measures against the Jews placed increasing pressure on them to emigrate.

In response, Polish Jews were experiencing their own brand of nationalistic fervour as they struggled to preserve their identity, even going so far as to demand that Yiddish and Hebrew be granted government status as national languages. Many Polish Jews became Zionists. Also worthy of note is the youth movement known as Hechalutz, which instituted a training program with the aim of preparing thousands of young Jewish men and women for immigration to Palestine. No less than half of Jewish immigrants to Palestine during this inter-war period hailed from Poland.

Two other major banners under which Polish Jewry aligned were the Agudas Yisroel and the Bund. Agudas Yisroel represented the more Orthodox sector of the Jewish masses and sought to strengthen Jewish life in Poland. The organization rejected both secularism and Zionism, deeming these as destructive forces that would soon shred the fabric of Jewish tradition. The Bund also rejected Zionism, but for a very different reason, deeming the movement to be nothing but a reactionary Utopian dream.

In 1939, with so many competing factions from within and pressures from without, the future of Polish Jewry was uncertain. Only a few of the most astute were able to predict what would happen next, and of those, none could have imagined its full horror.

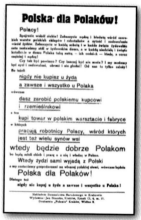

Announcement of the economic boycott of the Jews, 1936

PART 2:
THE HOLOCAUST

Understanding the Nazi Regime

Many people assume that the Nazi party came to power in the 1930s on an innovative anti-Semitic platform whose sole agenda was to exterminate the Jews and other "unacceptable" people. This is not quite the case. In taking a mature look at the Holocaust, one sees that there are a number of other dimensions to Hitler's Reich that should be considered. These include the culture of the times and its prevailing attitudes, how the Nazi party rose to power, what the Nazis sought to achieve and how they sought to achieve those goals.

In his book *Mein Kampf*, which he wrote while imprisoned for political crimes, Hitler expressed his hatred of what he believed to be the world's twin evils: communism and Judaism. However, these ideas were certainly not innovative. Hitler drew upon a long-standing tradition of German anti-Semitism in making Jews the scapegoat for Germany's troubles.

Hitler appointed chancellor, 30 Jan 1933

Since the early Middle Ages when Jews first arrived in Western Europe, their Christian hosts mistrusted them. When Jews refused to assimilate into local culture and rejected Christianity, mistrust often transformed into contempt. As detailed in Part 1 of this book, throughout the centuries, Jews had been the scapegoat of choice for German problems, such as the Black Death, economic depressions and missing children.

The founder of the Protestant movement, Germany's Martin Luther, paved the way for centuries of violent anti-Semitism:

What then shall we Christians do with this damned, rejected race of Jews? ...We must prayerfully and reverentially practice a merciful severity. Let me give you my honest advice. First, their synagogues or churches should be set on fire, and whatever does not burn up should be covered or spread over with dirt. Secondly, their homes should likewise be broken down and destroyed. They ought to be put under one roof or in a stable, like gypsies, in order that they may realise that they are not masters in our land. Thirdly, they should be deprived of their prayer books and Talmuds. Fourthly, their rabbis must be forbidden under threat of death to teach anymore. To sum up, dear princes and nobles who have Jews in your domains, if this advice of mine does not suit you, then find a better one so that you and we may be free of this insufferable devilish burden—the Jews.[49]

Title page and portrait from a 1581 edition of Martin Luther's writings.
He was the founder of the Protestant movement and an outspoken anti-Semite.

Martin Luther's remarks regarding the Jews continued to be quoted four centuries later in Nazi newspapers and pamphlets, but before they could represent the popular view, the stage first had to be set.

The German Empire was founded in 1871. The first few years of the new German nation witnessed an unprecedented economic boom. These halcyon years came to an abrupt end in 1873 when economic depression swept the globe. For a startling six years, Germany's gross national product declined. As a result, social and economic concerns took increasing precedence over political ones.

During the 19th century, Jews began to enter mainstream German society. The price of admission typically was their religious observance. Just when these "enlightened" Jews hoped that jettisoning their Jewish identity would eliminate the age-old "dislike of the unlike," a new form of anti-Semitism arose. Germans almost spontaneously redirected their suspicion from traditional Jews to acculturated ones. By the end of the century, a number of influential thinkers

Der Stürmer, depicting Jews draining the blood of German children. At the bottom of the page: "Die Juden sind unser Unglück!" — The Jews are our misfortune.

began to publish works that legitimized anti-Semitism.

Heinrich von Treitschke was one of the most prominent historians of nineteenth-century Germany, and also one of the most politically engaged. In 1879, he wrote a long essay claiming that the fundamental differences between German Jews and Christians could not be reconciled. He declared that "The Jews are our misfortune." His condemnation would become the motto of Julius Streicher's *Der Stürmer,* the Nazi newspaper and primary organ of Nazi propaganda.

Also in 1879, Wilhelm Marr, a German agitator and publicist, coined the term "anti-Semitism," arguing in his influential book, *The Way for Germandom to be Victorious over Judaism,* that assimilated Jews were undermining German culture and were responsible for Germany's bleak economic outlook.

In 1878, Adolf Stöcker, the court chaplain to Kaiser Wilhelm, founded Germany's first anti-Semitic political party: the Christian Social Party. Anti-Semitism was a minor theme in the party's early stages, but Stöcker discovered that the more he developed his anti-Semitic platform, the more popular his party became.

Soon, many Germans were advocating legal action against Germany's Jews, who at the time constituted less than 1% of the total German population. By the mid-1890s, legislation had been proposed in the Reichstag to limit Jewish education, Jewish participation in the professions and other basic rights that were afforded to other citizens. Though none of these proposals were enacted, anti-Jewish sentiment continued to fester and became acceptable in German society.

German anti-Semitism grew more sinister as it became intertwined with a perverse notion of "social Darwinism," which viewed all of history as a struggle for existence between human races in which only the "fittest" survive. In 1854, a French aristocrat, Joseph Arthur de Gobineau, wrote *An Essay on the Inequality of Human Races*, in which he developed the thesis of the "Aryan Master Race."

Gobineau's work influenced many. One of those particularly taken by his racial ideas was Houston Steward Chamberlain. Chamberlain was a member of German high society and the son-in-law of famed composer Richard Wagner. In 1899, Chamberlain wrote the best-selling *The Foundations of the Nineteenth Century*, in which he advanced various racist and especially anti-Semitic theories. In it, he contrasted the "typical" honest, loyal German with the "typical" greedy, immoral Jew.

Chamberlain's works were read widely throughout Europe, especially in Germany. His reception was particularly favourable among Germany's conservative elite. Kaiser Wilhelm II befriended Chamberlain, maintaining a correspondence and inviting him to stay at his court. The Kaiser ordered Chamberlain's book to be included in Germany's secondary school curricula and public libraries, and ensured that it was distributed to German soldiers.

Chamberlin's *Foundations* would prove to be a seminal work in German nationalism. Because of its popular success, and aided by Chamberlain's association with the Wagner circle, its ideas regarding Aryan supremacy and the struggle against Jewish influence spread widely. If it did not form the framework of later National Socialist ideology, at the very least it provided its adherents with a seemingly intellectual justification.

The signing of the Treaty of Versailles in 1918 brought the First World War to an end. One of its most significant and controversial provisions required Germany to accept sole responsibility for the war. Under the terms of Articles 231-248 (later known as the War Guilt Clauses), Germany was forced to make substantial territorial concessions and financial reparations, and was forced to undertake unilateral disarmament and severe military restrictions.

As was to be expected, the Treaty of Versailles brought shame and anger to the German people; but this was just the beginning of their problems. The Great Depression of the 1930s thoroughly destabilised Germany's already weak economy. The country was beset by hyperinflation of legendary proportions. The incumbent liberal Weimar Party failed to provide a stable government capable of ruling for more than a few months.

The people despaired. As an expression of their frustration, many voters turned their support to parties on the far right and far left of the political spectrum. The National Socialist German Workers' Party (NSDAP), better known as the Nazi Party, promised to address the problems that the German people faced. Its political platform advocated a strong authoritarian government that would undertake radical changes to promote economic stability, stem unemployment, expedite military rearmament, foster cultural renewal and above all, restore national pride.

With this backdrop in place, the political stage was set for a series of events that has been assessed as everything from utterly inevitable to outright miraculous: In 1933, Hitler and the Nazi Party, through a democratic process in one of the world's most "advanced" and "civilized" countries, assumed total, unmitigated control of Germany.

In *Mein Kampf*, Hitler embraced Gobineau's theory of the Aryan master race. This view, combined with the perverse doctrine of social Darwinism, led Hitler to argue that the German people had a moral obligation to rise up and rule the world. As such, the Nazis advocated a complete repudiation of the war reparations and a reclamation of forfeited territory—in direct defiance of the Versailles Treaty. Hitler believed that Aryan hegemony was

*Cover of Hitler's
Mein Kampf,
first edition 1925*

compromised by the very existence of a Jewish race, which represented everything he opposed. Although Jews constituted but 1% of the German population, he believed they were insidiously taking over the country.

Uniting the people by focusing them on a familiar common enemy, Hitler blamed the Jews and the communists for the failure of the Weimar government and for Germany's loss of dignity. Hitler alleged that the Jews were involved in a massive conspiracy, and that they were responsible for the German loss in World War I. He pointed to the successful bankers, financiers, media leaders and businessmen as examples of this Jewish conspiracy. Claiming that 75% of communists were Jews, he believed that the Jews were conspiring with the communists to take over the world. Hitler argued that the combination of Jews and communists had already been successful in Russia and now threatened the rest of Europe. Therefore, he promised the German electorate that he would cleanse the country of every trace of both Jews and communists.

Part of the Nazi regime's initial efforts to persecute minorities and "undesirables" included the formation of the Gestapo, the official secret police of Nazi Germany, in April 1934. Membership was voluntary, and by 1943, the Gestapo boasted some 50,000 members. Through its almost super-legal power to arrest and confine without any recourse to law whatsoever, the Gestapo was the Reich's principal means for eliminating enemies of the Nazi regime—especially the Jews. At first, separation and isolation were the primary means of persecution. Jews and other undesirables such as homosexuals and Jehovah's Witnesses, were required to wear badges in public, overtly designating their status. Almost all those who wore badges eventually found themselves in concentration camps.

The Gestapo alone, with "just" 50,000 operatives, would not have been capable of fulfilling the Nazi's genocidal ambitions throughout its would-be world empire. For that, Hitler required his Praetorian Guard, a paramilitary organisation known as the *Schutzstaffel* (protective units), or SS for short. In its early years, the SS was a relatively small cadre of thugs who served as Hitler's personal bodyguards. Under the stewardship of Heinrich Himmler, it was transformed into an organisation of almost one million men that wielded at least as much power as Germany's regular armed forces, the Wehrmacht. The men of the SS idolized Hitler and were infected with the most virulent strain of ideological virus that he sought to afflict upon the world. They were trained from their youth to be hateful, cruel and ruthless. The SS would be responsible for many of the most heinous crimes that the Nazis would commit against humanity.

Hitler and his cohorts believed that the combination of the Reich's invincible Wehrmacht, its inscrutable Gestapo and its indefatigable SS, would bring inevitable success in establishing the New Order they envisioned.

Although the Jews were their primary targets during the War, it must be noted that the Nazis and their collaborators also persecuted other groups for racial or ideological reasons. They viewed Poles and other Slavic peoples as inferior, and slated them for subjugation, forced labour and eventual annihilation. Like the Jews, the Roma (Gypsies) were persecuted on racial grounds. They were among the first to be killed in mobile gas vans at Chelmno, and more than 20,000 Gypsies were shipped to the death factories of Auschwitz-Birkenau. Through the so-called Euthanasia Program, the Nazis murdered an estimated 200,000 individuals with mental or physical disabilities. Christian church leaders who opposed Nazism, as well as thousands of Jehovah's Witnesses who refused to salute Adolf Hitler or to serve in the German army, were punished severely under the regime. Finally, the Nazis persecuted male homosexuals, whose behaviour they considered a hindrance to the preservation of the German nation.

Respect must be paid and consideration must be given to all the victims of the Nazi regime. This book has been designed to supplement Triumph and Tragedy, thus it will focus primarily on the story of Germany's all-out war against the Jews—a war that we call "The Holocaust."

Lexicon of the Holocaust

Aktion

A Nazi operation involving the mass assembly, deportation and murder of Jews.

Arbeit macht frei

German: Work makes [you] free. The sardonic slogan over the entrance gate at Auschwitz and other concentration camps.

"Arbeit macht frei" sign at Auschwitz

Aryan

Originally a technical linguistic term that was misappropriated by the Nazi regime to refer to the "master race." The Nuremberg Laws of 1935 established the legal definition of an Aryan as a "person of Germanic origin."

Crematoria at Auschwitz

Crematorium (plural: crematoria)

An oven for burning the dead.

Death Camp a.k.a. Extermination Camp

A concentration camp designed for systematic murder. Five such camps existed: Chelmno, Belzec, Sobibor, Treblinka and Auschwitz-Birkenau. All were

German civilians forced to walk past 30 starved Jewish bodies from a Death March

93

located in Poland. Sometimes, Majdanek is listed as a sixth extermination camp, because it also had apparatus designed for systematic murder; however, unlike the other five, this was not its primary purpose.

Death March

Forced evacuations of concentration camp prisoners over long distances under heavy guard and extremely harsh conditions.

Einsatzgruppen

Mobile killing squads of 600–1,000 men that followed the German armies into the Soviet Union in June 1941. These units were supported by units of the uniformed German Order Police and auxiliaries of volunteers (Estonian, Latvian, Lithuanian and Ukrainian). Their victims, primarily Jews, were executed by shooting and were buried in mass graves from which they were later exhumed and burned. At least a million Jews were killed by the Einsatzgruppen.

Endlösung a.k.a. Final Solution

Germany's plan to murder all the Jews of Europe. The term was employed at the Wannsee Conference (Berlin, 20 January 1942) where German officials discussed its implementation.

German soldiers of the Waffen-SS and the Reich Labour Service look on as a member of an Einsatzgruppe prepares to shoot a Ukrainian Jew sitting on the edge of a mass grave filled with corpses. Locale: Vinnitsa, 1942

Führer

German: Leader. This was Hitler's honorific title.

Generalgouvernement a.k.a. General Government

General Government refers to the Polish territories under German military occupation during World War II that were not annexed to Germany or other occupied areas.

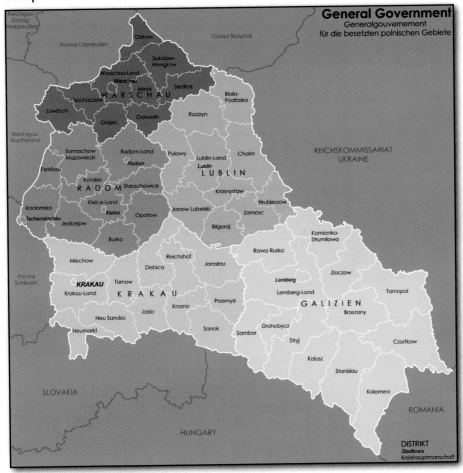

Gestapo

A contraction of *Geheime Staatspolizei,* "Secret State Police." Overseen by Heinrich Himmler, this was the official secret police of Nazi Germany.

Ghetto

A term dating back to medieval times. This was a "Jewish Quarter," established by occupying German forces, where all Jews from the surrounding areas were forced to reside. Usually surrounded by barbed wire or walls, and often sealed so that people were prevented from leaving or entering, the ghettos were characterized by overcrowding, starvation and forced labour. All were ultimately destroyed as the Jews were deported to death camps.

Hitler-Jugend a.k.a. Hitler Youth

From 1922 until 1945, a paramilitary organisation of the Nazi Party for boys aged ten to eighteen.

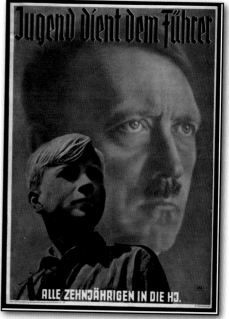

Judenfrei / Judeinrein

German terms for "free of Jews" and "clean of Jews," respectively. These terms were used by the Nazis to describe a location once all its Jewish residents had been deported or killed.

Judenrat

The Judenrat was the council of Jews appointed by the Nazis in each Jewish community or ghetto. A Judenrat was

Hitler Youth recruitment poster. The wording translates to: "Youth serves the leader. All ten-year-olds into the Hitler Youth."

established for every group of Jews in the occupied areas of Poland. They were typically led by existing community leaders who were expected to enforce Nazi decrees and liaise between Nazi authorities and the local Jewish population. These functions placed the Judenrat in a powerful but conflicted position. The morality of the decisions of many Judenrat leaders continues to be the subject of debate. Among the most controversial were Mordechai Rumkowski in Lodz and Jacob Gens in Vilna, both of whom justified the sacrifice of some Jews in order to save others.

Kanada a.k.a. Canada

As Jews were rounded up from around Europe and "relocated" to Auschwitz, they were told to bring their essential belongings on the transport. Upon arrival, these belongings were confiscated and sorted in large warehouses in a particular section of the camp. This section was nicknamed "Kanada" because it was a place of abundance. Here, a worker might find a suitable undergarment or morsel of food.

Kapo

An inmate in a concentration camp who was in charge of other inmates. Kapos received more privileges than regular prisoners, towards whom they were often brutal.

Konzentrazionslager a.k.a. KL, KZ, Concentration Camp

Immediately upon their assumption of power in 1933, the Nazis established camps for the imprisonment of all "enemies" of their regime: political opponents (e.g., communists, socialists and monarchists), Jehovah's Witnesses, Gypsies, homosexuals and other "asocials." Beginning in 1938, Jews were targeted for internment solely because they were Jews. The first three concentration camps established were Dachau (near Munich), Buchenwald (near Weimar) and Sachsenhausen (near Berlin).

Kristallnacht

German: the night of broken glass. The term refers to the anti-Jewish riots of 9-10 November 1938 in Germany and Austria. Kristallnacht was explained by the German government as a spontaneous popular reaction to the assassination of German diplomat Ernst vom Rath by Herschel Grynszpan, a German-born Polish Jew. In truth however, it was a pre-organised, coordinated attack on Jewish people and their property in

Street scene after Kristallnacht

which many Jews were murdered and 25,000–30,000 were arrested and placed in concentration camps. Two hundred and sixty-seven synagogues were destroyed, and thousands of homes and businesses were ransacked. These actions were carried out by the Hitler Youth, Gestapo, SS and SA.

Lebensraum

German: "living space." The Hitlerian doctrine that sought to justify expansion of the German Reich to satisfy Germany's need for land and resources.

Operation Reinhard

Nazi code name for the annihilation of the Jews in the Generalgouvernement (see above) in the extermination camps Belzec, Sobibor and Treblinka. These death camps had no organisational link to the massive concentration camp system, being controlled instead by the SS leadership of the Lublin District.

Pogrom

Violent, organised assault upon Jews, usually with the connivance of government officials.

Raus!

German: "Out!"

Selektion a.k.a. Selection

Euphemism for the process of choosing victims for the gas chambers in the Nazi camps by separating them from those considered fit to work.

Russian Jews awaiting selection

Shoah

Hebrew: devastation, ruin. This term is increasingly used by Jews and scholars to refer to the Jewish Holocaust, as the word Holocaust is increasingly appropriated to reference other genocidal and quasi-genocidal events.

Shtetl

Yiddish: a Jewish town or village.

Sonderkommando

A Jewish forced labour unit that worked in the death camps, assisting the extermination and cremation process until they themselves were killed and

99

replaced by fresh recruits. Among other tasks, they cleared the gas chambers, cremated bodies and sorted victims' clothing.

SS

An abbreviation for *Schutzstaffel* (Protective Units), usually written with two lightning bolts. Originally organised as Hitler's personal bodyguard, it was transformed by Heinrich Himmler into an organisation of almost one million men. The SS exerted as much political influence in the Third Reich as did Germany's regular armed forces.
Built upon Nazi ideology, the SS was responsible for the most heinous crimes against humanity perpetrated by the Nazis during World War II.

Storm troopers a.k.a. SA

An abbreviation for the *Sturmabteilung* (assault detachment). This paramilitary organisation of the Nazi Party was very important to Adolf Hitler's rise to power but was largely irrelevant after he took control of Germany in 1933, being effectively superseded by the SS.

Uberleben

German: to outlive. The will to survive.

Umschlagplatz

German: a collection point. It was a loading point in the Warsaw ghetto for all the products made in the ghetto. Later, this became the scene of extreme atrocities when Jews were rounded up for deportation to Treblinka.

Warsaw's Umschlagplatz

Untermensch

German: subhuman. A member of an "inferior race" in Nazi ideology.

Wannsee Conference

The meeting on 20 January 1942, of 15 Nazi officials (including Reinhard Heydrich and Adolf Eichmann) in the Berlin suburb of Grossen-Wannsee for the purpose of planning the Final Solution.

Wehrmacht

German: military or defence power. Term referring to Germany's military forces from 1935 to 1945.

Zyklon B

IG Farben's brand name for hydrogen cyanide a poisonous gas used in the gas chambers of the Nazi extermination camps.

Zyklon B canisters used in Auschwitz

Timeline of the Holocaust

1939

SEPTEMBER: On 1 September 1939, Hitler invades Poland, officially starting World War II. Two days later, Britain and France, obliged by treaty to help Poland, declare war on Germany. In less than four weeks, Poland collapses. Heydrich orders ghettos to be established in occupied Poland under Judenrats.

OCTOBER: A "Führer Decree" makes murder by medical personnel an official policy. Sick and crippled people are to be exterminated. The first deportation of Austrian/Moravian Jews to Poland takes place. Forced labour is decreed for Polish Jews aged 14 to 60, and the first Polish ghetto is established in Piotrkow, Poland.

NOVEMBER: Germans begin expulsion of Jews from Western Poland. They destroy the Yeshiva (Talmudic Academy) in Lublin and its huge library, which gave "so much pleasure to its conquerors that it was recalled with glee more than a year later." Wearing a distinctive yellow armband, "Judenstern" (Jewish star), becomes obligatory for all Jews in Central Poland.

Armbands

DECEMBER: Adolf Eichmann becomes the head of the Gestapo wing dealing with Jews. The Adult Euthanasia Program—The Reich Work Group of Sanatoriums and Nursing Homes known as T4— becomes systemized with the inventory and subsequent gassing of Jewish mental patients.

1940

JANUARY: First underground activities by Jewish Youth movements in Poland begin.

1940 Con't

FEBRUARY: Germans set up the Lodz ghetto. The first deportation of Jews from Germany to Poland.

APRIL: Himmler issues directive to establish a concentration camp at Auschwitz. The Lodz ghetto is sealed with 230,000 people in 1.6 square miles.

MAY: Rudolf Höss is appointed Commandant of Auschwitz and a concentration camp is established there.

JUNE: Germany conquers France.

OCTOBER: Anti-Jewish laws are passed by the Vichy government in France. The Warsaw ghetto is established.

NOVEMBER: The Warsaw ghetto is sealed off, ultimately containing half a million Jews.

1941

JANUARY: Gangs of Romanian Legionnaires hunt for Jews, loot and beat Jews in the street, desecrate 25 synagogues, destroy hundreds of homes and shops and butcher hundreds of Jews.

MARCH: Adolf Eichmann is appointed head of the Gestapo Department of Jewish Affairs. 3,600 Jews are arrested in Paris.

JUNE: Germany invades the Soviet Union. *Einsatzgruppen* (mobile killing squads) start conducting mass executions of Jews in German-occupied Soviet territory.

JULY: One of the Einsatzgruppen begins the systematic slaughter of

1941 Con't

Lithuanian Jewry. Ultimately, 70,000–100,000 Jews are shot in the forests near Vilna. Lithuanians assist the Germans in the murder of tens of thousands of Jews in Kovno and Slobodka. Heydrich is appointed by Goering to carry out the Final Solution.

SEPTEMBER: 34,771 Jews are killed by Germans and Ukrainians in the ravine of Babi Yar outside Kiev. The first gassing experiments are made at Auschwitz.

OCTOBER: Auschwitz II, known as Birkenau, is established. Theresienstadt ghetto in Czechoslovakia is established.

DECEMBER: An armed underground organisation is established in the Minsk ghetto. The first Jewish partisan group operates there.

1942

JANUARY: Wannsee Conference: A plan to annihilate all 11 million European Jews is drafted. A unified partisan organisation is established in the Vilna ghetto. A resistance organisation is established in the Kovno ghetto. Hitler speaks at the Sports Palace in Berlin, declaring that "the war will end with the complete annihilation of the Jews."

FEBRUARY: The Struma, a derelict ship with 769 Romanian Jewish refugees on their way to Israel is left adrift in the Black Sea and torpedoed by a Russian submarine whose crew suspected it was a German vessel. Only one person survived.

MARCH: One thousand Jews in the Theresienstadt camp are deported to the new Belzec death camp of which only six survive the war. In the following months another 41,000 will follow in their footsteps. Ten Jews are hanged in Zdunsk Wola near Lodz as substitutes for "the 10 hanged sons of Haman." The Jews of Lublin

**1942
Con't**

are deported to Belzec and extermination begins there. The Jews of Slovakia are deported to Auschwitz, and deportation of French Jews to Auschwitz begins.

APRIL: Einsatzkommando unit reports to Berlin that more than 90,000 Jews have been murdered in Crimea in the previous four-and-a-half months.

MAY: Extermination begins at Sobibor. By October 1943, 250,000 Jews will perish there.

JUNE: In the Warsaw ghetto, more than 100,000 Jews have died of disease and starvation. Treblinka opens. Eichmann officially notes that since December 1941, 97,000 people have been "processed" in three gas-vans. In reprisals for the assassination of Heydrich, the Czech town of Lidice is levelled and the entire population is murdered or deported. A second gas chamber is put into use at Auschwitz. The New York Times reports via the London Daily Telegraph that over 1,000,000 Jews have been killed by the Nazis.

JULY: Gizi Fleischman organises an underground "resistance group" in Czechoslovakia. Jews in Minsk, Lida and Slonim are massacred. The first deportees are sent from Germany and Holland to Auschwitz. The first medical experiments are performed at Auschwitz. Himmler sends a secret directive ordering the "resettlement" of the entire Jewish population of the General Government to be completed by 31 December. Beginning of the Warsaw ghetto Aktion where 6,000 to 7,000 people a day are deported to Treblinka for extermination.

AUGUST: Deportation from Belgium to Auschwitz begins. There is armed resistance during the liquidation of the Mir ghetto.

1942 Con't

AUGUST-SEPTEMBER: More than 250,000 Jews are killed at Belzec, and over 132,000 are killed in Eastern Territory pits.

SEPTEMBER: The Chief Rabbi of Norway, Julius Samuel, refuses to go into hiding and chooses to join 208 Norwegian Jews sent to Bergen-Belsen. New policy of open pit burning of bodies begins at Auschwitz. One hundred and seven thousand bodies are exhumed from mass graves and burned to prevent fouling ground water. Town of Tuczyn with 3,000 Jews stage ghetto-wide armed resistance against Nazis and escape to the forests. Most were ultimately shot by Nazis. Only 20 survived the war.

OCTOBER: Over 58,000 are killed in Belzec, 82,000 at Treblinka and 17,000 at Sobibor. Over 80,000 Jews are killed in Eastern Territory pits.

NOVEMBER: The U.S. State Department confirms the existence of Nazi extermination camps and the murder of two million Jews to date.

DECEMBER: Over 30,000 Yugoslavian Jews are starved, tortured and shot in four camps — 4,500 escape and join the partisans; of these, 1,318 are killed in battle.

1943

JANUARY: U.S. State Department is informed via Switzerland that in one Polish location 6,000 Jews a day are being killed. The first armed resistance in the Warsaw ghetto occurs.

FEBRUARY: The Bulgarian government signs an agreement with the Germans to allow deportations from Macedonia and Thrace; 11,000 Jews are deported.

1943 Con't

MARCH: Liquidation of the Krakow ghetto begins and lasts for two months. In northern Bulgaria, farmers threaten to lie down on the tracks to prevent the deportation of Jews. The Bulgarian Government rescinds the order to deport Northern Bulgarian Jews. Crematorium II at Birkenau is now ready for use.

APRIL: The third and last Macedonian transport reaches the Treblinka "resettlement"; all are gassed. Warsaw ghetto revolt takes place.

MAY: Nazi officer Jergen Stroop reports to his superiors that the Warsaw ghetto is no longer in existence. According to his calculations, 7,000 Jews have been killed in street fighting, 30,000 have been deported to Treblinka and 5,000-6,000 have perished in flames.

JUNE: Himmler orders the liquidation of all Polish and U.S.S.R. ghettos. Professor Clauberg in Auschwitz reports a sterilization rate of 1,000 women a day, mostly of Jewish women from Greece.

AUGUST: Revolt of Sonderkommando in Treblinka.

SEPTEMBER: Liquidation of the Minsk, Vilna and Riga ghettos begins. Most of the 2,000 deported Minsk Jews are killed in Sobibor.

OCTOBER: Orders are given for the expulsion of all Danish Jews. Thanks to Danish underground operations, only 415 Jews are captured by the Germans and 7,000 are evacuated to Sweden. In Sobibor's Camp #1, 600 prisoners revolt and try to escape. One crematorium is destroyed. Most of the escapees are eventually caught and killed.

1943 Con't

NOVEMBER: Within a few days, 50,000 Jews in the Lublin region are deported and shot in ditches behind the Majdanek gas chambers. Jewish underground in Budapest is set up including a workshop from which, by the end of 1944, 10,000 have been supplied with forged documents.

1944

JANUARY: "Report to the Secretary on the Acquiescence of this Government in the Murder of the Jews" is received by the American Secretary of the Treasury, Henry Morgenthau Jr. President Roosevelt establishes War Refugee Board.

MARCH: War Refugee Board evacuates 1,200 Romanian Jews and moves 48,000 to shelter.

MAY: In North Africa, the War Refugee Board opens the first refugee camp. Deportation of Hungarian Jews to Auschwitz begins.

JUNE: U.S. War Department refuses to bomb railroad tracks between Hungary and Auschwitz. Hanna Senesz, a Jewish girl originally from Hungary who had immigrated to Palestine, parachutes behind German lines to connect with Hungarian and Slovak resistance fighters. Caught on the Hungarian border, she dies knowing that her mission has given strength to those suffering in the camps. Since 15 May, 476,000 have been deported to Auschwitz. The allies are victorious on D-Day and it is the beginning of the end for the Third Reich.

JULY: Miklos Horthy, Regent of the Kingdom of Hungary, stops Hungarian deportations. Abortive attempt on Hitler's life by a group of Nazi officers. Russians liberate the Majdanek extermination camp.

1944 Con't

AUGUST: U.S. War Department issues a statement that bombing Auschwitz would divert air power from "decisive operations elsewhere." One hundred and twenty-seven Flying Fortress Bombers drop high-explosives on the factory areas at Auschwitz, less than five miles east of the gas chambers.

OCTOBER: Inmates in Auschwitz rebel; one crematorium is blown up.

NOVEMBER: Last group of Jews is deported from Theresienstadt to Auschwitz. The remainder of the prisoners, approximately 2,300, are deported to Ravensbruck and Bergen-Belsen to meet the growing slave labour demand. Nazis try to hide evidence of death camps.

1945

JANUARY: Death marches to the interior of Germany begin, taking 250,000 Jewish lives. Swedish diplomat Raoul Wallenberg, who saved tens of thousands of Hungarian Jews, is last seen alive with Soviet troops. Approximately 800 prisoners remaining in the Lodz ghetto (after 74,600 had been deported to Auschwitz) are liberated by Soviet troops. Inmates are forced on a death march from Stutthoff concentration camp. Soviet troops arrive at Auschwitz to discover 7,600 survivors and 648 corpses. Most of the prisoners in Auschwitz had been sent out on a death march eight days before.

Children from Auschwitz liberated by the Red Army in January 1945. Although usually most children were killed immediately upon arrival, this group includes Jewish twins kept alive to be used in Mengele's medical experiments.

FEBRUARY: The Gross-Rosen complex is evacuated. Thousands of the 40,000 prisoners who left for other

1945
Con't

camps are murdered en route. Recha Sternbuch initiates the Musy-Himmler negotiations, releasing 1,210 Theresienstadt inmates. Soviet forces capture Budapest, saving 120,000 Jews.

MARCH: Anne Frank dies of typhus in the Bergen-Belsen concentration camp. Hitler orders the destruction of all Germany, believing it to be unworthy of surviving him. His order mandates the destruction not only of military installations, but also of all stores, industries and transportation and communication installations. Nothing is to fall into enemy hands.

APRIL: Most of the Jewish prisoners remaining at the Buchenwald concentration camp in Germany are forced out on death marches. On his last visit to Theresienstadt, Adolf Eichmann is heard to say, "I shall gladly jump into the pit, knowing that in the same pit there are five million enemies of the state." U.S. troops liberate approximately 20,000 prisoners from Buchenwald. British troops liberate Bergen-Belsen and then move on in pursuit of German forces. U.S. troops occupy Munich. Hitler commits suicide. Dachau is liberated by American troops.

30 April 1945, Germany surrenders, bringing an end to the Third Reich.

Frequently Asked Questions

(Note: This material was adapted from The Simon Wiesenthal Centre's "36 Questions about the Holocaust.")

When speaking about the "Holocaust," to what time period are we referring?

The "Holocaust" refers to the period from 30 January 1933, when Hitler became Chancellor of Germany, to 8 May 1945 (V-E Day), the end of the war in Europe.

What was Hitler's ultimate goal in launching World War II?

Hitler's ultimate goal in launching World War II was the establishment of an Aryan empire from Germany to the Urals. He considered this area the natural territory of the German people, an area to which they were entitled by right, the *Lebensraum* (living space) that Germany needed so badly for its farmers to have enough soil. Hitler maintained that these areas were needed for the Aryan race to preserve itself and assure its dominance.

Did the Nazis plan to murder the Jews from the beginning of their regime?

This question is one of the most difficult to answer. While Hitler made several references to killing Jews, both in his early writings (Mein Kampf) and in various speeches during the 1930s, it is fairly certain that the Nazis had no operative plan for the systematic annihilation of the Jews before 1941. The decision on the systematic murder of the Jews was apparently made in the late winter or the early spring of 1941, in conjunction with the decision to invade the Soviet Union.

How many Jews were murdered during the Holocaust?

While it is impossible to ascertain the exact number of Jewish victims, statistics indicate that the total was over 5,860,000. Six million is the round figure accepted by most authorities. Every Jewish community in occupied Europe suffered losses during the Holocaust. The Jewish communities in North Africa were persecuted, but the Jews in these countries were neither deported to the death camps, nor were they systematically murdered.

COUNTRY	Estimated pre-war Jewish population	Estimated Jewish population annihilated	Percent killed
POLAND	3,300,000	3,000,000	90
BALTIC COUNTRIES	253,000	228,000	90
GERMANY & AUSTRIA	240,000	210,000	90
BOHEMIA & MORAVIA	90,000	80,000	89
SLOVAKIA	90,000	75,000	83
GREECE	70,000	54,000	77
NETHERLANDS	140,000	105,000	75
HUNGARY	650,000	450,000	70
BYELORUSSIAN SSR	375,000	245,000	65
UKRAINIAN SSR	1,500,000	900,000	60
BELGIUM	65,000	40,000	60
YUGOSLAVIA	43,000	26,000	60
ROMANIA	600,000	300,000	50
NORWAY	2,173	890	41
FRANCE	350,000	90,000	26
BULGARIA	64,000	14,000	22
ITALY	40,000	8,000	20
LUXEMBURG	5,000	1,000	20
RUSSIAN SFSR	975,000	107,000	11
DENMARK	8,000	52	<1
FINLAND	2,000	22	1
Total	8,861,800	5,933,900	67

How many non-Jewish civilians were murdered during World War II?

While it is impossible to ascertain the exact number, the recognised figure is approximately five million. Among the groups which the Nazis and their collaborators murdered and persecuted were: Gypsies, Serbs, Polish intelligentsia, resistance fighters from all of the nations, German opponents of Nazism, homosexuals, Jehovah's Witnesses, habitual criminals and the "anti-social" (e.g., beggars, vagrants) and the handicapped.

What does the term "Final Solution" mean and what is its origin?

The term "Final Solution" (*Die Endlösung*, in German) refers to Germany's plan to murder all the Jews of Europe. The term was employed at the Wannsee Conference (Berlin; 20 January 1942) where German officials discussed its implementation.

When did the "Final Solution" actually begin?

While thousands of Jews were murdered by the Nazis or died as a direct result of discriminatory measures instituted against Jews during the initial years of the Third Reich, the systematic murder of Jews did not begin until the German invasion of the Soviet Union in June 1941.

How did the Germans define who was Jewish?

On 14 November 1935, the Nazis issued the following definition's of a Jew: anyone with three Jewish grandparents; someone with two Jewish grandparents who belonged to the Jewish community on 15 September 1935, or joined thereafter; was married to a Jew or Jewess on 15 September 1935, or married one thereafter; was the offspring of a marriage or extramarital liaison with a Jew on or after 15 September 1935.

When was the first concentration camp established and who were the first inmates?

Crematorium in Dachau

The first concentration camp, Dachau, opened on 22 March 1933. The camp's first inmates were comprised mostly of the non-Jewish groups that the Nazi regime would oppress throughout the War. Among them were political prisoners (e.g., Communists or Social Democrats), habitual criminals, homosexuals, Jehovah's Witnesses and "anti-socials" (beggars, vagrants, hawkers). Others who were considered problematic by the Nazis (e.g., Jewish writers and journalists, lawyers, unpopular industrialists, and political officials) were also imprisoned.

What was the difference between the persecution of the Jews and the persecution of other groups classified by the Nazis as enemies of the Third Reich?

The Jews were the only group singled out for total, systematic annihilation by the Nazis. The only way for Jews to escape the death sentence imposed by the Nazis was to flee from Nazi-controlled Europe. According to the Nazis' Final Solution, every single Jew was to be killed.

Other enemies of the Reich were persecuted as individuals. Their families were usually not held accountable for the crimes—real or alleged—of their relatives. Thus, if a person were executed or sent to a concentration camp, it did not mean that each member of his family would meet the same fate. Moreover, the Nazis' enemies were usually classified as such because of their actions or political affiliation (actions and/or opinions which could be revised). The "crime" of the Jews was their racial origin, which could never be changed.

Why were the Jews singled out for extermination?

The explanation of the Nazis' implacable hatred of the Jew rests on their distorted world view which saw history as a racial struggle and which should culminate in the triumph of the superior Aryan race. They considered the Jews a race whose goal was world domination and who, therefore, were an obstruction to Aryan dominance. Regarding the Jews as a threat, the Nazi's felt duty-bound to eliminate them. Moreover, the Jews' racial origin was seen as making them habitual criminals who could never be rehabilitated and who were hopelessly corrupt and inferior.

Did the Jews in Europe realize what was going to happen to them?

Regarding the potential victims' knowledge of the Final Solution, several key points must be kept in mind. First of all, the Nazis did not publicize the Final Solution, nor did they ever openly speak about it. Every attempt was made to fool the victims and thereby prevent or minimize resistance. Deportees were always told that they were going to be "resettled." They were led to believe that they were being sent to "the

Captured Jewish women, Budapest, Hungary 1944

East" where conditions would be better than those in the ghettos. Following arrival in certain concentration camps, the inmates were forced to write home about the wonderful conditions in their new place of residence. The Germans made every effort to ensure secrecy. In addition, the notion that human beings— let alone the civilized Germans—could build camps with special apparatus for mass murder seemed unbelievable in those days. Escapees who did return to the ghetto frequently encountered disbelief when they related their experiences. Even Jews who had heard of the camps had difficulty believing reports of what the Germans were doing there. Thus, there is no doubt that many European Jews were not aware of the Final Solution, especially in its early stages. This fact has been corroborated by German documents and the testimonies of survivors.

What did people in Germany know about the persecution of Jews and other enemies of Nazism?

Certain initial aspects of Nazi persecution of Jews and other opponents were common knowledge in Germany. For example, everyone knew about the Boycott of 1 April 1933, the Laws of April and the Nuremberg Laws, because they were fully publicized. Moreover, offenders were often publicly punished and shamed. The same holds true for subsequent anti-Jewish measures. Kristallnacht (The Night of the Broken Glass) was a public pogrom, carried out in full view of the entire population. While information on the concentration camps was not publicized, a great deal of information was available to the German public, and the treatment of the inmates was generally known, although exact details were not easily obtained.

As for the implementation of the Final Solution and the murder of other undesirable elements, the situation was different. The Nazis attempted to keep the murders a secret and, therefore, took precautionary measures to ensure that they would not be publicized. Their efforts, however, were only partially successful. For example, public protests by various clergymen led to the halt of the euthanasia program in August of 1941. These protests were obviously the result of the fact that many were aware that the Nazis were killing the mentally ill in special institutions.

It was common knowledge in Germany that the Jews who had been sent to the East had "disappeared." While large segments of the German population did not know what had actually happened to the Jews, there were thousands upon thousands of Germans who participated in and/or witnessed the implementation of the Final Solution: members of the SS, the Einsatzgruppen, death camp or concentration camp guards, police in occupied Europe and some members of the Wehrmacht.

Did all Germans support Hitler's plan for the persecution of the Jews?

While some Germans who opposed Hitler agreed with his anti-Jewish policies, many others were against his persecution of the Jews. Despite this opposition, there is no evidence of any large-scale protest regarding the treatment of the Jews. There were Germans who defied the 1 April 1933 boycott, and purposely patronized Jewish stores. Some Germans helped Jews escape or hide, but their numbers were very small. The Nazis sent a Berlin priest, Dompropst Bernhard Lichtenberg, to a concentration camp for having prayed daily for the Jews. Other priests were deported for their failure to cooperate with Nazi anti-Semitic policies; however, the majority of the clergy complied with the directives against German Jewry and did not openly protest.

Did the people of occupied Europe know about Nazi plans for the Jews? What was their attitude? Did they cooperate with the Nazis against the Jews?

The attitude of the local conquered populations vis-à-vis the persecution and destruction of the Jews varied from zealous collaboration with the Nazis to active assistance to Jews; thus, it is difficult to make generalizations. The situation also varied from country to country. In Eastern Europe and especially in Poland, Russia and the Baltic States (Estonia, Latvia, and Lithuania), there was much greater knowledge of the Final Solution because it was implemented in those areas. Elsewhere, the local population had less information on the details of the Final Solution.

In every country they occupied, with the exception of Denmark and Bulgaria, the Nazis found many locals who were willing to cooperate fully in the murder of the Jews. This was particularly true in Eastern Europe, where there was a long-standing tradition of virulent anti-Semitism, and where various national groups which had been under Soviet domination (Latvians, Lithuanians and Ukrainians) fostered hopes that the Germans would restore their independence. In several countries in Europe, there were local fascist movements which allied themselves with the Nazis and participated in anti-Jewish actions; for example, the Iron Guard in Romania and the Arrow Guard in Slovakia. On the other hand, in every country in Europe, there were courageous individuals who risked their lives to save Jews. In several countries, there were groups that aided Jews, e.g., Joop Westerweel's group in the Netherlands, Zegota in Poland and the Assisi underground in Italy.

Did the Allies and the people in the Free World know about the events going on in Europe?

The various steps taken by the Nazis prior to the Final Solution were all taken publicly and were, therefore, reported in the press. Foreign correspondents commented on all the major anti-Jewish actions taken by the Nazis in Germany, Austria and Czechoslovakia prior to World War II. Once the war began, obtaining information became more difficult, but reports, nonetheless, were published regarding the fate of the Jews. Thus, although the Nazis did not publicize the Final Solution, less than one year after the systematic murder of the Jews had begun details began to filter out to the West. The first report which spoke of a plan for the mass murder of Jews was smuggled out of Poland by the Bund (a Jewish socialist political organisation) and reached England in the spring of 1942. The details of this report reached the Allies from Vatican sources as well as from informants in Switzerland and the Polish underground. (Jan Karski, an emissary of the Polish underground, personally met with Franklin Roosevelt and British Foreign Minister Anthony Eden.) In June 1942, The New York Times reported that over one million Jews had been killed by the Nazis. Eventually, the American government confirmed the reports to Jewish leaders in late November 1942. They were publicized immediately thereafter. While the details were neither complete nor wholly accurate, the Allies were aware of what the Germans were doing to the Jews at a relatively early date.

What was the response of the Allies to the persecution of the Jews? Could they have done anything to help?

The response of the Allies to the persecution and destruction of European Jewry was inadequate. Only in January 1944 was an agency, the War Refugee Board, established for the express purpose of saving victims of Nazi persecution. Prior to that date, little action was taken. On 17 December 1942, the Allies issued a condemnation of Nazi atrocities against the Jews, but this was the only such declaration made prior to 1944.

No attempt was made to call upon the local population in Europe to refrain from assisting the Nazis in their systematic murder of the Jews. Even following the establishment of the War Refugee Board and the initiation of various rescue efforts, the Allies refused to bomb the death camp of Auschwitz and/or the railway lines leading to that camp, despite the fact that Allied bombers were at that time engaged in bombing factories very close to the camp and were well aware of its existence and function.

Tens of thousands of Jews sought to enter the United States, but they were barred from doing so by stringent American immigration policies. Even the relatively small quotas of visas which existed were often not filled, although the number of applicants was usually many times the number of available places. Conferences held in Evian, France (1938) and Bermuda (1943) to deal with the refugee problem did not provide a solution. At the French meeting, the participants who had been invited by the United States and Great Britain were told that no country would be asked to change its immigration laws. Moreover, the British agreed to participate only if Palestine was not to be considered as an option for Jewish immigration. In Bermuda, the delegates did not deal with the fate of those still in Nazi hands, but rather with those who had already escaped to neutral lands.

Who are the "Righteous Among the Nations"?

"Righteous Among the Nations" or "Righteous Gentiles" refers to those non-Jews who aided Jews during the Holocaust. These people were to be found in every country overrun by or confederate with the Nazis, and their deeds often led to the saving of Jewish lives. Yad Vashem, the Israeli national remembrance authority for the Holocaust, bestows special honours upon these individuals. To date, after carefully evaluating each case, Yad Vashem has recognised approximately 10,000 Righteous Gentiles in three different categories of recognition. The country with the most Righteous Gentiles is Poland. The country with the highest proportion (per capita) is the Netherlands. The figure of 10,000 is far from complete as, in many cases, those who were helped died before reporting their stories. Moreover, this figure only includes those who actually risked their lives to save Jews and not those who merely extended aid.

How many Jews were able to escape from Europe prior to the Holocaust?

It is difficult to arrive at an exact figure for the number of Jews who were able to escape from Europe prior to World War II, since the available statistics are incomplete. From 1933 to 1939, 355,278 German and Austrian Jews left their homes. (Some immigrated to countries that were later overrun by the Nazis.) In the same period, 80,860 Polish Jews immigrated to Palestine, and 51,747 European Jews arrived in Argentina, Brazil and Uruguay. During the years 1938-1939, approximately 35,000 emigrated from Bohemia and Moravia (Czechoslovakia). Shanghai, the only place in the world for which one did not need an entry visa, received approximately 20,000 European Jews (mostly of German origin) who had fled their homelands. Immigration figures for countries of refuge during this period are not available. In addition, many countries did not provide a breakdown of immigration statistics according to ethnic groups. It is impossible, therefore, to ascertain a complete answer to this question.

What efforts were made to save the Jews fleeing from Germany before World War II began?

The United States and Great Britain convened a conference in 1938 at Evian, France, seeking a solution to the refugee problem. With the exception of the Dominican Republic, the nations assembled refused to change their stringent immigration regulations, which were instrumental in preventing large-scale immigration.

Various organisations attempted to facilitate the emigration of the Jews (and non-Jews persecuted as Jews) from Germany. Among the programs launched were the "Transfer Agreement" between the Jewish Agency and the German government, whereby immigrants to Palestine were allowed to transfer their funds to that country in conjunction with the import of German goods to Palestine. Other efforts focused on retraining prospective emigrants in order to increase the number of those eligible for visas, since some countries barred the entry of members of certain professions. Other groups attempted to help in various phases of refugee work: selection of candidates for emigration, transportation of refugees, aid in immigrant absorption, etc. Some groups enlisted the help of governments and international organisations in seeking havens for refugees, in order to increase Jewish emigration. The League of Nations established an agency to assist refugees, but its success was extremely limited due to a lack of political power and inadequate funding.

Efforts were made for the illegal entry of Jewish immigrants to Palestine as early as July 1934, but

Struma Memorial Holon, Israel. Tens of thousands of Jews were rescued from the Nazis by shipping them to Palestine in rickety boats. Many of these boats were intercepted. The last immigrant boat to try to enter Palestine during the war was the Struma, torpedoed in the Black Sea by a Soviet submarine in February 1942.

were later halted until July 1938. Large-scale efforts were resumed by the Mosad l, Aliya Bet, Revisionist Zionists and private parties. Attempts were also made, with some success, to facilitate the illegal entry of refugees to various countries in Latin America.

Why were so few refugees able to flee Europe prior to the outbreak of World War II?

Two important factors should be noted. First, prior to the outbreak of World War II, the Germans were in favour of Jewish emigration. At that time, there were no operative plans to kill the Jews. The goal was to induce them to leave—even by the use of force. Second, it is important to recognise that in the early to mid-1930s, many German Jews were reluctant to emigrate. The majority sought to do so following Kristallnacht (The Night of Broken Glass), 9–10 November 1938. Had more havens been available at that time, more people would certainly have emigrated.

The relatively low number of refugees leaving Europe prior to World War II was the result of strict immigration policies adopted by the prospective host countries. Great Britain took measures to severely limit Jewish immigration to Palestine. In May 1939, the British issued a "White Paper" stipulating that only 75,000 Jewish immigrants would be allowed to enter Palestine over the course of the next five years (10,000 a year, plus an additional 25,000). This decision prevented hundreds of thousands of Jews from escaping Europe. In the United States, the number of immigrants was limited to 153,744 per year, divided by country of origin. Moreover, the entry requirements were so stringent that available quotas were often not filled. Schemes to facilitate immigration outside the quotas never materialized, as the majority of the American public consistently opposed the entry of additional refugees. Other countries, particularly those in Latin America, adopted immigration policies that were similar or even more restrictive, thus closing the doors to prospective immigrants from the Third Reich.

Was there any opposition to the Nazis within Germany?

Throughout the course of the Third Reich, there were different groups who opposed the Nazi regime and certain Nazi policies. They engaged in resistance at different times and with various methods, aims and scope. From the beginning, leftist political groups and a number of disappointed conservatives were in opposition; at a later date, church groups, government officials, students and businessmen also joined. After the tide of the war had turned, elements within the military played an active role in opposing Hitler. At no point, however, was there a unified resistance movement within Germany.

Did the Jews try to fight against the Nazis? To what extent were such efforts successful?

Despite the difficult conditions to which Jews were subjected in Nazi-occupied Europe, many engaged in armed resistance against the Nazis. This resistance can be divided into three basic types of armed activities: ghetto revolts, resistance in concentration and death camps and partisan warfare.

While the Warsaw ghetto revolt, which lasted for about five weeks beginning on 19 April 1943, is probably the best-known example of armed Jewish resistance, there were many other ghetto revolts in which Jews fought against the Nazis as well.

Despite the terrible conditions in the death, concentration and labour camps, Jewish inmates fought against the Nazis at the following sites: Treblinka (2 August 1943); Babi Yar (29 September 1943); Sobibor (14 October 1943); Janowska (19 November 1943); and Auschwitz (7 October 1944).

Jewish partisan units were active in many areas, including Baranovichi, Minsk, the Naliboki forest and Vilna. While the sum total of armed resistance efforts by Jews was not militarily overwhelming and did not play a significant role in the defeat of Nazi Germany, these acts of resistance did lead to the rescue of an undetermined number of Jews and resulted in Nazi casualties and untold damage to German property and self-esteem.

Did the International Red Cross aid victims of Nazi persecution?

During the course of World War II, the International Red Cross (IRC) did very little to aid the Jewish victims of Nazi persecution. Its activities can basically be divided into three periods:

1. September 1939–22 June 1941:

The IRC confined its activities to sending food packages to those in distress in Nazi-occupied Europe. Packages were distributed in accordance with the directives of the German Red Cross. Throughout this time, the IRC complied with the German contention that those in ghettos and camps constituted a threat to the security of the Reich and, therefore, were not allowed to receive aid from the IRC.

2. 22 June 1941–Summer 1944:

Despite numerous requests by Jewish organisations, the IRC refused to publicly protest the mass annihilation of Jews and non-Jews in the camps or to intervene on their behalf. It maintained that any public action on behalf of those under Nazi rule would ultimately prove detrimental to their welfare. At the same time, the IRC attempted to send food parcels to those individuals whose addresses were known to it.

3. Summer 1944–May 1945:

Following intervention by such prominent figures as President Franklin Roosevelt and the King of Sweden, the IRC appealed to Miklos Horthy, Regent of Hungary, to stop the deportation of Hungarian Jews.

The IRC did insist that it be allowed to visit concentration camps, and a delegation did visit the "model ghetto" of Terezin (Theresienstadt). The IRC request came following the receipt of information about the harsh living conditions in the camp. The IRC requested permission to investigate the situation, but the Germans only agreed to allow the visit nine months after submission of the request. This delay provided time for the Nazis to complete a "beautification" program, designed to fool the delegation into thinking that conditions at Terezin were quite good, and that inmates were allowed to live out their lives in relative tranquillity.

The visit, which took place on 23 July 1944, was followed by a favourable report on Terezin to the members of the IRC, to which Jewish organisations protested vigorously, demanding that another delegation visit the camp. Such a visit was not permitted until shortly before the end of the war.

How did Germany's allies, the Japanese and the Italians, treat the Jews in the lands they occupied?

Neither the Italians nor the Japanese cooperated regarding the Final Solution. Although the Italians did, upon German urging, institute discriminatory legislation against Italian Jews, Mussolini's government refused to participate in the Final Solution and consistently refused to deport its Jewish residents. Moreover, in their occupied areas of France, Greece and Yugoslavia, the Italians protected the Jews and did not allow them to be deported. However, when the Germans overthrew the Badoglio government in 1943, the Jews of Italy, as well as those under Italian protection in occupied areas, became subject to the Final Solution.

The Japanese were also relatively tolerant toward the Jews in their country, as well as in the areas which they occupied. Despite pressure by their German allies urging them to take stringent measures against Jews, the Japanese refused to do so. Refugees were allowed to enter Japan until the spring of 1941, and Jews in Japanese-occupied China were treated well. In the summer and fall of 1941, refugees in Japan were transferred to Shanghai, but no measures were taken against them until early 1943, when they were forced to move into the Hongkew ghetto. While conditions were hardly satisfactory, they were far superior to those in the ghettos under German control.

What was the attitude of the churches vis-à-vis the persecution of the Jews? Did the Pope ever speak out against the Nazis?

The head of the Catholic Church at the time of the Nazi rise to power was Pope Pius XI. Although he stated that the myths of "race" and "blood" were contrary to Christian teaching (in a papal encyclical, March 1937), he neither mentioned nor criticized anti-Semitism. His successor, Pius XII (Cardinal Pacelli), was a Germanophile who maintained his neutrality throughout the course of World War II. Although as early as 1942 the Vatican received detailed information on the murder of Jews in concentration camps, the Pope confined his public statements to expressions of sympathy for the victims of injustice and to calls for a more humane conduct of war.

Despite the lack of response by Pope Pius XII, several papal nuncios played an important role in rescue efforts, particularly the nuncios in Hungary, Romania, Slovakia and Turkey. It is not clear to what extent, if any, they operated upon instructions from the Vatican. In Germany, the Catholic Church did not oppose the Nazis' anti-Semitic campaign. Church records were supplied to state authorities, who used them in the detection of people of Jewish origin. While Catholic clergymen protested the Nazi euthanasia program, few, with the exception of Bernhard Lichtenberg, spoke out against the murder of the Jews.

In Western Europe, Catholic clergy spoke out publicly against the persecution of the Jews and actively helped in the rescue of Jews. In Eastern Europe, however, the Catholic clergy was generally more reluctant to help. Dr. Jozef Tiso, the head of state of Slovakia and a Catholic priest, actively cooperated with the Germans as did many other Catholic priests.

The response of Protestant and Eastern Orthodox churches varied. In Germany, Nazi supporters within Protestant churches complied with the anti-Jewish legislation and even excluded Christians of Jewish origin from membership. Pastor Martin Niemöller's Confessing Church defended the rights of Christians of Jewish origin within the church. With the exception of a memorandum sent to Hitler in May 1936, this Church did not publicly protest the persecution of Jews nor the measures taken against them.

In occupied Europe, the position of the Protestant churches varied. In several countries (Denmark, France, the Netherlands, and Norway), local churches and/ or leading clergymen issued public protests when the Nazis began deporting Jews. In other countries (Bulgaria, Greece, and Yugoslavia), some Orthodox church leaders intervened on behalf of Jews and took steps which, in certain cases, led to the rescue of many.

What were the Nuremberg trials?

The term Nuremberg Trials refers to two sets of trials of Nazi war criminals conducted after the war. The first trials were held from 20 November 1945 to 1 October 1946 by the International Military Tribunal (IMT), composed of representatives from France, Great Britain, the Soviet Union, and the United States. It prosecuted the political, military, and economic leaders of the Third Reich who had been captured by the Allies. Among the defendants were many of the most prominent Nazis: Göring, Rosenberg, Streicher, Kaltenbrunner, Seyss-Inquart, Speer, Ribbentrop, and Hess.

Defendants in their dock, Nuremberg Trials. The main target of the prosecution was Hermann Göring (at the left edge on the first row of benches), considered to be the most important surviving official in the Third Reich after Hitler's death.

(Hitler, Himmler and Goebbels were not brought to trial as they had committed suicide.) The second set of trials, known as the Subsequent Nuremberg Proceedings, was conducted before the Nuremberg Military Tribunals (NMT), established by the Office of the United States Government for Germany (OMGUS). While the judges on the NMT were American citizens, the tribunal considered itself international. Twelve high-ranking officials were tried, among whom were cabinet ministers, diplomats, doctors involved in medical experiments and SS officers involved in crimes in concentration camps or in genocide in Nazi-occupied areas.

How many Nazi criminals were there? How many were brought to justice?

We do not know the exact number of Nazi criminals, since the available documentation is incomplete. The Nazis themselves destroyed many incriminating documents, and there are still many criminals who are unidentified and/or unindicted.

Those who actually implemented the Final Solution include the leaders of Nazi Germany, the heads of the Nazi Party and the Reich Security Main Office. Also included are hundreds of thousands of members of the Gestapo, the SS, the Einsatzgruppen, the police and the armed forces, as well as those bureaucrats who were involved in the persecution and destruction of European Jewry. In addition, there were thousands of individuals throughout occupied Europe who cooperated with the Nazis in killing Jews and other innocent civilians.

Although we do not have complete statistics on the number of war criminals brought to justice, the number is certainly far less than the total of those who were involved in the Final Solution. The leaders of the Third Reich who were caught by the Allies, were tried by the International Military Tribunal in Nuremberg and the Subsequent Nuremberg Proceedings. In total, 5,025 Nazi criminals were convicted between 1945–1949 in the American, British and French zones, in addition to an unspecified number of people who were tried in the Soviet zone.

In addition, the United Nations War Crimes Commission prepared lists of war criminals who were later tried by the judicial authorities of various Allied countries and those countries under Nazi rule during the war. The latter countries have conducted a large number of trials regarding crimes committed in their lands. The Polish tribunals, for example, tried approximately 40,000 persons, and large numbers of war criminals were tried in other countries. In all, about 80,000 Germans have been convicted for committing crimes against humanity, while the number of convicted local collaborators is in the tens of thousands. Special mention should be made of Simon Wiesenthal, whose activities led to the capture of over one thousand Nazi criminals.

Profiles in Evil: Leading Perpetrators of the Holocaust

Adolf Hitler – The Face of the Holocaust

Adolf Hitler (1889-1945)

As chancellor and Führer of Nazi Germany from 1933-1945, Adolf Hitler was one of the most demonic dictators the world has ever known. He initiated World War II, the most destructive event in human history, which ultimately cost the lives of some 75 million people. His armies conquered most of Europe and North Africa in a few short years and were responsible for killing as many as 17 million civilians, six million of whom were Jews.

Hitler claimed that Jews were enemies of the Aryan race. He held them responsible for the German economic and political crises and its military defeat in World War I. In 1919, Hitler joined the small and insignificant National Socialist German Workers Party (NSDAP), popularly known as the Nazi Party. In 1921, he became its leader by gaining broad support for his promotion of German nationalism and supremacy, anti-Semitism and anti-communism. Using his uncanny oratorical magnetism, Hitler inspired a frightful hatred amongst his growing audiences. In 1933, he was appointed Chancellor of Germany and quickly transformed the country into a dictatorship known as the Third Reich.

In his words: "The efficiency of the... national leader consists primarily in [concentrating]... the attention of a people on a single enemy." For Hitler, that enemy was the Jews. But to Hitler, the Jews were more than just a scapegoat and a political expedient. He perceived his confrontation with Jewry as humanity's central concern; "The struggle for world domination is between me and the Jews. All else is meaningless. The Jews have inflicted two wounds on the world: circumcision on the body and conscience on the soul. I come to free mankind from their shackles."[53]

In the final days of the War, Hitler showed that even by the Nazis' wretched standards, he was a treacherous, evil, back-stabbing, self-serving megalomaniac of the highest degree. When he perceived Germany's imminent defeat, he ordered the complete destruction of Germany's entire industrial infrastructure so it would not fall into Allied hands, saying that Germany's failure to win the war forfeited its right to survive. Execution of this scorched earth plan was entrusted to arms minister Albert Speer, who disobeyed the order.

On 30 April 1945, when Soviet troops were within a block or two of the Reich Chancellery, Hitler committed suicide by shooting himself in the temple while simultaneously biting into a cyanide capsule. Hitler's body and that of Eva Braun (his mistress whom he had married the day before) were put into a bomb crater, doused in gasoline, and set alight as the Red Army advanced and shelling continued.

Heinrich Himmler – The Greatest Mass Murderer of All Time

German news magazine *Der Spiegel* named Himmler "the greatest mass murderer of all time." As Reichsführer-SS, he was in charge of the Gestapo and personally oversaw the concentration camps extermination camps and Einsatzgruppen. Through these agencies, he coordinated the killing of some six million Jews, between 200,000 and 500,000 Roma, many prisoners of war and possibly another three to four million Poles, communists and other groups whom the Nazis deemed unworthy to live or who simply were "in the way," including homosexuals, people with physical and mental disabilities and members of the Confessing Church.

Heinrich Himmler (1900-1945) inspecting Dachau concentration camp in 1936

Himmler attended a Gymnasium where he studied classical literature. His father, the principal, sent him to spy on and punish other pupils. His father even called him a born criminal.[54]

In 1925, after failing as a chicken farmer, Himmler joined Hitler's personal bodyguard brigade, the black-shirted Schutzstaffel (SS). He was appointed head of the SS in 1929, which at that time consisted of only 280 men. It would soon become the most powerful body in the state, charged with "safeguarding the ... embodiment of the National Socialist idea"—in other words, putting the Nazi principles of Aryan supremacy into action. In 1933, he set up the first concentration camp in Dachau and quickly began filling it.

Himmler believed that he was the reincarnation of Henry the Fowler, the founder of the Holy Roman Empire.[55] He dreamed of a pure, blond-haired, blue-eyed race of heroes who would conquer the inferior races according to the process of natural selection. He viewed the SS man as a warrior, scholar and leader, all in one. Himmler established the state-registered human stud farm known as Lebensborn, where he hoped to breed a race of supermen, by selecting the most beautiful girls with perfect Nordic traits, and breeding them with SS men.[56] He bade all women to act out of their moral conscience to bear Aryan children, and he proposed that soldiers should be allowed a second wife.

In 1939, Hitler appointed Himmler as Reich Commissar for the "Strengthening of Germandom," and he was given absolute control over the newly annexed Poland. Himmler rationalized mass murder as a moral duty, saying, "We had the moral right. We had the duty to our people to destroy this people. We have fulfilled this most difficult duty for the love of our people."

A recording still exists of a speech Himmler made in Posen in 1943. It provides tremendous insight into the minds not just of Himmler, but of the Nazis in general.

"I also want to refer here very frankly to a very difficult matter. We can now very openly talk about this among ourselves, and yet we will never discuss this publicly....

"I am now referring to the evacuation of the Jews, to the extermination of the Jewish people. This is something that is easily said: 'The Jewish people will be exterminated,' says every Party member, 'this is very obvious. It is in our program—elimination of the Jews, extermination, a small matter.' And then they turn up, the upstanding 80 million Germans, and each one has his decent Jew. They say the others are all pigs, but this particular one is a splendid Jew. But none has observed it, endured it. Most of you here know what it means when 100 corpses lie next to each other, when there are 500 or when there are 1,000. To have endured this and at the same time to have remained a decent person— with exceptions due to human weaknesses—has made us tough, and is a glorious chapter that has not and will not be spoken of. Because we know how difficult it would be for us if we still had Jews as secret saboteurs, agitators and rabble rousers in every city, what with the bombings, with the burden and with the hardships of the war. If the Jews were still part of the German nation, we would most likely arrive now at the state we were at in 1916 and '17".

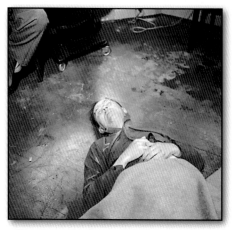

Shortly before the end of the war, Himmler attempted to negotiate peace with the Allies. It was he who surrendered Germany to the Western Allies. After being arrested by British forces, he committed suicide before he could be questioned.

Himmler on the floor at British 2nd Army HQ after his suicide on 23 May 1945

Joseph Goebbels – Spin Doctor of Death

Paul Joseph Goebbels served as the Minister of Propaganda in Nazi Germany from 1933 to 1945. He was the mastermind responsible for waging an all-encompassing media campaign to arouse the German masses in support of Hitler and his war against the Jews. Prior to the war, Goebbels had been an English literature scholar but was frustrated as a writer and failed as a playwright. He turned his literary talents to support the fledgling Nazi Party in its rise to absolute power. Goebbels was personally enamoured with Hitler. In his private writings, Goebbels wrote of Hitler, "I love him... He has thought through everything. Such a sparkling mind can be my leader. I bow to the greater one, the political genius."

Joseph Goebbels (1897-1945)
Minister of Propaganda

Goebbels proved himself a master of the "Big Lie" technique—a phrase coined by Hitler himself in Mein Kampf, in reference to the imagined Jewish attempt to corrupt society—that any lie, no matter how outlandish, if told repeatedly to the masses would eventually be believed.

In November 1938, Goebbels found the opportunity he was looking for to rally a nationwide, government-sanctioned pogrom against the Jews of Germany. A Jewish young man, Herschel Grynszpan, had shot and killed a German official in revenge for the deportation of his family. Goebbels used the assassination as an excuse to organise and orchestrate the rampage known as Kristallnacht in which thousands of synagogues and hundreds of Jewish homes and businesses were destroyed, and 30,000 Jews were detained and later deported to concentration camps. Goebbels claimed that anti-Jewish violence had spontaneously erupted across the country in response to the assassination.

Throughout the war period, Goebbels manipulated the collective consciousness of the German people through comprehensive, insidious control of every media outlet. In 1941, in his newspaper *Das Reich*, he referred to Hitler's "prophecy" that German Jewry "is now suffering the gradual process of annihilation which it intended for us." On numerous occasions he publicly stated that the war against the Jews was a justified response to Jewish provocation intended to destroy the Aryan race.

Upon hearing of Hitler's death, Goebbels lamented, "The heart of Germany has ceased to beat." As per Hitler's written will, Goebbels assumed the role of Reich Chancellor—a post that he served for only one day. With Russian troops already at the gates of Berlin, Goebbels attempted in vain to arrange a truce with Stalin. After his offer was rejected, he decided there was no hope for him and his family. "For us, everything is lost now, and the only way left for us is the one which Hitler chose. I shall follow his example." Hours before the Russians entered Berlin, Goebbels took the lives of his wife and six children and then committed suicide.

Reinhard Heydrich — Father of the Final Solution

Reinhard Heydrich was born in the quaint town of Halle on the western border of Germany. There he nurtured his great love for music and became an accomplished violinist. His greatest joy, however, was cold-blooded murder. He killed with a passion, gaining nicknames such as the "hangman" and the "blonde beast."

In 1931, Heydrich was recruited into the Nazi Party to head the first counter-intelligence division of the SS. He created a massive network of spies and informers and began amassing thousands of index cards with information about every possible enemy of the party, for use in blackmail. He soon became one of the most powerful men in Germany—the right-hand man of Heinrich Himmler

Reinhard Heydrich
(1904-1942)

himself. At one point during his rise to power, Heydrich's enemies began to circulate rumours that he was descended from Jews. A thorough investigation into his genealogy revealed only "pure" blood; however, the allegations haunted him until his death.

With Hitler's rise to power in 1933, political opponents began to be arrested. Heydrich filled the prisons with "offenders," leading to the construction of the first concentration camps. He was given the order from Hitler that "all means, even if they are not in conformity with existing laws and precedents, are permitted if they serve the will of the Führer." Heydrich was soon appointed the head of the Gestapo, and political activists and other "undesirables" began disappearing throughout Germany. Most of the time, their families never saw them again; on occasion, families would receive an urn containing the ashes of a relative who had disappeared.

Heydrich was instrumental in developing the Final Solution. In 1938, he stated that the only solution to the problem of the Jews, whom he called "the eternal sub-humans," was total annihilation. On 20 January 1942, Heydrich invited senior Nazi officials to a conference in Wannsee, Berlin. There, he revealed his plan for the Final Solution, which included combing Europe "from west to east for Jews." His plan consisted of building camps for Europe's eleven million Jews who would be used for slave labour. Many would "fall away through natural selection" and those who survived would "be dealt with appropriately." Heydrich never mentioned how to deal with Jews who were unfit for work, but according to attendee Adolf Eichmann, the answer was implied and obvious to all.

Heydrich's personal reign of terror was put to an end when two members of the Czech resistance assassinated him in Czechoslovakia in 1942. His murderous legacy, however, lived on in Operation Reinhard—the plan to establish the heinous initial trio of extermination camps Treblinka, Sobibor and Belzec.

Adolf Eichmann – The Architect of the Holocaust

Adolf Eichmann joined the Austrian branch of the Nazi Party in 1932 and soon became a member of the notorious SS. In the years that followed, he went on to serve as a security police officer and was assigned to the headquarters in Berlin as a squad leader and finally as a lieutenant. In 1937, Eichmann was sent to Palestine to ascertain if a mass emigration of German Jews to Palestine was possible. Considering the strong British objection to the idea of a Jewish state, the idea was soon abandoned.

In 1938, he was selected to head the Central Office for Jewish Emigration, and charged with the forcible deportation of Austrian Jews. On 15 August, Eichmann released a draft entitled the "Madagaskar Projekt," based on a much older concept, which called for the resettlement of one million Jews per year over four years to the African island of Madagascar. The plan envisioned taking control of the fleet of the British Royal Navy. With the victory of Britain over the Vichy forces in Madagascar in 1942, the plan was effectively abandoned. If things had gone differently, there might never have been a Holocaust as we know it.

Adolf Eichmann
(1906-1962)

Eichmann acted as recording secretary of the Wannsee Conference where the policy for official genocide was decided. Eichmann was given the position of Transportation Administrator of the Final Solution to the Jewish Question and was placed in charge of all trains carrying Jews to the death camps. In 1944, Eichmann was sent to Hungary where he organised the transport of 430,000 Hungarians to Auschwitz in a span of 10 weeks. By 1945, General Himmler ordered cessation of all Jewish extermination and for the evidence of the Final Solution to be destroyed; yet Eichmann continued his work with zeal, against official orders.

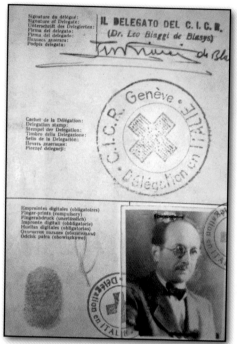

Red Cross identity document Adolf Eichmann (1906–1962) used to enter Argentina under the fake name Ricardo Klement in 1950, issued by the Italian delegation of the Red Cross of Geneva

After the war, Eichmann escaped American forces and fled to Italy. In 1950, he travelled to Argentina with falsified entrance visas and eventually brought his entire family to Argentina, settling in the suburbs of Buenos Aires.

In 1959, news of Eichmann's whereabouts reached the Mossad in Israel, which succeeded in capturing Eichmann and bringing him back to Israel for trial.

Eichmann's Israeli trial began in Jerusalem on 11 April 1961. He was indicted on 15 criminal charges, including crimes against humanity, crimes against the Jewish people and membership in an outlawed organisation. During the entire trial, Eichmann insisted that he was only "following orders," and that he "never did anything, great or small, without obtaining in advance express instructions from Adolf Hitler or any of my superiors." During cross examination, Eichmann was asked if he felt guilty for the murder of millions of Jews. He replied, "Legally not, but in the human sense ... yes, for I am guilty of having deported them." The prosecution responded with a quote from Eichmann in 1945 stating: "I will leap into my grave laughing because the feeling that I have five million human beings on my conscience is for me a source of extraordinary satisfaction." Eichmann responded that he was only referring to "enemies of the Reich."

After 14 weeks of testimony with more than 1,500 documents and 100 prosecution witnesses, the court found Eichmann guilty of all counts and sentenced him to death, stating that "Eichmann received no superior orders at all. He was his own superior and he gave all orders in matters that concerned Jewish affairs ... The so-called Final Solution would never have assumed the infernal forms of the flayed skin and tortured flesh of millions of Jews without the fanatical zeal and the unquenchable blood thirst of the appellant and his associates." Eichmann was hanged on 31 May 1962, and his execution remains the only case of capital punishment ever carried out in Israel.

Adolf Eichmann on trial

Hans Frank — Governor of Occupied Poland

Hans Frank (1900–1946) in his cell at the International Military Tribunal trial of war criminals at Nuremberg in 1945

Hans Frank served the Reich as Governor-General of occupied Poland from 1939 to 1945. He oversaw the segregation of Polish Jewry to ghettos, including the infamous Warsaw ghetto, as well as the drafting of Polish civilians into forced labour.

Frank was a lawyer by training. In the early part of his career, during the 1920s and 1930s, he provided legal services for the Nazi Party. Later, he was appointed Hitler's personal legal advisor. In 1930, Hitler responded to allegations that his father was half-Jewish by entrusting Frank to research his ancestry and dispel the rumours. Frank's inquiry revealed that Hitler's paternal grandmother, Maria Anna Shicklgruber, had worked as a cook for a Jewish family. At the age of 42, she had borne a child out of wedlock while working for them, and the Jewish family had financially supported the child until he turned 14. Frank concluded that the money was bribe money to avoid a scandal, and that in truth the father of the child was a local factory worker who later married Shicklgruber. During the Nuremberg trials, however, he admitted that it was quite probable that Hitler indeed had some Jewish blood.

As one of Hitler's most trusted confidants, Frank was appointed the Governor-General of the occupied Polish territories immediately following the German invasion of Poland in 1939. He made the Wavel Castle in Krakow his headquarters and ruled Poland with an iron fist as friend to neither Pole nor Jew. Of the Poles, he said, "Poland will be treated like a colony; the Poles will become slaves of the

Greater German Reich." Of the Jews he was even less charitable, writing, "A problem that occupies us in particular is the Jews. This merry little people, which wallows in dirt and filth, has been gathered together by us in ghettos and quarters, and will probably not remain in the Government-General for very long ... Since the Jews moved away from Jerusalem, there has been nothing for them except an existence as parasites; that has now come to an end ... In 1919, at our first meetings in Munich, we proclaimed the motto: an end must be put to the rule of the Jews in Europe."

After the war, Frank was prosecuted at the Nuremberg trials and found guilty of his crimes against humanity. He wrote that if he would put up posters for every Pole that he had executed, "the forests of Poland would not be sufficient to manufacture the paper." In his memoirs, written during his time on death row, he wrote, "a thousand years will pass and still Germany's guilt will not have been erased." He was executed on 16 October 1946.

Rudolf Höss — Commander Of Auschwitz

Rudolf Höss (1900-1947) at the Supreme National Tribunal of Poland

Rudolf Höss was born to a strict Catholic family who fervently hoped he would someday become a priest. After leaving the Church as a teenager, he joined the German war effort in World War I and quickly rose through the ranks. Following the war, Höss joined the Nazi party and the SS. He was ultimately appointed the first commandant of Auschwitz where he served from May 1940 until November 1943.

In 1941, Hitler's henchmen selected the Polish town Oswiecim, which was centrally located and a major nexus of the Polish railway system, to be the hub of Hitler's Final Solution. The Germans called it Auschwitz. After receiving personal orders from Himmler to begin the extermination of Europe's Jews, Höss worked on perfecting the techniques of mass killing to make them as quick and efficient as possible.

Höss was singlehandedly responsible for transforming Auschwitz from a regular prison camp to a death factory, the likes of which had never been seen before. He oversaw the construction of four large gas chambers in Birkenau and attendant crematoria, which he employed to murder and incinerate some 20,000 people a day. Höss experimented with a variety of gassing methods before choosing Zyklon B, which only took 3 to 15 minutes to overcome its victims. "We knew when the people were dead because they stopped screaming," he said.

Perhaps his most fiendish innovation was designing Auschwitz in such a way that its victims had little idea what was happening until it was too late. In Höss's own words, "We endeavoured to fool the victims into thinking that they were to go through a delousing process. SS guards at Auschwitz were expected to carry out

> I COMMANDED AUSCHWITZ UP UNTIL 1 DECEMBER 1943, AND ESTIMATE THAT AT LEAST 2 ½ MILLION VICTIMS WERE EXECUTED OR ELIMINATED THERE BY GASSING AND BURNING. AT LEAST A FURTHER HALF A MILLION DIED AS A RESULT OF HUNGER AND ILLNESS, WHICH MAKES A TOTAL OF ABOUT 3 MILLION. THIS FIGURE REPRESENTS ABOUT 70 OR 80 PER CENT OF ALL PEOPLE WHO WERE SENT AS PRISONERS TO AUSCHWITZ. THE REST WERE SELECTED FOR SLAVE LABOUR IN THE FACTORIES AND WORKSHOPS IN THE CONCENTRATION CAMP.
>
> RUDOLF HÖSS, AFFIDAVIT OF 5 APRIL 1945

their diabolic duties in utmost secrecy. However, Höss himself recalled, "the foul and nauseating stench from the continuous burning of bodies permeated the entire area and all of the people living in the surrounding communities knew that exterminations were going on at Auschwitz."

Höss went into hiding immediately after the war. He was eventually discovered when his wife disclosed his whereabouts to the British. On 25 May 1946, he was handed over to the Polish authorities and was sentenced to death by hanging by the Supreme National Tribunal in Poland. In an ironic twist, Höss was hanged on a gallows adjacent to one of the crematoria at Auschwitz. Only in the solitude of his prison cell, just days before his execution, did Höss finally come to the recognition that he "sinned gravely against humanity."[57]

Höss immediately before being hanged Auschwitz, 16 April 1947

PART 3:
PLACES WE WILL GO

Major Jewish Centres JRoots Visits in Poland

Bialystok

Bialystok was one of Poland's principal centres of Jewish life. At the community's peak, on the eve of the First World War, almost 70% of Bialystok's population was Jewish (61,500 out of a total population of 89,700).

In the century before World War II, the city grew into an industrial centre, specializing in textiles. The smoke-filled skies of Bialystok always appeared grey. The river Biala which crosses the city, and from which the city's name is derived, was shallow and polluted by industrial waste from factories.

The first Jewish textile mills were established in 1850. Although initially staffed by German specialists, Jewish labour slowly took over as Jews acquired skills as spinners, weavers, knitters and dyers. By 1898, of the 372 mills in Bialystok, 299 (83%) were Jewish-owned, employing more than five thousand Jewish workers. At that time, Bialystok's total population was about 63,000, of which 48,000 were Jews.

Outside the textile industry, Jews dominated the economic life of the city as well. Of the 3,628 merchants and shopkeepers in the city in 1897, 88% were Jews. In 1921, 93% of the businessmen were Jewish, and 89% of the industrial plants were Jewish-owned.

In the 19th century, when Bialystok was governed by Prussia, contact with German Jewry had introduced the spirit of enlightenment (Haskalah) into Jewish circles. Many prominent Maskilim (people who subscribed to the ideology of the Haskalah) emerged here, including Elazar Ludwig Zamenhof, the creator of the international language, Esperanto. (See his biographical profile in Part 4.)

Bialystok was a city of exemplary cultural institutions and charitable foundations, of erudite Torah scholars and masters of the arts and sciences. Ideological streams from the secular socialist Bund labour and Marxist Zionistic Po'alei Zion, to the religious Zionist Mizrahi and ultra-Orthodox Agudas Yisroel, were active and hosted vast and varied communal activities. It was the city of Rabbi Shmuel Mohliver, founder of the Hibat Zion movement, and of Nahum Tzemach, father of the Habima Theatre. Of all the Polish cities in the 1930s, Bialystok had the highest percentage of Hebrew speakers.

The Jewish labour movement found especially strong support in Bialystok, and starting in 1897 many Jewish workers there became active members of the Bund. They published their own influential underground newspaper: *Der Bialystoker Arbeiter* (The Bialystok Worker). Activism, however, had a price. Intensive activities of Bialystok's labour movement during the Russian revolution of 1905-06 provoked a savage Russian reprisal. Between June 1 and 3, 1906, a pogrom took the lives of 70 Jews, in addition to gravely injuring 90 others.

Unlike the majority of Jewish Poland which was dominated by Hassidism, most of Bialystok's Jews were known as Litvaks (Lithuanian-minded), meaning they were either Mitnagdim (opposed to the Hassidic movement), or Maskilim ("enlightened" reformist Jews). Bialystok had a Beit Yaakov school for women and a large yeshiva with twelve grades in the Talmud Torah and four yeshiva grades with 20 to 30 students in each. There were also a number of Batei Medrash (Jewish study halls) in the vicinity of the Great Synagogue. However, its most significant lasting effect on Jewish culture would come from a foreign yeshiva that was "transplanted" there.

One of the most significant pre-war yeshivas was located in Navaredok (now in Belarus, but then in Russia). The yeshiva placed a heavy focus on *mussar* (the perfection of one's character). After the Bolshevik revolution in 1917, the Navaredok yeshiva was forced to relocate in Bialystok. Aside from intense Talmudic study, its 200 students went to great extremes to negate their egos. At times, their methods were viewed as highly unconventional, yet the relatively small institution made an enormous lasting impact on Orthodox Jewry. The institution produced some of the leading rabbinic figures of the 20th century, including Rabbi Yaakov Yisrael Kanievsky (1899-1985) known as "The Steipler."

Rabbi Kanievsky relocated from Bialystok to Israel in the 1930s. There, he was instrumental in founding the Jewish community of Bnei Brak, where he served as the head of its two main yeshivas for many years.

A glimpse of the world that was: This photo, taken in Bialystok on 20 November 1932, shows homemakers carrying their cholent, a traditional a dish of meat, potatoes and beans. The baker's oven would become the community's oven on Friday afternoons where their cholents would stew until the next day so families could enjoy warm Sabbath meals.

Shortly after the outbreak of World War II, the Germans entered Bialystok but transferred it to the Soviets after just one week. When the Germans reoccupied the city on 27 June 1941, some 50,000 Jews still lived here.

The Germans acted swiftly. On the day following the second German occupation, known as "Red Friday," the Germans burned down the Jewish quarter, including the Great Synagogue. Before the end of the week, 300 of the Jewish intelligentsia had been rounded up and taken to Pietrasze, a field outside the town, and murdered. The following week, about 3,000 more Jewish men were killed there. A Judenrat was established on 26 July 1941. On 1 August, the remaining Jewish population was shut into a ghetto where every Jew aged 15 to 65 began forced labour.

The Bialystok Great Synagogue was built on Suraska Street, between the years 1908 and 1913. From the beginning, it was only open on Saturdays and holidays. After World War I, a choir and organ were introduced. National holidays were celebrated with services attended by the likes of the city mayor and regional governor. The last official rabbi of Bialystok, Dr. Gedalia Rozenman, would end prayer services with Hatikva, followed by the Polish national anthem. Before burning the synagogue in June 1941, the Germans locked at least 700 Jewish men inside. Gasoline was poured at the entrances, and a grenade was tossed into the building, igniting an enormous fire. The conflagration spread to nearby homes, where Jews in hiding were burned alive. The following day, 30 wagonloads of corpses were taken to a mass grave in which some 2,000 Jews were buried.

In November 1942, the Warsaw underground sent Mordechai Tenenbaum (Tamaroff) to organise a resistance movement in Bialystok. Unfortunately, Jewish disunity stymied his efforts, and when the first Aktion took place in February 1943, the resistance movement was unprepared.

One thousand Jews were killed in Bialystok during the first Aktion and another 10,000 were deported to Treblinka. For economic reasons, the final destruction of the Bialystok Ghetto was delayed for six months and was scheduled for 16 August 1943.

It was not until July 1943, that the various underground factions united under Tenenbaum. On 16 August 1943, the final liquidation of the ghetto commenced. The underground engaged in an open battle with the Germans and held out for a month. After quashing the uprising, the Germans completed the Aktion, sending some 40,000 Jews to Treblinka and Majdanek.

Only about 1,000 Bialystok Jews survived the war.

Czestochowa

What put Czestochowa on the map—and what has kept it there for at least six centuries—is the monastery of Jasna Gora (Bright Mountain). The ancient edifice houses what Catholics consider Poland's most sacred relic: the Black Madonna. Every year, millions of pilgrims flock to view this painting of Mary and child, which is said to have miraculous powers.

Until the 18th century, Czestochowa had the legal status of *"de non tolerandis Judaeis"* (non-tolerance of Jews). When Jews were finally permitted to settle there around 1700, they immigrated rather hesitatingly. A century later the Jewish population reached 500 (15% of the town's total), and in 1806, a Jewish school was established. Around this time, many German artisans and capitalists came to Czestochowa from nearby Silesia. Among them were entrepreneurial and well-heeled Jews who established local factories. Jewish peasants from surrounding villages descended upon the city in search of employment, and within a generation the Jewish community numbered some 3,000.

Differences between the poor, native Polish Jews and the newly arrived wealthier ones were readily apparent. As has happened countless times in Jewish history, the more affluent Jews related to their Jewish heritage liberally, while the less well-off tended to be more traditional. In the 1830s, the community appointed Hertz Kon, a prosperous Jew of German origin, as Chairman of the Kehilla (Jewish community). Kon was a progressive who viewed Judaism as a hindrance to social advancement and openly advocated assimilation. By the mid-19th century, a dramatic rise in Catholic conversions plagued the Czestochowa community.

Socio-economic problems persisted, and 1847-1848 proved to be particularly difficult economically. The Jewish population declined when many were forced to migrate to Lodz in search of work. Nevertheless, the final third of the century saw renewed economic vigour amongst Jewish industrialists, and once again, the masses began to arrive in Czestochowa. By the end of the 19th century, wealthy Jews had established major printing, textile, glass and haberdashery industries that employed thousands. Census data record that the Jewish population which stood at 3,360 in 1862 had more than tripled to 11,764 by the year 1900.

In the 20th century, industrialists continued to profit, while anti-Semitic sentiment surged. On 27 May 1919, anti-Jewish rioting left seven Jews dead and 32 seriously injured. Again, on 19 June 1937, 46 shops, 21 homes and a synagogue were destroyed. This was not the work of a few Polish hooligans; according to police records, around 15,000 Poles participated in the destruction.

When the Germans arrived in Czestochowa on 3 September 1939, there were about 28,500 Jews out of a total population of around 135,000. The following day, a horrendous pogrom known as "Bloody Monday" left some 180 Jews dead. Countless Jews were beaten, robbed and raped. Later that month, the Nazis destroyed the Old Synagogue, and in December, drunken Poles (encouraged by German officers) set the New Synagogue ablaze.

Starting in August 1940, Nazis began deporting able-bodied young men as slave labourers. The first thousand were dispatched to build a highway in the Lublin District; few survived. In total, about 3,000 were relocated from Czestochowa to various labour camps.

On 9 April 1941, the Nazis established the Czestochowa ghetto, which remained "open" until 23 August 1941. After this time, any of its 48,000 prisoners who attempted to escape were liable to summary execution. Even contact with the Polish "Aryan" population was totally forbidden. Enslaved, the Jews laboured primarily in metal and ammunition factories. Most believed their work was necessary for the German war effort, and few believed they faced imminent deportation. Even when Warsaw ghetto escapees arrived in the summer of 1942 with tales of the deportations to Treblinka, most dismissed the stories as "imaginations of sick minds." Despite their denial, on Yom Kippur, 21 - 22 September 1942, liquidation began. In a few weeks, SS officers aided by

The New Synagogue was completed in 1893 and burned on 25 December 1939. In 1955 the Czestochowa City Council decided to build a philharmonic hall on its ruins.

Ukrainians and Latvians transported 38,250 Jews from the "Big Ghetto" to Treblinka, and 2,000 others were murdered locally. Jewish resistance efforts attempted to stave off the liquidation but with minimal results. Fighters continued to resist in vain until June 1943.

Roundup of Jews in Czestochowa

In November 1942, the 5,000 Jews who had survived the initial liquidation were relocated to the "Small Ghetto" to continue as slave labourers in the local HASAG-Pelcery ammunition factory. Another 1,000 or so "illegals" snuck into the ghetto with them. The inmates faced periodic selections and deportation, and by July 1943 most had been sent to Treblinka.

Deportation of Jews from Czestochowa 1942

In 1944, many other Jews were relocated from Lodz, Radom and Kielce to work in the expanding Czestochowa munitions plant. By the end of that year, Czestochowa had become the site of one of the largest work camps in the Generalgouvernement with about 10,000 Jewish prisoners.

The surprise Soviet offensive in early 1945 forced Nazis to abandon the camp. They dispatched half of the inmates to concentration camps in Germany. The remaining 5,000 Jews were still alive when the Red Army liberated Czestochowa on 17 January 1945—among them were 1,500 Jews from Czestochowa itself.

Gora Kalwaria ("Gur")

In the early 19th century, the long-standing ban on Jewish settlement was lifted in Gora Kalwaria, and Jews quickly became the predominant constituency of the town. It soon became one of the major centres of Hassidic Judaism and home to the Gur Hassidic dynasty. Prior to the Holocaust, Ger, with some 200,000 adherents, was the largest and most important Hassidic sect in Poland, and possibly in the world.

The Gur dynasty was founded by Rabbi Yitzhak Mayer Rothenberg Alter (1798–1866), better known as the "Chidushei HaRim." His father was the town's rabbi and had been a disciple of the famed Hassidic master, Levi Yitzhak of Berdichev. The Chidushei HaRim was both an inspirational figure and a Talmudic genius. One of the pillars of his worldview was that every person is born with a specific heavenly assignment regarding how he or she must improve the world (i.e., to make a "*tikkun*"). Moreover, he believed that each person is uniquely qualified for his or her mission, and should one fail, the mission would never be accomplished.

The Chidushei HaRim had 13 or 14 children, most of whom died in infancy, and all of whom died during the Chidushei HaRim's lifetime. Yehudah Aryeh Leib (1847–1905), the son of the Chidushei HaRim's oldest son, was orphaned as an infant, and was raised by his grandfather. Yehudah Leib was a child prodigy and studied without interruption for 18 hours at a time. When he was 19, the Chidushei HaRim passed away, and pressure was exerted on Reb Yehudah Leib to assume the mantle of leadership. He felt unworthy and declined. Four years later, when the interim successor died, Reb Yehudah Leib felt that he had no choice but to comply with the wishes of the Hassidim, and he became the leader of Ger.

Under Rabbi Yehudah Leib's guidance, Gur became the largest Hassidic group in Poland. He came to be known as the "Sfas Emes" (lips of truth), a title taken from his magnum opus. Like his grandfather, he also played a role in public affairs, concerning himself with contemporary Polish Jewish problems. As a distinguished scholar of exceptional personal character, he won the confidence of rabbis and Jewish communal leaders. The Sfas Emes wielded wide influence and even succeeded in garnering seats for Gerrer Hassidism in the Polish Congress.

On 8 September 1939, Gora Kalwaria with its Jewish population of 3,500 was occupied by the Germans. Local Jews were immediately subject to persecution and anti-Jewish decrees. On 15 January 1940, the Germans ordered the establishment of a Judenrat (Jewish Council), whose principal task was to provide a consistent supply of manpower for forced labour. In February 1940, the Jews were moved to a "Jewish quarter," to which Jews from the surrounding villages and refugees from other cities were also brought.

In February 1941, the Jews of Gora Kalwaria were deported to the Warsaw Ghetto; 1,600 were deported on 25 February, and another 1,349 the following day. The Jews were gathered in the market square, and from there, they marched to the railway station carrying only clothes and a little food. The sick and feeble and those who tried to hide and evade deportation were shot on the spot. Over the next year and a half, hundreds of Gora Kalwaria

Jews from Gora Kalwaria, Poland, being deported to the Warsaw Ghetto

refugees died in the Warsaw ghetto. Those who didn't perish from starvation or epidemics were deported from Warsaw to the Treblinka death camp during the Great Deportation in the summer of 1942.

Although almost all Gerrer Hassidim in Europe perished during the Holocaust, the Sfas Emes' son, Rabbi Avraham Mordechai Alter (1866–1948) known as the "Imrei Emes," managed to escape and quickly set about rebuilding the movement in Palestine. Today, the Gur dynasty—based in Jerusalem—is once again a substantial force in the Hassidic world. Although accurate population figures for Hassidim are hard to come by, it is estimated that in 2010 there were about

500,000 Hassidim worldwide, approximately 5% of which were Gerrer Hassidim. On major occasions, as many as 12,000 Gur Hassidim may gather in the main Gerrer Beit Medrash (study hall) in Jerusalem.

Grand Rabbi Avraham Mordechai Alter of Ger, known as the "Imrei Emes." The picture was taken in Europe prior to his escape to Palestine.

Wedding of one of the Gerrer Rebbe's granddaughters, 2008

Izbica

Situated in the Lublin region of Poland, Izbica was unique among the Jewish *shtetls* of Poland. Until the German occupation and the onset of WWII in 1939, Izbica remained almost entirely Jewish and predominantly Orthodox. Although the earliest references to Izbica date back to the 15th century, the town was officially established only in the mid-1700s as a haven for Jews expelled from the nearby town of Tarnogora.

By the mid-1800s, the population in Izbica was expanding rapidly. The Hassidic master, Rabbi Mordechai Josef Leiner, author of the well-known work Mei Ha-Shiloach, established his court there. The frequent visits of his Hassidim to the area greatly supported the economic growth of the poor town. By 1860, the *shtetl's* population numbered 1,450. Most of the residents lived in small wooden homes around the town's most impressive building: the brick synagogue.

The interwar years saw rapid development in Izbica—especially on the political front. Movements such as Mizrahi (religious Zionism), the Zionist Organisation, and the socialist Bund sprang up. However, due to the religious orientation of most Izbica Jews, the most powerful group was the Orthodox Agudath Israel political movement. Communally, there was growth as well. Many charitable organisations were established including a Bikur Cholim society (aid to the sick) and a Linat HaTzadek (aid for the poor). Despite the political changes, Izbica, which had grown to a population of over 5,000, retained its character as a small town where everyone knew each other.

Life—as they had known it—came to an abrupt end shortly after the German invasion in the fall of 1939. A ghetto was established, and though it was not formally closed off, the topography of the area made escape almost impossible.

Izbica ghetto

In 1941, Kurt Engels, the brutal head of the Gestapo, moved the regional Gestapo headquarters to Izbica. One of his first items of business was to desecrate the local Jewish cemetery. He forced Jewish slave labourers to dismantle its tombstones and use them to build the Gestapo command centre. His cruelty towards the Jews of Izbica knew no bounds.

Space was limited and food was scarce. Living conditions quickly became horrendous. There was simply no room to support the large population in the small *shtetl*. People were forced to live in the streets, huddling in doorways. Disease and famine were rampant. Without a hospital, the Jews were compelled to transform the synagogue into a makeshift medical facility.

Izbica was converted into a transit ghetto; a sort of hub of death that linked displaced Jews from the west with the Operation Reinhard death camps in the east. In March 1942, deportations from Central Europe to the new death camp at Belzec began. The first transport consisted of 1,001 Jews from Theresienstadt, who after a two day's journey, arrived in Izbica. There, they were forced to clear rubble before being sent on to their fate at Belzec. Of the 1,001 Jews in that first deportation, only six survived the war. In the ensuing months, thousands of Jews from Germany, Austria and Czechoslovakia passed through Izbica en route to their deaths.

By the end of 1942, the entire Jewish population of Izbica had been transported to the Belzec or Sobibor death camps.

Jedwabne

The Jewish community of Jedwabne was established in the 18th century. According to the 1921 census, the town had a Jewish population of 757 people, or 62% of Jedwabne's total population. It was a typical *shtetl* of pre-war Poland.

Almost immediately after the onset of World War II, Jedwabne was transferred to the Soviets as part of the German-Soviet Boundary Treaty of 28 September 1939. Initially, many Polish Jews were relieved to learn that the Soviets, rather than the Nazis, were to occupy their town; so unlike the gentile Polish population, they publicly welcomed the Red Army as their protector. However, following Nazi Germany's invasion of the Soviet Union on 22 June 1941, German forces immediately overran Jedwabne along with the rest of the Polish lands that had been occupied by the Soviets.

The Germans encouraged local Poles to commit anti-Jewish pogroms and robberies with total impunity. On the morning of 10 July 1941, by the order of Jedwabne's Polish mayor Marian Karolak, a group of Polish men from Jedwabne and environs rounded up the Jews in Jedwabne. The defenceless Jews were taken to the square in the centre of the town, where they were ordered to pluck grass while they were beaten. About 40 Jewish men were then forced to demolish a statue of Lenin that had been erected by the Soviets.

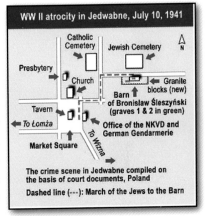

WW II atrocity in Jedwabne, July 10, 1941

The crime scene in Jedwabne compiled on the basis of court documents, Poland

Dashed line (---): March of the Jews to the Barn

Then, led by the local rabbi, the Jews were forced to carry Lenin's bust out of town while singing Soviet songs. Upon their return, they were taken to an empty barn, where they were shot.

Later that day, the Polish mob (in the presence of German Ordnungspolizei) locked the remaining Jews—mostly women and children—in the same barn and burned them alive.

For many, a particularly troubling aspect of this already horrific story is that the crimes were carried out by a mob of Polish gentiles acting out of their own volition, and not under the command of the Germans. German forces were certainly complicit; documentary evidence suggests that eight German gendarmes stood by and shot those who tried to escape the barn. However, the fact remains that the massacre was wilfully carried out by Polish civilians.

In 2000, Princeton sociologist and historian Jan T. Gross published a book entitled *Neighbors: The Destruction of the Jewish Community in Jedwabne, Poland*, in which he describes how the massacre was perpetrated by Polish civilians and not by the German invaders, as had previously been assumed. *Neighbors* inspired a wide-ranging debate in Poland regarding the Polish people's role in the Holocaust. A subsequent investigation conducted by the Polish Institute of National Remembrance (IPN) largely supported Gross' conclusions, though it questioned

Gross's estimate of 1,600 victims. The total number of Jewish victims has variously been given as ranging from 250 to 2,000.

Monument to the victims of the Jedwabne massacre

Krakow

Krakow became the capital of Poland in 1038. The first references to a Jewish presence there date from 1304. It was a generation later, during the reign of King Kasimir III (Kazimierz), that Krakow became a centre for both Jewish and secular culture. In 1364, King Kasimir selected the city as the site for Poland's first university—the Krakow Academy. Kasimir also supported the development of an adjacent independent town named Kazimierz, in honour of himself. Krakow gained prominence as a large, politically powerful and multicultural city; a place in which original thinkers such as Nicolas Copernicus would later thrive, and one which permitted a flourishing Jewish culture.

By the late 15th century, more than 40% of the university's student population hailed from beyond Poland's borders, engendering a climate of diversity. However, a large proportion of Krakow's native population was German in origin and maintained strong Germanic ties; thus the waves of anti-Jewish sentiment in Germany reached Poland. By the end of the 15th century, there had been several incidents of appropriation of Jewish property and even murder. Poland's rulers

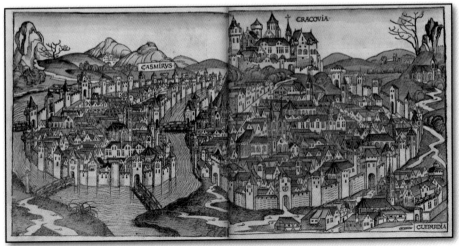

Woodcut from 1493 showing western view of Kazimierz (left)
across the Vistula River from Krakow

and Krakow's authorities condemned these anti-Semitic acts and put to death those who were convicted of the crimes. Despite governmental support of the Jews, resentment of the competition Jewish merchants posed to Polish traders continued to grow. In 1495, after a fire devastated a large part of Krakow, rumours blaming the Jews of treachery spread. Pogroms erupted and Jews were forced to move from Krakow to neighbouring Kazimierz.

The move to Kazimierz had a dramatic impact on Jewish life. The community acquired larger living quarters and a substantial degree of self-rule. Administrative autonomy also enabled the community to absorb refugees from Central Europe during the mid-16th to mid-17th centuries, and those who had fled Ukraine and Podolia during the Chmielnicki massacres of 1648–1656.

Kazimierz developed into a leading religious centre. The first yeshiva was established by Rabbi Yaakov Pollack in the late 15th century. Over the next century, several other yeshivas of comparably excellent repute emerged, making Kazimierz a premier centre for Talmudic study and attracting scholars whose commentaries and correspondence are still studied today. Among these notables are the Rema, Bach, Pnei Yehoshua and Tosefos Yom Tov. (See Part 1 on the Golden Age of Poland for more on Jewish life during the period and Part 4 for Profiles on the Rema and Tosefos Yom Tov.)

The first synagogue in Kazimierz took the form of a "Fortress Synagogue"—a building designed not only for worship and study but also for physical protection. The military design is testimony to the level of threat under which the Jewish community lived. Now known as the Old Synagogue of Krakow, Kazimierz' fortress synagogue has windows high above ground level, thick masonry, and heavy buttressing. It is the  *oldest of a number of fortress synagogues in Poland. Rebuilt in 1570, it remained in use until the Nazi invasion of Poland in 1939.*

In 1553, the Jewish community had to respond to threats from Krakow's Christian population. They successfully petitioned the Kazimierz town council for the right to build a defensive interior wall that would cut across the western end of the older defensive walls. The area between the two walls became known as the *Oppidum Judaeorum*—Jewish City. This was not a ghetto, however, and there were always some Jews living outside the walls and in the surrounding countryside. Those who lived outside the walls were typically the wealthier representatives of the community including the royal bankers, who lived alongside members of the Polish gentry in Krakow itself. The walls were expanded in 1608 due to the ongoing growth of the community. Subsequent requests to expand the walls, however, were declined, leaving the "city" severely overcrowded.

The demise of the Oppidum as an independent community began when the Austrian Emperor Joseph II, as part of his Enlightenment reforms, disbanded its administration. When Kazimierz itself lost its status as a separate town in 1791 and was integrated into

"As many sukkot as there are families..." A Scene in Krakow during the Holiday of Sukkot, 1937

the main city of Krakow, the more affluent Jewish families took advantage of the merger and moved out of the old Jewish district. However, the core of the Jewish community remained close to the existing synagogues and communal facilities even after the walls of the old Oppidum were torn down in 1822. The community gradually spread out over the next century. By the 1930s, Krakow's 120 officially registered synagogues were to be found in every corner of the city.

Persecution of the Jewish population of Krakow began soon after the German troops entered the city on 6 September 1939. From the first days of the occupation, Jews were obliged to take part in forced labour. In November, all

Jews over 12 years of age were required to wear identifying armbands. Throughout Krakow, synagogues were closed, and all their valuable content confiscated.

In May 1940, the Nazi occupation authority announced that Krakow would become the "cleanest" city in the General Government (the occupied, but unannexed part of Poland). Most local Jews were ordered to leave the city. Of the more than 68,000 Jews then in Krakow, only 15,000 workers and their families were permitted to remain. The rest were relocated in the surrounding rural areas.

Forced labour in Krakow ghetto

The Krakow ghetto was formally established on 3 March 1941, in the Podgorze district rather than the Jewish district of Kazimierz. This meant that almost all Jews were forced to abandon their homes and much of their property. 15,000 Jews were crammed into an area previously inhabited by 3,000 people. One apartment was allocated to every four Jewish families, and many of the less fortunate lived on the street.

Tombstone-shaped wall preserved from the Krakow ghetto with a typical ghetto home in the background

The ghetto was surrounded by imposing walls. All windows and doors that provided access to the Aryan side were bricked up. Only four guarded entrances permitted traffic to pass through. In a grim foreshadowing of the fate of the inmates, the walls contained panels designed in the shape of tombstones.

Young people of the Akiva youth movement produced an underground newsletter, *HaChalutz HaLochem* (the fighting pioneer). They joined forces with other Zionists to form a local branch of the ZOB (Jewish Fighting Organisation), which organised resistance in the ghetto. Their efforts were supported by the Polish underground Armia Krajowa. The ZOB in Krakow carried out a variety of resistance activities including the bombing of the Cyganeria café, a gathering place of Nazi officers; however, their efforts did not lead to a general uprising before the ghetto was liquidated (as had happened in Warsaw).

From 30 May 1942 onward, the Nazis implemented systematic deportations from the ghetto to the Belzec death camp. The first transport in June 1942 consisted of 5,000 people. In the second Aktion in October, another 6,000 were deported, and the patients of the Jewish hospital, the residents of the old age home and the 300 children at the orphanage were murdered locally.

Jews gathered and waiting deportation

On 13-14 March 1943, the final liquidation of the ghetto's more than 10,000 inmates was carried out under the command of Amon Göth, commandant of the nearby Plaszow labour camp. Of these, 8,000 Jews who were deemed fit to work were transported to

Bundles abandoned by Jewish deportees from the Krakow Ghetto, March 1943

Plaszow. Some 2,000 others were considered unfit for work and were murdered in the streets of the ghetto. Those who remained were sent to Auschwitz.

Pankiewicz's "Under the Eagle" pharmacy

At the time that the Krakow ghetto was confined to the Podgorze district, there had been four pharmacies owned by non-Jews. One of these was owned by Tadeusz Pankiewicz, the only proprietor to decline the German offer of relocating to the Aryan side of the city. He was given permission to continue operating his establishment in the ghetto and to reside on the premises. There, he supplied medicine to the ghetto's inhabitants and, whenever possible, aided their escape. The supply of often-scarce medications and pharmaceuticals to the ghetto's residents (often free of charge) substantially improved their quality of life and contributed to survival itself. After the war, Yad Vashem recognised Pankiewicz as one of the Righteous Among the Nations for rescuing countless Jews.

Also well-known is Oskar Schindler, who saved the Jewish slave labourers employed in his factory in Krakow from deportation to the Plaszow concentration camp. His story is recounted in Steven Spielberg's movie Schindler's List, which was filmed on site in Krakow. (See Schindler's profile in Part 4.)

Krasnik

Krasnik Great Synagogue

For much of its history, Krasnik was a small town with a big Jewish population. At the start of World War II, a full 50% of its 10,000 inhabitants were Jewish. Today, no Jews remain; yet the two beautiful old synagogues and other architectural vestiges have a fascinating story to tell.

The first presence of Jews in Krasnik dates back to the 1530s. In 1587, Jews received official permission to reside in Krasnik without any formal restrictions. They began to take up residence in the market square, Lubelska St. and Żydowska St. ("Żydowska" means Jewish), as well as in houses along the perimeter of the town walls. Aside from the religious facilities found in virtually every Jewish community, such as a mikvah (ritual bath) and Jewish cemetery, the Krasnik community also benefitted from a dedicated Jewish hospital.

Main Hall of the Great Synagogue

Main Hall of the Small Synagogue

A wooden synagogue served the community and stood close to the market square. In 1637, a fire broke out in Krasnik, consuming the synagogue along with much of the town. A certain Baruch (a common Jewish man's name) was accused of having set the fire as an act of arson. In retaliation, municipal and church authorities imposed a ban against the reconstruction of Jewish homes and stalls in the marketplace. It took some 35 years before the community had both the money and permission to rebuild their homes and a new synagogue out of brick.

In the first half of the 19th century, a second, smaller synagogue was erected. Around this time, Krasnik became a significant Hassidic centre.

During World War I, several anti-Jewish riots occurred in the town. The attacks took a heavy toll on the Jewish community in terms of both property and lives. Amongst the dead were the two local rabbis who were murdered by Russian soldiers. The war also brought general poverty to most of the Jewish inhabitants.

During the interwar period (1918-1939), Krasnik became one of the most influential Jewish communities in the Lublin region, (though not necessarily in the religious arena). Assimilation progressed at a rapid pace in the 1930s, with the establishment of a joint school for Polish and Jewish children in 1935. By 1939, 40% of the school (314 students) were Jewish.

On 9 September 1939, the Germans invaded Krasnik. In August 1940, a ghetto was established in which Jews from the town and its outlying areas were forced to live. By February 1942, ghetto inmates numbered some 6,000. Living conditions in the Krasnik ghetto—like ghettos throughout Poland—were abhorrent. Death, hunger and illness were widespread.

Liquidation of the Krasnik ghetto began in April 1942 when about 6,000 people were sent to Belzec. There were further deportations in October and November. Around the same time, about 600 residents were sent to a forced labour camp in Krasnik. Ultimately, almost all who had survived the ghetto, including those who had been sent to the forced labour camp, ended up in Belzec. The only significant exceptions were the several hundred people who were shot in the Jewish cemetery on Szewska Street in the final stage of liquidation, and a tiny number who managed to survive the war.

Lancut

Jews first arrived in Lancut in the 14th century and quickly became an important part of the town's economic life. Jews worked as merchants, glaziers and wood-carvers. In the 19th century, Lancut became a significant hub of Hassidic life. It was a typical *shtetl*, and before World War II, Lancut boasted 1,925 Jews—more than one-third of the town's population.

Lancut was home to a number of Hassidic luminaries, and it was the Hassidim who set the tone of Jewish life in the town. Perhaps the most famous leader was Rabbi Elimelech of Lizhensk who lived there for a time. (See upcoming section on Lizhensk and biographical profile of Rabbi Elimelech in Part 4.) The second most famous was Rabbi Yaakov Yitzhak, a Hassidic rebbe who would come to be known as the "Chozeh (seer) of Lublin." Rather than recount the biographical details of his life, let us savour a story of the Chozeh from which we can learn so much more about him.

> The Chozeh of Lublin and his disciples had set out on a long journey. As the sun was setting on Friday afternoon, they found themselves at an unfamiliar crossroads. Dismounting from their wagons, they debated which way to turn. The Chozeh interrupted the discussion and advised them to let the horses' reins go free and let the horses go where they would. The disciples did as he said, and they travelled quite a few miles on the road before meeting a peasant who told them that the town which they had reached was not the one they had been searching for.
>
> Nevertheless, as the Shabbat was quickly approaching, they had no choice but to stop and find some lodging for the night. At that point, the Chozeh announced to his Hassidim, "This Shabbat, I am not to be known as a Rebbe." From this they understood that, for reasons of his own, he wanted to be incognito. It was also understood that they should arrange their own accommodations. So, they entered the town and made their way to the synagogue, knowing that, according to the time-honoured custom, strangers always received an invitation from some villager for the Shabbat meal. Sure enough, they all received invitations, except for the Chozeh, who, in his usual fashion, prolonged his prayers until all the congregants had left. There was, however, one very old man who also remained in the synagogue and sat singing the traditional Shabbat tunes. The old man noticed the stranger and asked him, "Where will you be having your meal?" The Chozeh replied, "I don't know yet." "Well, I would suggest that you have your Shabbat meals in the local inn, and after the Shabbat

ends, I will go around and collect the money to pay the bill." "No," replied the Chozeh, "in that inn, they don't even light Shabbat candles. No, I wouldn't make Kiddush in such a place." "Well, I would invite you to my own home, but we really don't have much of anything to eat or drink." "Don't worry, I don't eat very much, and I don't drink very much either." "All right, so, you'll come home with me," said the old man, still sitting with his prayer book in hand.

"Tell me, where do you come from?" "I come from Lublin." "You don't say! Why, you don't happen to know the tzaddik, the Chozeh, do you?" "It so happens that I know him very well. I spend all of my time with him." The old man's eyes lit up like a fire. "I would like very much to be able to see him in his glory, but I don't know how it can be. I'm very poor and I've become weak in my old age, so it is impossible for me to make the journey to Lublin. Nevertheless, my desire is so strong; I fast one day a week that I should have the merit to see him with my own eyes. Please, what can you tell me about him?" "Well, what kind of things do you want to know?" asked the Chozeh. "You see, many years ago, when he was just a little boy, I was his teacher. In those days he was a regular boy, just like all the rest. But now, I hear he performs miracles and is a great tzaddik. Every day, when his turn came to read from the prayer book, he would be missing. And when he would finally show up, I would spank him. Then, one day I decided to follow him. I was curious to see where he went all the time. So,

I walked a little distance behind him, and followed him into the forest. There, he sat down and cried out from the depths of his heart, 'Shema Yisrael, Hashem Elokeinu, Hashem Echad!' (Hear O Israel, The Eternal is our G-d, The Eternal is One!) From that day on I never spanked him again."

The Chozeh was greatly moved by the old man's recollection, and it was clear to him why G-d had directed his path to this out-of-the-way little village. He revealed to the old man his real

Late 18th century painting of Lancut's synagogue by Polish artist Zygmunt Vogel (1764-1826)

identity, and the old man fainted. After he was revived, the old man told the Chozeh not to reveal to anyone who he was. After the end of Shabbat, the Chozeh and his followers continued on their journey. They arrived at an inn and enjoyed the Melave Malka meal (a ritual meal following the Sabbath, bidding goodbye to the "Shabbat Queen"). When they had finished, the Chozeh told them, "Let's return to the village now, for it is time for us to pay our last respects to the old man I stayed with. He has just departed from this world." They returned and eulogized the old man who had such a burning love for righteous people that G-d granted him his greatest wish.

The Lancut synagogue was set ablaze during World War II, but because it is masonry, the building was not destroyed. It was used for grain storage during the war, and probably for storage purposes for some years afterwards. In 1956, with no Jews residing in Lancut, the town council proposed to destroy the building. Dr. Stanislaw Balici persuaded the council to

View of the Lancut synagogue after restoration

preserve the building as a museum and memorial to Lancut's destroyed Jewish community.

Lizhensk/Leżajsk

The second half of the 1700s marked the high point in the community's history. It was then that the famed Rabbi Elimelech established his court in Lizhensk, transforming the small town into a major Hassidic centre. (For more about Rabbi Elimelech, see his profile in Section IV.) After his passing, annual spring

pilgrimages to his tomb became a central event on Lizhensk's annual calendar. Wealthier pilgrims would bring welcomed business, and in their wake followed impoverished Jews from across Poland hoping to receive charitable donations.

Tomb of R' Elimelech of Lizhensk

At the start of World War II, Poland was divided between Germany and Russia, with Lizhensk assigned to the German zone. The Germans burned down the synagogue and destroyed Jewish homes. Even the cemetery was looted and vandalized. At that time, the Germans brutally expelled most of the Jews to Russian territory. The few hundred Jews who remained were imprisoned in a ghetto which was liquidated in 1942. Nine natives of Lizhensk who returned after the war were murdered by local Polish anti-Semites. The Jewish community of Lizhensk was never re-established.

Lodz

Lodz is currently the third largest city in Poland and is centrally located near Warsaw. During the 19th century, while under Russian rule, the tiny settlement of Lodz developed into a modern, industrial city. A nascent textile industry emerged in the early 1820s and within a few years, Lodz became known as one of the most active textile producers in Europe. The city grew rapidly. The population quintupled from around 800 in 1820 to 4,300 residents a decade later. Over the course of the next century, the population had increased 150-fold to more than 600,000 residents.

In 1809, a Jewish community was founded in Lodz. In the late 1820s, Jews were granted permission to acquire and develop property, and in 1861, they received permission to settle throughout the city. During the period of rapid expansion, Lodz became an attractive city for Jewish industrialists. Soon, one-third of the city's residents were Jews. In 1914, one-third of the city's factories, and nearly one quarter of its small workshops, were owned by Jews. Although Jews wielded considerable industrial and economic influence, Jewish entrepreneurs were limited by many anti-Jewish laws and policies. Nevertheless by 1931, the Jewish population in the city numbered over 200,000.

The Jewish community in Lodz continued to develop and thrive throughout the years leading up to the Holocaust. There was a vast Jewish infrastructure, including educational institutions, a kosher slaughterhouse, a mikvah (ritual bath) and charitable and cultural organisations. There were a number of synagogues built in the city throughout the 1800s, including the Orthodox Stara synagogue (Alte Shul), the Great Synagogue and the Ezras Yisrael synagogue (Wolynska Shul). Tragically, the Nazis destroyed all of these synagogues during their occupation of Lodz.

In 1912, Markus Braude built the first Hebrew Secondary School in Lodz. It was modelled after the European "gymnasium" schools (academic high schools that prepared students for university). In 1918, a Yiddish school was opened, followed by a Jewish school for girls in 1924.

The city became an major Jewish cultural centre, home to theatre and drama groups, and many famous Yiddish actors and musicians including world-renowned pianist, Arthur Rubinstein.

While Jews were afforded relative freedom in Lodz during the years of industrial prosperity, they were never considered fully equal citizens. For example, Jewish manufacturers were not granted government assistance to rebuild businesses that were damaged in World War I, while their non-Jewish counterparts were.

Anti-Semitism was prevalent and increased dramatically during the interwar years. In the early 1930s there were attacks against Jews, and anti-Jewish laws and policies were gradually but systematically instituted throughout the decade. By 1938, gentile customers were forbidden to enter shops owned by Jewish merchants. These policies had nothing to do with Nazi Germany.

On 8 September 1939, the German army reached Lodz. The Nazis immediately passed a series of severe anti-Jewish decrees. Jewish businesses were expropriated and Jewish bank accounts were frozen. Freedom of movement was restricted as were employment opportunities. Even synagogue prayer services were outlawed.

By the end of 1939, approximately 70,000 Jews had relocated from Lodz to Warsaw and surrounding areas. On 1 March 1940, the 160,000 remaining Jews were brutally forced into the enormous Lodz ghetto. When it was officially sealed in May, the Lodz ghetto was second only to the Warsaw ghetto in total population. As in other ghettos throughout Poland, starvation and disease were widespread. Those who were caught attempting to escape were summarily executed.

In October of 1939, the Nazis established a Jewish Council, or Judenrat, as their liaison to the Jewish community. As its chairman, they appointed 70-year old Mordechai Chaim Rumkowski.

Rumkowski believed the best chance Jews had for survival was to ensure they were employed and providing real economic value to the Germans. In a speech he delivered in February 1941 he explained, "My main slogan has been to give work to the greatest possible number of people." The workers were carpenters, tailors, shoemakers and the like, all producing goods for Germany. Through his efforts, Rumkowski built a profitable manufacturing empire comprised of some 120 full-time plants employing tens of thousands within the walls of the ghetto. "They respect us because we constitute a centre of productivity ... The plan is work, work, and more work!" His domain was vast and bolstered by a small army of Jewish police. He became known as "King Chaim."

His efforts were certainly not in vain. Rumkowski obtained permission to open schools for 5,000 students to be taught in Hebrew and Yiddish. For seven months in 1941 and 1942 he was able to arrange for a Jewish postal service that enabled those trapped within the ghetto to have a sense of hope, security and connection with the outside world. He arranged for Jewish services to lift spirits, and he cared for incoming refugees as brethren.

Periodic deportations to the Chelmno extermination camp began in January 1942. At the time of each new Aktion, those who could not work were selected for deportation. By May of that year about 40,000 Jews from Lodz had been sent to their deaths.

From the start, Rumkowski emerged as a controversial figure. The controversy arose not from his strident efforts to aid the Germans as much as his willingness to sacrifice individuals for the sake of what he believed was the greater good. At its most extreme, when facing German demands to deport some 20,000 Jews, Rumkowski told the people to hand over their children under 10 years of age and adults over 65. Rumkowski lamented, "I simply must cut off the limbs to save the body. I have to take away children, because otherwise others will also be taken." Contemporary accounts report that while Rumkowski spoke "with a broken heart," his decision was ultimately carried out, and about 16,000 children, elderly and infirm Jews were forcefully deported from Lodz to Chelmno in September 1942.

Jewish families wait in the snowfall with their belongings packed for relocation, March 1940

The population of the ghetto continued to decline rapidly, and it was transformed from a

Rumkowski testing soup in the ghetto

concentration camp into a labour camp in which only adults who were fit to work remained. Deportations continued until 30 August 1944, when the last transport left Lodz for Auschwitz. Rumkowski himself was amongst those deported to Auschwitz in 1944. According to some accounts, the aggrieved and unforgiving parents of those unfortunate children he had ordered deported two years prior ensured he would not survive to even see Auschwitz.

After the final transport, a handful of Jews remained in the camp, organising the remaining possessions of the dead and dismantling the factories in Lodz so they could be relocated to Germany. When the Soviets liberated the camp on 19 January 1945, there were fewer than 800 survivors.

After the war, 40,000–50,000 Jews returned to Lodz, primarily from the Soviet Union; however, their stay was temporary. Ongoing economic hardship and anti-Semitism pushed many to emigrate. Within five years, half of the Jewish population in Lodz had resettled in Israel. By 1969, most of those who had initially remained also left Poland.

The once vibrant Jewish community in Lodz now consists of but a few hundred Jews. There is one active synagogue, which was built in the 18th century. Hidden within the ghetto, it miraculously survived the Holocaust. There are also a number of other Jewish sites of interest remaining throughout the city, including the former *beit midrash*, a kosher slaughterhouse, a Jewish cemetery and the mansions of several famous Jewish industrialists.

Lublin

Lublin had been a key city for the Jews of Poland since the Golden Age in the 1500s. A significant yeshiva was established here in 1515. By 1600, Lublin was home to several thousand Jews, including the famous Talmudic scholar and Jewish legal authority, Rabbi Meir Lublin (the Maharam), whose rulings are still followed today. Being a major trade centre, Lublin was chosen to host the annual meetings of the semi-autonomous Jewish parliament, known as the "Council of the Four Lands." Lublin Jews held prominent positions in the Council, including the role of Speaker.

Lublin's Jews suffered greatly during the Chmielnicki massacres of 1648–1649. (See Part 2.) Over time, the Jewish population gradually recovered, and in the late 1700s, Lublin attained new prominence with the growth of the Hassidic movement.

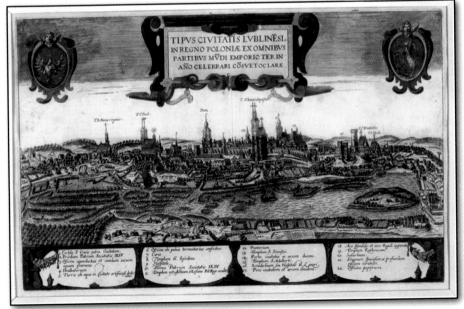

Drawing of Lublin in the 16th century

179

During the 1800s and early 1900s, the Jewish population of Lublin grew as the city's industrial and commercial activities increased. Lublin's reputation as a Hassidic centre was bolstered by the presence of such luminaries as the Chozeh (seer) of Lublin, of whom it was said he could see directly into the souls of people, and Rabbi Tzadok of Lublin, a notable Jewish thinker whose writings are still popular today.

The Jewish quarter in the old section of Lublin, 1938

Before the war, Lublin was a major intellectual and commercial centre. Lublin's Jewish community included numerous synagogues, schools, cemeteries, a hospital, an orphanage and an old-age home. There were two Yiddish-language newspapers, and Jews were represented on the Lublin town council. Jews owned 50% of the town's factories and 30% of its workshops.

A "cheder" (religious school for boys) in Lublin, 1924

Most of the large pre-war population was killed during the Holocaust. Of the 40,000 Jews who lived in Lublin prior to the war, only 200-300 survived in hiding or in camps, and another 1,000 survived the war in areas held by the Soviets.

Rabbi Meir Shapiro and Yeshivat Chochmei Lublin

Lublin is often associated with Rabbi Yehuda Meir Shapiro, one of the most notable religious Jewish personalities of the early 20th century.

Rabbi Shapiro introduced and promoted the idea of learning the "Daf Yomi" (the page of the day), by which the same one page of the Talmud is studied daily everywhere in the world. A new page is studied every day, 365 days a year, and the entire Talmud is completed over the course of seven-and-a-half years. It is an

Rabbi Yehuda Meir Shapiro

Drawing of Yeshivat Chochmei Lublin in the 1930s

idea that has become increasingly popular amongst Orthodox Jewry. The program began its 13th cycle in 2012 and has tens of thousands of participants worldwide.

Rabbi Shapiro devoted much of his energy to raising the level of Jewish scholarship in Poland. In every city where he served as rabbi, he established a yeshiva and attracted many promising scholars. In 1930, he founded the yeshiva Chochmei Lublin (the wise of Lublin). Seeking to raise the prestige of yeshiva students and Torah study, he built an extraordinary facility offering students modern accommodations and quality meals. The six-storey building had 120 rooms and a huge auditorium. It even housed a model of the Temple in Jerusalem. The yeshiva grew from 200 students at the time of its founding to nearly 500 students in 1939. The opening of this palatial, modern yeshiva building marked a high point in the religious life of Polish Jewry.

Sadly, Rabbi Shapiro died of typhus just three years after the yeshiva's opening. At the time of his death, the yeshiva's future was threatened by heavy debts. Fortunately, Rabbi Shapiro had arranged for the yeshiva to benefit from his life insurance policy. In 1940, the Nazis created an enormous bonfire in front of the school building and burned all 55,000 volumes of the yeshiva's enormous book collection.

Today the building of Yeshivat Chochmei Lublin serves as a resource to the Polish Jewish community

When the Germans invaded Lublin in September, 1939, there were 37,830 Jews in the city (40% of the population). The Nazis established a ghetto in Lublin in March 1941. Until March of the following year, the closure of the ghetto was not strictly enforced, and illegal trade with the outside world contributed to better living conditions than those of many other ghettos. On 16 March 1942, liquidation of the ghetto began. Two hundred children from the Lublin Jewish orphanage were killed and hundreds of hospital patients were murdered. Deportations proceeded at a rate of 1,500 people per day. By April of the same year, 30,000 Lublin Jews had been sent to Belzec.

Majdanek Labour and Concentration Camp

Entrance to Majdanek Camp

The Nazis established the Majdanek concentration camp just outside the city of Lublin in October 1941. Originally, the camp was designed to hold 25,000–50,000 Russian soldiers captured during the German invasion of the Ukraine. One hundred and fifty local Jewish men were forced to work alongside these Russian prisoners of war to build the camp. Due to atrocious conditions, this first group of workers all died from disease within a few months.

In 1942, three extermination camps, Belzec, Sobibor and Treblinka, began operations to eliminate Polish Jewry under a secret program called Operation Reinhard. Due to the need for Jewish manpower in the war effort, some Jews were temporarily spared and were sent to one of a large network of labour camps. Majdanek was one such labour camp. Here, work was primarily done at the Steyr-Daimler-Puch weapons/munitions factory. Within the framework of Operation Reinhard, Majdanek also served as a sorting and storage depot for property and valuables taken from the victims at the killing centres in Belzec, Sobibor and Treblinka.

At Majdanek, the Nazis made no attempt to hide the purpose of the camp from

The view of Lublin from Majdanek

the surrounding population. The camp was located at the side of a major road, only a few miles from the centre of Lublin, with no trees or hills to conceal it from passersby. Cruel treatment of the prisoners and smoke from the crematorium would have been clearly visible from the road.

According to the data from the official Majdanek State Museum, a total of 300,000 people were inmates during the period of the camp's operation. Although Majdanek also occasionally functioned as a killing centre for Jews, this was not as systematic as in the extermination camps. Of the approximately 3,000,000 Polish Jews murdered, 59,000 were killed in Majdanek.

Super-wide-angle photograph of the gas chamber in Majdanek

Operation Reinhard continued until November 1943, when the last Generalgouvernement Jews were exterminated as part of Operation "Harvest Festival." Many of these last remaining Jews had been imprisoned at Majdanek. On 3 November 1943, as part of the Harvest Festival "celebration," 18,400 Jews—some of Poland's last—were shot here on a single day.

When Soviet forces rapidly approached Lublin in late July 1944, the Germans were taken by surprise. They hastily attempted to evacuate Majdanek, marching some of the inmates to Auschwitz and leaving others behind to destroy the evidence of their crimes. Majdanek was the first major concentration camp to be liberated by Allied forces. Because the Germans were unable to destroy the crematorium and other evidence before the Red Army arrived, Majdanek is also one of the best-preserved concentration camps.

Plaszow Labour and Concentration Camp

Memorial at Plaszow

The Plaszow concentration camp, located near Krakow, was established by the Germans soon after their invasion of Poland. Originally a Jewish cemetery, the Nazis first converted it into a forced labour camp to supply manpower to several armament factories and a stone quarry. Later, in 1943, it was converted into a concentration camp. The death rate in the camp was high, as many prisoners succumbed to starvation and typhoid. Plaszow is notorious for the executions carried out there, and many of the Jews who died in the camp were victims of individual or mass shootings.

Commander Amon Göth on the balcony of his house in Plaszow

On 13 March 1943, Amon Göth, an SS officer and commander of the camp, personally oversaw the liquidation of the Krakow ghetto, sending its stronger inhabitants to work in Plaszow. Those deemed unfit for work were killed. There is much testimony describing Göth's particularly cruel treatment of prisoners.

When the Nazis learned that the Russians were nearing Krakow, they completely dismantled the camp, leaving only an empty field. The bodies that had been buried there in mass graves were exhumed and burned on site. In January of 1945, the remaining inmates and camp staff left Plaszow on a death march to Auschwitz. Germany succeeded in hiding the atrocities of Plaszow and upon entering the camp on 20 January 1945, the Red Army found no evidence of what had once been there.

The area where the camp had once been now consists of sparsely wooded hills and fields. Today, a large memorial and a small plaque mark the site where mass destruction had taken place. Plaszow is the camp depicted in Schindler's List, a movie describing the life and wartime experiences of Oskar Schindler. (See profile on Schindler in Part 4.)

Rzeshov

The Jewish community of Rzeshov dates back to the 15th century. During the 19th century, the community flourished as a major Hassidic centre: home to five Rabbis, two synagogues, four *shteiblach* (smaller, private synagogues) and four cemeteries. At that time, most of Rzeshov's Jews, (close to half of the town's general population) were Hassidim, many of whom were followers of the Sanz and Sadigora Rebbes.

Rzeshov synagogue

In addition to Hassidism, the Haskalah as well as Zionism gained currency here in the late 19th and early 20th centuries. Between the two world wars, numerous political organisations and youth movements thrived. There was a Jewish hospital, a Jewish Music and Drama Association, a Jewish Academic Union, artisan guilds and the like.

The Germans occupied Rzeshov, then home to some 15,000 Jews, just before the High Holy Days in September 1939. On Rosh Hashanah and Yom Kippur, the Nazis drove Jewish men, still wrapped in their prayer shawls, out of the synagogues and murdered many of them for sport.

Life for the Jews in Rzeshov deteriorated rapidly. By the end of 1939, there were 10 forced labour camps in the Rzeshov region. Jews were forced to wear yellow stars and Jewish businesses had to be clearly marked. In December 1941, the Germans established a ghetto to imprison 25,000 Jews from Rzeshov and the surrounding region. In July 1942, the ghetto was liquidated. About 22,000 were deported to the Belzec death camp, while another 1,000 were taken to the nearby forest and shot. In November 1943, the ghetto was transformed into a slave labour camp. Most of the inmates were eventually deported to Auschwitz.

Tarnow

Tarnow touts itself as a Polish "hot spot," offering nightlife, hotels and museums. StayPoland.com beckons tourists: "The winding streets of the mediaeval town ... create a magical atmosphere which can be experienced in no other place in the country." For Jews, however, Tarnow is still a particularly striking example of the horrors of the Holocaust: a city where Jews had lived for centuries, only to be swiftly decimated by the Nazis' singular cruelty.

Tarnow is in southern Poland, 45 miles east of Krakow. Historical records indicate that Jews had lived here since the mid-15th century. Tarnow and its surrounding region formed a significant religious centre in Southern Poland, particularly for Hassidic Jews. Its Jewish community had synagogues, schools and a rich social and religious life.

Before World War II, Tarnow was home to 25,000 Jews, about half of the total population. The Jewish community was ideologically diverse and included both religious Hassidim and secular Zionists. It was an important centre of religious life with synagogues and houses of study. Although most of Tarnow's Jews were poor, a significant number were part of the city's intellectual and cultural

Postcard of Tarnow's "New Synagogue" at the turn of the century

elite. They were lawyers and doctors, musicians, teachers and industrialists. There was a rich social life and infrastructure, complete with Jewish schools, newspapers and cultural and social organisations.

The tragedies of Tarnow began on 8 September 1939, when the Germans occupied the town. By the following day, synagogues and Jewish homes had been burned down. Like Jews throughout Poland, Tarnow's Jews were subjected to degradation and humiliation and were forced to wear identifying yellow stars.

In May 1940, the first deportation from Tarnow took place—the very first transport to the recently opened Auschwitz concentration camp. It included Polish political prisoners, amongst whom were many of the Tarnow Jewish community's leaders. Upon arrival, Auschwitz's deputy commander—the man who would later innovate the use of Zyklon B—announced, "This is Auschwitz Concentration Camp ... Any resistance or disobedience will be ruthlessly punished. Anyone disobeying superiors or trying to escape, will be sentenced to death. Young and healthy people don't live longer than three months here. Priests one month, Jews two weeks. There is only one way out — through the crematorium chimneys."[60]

By March 1941, the Jews of Tarnow and the surrounding region were forced into the Tarnow ghetto. The small enclave's population soon swelled to 40,000. There was neither enough room nor enough food to sustain the population, and starvation and disease grew rampant. Jews were forbidden, on pain of death, to smuggle food into the ghetto. Adding insult to injury, the Germans levied huge collective fines from the Jewish community. Over the months, roundups for forced labour became increasingly frequent, and German brutality went from extreme to unimaginable: beyond beatings, pedestrians were periodically shot in the streets for no reason whatsoever.

In June 1942, the concerted effort to liquidate Tarnow's Jews began. About 12,000 were sent to the Belzec extermination camp. During the deportation operations,

Nazis humiliate Jews in Tarnow in 1940. Local onlookers look disturbingly pleased to be part of the photograph.

189

the German forces killed wantonly and arbitrarily, massacring hundreds of Jews in the streets, in the marketplace, in the Jewish cemetery and in the woods nearby. Around this time, a group of Jews in Tarnow organised a resistance movement. Some joined partisans in the forests, but were later killed by SS units. Others tried to escape to Hungary—most unsuccessfully.

Further large deportations to Belzec were carried out in September and November 1942. The Germans finally liquidated the ghetto in September of 1943. The last 10,000 Jews were deported: 7,000 to Auschwitz for extermination and 3,000 to the Plaszow labour camp for further exploitation. During the liquidation, fifty Jews tried to smuggle small children out of the ghetto. Tragically, they were all separated from the transport and gunned down. Late in 1943, Tarnow was declared Judenrein.

The overwhelming majority of Tarnow's Jews were murdered by the Germans. After liberation, 700 Jews returned to Tarnow, but continuing anti-Semitism forced them to leave shortly thereafter. Most of them immigrated to Israel.

Tykocin

Tykocin lies on the bank of the Narew River, a natural boundary between Poland and Lithuania. During the Middle Ages, the Narew served as a principal artery of communication and transport for the region, and Tykocin developed rapidly. In 1522 the Gashtold family, which owned Tykocin at the time, invited 10 Jewish families from Grodno (located 55 miles northeast in modern day Belarus) to settle there. The families were given sites for homes and were later permitted to establish shops, a synagogue and a cemetery. The community prospered. Most of its members earned their livelihoods as traders or artisans, while others were involved in the trade of salt, spices and cloth. By 1576, there were 54 houses in Tykocin owned by Jews.

As in other Polish cities, there was ongoing economic rivalry between the Jews and Polish burghers (middle class) of Tykocin. The conflict in Tykocin, however, grew particularly intense. At one point, anti-Semites even made use of the 1657 blood libel in nearby Rozanystok as an excuse to organise

Tykocin's synagogue was built in 1642, and is considered one of the most beautiful synagogues in Poland. It is distinguished by its external simplicity and the harmony of its baroque interior. Until 1740, it was the finest building in the town. The Germans converted the antique synagogue into a storehouse for holding the household goods plundered from the local Jews. The synagogue was thoroughly restored in the late 1970s along with its historic wall paintings and decorative texts.

riots against the Tykocin Jews and threatened them with expulsion. Although no expulsion was carried out in Tykocin, two of the leaders of the Rozanystok Jewish community were executed.

In many ways, the Tykocin Jewish community was a model community. In the 17th century, the Jewish Council of the Four Lands referred to it as "magnificent, talented and complete." The importance of the Tykocin community is evident from the stature of its rabbis over the centuries. Among these were the famed Talmudist, Rabbi Shmuel Eliezer Eidels (1555-1631), better known as the "Maharsha"; the founder of the Belz Hassidic dynasty, Rabbi Shalom Rokeach (1779-1855); and prolific commentator, Rabbi Yehoshua Shapiro (1801-1873).

Until the beginning of the 20th century, Tykocin Jews lived very traditionally. Religious institutions were the centre of social and cultural life. Tykocin's first Zionist organization was founded in 1904. A few years later, HaMizrachi, Po'alei Zion and the Bund increased the number and scope of Jewish organisations in Tykocin. The first modern Jewish public library was opened here in 1912. While the interwar years were economically very difficult, the cultural and social life of the Jews of Tykocin blossomed further, and Zionist activity increased dramatically.

In the 1930s, anti-Semitic violence and the boycotting of Jewish merchants and artisans intensified. Anti-Jewish riots took place in 1936, and lasted several days; they recurred in 1938. Gangs of anti-Semitic youth stoned the synagogue and Jewish homes. Respite came in the autumn of 1939 when Tykocin was transferred to Soviet control, and anti-Semitic activity decreased.

The reprieve of the Soviet period was, of course, the calm before the storm. In June 1941, after the outbreak of the German-Soviet war, Tykocin was captured by the Germans. With the encouragement of the Nazis, the Poles immediately unleashed a pogrom against the local Jewish community and looted Jewish property. Five German gendarmes arrived in Tykocin on 16 August 1941, and pretended that they had come to protect the Jews from their Polish attackers. When they ordered the Poles to return the stolen property, many Jews began to believe in the Germans. The ruse went so far that Poles started to complain that the Germans had sold themselves to the Jews for bribes. Within days, however, Tykocin's Jews understood the gendarmes' game. They prohibited Jews from leaving the town, and simultaneously ordered the digging of three large pits in the nearby Lupochowo forest.

On 24 August 1941, the Germans proclaimed that the next morning at 6:00, Jews were to report to the market square. This caused a great deal of panic, but only a few of the community were able to escape to the surrounding forest. After a Selektion, about 1,400 Jews were told that they were being relocated to the Bialystok ghetto, and that each could take a package of as much as 25kg. Four Nazi trucks arrived and escorted the men who were to be "relocated." They marched to the village of Zawod where they were locked up in the local school. The trucks later transported them to the pits in Lupochowo forest, where they were murdered. On the same day, the women and children of Tarnow were also murdered in the Lupochowo forest. The Germans then rounded up the 700 Tykocin Jews who had not reported to the market square as ordered, including the elderly and sick, and murdered them at Lupochowo as well.

About 150 Jews succeeded in fleeing Tykocin before the liquidation of the community, but most of them were captured by local Polish peasants who handed them over to the Germans. The few who escaped made it to Bialystok only to suffer the same fate as its Jews when that ghetto was liquidated. Only seventeen Jews of Tykocin survived the Holocaust.

Warsaw

While Jewish settlement in Warsaw first began in the 14th century, few Jews lived there until the early 1800s. In 1809, a Jewish Quarter was established; but initially only wealthy Jews, who dressed in European garb, who could read and write in Polish, German or French and who sent their children to state

Great Synagogue in the 1910s

schools, were permitted to reside there. From 1818-1918, Warsaw's Jewish population grew at an explosive pace. Within a century, it became the largest Jewish community in Europe and second only to New York in the world. Most of the Jews living in Warsaw in the 19th century had been Orthodox—many were Hassidim of the Rabbi of Gur, who lived in a nearby suburb. But with each passing year, the population tended further towards secularism.

By the end of World War I, almost 350,000 Jews lived in Warsaw, comprising about a third of the city's total population. In the wake of World War I, many more Jewish refugees fled to Warsaw. During the interwar period, the community once again enjoyed marked growth and relative freedom, despite anti-Semitism and economic hardship.

In the years leading up to World War II, Warsaw's Jews were infused with creative energy. As Warsaw's status as a major European cultural centre rose, Jews were very much a part of the scene. It was the

A shoemaker in Warsaw, 1927

Okopowa Street Cemetery
Arguably the most beautiful place in Warsaw

heyday of Yiddish theatre. The city hosted international piano and violin competitions. Jewish weekly newspapers emerged in both Yiddish and Polish, and Warsaw became the centre for Hebrew publishing in both Poland and Russia. Many famous Jewish writers, including Isaac Bashevis Singer (1902-1991), lived or worked in Warsaw.

Although the period before the war was marked by inflation and political instability, many Jews were part of the city's middle- and upper-classes and were active in commerce and professional life. Jews played major roles in the local banking industry and in the sales of salt and alcoholic beverages. Wealthy Jews and the intelligentsia were attracted to the Great Synagogue, the largest, most beautiful synagogue in Warsaw, which offered a Reform service in Polish.

Politically, Warsaw's Jews were deeply involved in Zionist and Jewish socialist

Mass grave at Okopowa Street Cemetery

activities. The Zionists promoted their agenda of returning the Jewish people to the Land of Israel. Jewish socialism, with its emphasis on Jewish culture and the use of Yiddish as the Jewish national language, appealed to large numbers of Warsaw's artisans, Jewish labourers and members of the Jewish intelligentsia.

The Okopowa Street Cemetery

The main Jewish cemetery in Warsaw was the Okopowa Street cemetery, established in 1803. It is an enormous, sprawling testament to the life that once was, occupying 83 acres and containing over 200,000 individually marked graves. Here, simple gravestones inscribed in Hebrew lie alongside elaborately carved tombs and towering mausoleums in styles ranging from Egyptian revival to art deco. Of interesting note, the cemetery was one of the first to allow family burial plots, with men and women buried next to each other.

Countless of Jewish history found their final resting place here. Amongst the noteworthy rabbis are Rabbi Naftali Tzvi Yehudah Berlin (the "Netziv") who is buried next to his famous grandson-in-law, the Rabbi of Brisk, Chaim Soloveitchik. Many members of the Gur Hassidic dynasty are buried here, as is the Modzitzer Rabbi, who is famous for his musical compositions. Other gravesites are those of: historian Meir Balaban; Yiddish writer I.L. Peretz; head of the ghetto's Judenrat, Adam Czerniakow; and Ludwik Zamenhof, who attempted to promulgate the universal language Esperanto. (See Part 4 for biographical sketches of Rabbi Naftali Tzvi Yehudah Berlin, I.L. Peretz, Adam Czerniakow and Ludwik Zamenhof.)

Aside from the thousands of individually marked graves, there are enormous unmarked mass graves of victims of the Warsaw ghetto, where perhaps more than 100,000 bodies were dumped.

Although most of the cemetery has become overgrown with trees in the years since the World War II, a small portion of it is still in use, serving the renewed Jewish community of Warsaw.

The Nozyk Synagogue

Nozyk Synagogue Exterior

Interior of the Nozyk Synagogue

The Nozyk Synagogue on Twarda Street is the only remaining synagogue (out of more than 400) that was not destroyed by the Nazis and is still standing in Warsaw. It was built with funds donated by Zalman Nozyk, a wealthy Warsaw merchant, and his wife Rivka, and was opened in 1902. In 1923, a semi-circular area was added alongside the eastern wall allowing for a choir, and helping it develop into a renowned venue for Jewish music and song.

During the early years of the war, the ghetto included the Nozyk; but later, when the borders of the ghetto were redrawn, the building became part of Aryan Warsaw. German forces then used the building as a horse stable—a common wartime display of Nazi contempt for Judaism.

After the war, the synagogue was returned to the Jewish community and was reopened in 1983 on the 50th anniversary of the Warsaw Ghetto Uprising. Though there was relatively little activity there at first, the Polish Jewish community has undergone a veritable renaissance in recent years, much of it centred around the Nozyk. In 1992, Rabbi Michael Schudrich moved to Warsaw and set out to revitalise the local Jewish community. In December 2004, he was appointed the first Chief Rabbi of Poland since the war and has been instrumental in rebuilding the communities of Warsaw, Lodz and Krakow. Today, one can find daily services held at the Nozyk synagogue as well as an adjacent kosher canteen, kosher shop and cultural centre.

The Warsaw Ghetto

On 30 September 1939, within a month of invading Poland, German forces entered Warsaw. At the time, Warsaw had the largest Jewish population of any city in Europe: 400,000 people. Almost immediately, the Nazis issued anti-Jewish decrees and set out to establish a ghetto to sequester the Jewish community. Despite the fact that Jews constituted about a third of Warsaw's total population (even before considering the substantial number of Jewish refugees who had fled to Warsaw throughout the preceding month), only about 2.4% of the city was allocated for the ghetto.

The Warsaw ghetto was split into two areas: the "small ghetto," generally inhabited by richer Jews, and the "large ghetto." The two sub-ghettos were

Remnants of the Warsaw ghetto's wall

linked by a single footbridge. On 16 November 1940, both were closed off from the outside world by a high brick wall and armed guards around the perimeter.

Conditions in the ghetto were desperate. Perhaps 100,000 of its victims died from starvation, epidemics (especially typhus) and random Nazi killings. Smuggling was often the only source of subsistence. Hundreds of four- and five-year-old children snuck into the Aryan side of the city, sometimes several times a day, smuggling food back into the ghettos. They often returned with loads of goods that weighed more than they did.

Although life was chaotic in the ghetto, there was an official organising body known as the Judenrat (the ghetto's Jewish council), which was responsible for rationing food, organising forced labour and the administration of general community services. The Judenrat's 24 members came from a cross-section of the Warsaw Jewish community and were directed by the controversial Adam Czerniakow. (See his profile in Part 4.) Together, they were faced with the difficult task of cooperating with the Germans enough to avoid major killings and deportations, while doing their best to avoid the implementation of the oppressive Nazi decrees. Many saw members of the Judenrat as traitors, while others were sympathetic to the difficult situation in which the Judenrat members had been placed.

Despite the dire hardships, life in the ghetto was much richer than one might have expected. Underground organisations promoted educational and cultural activities. Others established hospitals, public soup kitchens, orphanages, refugee centres and recreational facilities. Schools for children emerged under the guise of soup kitchens, hidden libraries cropped up around the ghetto and secret yeshivot were housed in underground bunkers. The ghetto even had a clandestine symphony orchestra.

Life in the ghetto continued in this fashion until the summer of 1942, when the Nazis began liquidating the ghetto. From Tisha B'Av (23 July) to Yom Kippur (21 September) of 1942, between 250,000 and 300,000 civilians were "relocated" to Treblinka, where they were murdered. By the end of 1942, it was clear to those

who had survived the first wave of deportations that "relocation" was fatal. The idea of armed resistance against the Nazis began to gain currency among the ghetto inhabitants.

On 18 January 1943, the first bout of armed resistance flared when the Germans attempted to initiate a second round of deportations. The fighting was organised primarily by two groups: the ZZW (Jewish Military Union) headed by David Apfelbaum, and the ZOB (Jewish Fighting Organisation) led by Mordechai Anielewicz. (See profile on Anielewicz in Part 4.) Armed with little more than handguns, their operatives joined a group of Jews selected for deportation and opened fire on the unsuspecting German soldiers who were readying them for the trains. Even though the ZZW and ZOB suffered heavy losses, the German force succumbed after four days, and the deportation was halted.

The ZOB and ZZW immediately took control of the ghetto. They built dozens of fighting posts and executed individuals who had collaborated with the Germans: Jewish police officers; members of German-sponsored and controlled organisations; and Gestapo agents. They prepared themselves for the day when the Germans would inevitably return to the ghetto.

Three months later, the Germans announced a final deportation. On the eve of Passover, 19 April 1943, several thousand Ukrainian and Latvian SS troops entered the ghetto. The Jewish fighters, numbering perhaps as many as 1,000, responded with the largest Jewish resistance effort of the Holocaust period. They only had short-range arms such as pistols and revolvers and minimal ammunition. These weapons were of limited value in combat and were practically useless at larger distances. Thus, the freedom fighters relied heavily on improvised explosive devices and Molotov cocktails. Notwithstanding their hopeless odds, the Jewish resistance in Warsaw held out longer than the Polish army had held out against the invasion of Poland in September 1939.

After initial setbacks, the Germans, under Commander Jürgen Stroop, systematically burned and blew up the ghetto buildings, block by block, capturing or murdering anybody they found. The Nazi operation officially ended on 16 May with the symbolic demolition of the Great Synagogue of Warsaw. According to the official report, at least 56,065 people were killed by German forces in the ghetto or were deported to concentration and death camps, most of them to Treblinka.

Jürgen Stroop's internal SS daily report written on 16 May 1943, stated:

One hundred and eighty Jews, bandits and sub-humans, were destroyed. The former Jewish quarter of Warsaw is no longer in existence. The large-scale action was terminated at 20:15 hours by blowing up the Warsaw Synagogue ... Total number of Jews dealt with 56,065, including both Jews caught and Jews whose extermination can be proved ... Apart from eight buildings (police barracks, hospital and accommodations for housing working-parties), the former ghetto is completely destroyed. Only the dividing walls are left standing where no explosions were carried out.

JRoots student group at Mila 18, site of command bunker of Mordecai Anielewicz's ZOB Warsaw Ghetto fighters' last stand

The Extermination Camps

As soon as the Nazi party rose to power in 1933, it became common practice to intern anyone seen as a threat to the Party in concentration camps. The first of the inmates were "political prisoners" in the loosest sense of the term. These early camps were, in effect, prisons that provided the Reich with slave labour. Amongst the first to be opened were Dachau, located just outside of Munich (1933) and Sachsenhausen, a few miles north of Berlin (1936).

Although the camps built before the end of 1941 were supposedly intended to be labour or transit camps—designed to exploit, rather than exterminate their inmates—conditions in the camps were so brutal and inhumane, that the mortality rate was exceptionally high. Prisoners died from disease, malnutrition and exhaustion. Many were executed without due process, and some were subjected to frightful medical experiments.

In the summer of 1941, Hitler ordered the "Final Solution to the Jewish Question"— the extermination of all the Jews of Europe. Killing squads, known as Einstatzgruppen, followed the German army as it invaded the Soviet Union. In each newly conquered town or village, the entire Jewish community, including men, women and children, was rounded up and marched to a nearby forest. There, they were forced to dig a large pit. After stripping off their clothing, they were shot into the mass grave.

In 1941, the mobile killing squads murdered over a million Jews and thousands of Soviet partisans and Roma (Gypsies). However, the Germans estimated there were some 11 million Jews in Europe, and they sought to annihilate them all. A more efficient plan was needed.

The mobile death squads were considered too inefficient for killing large numbers of people. Shooting was too resource intensive for the Reich and too psychologically taxing on the murderers. Moreover, mass shootings attracted the attention of both the local populations and regular German soldiers, and rumours of the killings filtered back to Germany. As Hitler wanted to hide his "Final Solution" from the German people and the world at large, an alternate plan for exterminating the large Jewish population of Poland was sought.

In late 1941 and early 1942, the Nazis opened five death camps in Poland: Belzec, Sobibor, Treblinka, Chelmno and Auschwitz-Birkenau. These camps were not intended as labour camps, nor as prisons for punishing criminal actions. They were intended for one purpose only: to facilitate genocide—the annihilation of the Jewish People and other "undesirables."

Original boxcar used for transport to the concentration camps described by Tzvi Sperber to a JRoots group

At the end of 1941, a new method of extermination was introduced in which victims were asphyxiated in the sealed compartment of a lorry into which carbon monoxide from the running engine was funnelled.

In January of 1942, top Nazi officials gathered at a resort on the shores of Lake Wannsee, near Berlin, to coordinate a network of "killing centres" where millions of Jews and other enemies of the German Reich could be executed efficiently and secretly. These death camps would differ in purpose and function from the existing concentration camps.

The death camps were quite literally factories of death. The vast majority of those who entered their gates were killed within hours of their arrival. Jews were transported to the camps by train and trucks where they were met by guards who explained that they would be bathed and disinfected before entering the camp. The Jews were forced to relinquish their valuables and to undress. The women's hair was shaved. They were then crowded into sealed chambers into which poisonous gas was released, initially using the same carbon monoxide method as had been used in the mobile vans.

Murder was postponed for a few of the strongest and healthiest who were first exploited as slaves. These so-called Sonderkommando—literally, "special unit," a term consistent with the Nazi practice of euphemism and deception—were forced to assist in the most dreadful of tasks such as removing their lifeless brethren from the gas chambers and burning their bodies. The clothing, hair and personal effects of the victims were collected and sorted by Sonderkommando, and then sent to Germany. Most of the victims of these camps were Jews, but many others, including many Roma (Gypsies), were executed as well.

Chelmno

The first death camp was opened on an abandoned estate in the town of Chelmno, about an hour northwest of Lodz. Its function was the liquidation of the substantial Jewish population of Lodz and its environs.

The SS and its auxiliaries began killing operations at Chelmno on 8 December 1941. The first people brought to the camp to be murdered were the 2,000 Jews who lived in the nearby town of Kolo. They were brought to Chelmno in stages by truck. Upon arrival, they were instructed to undress and then were led out the back of the manor into the rear-end of a large lorry where they were asphyxiated by carbon monoxide. The lorry then transported the dead bodies to the forest where they were buried and later dug up and burned.

A gas van in Chelmno extermination camp

Beginning in January 1942, Jews were taken from the Lodz ghetto to their deaths at Chelmno. These included Jews from Germany, Austria, Bohemia, Moravia and Luxemburg who had been interned in Lodz. Many Roma were sent to Chelmno as well. Although the facility was closed in March 1943, it was reopened in the summer of 1944 for the final liquidation of the ghetto.

Lodz, Poland, September 1942. Family members say goodbye to a child through a fence at the ghetto's central prison where children, the sick, and the elderly were held before deportation to Chelmno during the "Gehsperre" action.

The secretary of the local council, Stanislaw Kaszynski, and his wife tried to bring public attention to what was being perpetrated at the camp. In late January 1942, they were arrested and executed three days later.

The Operation Reinhard Camps

Operation Reinhard was the code name given to three extermination camps—Belzec, Sobibor and Treblinka—established for the sole purpose of exterminating the approximately two million Jews then living in the General Government district (the unannexed part of Poland taken over by the Germans during World War II). The guards in all three camps were Soviet prisoners of war or Polish civilians. The SS trained these guards to be ruthless killers.

These camps were designed to hide their true function from both the outside world and their victims. The reception area and the killing centre (including gas chambers and mass graves) were separated by a narrow, enclosed passage known as "the tube." After undressing and handing over their valuables, the prisoners were forced to run naked from the reception area through the tube into the gas chambers. The camps were surrounded by barbed wire fences interwoven with branches and surrounded by trees to camouflage them.

In 1943, the Sonderkommando in both Sobibor and Treblinka, revolted. Those few who managed to escape and evade recapture were virtually the only survivors of Operation Reinhard, which murdered some 1.7 million Jews between March 1942 and October 1943. Operation Reinhard ended in November 1943—after almost all of Polish Jewry had been annihilated.

Forest leading to Treblinka. Concrete sleepers commemorate the train tracks leading here

Concurrent with the latter phase of Operation Reinhard was "Aktion 1005" which was designed to remove all traces of the mass murders. In each camp, prisoners were forced to exhume mass graves and cremate the buried bodies, using giant grills made from wood and railway tracks. Afterwards, bone fragments were ground up in specialized milling machines, and all remains were then re-buried in freshly-dug pits. For this reason, when visiting the Operation Reinhard camps, there is virtually nothing left to see of the camps themselves.

Belzec

Originally established in 1940 as a labour camp, Belzec was converted into a death camp in late 1941, making it the first of the Operation Reinhard camps to go into operation. It would also serve as the model for the two others.

The wooden gas chambers were disguised as the barracks and showers of a labour camp, so that the victims would not realize the true purpose of the site. To preempt revolt, the process was conducted as quickly as possible: people were forced to run from the trains to the gas chambers, leaving them no time to absorb where they were or to plan a revolt. A handful of Jews were selected to be Sonderkommandos who would perform all the manual work involved with extermination: removing the bodies from the gas chambers, burying them, sorting and repairing the victims' clothing, etc. These workers were periodically killed and replaced by new arrivals, so that they too could not organise a revolt.

Between March and December 1942, approximately 434,500 Jews from Lvov, Lublin and their surrounding areas, were murdered in Belzec. In total, the death camp operated for about 13 months during which a shocking 600,000 people were gassed. In the spring of 1943, the camp was dismantled and converted into a farm, which was tended by a former guard.

Only two Jews are known to have survived Belzec: Rudolf Reder and Chaim Hirszman.

The Operation Reinhard Camps: Sobibor

Located in the Lublin district in eastern Poland, Sobibor was established in May 1942. Jews were transported to the camp from Lublin, Moravia, Moldavia, Slovakia, France, the Netherlands and the ghettos of Belarus and Vilna.

The camp operated in a similar fashion to Belzec. Trains entered the railway station, and the Jews onboard were told they were in a transit camp. They were forced

Thomas "Toby" Blatt, Sobibor survivor seen here speaking to a JRoots group in Sobibor

to undress and hand over their valuables before being led along the 100-metre-long "Himmelstrasse" (road to heaven), which led to the gas chambers. There they were gassed using carbon monoxide released from the exhaust pipes of a dismounted tank engine.

Sobibor was the site of one of two successful uprisings by Jewish prisoners in Nazi extermination camps. There had been a similar revolt at Treblinka on 2 August 1943. (A revolt at Auschwitz-Birkenau in October 1944 led to one of the crematoria being blown up, but nearly all the escapees were killed.)

Portrait of Sobibor uprising survivors taken in 1944

On 14 October 1943, members of the Sobibor underground succeeded in covertly killing 11 German SS officers and a number of camp guards. The uprising began in the tailor shop and the shoemakers' room where the Commander-in-chief of the camp and the head of the Ukrainian guards were knocked out and relieved of their weapons. Although the plan was to kill all the SS and walk calmly out of the main gate of the camp, the killings were discovered and the inmates had to run for their lives under heavy machine-gun fire from guards.

Fewer than 300 out of the 500 prisoners in the camp succeeded in escaping to the forests. Many died in the minefields surrounding the site, and some were recaptured and executed by the Germans over the next few days. Only 50 to 70 escapees survived the war.

The day after the uprising, the camp was permanently closed. Estimates of the number of Jews killed in Sobibor are as high as 250,000. There are very few survivors. Thomas "Toby" Blatt is one of them. He was the only living witness from Sobibor in the 2009/2010 Demjanjuk trial.

Treblinka

In 1941, a labour camp was established near the town of Treblinka in northeast Poland. The camp continued to function until 1944. In July 1942, a death camp known as Treblinka II, together with the Warsaw-Bialystok railway line, were built near the labour camp. The two camps functioned under different authorities but worked in tandem; prisoners at the death camp who were selected for work were transferred to the labour camp, and prisoners of the labour camp who could no longer work were sent to the death camp.

In the two months from July to September 1942, approximately 265,000 Jews were transported from the Warsaw ghetto to their deaths in Treblinka. From August to November of the same year, about 340,000 Jews were transported to Treblinka from the Radom district. Until May 1943, thousands more arrived at

Treblinka from Bialystok, Greece and Macedonia. In total, nearly 900,000 Jews were murdered at Treblinka between July 1942 and November 1943. Upon its closure in the fall of 1943, the Nazis destroyed the entire camp in an effort to conceal all traces of their crimes.

Edi Weinstein (centre), one of the very few known survivors of Treblinka. He is flanked by JRoots directors Rabbi Naftali Schiff (left) and Tzvi Sperber.

Auschwitz-Birkenau

Auschwitz has come to symbolize the Holocaust. Its infamy derives from the sheer enormity of the "killing complex" and the number of people murdered there. Auschwitz was comprised of three camps and numerous sub-camps. The main camp, known as Auschwitz I, was opened in May 1940 as a concentration and labour camp.

The Nazis first experimented with the use of Zyklon B in the Auschwitz gas chambers in the summer of 1941. Though certain targeted groups were gassed there, Auschwitz I remained, in essence, a concentration and labour camp. In the spring of 1942, a second camp, created within the Auschwitz complex, was designated as a killing centre, and was the final destination for all Jews from areas not included in Operation Reinhard. This camp was known interchangeably as Auschwitz II or Birkenau. Birkenau was originally equipped with two gas chambers. Four new gas chambers using Zyklon B were opened in early 1943. Alongside the gas chambers were crematoria—ovens to burn the bodies.

Eva Neuman as she enters Auschwitz in 1943 from Hungary as a 15-year-old girl.

Immediately upon their arrival at Auschwitz, the victims were subjected to a selection process. It was here that the notorious Doctor Mengele plied his murderous trade. Those selected for work were sent to one of its many associated labour camps.

Mrs Eva "Bobby" Neuman pictured here 55 years later speaking to a JRoots group. (Background is a boxcar outside Auschwitz.)

Those deemed unfit to work were immediately sent to the gas chambers.

The conditions in the labour camps were unbearable, and prisoners who did not pass daily selections were gassed. Unlike the other death camps, Auschwitz-Birkenau itself functioned as both a concentration camp and an extermination camp. There were many individual acts of resistance and defiance by the prisoners. In October 1944, the Jewish Sonderkommando revolted, destroying one of the crematoria.

Remains of crematorium in Birkenau

Auschwitz survivor Martha Grunwald

Between 1942 and 1944, transports of Jews arrived in Auschwitz from every part of Nazi-controlled Europe. Many Jews were transferred from other concentration camps to the killing centre at Birkenau. After the closure of the three Operation Reinhard camps in late 1943, Auschwitz-Birkenau was to be the final destination for all the remaining Jews of Europe.

All four gas chambers at Birkenau were put into round-the-clock use in the spring and summer of 1944 to wipe out Hungary's Jews and the last survivors of the ghettos. At that point, up to 6,000 Jews a day were being put to death in each of the four. By the time the gas chambers were destroyed in November 1944, over one million Jews had been murdered at Auschwitz, most of them immediately upon arrival. Tens of thousands of Poles, Roma and prisoners of war were also killed there. The camp was liberated by the Soviets on 27 January 1945.

JRoots group by "The Gate of Death" - Birkenau

213

PART 4:
PEOPLE WE WILL "MEET"

Profiles in Dedication: Rabbinic Leadership in the 16th-19th Century

16th Century: Rabbi Moshe Isserles—The "Rema" Of Krakow

Moshe Isserles (1530-1572), known by the acronym "ReMA" (for Rabbi Moshe Aesserles, in Hebrew), was born into one of Krakow's most prestigious Jewish families. His father was a prominent Torah scholar, as well as a successful businessman and a leading philanthropist.

Rabbi Moshe Isserles
(1530-1572)

Moshe was very precocious, and as a young boy, was sent to the world-renowned yeshiva (Torah academy) of Rabbi Shalom Shachna in Lublin. There, he exhibited such extraordinary abilities that Shachna took him for a son-in-law when he was only 14 years old.

After his years in Lublin, the Rema returned to Krakow. At the age of 20, he was appointed Chief Rabbi of the city—an astoundingly prestigious post for someone so young. Only two years later, in 1552, the city was struck by a plague that took the lives of almost a fifth of the city's Jewish population. Amongst the casualties were his grandmother, his mother and his 20-year-old wife. The synagogue his father built to perpetuate their memories came to be known as the Rema's shul (synagogue).

At the age of 30, the Rema founded his own yeshiva in Krakow. Having inherited great wealth from his father, the Rema supported the pupils of his yeshiva at his own expense. His students cherished his warmth and fatherly concern. One student fondly recalled how the Rema would enter his room at night and, with utmost care, gently cover him with a blanket.

The Jews of Poland greatly revered the Rema, recognising his total mastery of Jewish Law and great secular knowledge. In addition to Talmud and Halacha (Jewish Law), the Rema was an avid student of Kabbalah, philosophy, astronomy and history. From 1580-1764, the Vaad Arba HaAratzot, (the Council of the Four Lands), met twice a year

The Rema's shul, still in use today

to discuss issues of importance to Poland's Jewish community. There were often great disagreements amongst the various rabbis in the council; but, during the 22 years that the Rema was in Krakow, all decisions issued by the Vaad were unanimous.

All these stories are beautiful; similar ones are told of many great rabbis throughout the ages. The Rema's eternal significance, however, arose from his ability to unify two Jewish worlds in a most unexpected way...

By the 16th century, a number of competing Talmudic commentaries existed, making it difficult for the average Jew to know which to follow and how to act. Unbeknownst to each other, two of Jewry's greatest scholars, the Rema in Poland and Rabbi Yosef Caro in Israel, undertook the tremendous task of creating a clear, comprehensive code of Jewish conduct that integrated the various commentaries into a cohesive whole.

The Rema worked for many years to create what he thought would be his great contribution to Jewish civilization. Before he finished the work, however, Rabbi Caro completed his own code, which he called, the Shulchan Aruch (literally, the "set table"). One of the Rema's students obtained an early copy of it, and presented it to the Rema as a gift.

The Rema relates in the introduction to his work, that he went into a deep depression upon receiving the gift. He could not understand how he had spent so many years in vain, and begged Heaven to provide him with an answer. And then, it struck him...

Sephardic and Ashkenazic Jews had been relatively isolated from each other for almost 500 years. The two communities were hosted by two vastly different cultures. Sephardim lived in the Muslim countries of North Africa, Spain, and the Middle East, while the Ashkenazim lived among Christians in Europe. Although both groups adhered to Jewish law as derived from the Talmud and its commentaries, over the centuries, the two communities had developed numerous differences in their practices and customs.

Caro's code was based on several major medieval commentaries, but generally reflected Sephardic tradition, since Rabbi Caro was himself originally from Spain. Therefore, as a code of Jewish Law, the Shulchan Aruch was only of practical use to those Jews of Sephardic descent.

In an act of remarkable selflessness, rather than publish a competing work—as so many have done before—the Rema chose to restructure his work to supplement Caro's work. In it, he showed where Ashkenazic practice differed from the Sephardic tradition. In an incredible display of his humility, he called his work the Mapah (the "tablecloth"), which would adorn Caro's Shulchan Aruch ("set table").

In an epic demonstration that "everything is for the best," the Rema's notes transformed the Shulchan Aruch from one individual's presentation of Jewish law to the authoritative code for the entire Jewish people. For the first time, Ashkenazic and Sephardic Jews were united by a single code of law. The Shulchan Aruch, including the glosses of the Mapah, remains the undisputed basis of practical Jewish law until today.

The Rema died when he was only 42 years old. His tombstone reads, "*MeMoshe ad Moshe, lo kam k'Moshe,*" —From Moses to Moses, none arose like Moses. This epitaph had been used once before, for one of the greatest rabbinic commentators of all time: Maimonides (Rabbi Moses ben Maimon). The Rema's contemporaries considered him the "Maimonides of Polish Jewry." Like Maimonides, his knowledge was all-encompassing, and his personal character was sterling, like that of the biblical Moses—the most humble man on earth.

The Rema's tombstone

17th Century: Rabbi Yom Tov Lipmann—The "Tosefos Yom Tov"

Gershon Shaul Yom Tov Lipmann Heller was born in 1579 in Wallerstein, (now Mulhausen, Bavaria) where his father was the Chief Rabbi. As a young man, he journeyed to Prague to study in the yeshiva of the renowned Maharal. From a young age he served as one of Prague's rabbinic judges. In 1625, the accomplished scholar moved to Vienna, where he was elected Av Bet Din, the head of the Jewish court. He went on to serve as Chief Rabbi of Prague and then later of Krakow. He was instrumental in solving legal problems that arose from the Chmielnicki massacres of 1648-1649 and wrote a famous eulogy for its victims.

The tombstone of Rabbi Yom Tov Lipmann Heller (1579-1654) in Krakow

Rabbi Heller's best known work is the Tosefos Yom Tov (Yom Tov's Additions), a commentary on the Mishna (the redaction of Jewish Oral Law). The Mishna was written using extremely terse, cryptic language that could only be understood with the help of a scholarly teacher. A masterfully brief commentary had been written by Rabbi Ovadia of Bartenura to provide a key to the Mishna; but that work glossed over many apparent contradictions in the Mishna and Talmud. Rabbi Heller wrote a supplement (tosefet) to Rabbi Ovadia's commentary, in which he combined Talmudic exposition with medieval commentaries on the Talmud and Mishna. He grappled with some of the thorniest problems that emerged from careful analysis of the Mishna text. As his book was quickly accepted as an indispensable companion to the Mishna, Rabbi Heller himself is often referred by the name of his work, "The Tosefos Yom Tov."

The Tosefos Yom Tov died in Krakow, Poland, in 1654. Surprisingly, he requested to be buried in the section of the cemetery reserved for the lower classes of Jewish society. The reason why he had made this choice is a fascinating story—so don't forget to ask about it when you are there!

18th Century: Rabbi Elimelech of Lizhensk

Elimelech Weisblum was born in 1717 in the Polish province of Galicia, an area then famous as a centre of Torah study. The Hassidic movement had just been born some 400 kilometres to the east, in modern day Ukraine. Rabbi Elimelech was captivated by Hassidic thought, and he in turn inspired many other Jews to become Hassidim. Under Rebbe Elimelech's leadership, Galicia became an important Hassidic centre.

A Hassidic Rebbe prays at the Tomb of R Elimelech of Lizhensk (1717-1786)

For centuries, Rebbe Elimelech's burial site in Lizhensk has drawn pilgrims from near and far and is associated with many miracles. Its walls are adorned with Rebbe Elimelech's moving "Prayer before Prayer" which some Hassidic Jews recite daily. Many consider the site to be particularly auspicious for ensuring one's prayers be answered and journey there in hopes that Heaven will fulfil their requests in the merit of Rebbe Elimelech.

Much of Hassidic culture revolves around marvellous, thought-provoking, inspiring stories. It is not surprising then, that the circumstances of R' Elimelech's birth are themselves the subject of a typical Hassidic tale. One can perhaps learn even more about R' Elimelech and Hassidus from the medium than from the story itself.

> *In the Galician hills, there was a small village, wherein lived a contented, though impoverished community of righteous Jews. Among the poorest were the village's two water carriers. They earned their livelihoods by schlepping weighty buckets up from the river to all who could afford their services. Of*

the two, Reb Eliezer Lippa eked out a few more kopeks each week, since he serviced the four wealthiest families of the village. His counterpart, Reb Zalman Dov, serviced the shtetl's four small shteiblach (synagogues), providing them with water with which to wash people's hands before prayers.

Reb Eliezer Lippa was a G-d-fearing man, and after hearing a wonderful story about the Holy Temple in Jerusalem from a maggid (itinerant storyteller), he was inspired to do something to bring himself closer to his Creator. He proposed to Reb Zalman Dov that they should exchange two of their water rounds with each other. Reb Eliezer Lippa could thus partake in the mitzvah of the synagogue deliveries, and in exchange, Reb Zalman Dov could provide for two high-paying customers.

The humble men agreed with joy, and each day Reb Eliezer Lippa would haul his overflowing, synagogue-bound buckets with a deep, inner satisfaction, knowing that he was participating in a mitzvah. Reb Eliezer Lippa's wife had, until this time, been barren, but his joy and enthusiasm opened the heavenly gates and she soon gave birth to two sons. One of them was Rebbe Elimelech and the other was his saintly brother, Rebbe Zusha.[60]

Rebbe Elimelech used to spend many hours each day preparing for prayer by meditating and focusing on the greatness of G-d, in order to place his personal significance in proper perspective. He sought an almost purely spiritual life, often forsaking food and sleep to study Torah. Over time, he became known as the consummate *tzaddik* (holy man).

When Rabbi Dov Ber (the Maggid of Mezeritch) succeeded his teacher, The Baal Shem Tov, as the leader of the Hassidic movement, he hoped to inspire and uplift the downtrodden Jews of Europe. He chose Rebbe Elimelech, one of his most dedicated and saintly students, to help him spread the light and joy of Hassidism in Poland.

Wherever R' Elimelech went, he spread kindness, tolerance and wisdom. His deeds continue to be recounted in countless Hassidic tales. Many of these stories tell of the experiences of R' Elimelech and his brother R' Zusha as they travelled the Galician countryside, inspiring the masses to spiritual greatness.

Rebbe Elimelech's book, *Noam Elimelech,* contains comments on the weekly Torah portions and explores many lofty and mystical topics. It became a central book of Hassidic thought, and R' Elimelech came to be called "The Noam Elimelech." Since Rebbe Elimelech was such a self-effacing man, it is hard to imagine that he would countenance a request to tell us a story about himself. But if he were to agree, perhaps the following is the story he would tell:

A visitor from Hungary stopped a passerby on a street in the town of Lizhensk with the query: "Can you please direct me to the home of the great Rabbi Elimelech?"

The man raised his eyes in astonishment: "You mean to tell me that you journeyed all the way from Hungary to see this Rebbe of Lizhensk? Have the exaggerations and embellishments about this man travelled that far already? I know this Rabbi Elimelech personally, and the man is an absolute nothing. I'm afraid that you've wasted your time and money on these silly rumours."

The visitor was outraged. "You lowly, despicable man!" he thundered. "What do you know? You obviously have no understanding of anything holy and spiritual!" Still fuming, the visitor stormed off.

Later that day, when he entered Rabbi Elimelech's study for his appointed audience, he nearly fainted in shame and remorse. The man he had derided earlier on the street was none other than Rabbi Elimelech himself! With tears in his eyes, he begged the Rebbe's forgiveness.

"Why are you so upset?" asked Rabbi Elimelech. "There's no need to apologise. I told you the simple truth, and everything you said was also true..." [61]

19th Century: Rabbi Naftali Tzvi Yehudah Berlin — The "Netziv"

Rabbi Naftali Tzvi Yehudah Berlin, commonly known by the acronym the "NeTZiV" ("the pillar"), was the Rosh Yeshiva (dean) of the famed Volozhin Yeshiva for almost 40 years. Under his leadership, the Yeshiva flourished, increasing from 100 to 400 students.

The Netziv (1816-1893)

In 1892, the Russian government, influenced by the Jewish Maskilim, demanded that the yeshiva modify its curriculum to include Russian language and other secular studies. It also demanded the yeshiva reduce the size of its student body. Unwilling to compromise the character and content of the yeshiva by limiting Torah study, the Netziv refused to accede to these demands. As a result, the authorities closed the yeshiva. The Netziv's life had been so intertwined with the yeshiva, that shortly after its closing, his health began to decline, and he passed away within two years.

When the Netziv had completed his first major work, *Ha'Emek Sheilah*, he invited a group of friends and students to participate in a *siyum*, a festive meal traditionally made to celebrate the completion of a Torah accomplishment. During the meal, he revealed a moving incident from his youth. As retold by Rabbi Paysach Krohn, the Netziv began:

> *When I was a young child, I was once playing at home when I heard my father crying. My parents had been talking in the kitchen, unaware that I could hear them. Since I overheard them mention my name, I paid close attention to the rest of the conversation. My father said, "I don't know how to handle the situation. I've tried every possible way to get Hirsh Leib (a Yiddish nickname by which the Netziv was often called) interested in learning. I have offered him prizes, but nothing seems to work. It was my fervent dream that he should become a Talmid Chacham (Torah scholar). I guess we'll just have to train him to be a ba'al melachah (craftsman).*
>
> *I was shaken by my father's pain and tears, and when he finished talking I ran in and promised him that from then on I would devote my time to learning Torah.*
>
> *Imagine for a moment where I would be today had I not heard my father's anguish. I would have grown up to be a shoemaker, a tailor or a carpenter.*

Coming from the family that I do, I would have been honest in business, and each night when I would have come home from work, I probably would have looked into a Mishnayos (redaction of the Oral Torah), studied some Chumash (the Five Books of Moses) and maybe even some Ein Yaakov (compendium of the non-legalistic portions of the Talmud, consisting mainly of anecdotes and stories), and that would have been the extent of my Torah learning. Every Yom Kippur I would have asked Hashem (G-d) for forgiveness for the sins that I might have committed that year, and before my death I would have recited viduy (confession).

But the Heavenly Court would have asked me why I hadn't written Ha'Emek Sheilah—and that would be something that, as a craftsman, I would never have imagined I was capable of doing. Yet the Heavenly Court would have been right. For indeed, you see that I actually did write it. Therefore, the reason for this siyum (festive meal) is twofold: first to celebrate the completion of this work; and second, to express gratitude to Hashem (G-d) that he led me on the path to fulfil the potential within me, which otherwise would have lain dormant in me forever.

Profiles In Idealism: Cultural Leadership in Pre-War Poland

Isaac Leib Peretz — A Voice for Self-Determination

Isaac Leib Peretz (1852-1915)

Isaac Peretz, best known as I.L. Peretz, was a Yiddish language author and playwright. Peretz, Mendele Mokher Seforim and Sholem Aleichem, were the three great classical Yiddish writers.

Peretz was born in the *shtetl* of Zamosc and raised in an Orthodox home. At a young age, he chose to jettison Orthodoxy, and by the age of 15 he became a member of the Haskalah movement. He delved into secular learning, reading history, philosophy and literature in Polish, Russian, German and French.

Peretz began writing poetry in Polish and Hebrew. The pogroms of 1881 awakened a nationalist sentiment in Peretz. He began to write in Yiddish and moved to Warsaw where he edited a Yiddish literary journal. His first Yiddish poem, "Monish," (1888) is considered a milestone of Yiddish literature. Peretz's work appealed to Jewish intellectuals who had left the *shtetls* for life in the thriving cities. He viewed himself primarily as a writer of Jewish ideals, based on the unique tradition and history of the Jewish people.

Many Maskilim endorsed a concept of cultural universalism, which translated into a desire to assimilate fully into non-Jewish culture. Peretz, however, was against cultural universalism. He felt that every nation contributes a unique culture and character to the world and must therefore remain distinct. Unlike most of his peers, he had respect for Hassidic Jews. He saw in them a uniquely Jewish spirit, rising up with joy in the face of adversity. He adopted the style of the Hassidic tales and many of his stories emphasized the importance of sincere faith rather than empty ritual. While many Jewish intellectuals supported the Russian Revolution of 1905, Peretz feared that the universalist ideals of the revolutionaries would leave little room for Jewish cultural identity.

Amongst Peretz's most important short stories is "Bontshe Shvayg" (Bontsche the Silent). It is the story of Bontshe, an extremely meek and modest man, downtrodden on earth but exalted in heaven. In recognition of his sterling character, the celestial assembly offers Bontshe any reward he might choose. "What I'd like most of all," requested Bontshe, "is a warm roll with fresh butter every morning."

Peretz's grave in Warsaw's Okopowa Street Jewish cemetery

Bontshe came to symbolize the passivity and small mindedness of the typical *shtetl* Jew in the eyes of the Maskilim.

Sholem Aleichem — The Mark Twain of Eastern Europe

One of history's most humorous Jews was given the befittingly humorous Jewish name, Sholem Naumovich Rabinovich. Not surprisingly, he preferred to be known by his pen name, Sholem Aleichem (literally, "peace be upon you"). He became one of the most popular Yiddish authors and playwrights of all time. He is best known for his entertaining short stories depicting Eastern European Jewish life, the most famous of which, "Tevye's Daughters," became the basis of the play *Fiddler on the Roof.*

Sholem Aleichem (1859-1916)

Sholem Aleichem was born in the Ukraine in 1859. He wrote his first work, a Yiddish version of Robinson Crusoe, at the age of 15. After his initial literary foray, he chose to write in the newly resurrected Hebrew language. Later, however, he reverted to Yiddish, the language of his childhood. He chose the comical pseudonym Sholem Aleichem to conceal his identity from his father who, as an avid Maskil, scorned Yiddish as the language of the backward-thinking Jew. Rabinovich senior preferred Hebrew as a symbol of the modern, cosmopolitan Jew. Interestingly, many other Yiddish writers also wrote anonymously or under pen names, to avoid offending the Jewish intelligentsia of Russia, who spoke and wrote primarily in Russian.

Sholem Aleichem married into a wealthy family and used his money to help support many new Yiddish writers. He was often called the "Jewish Mark Twain" because of the two authors' similar styles. When the two met face-to-face later in life, Mark Twain commented that he was considered the American Sholem Aleichem!

In August 1904, Sholem Aleichem edited *Hilf: a Zaml-Bukh fir Literatur un Kunst* (Help: An Anthology for Literature and Art), a compilation of contemporary works, published to aid the victims of the Kishinev pogrom. A year later, the wave of pogroms that swept through the Jewish communities of Russia forced Sholem Aleichem and his family to flee Russia. The family settled in Geneva for ten years before immigrating to America in 1914.

By the time he died in 1916 at the age of 57, Sholem Aleichem had made a profound impact on the world of Yiddish culture. His funeral was one of the largest in New York City's history, with an estimated 100,000 mourners in attendance. The following day, his last will and testament was printed in the New York Times and was read in the US Congress. The will contained instructions for how his annual yahrzeit—the anniversary of his death—should be commemorated. He told his friends, family and followers to get together to read his will along with one of his stories. "One of the very merry ones," he wrote, "and recite it in whatever language is most intelligible to you ... Let my name be recalled with laughter, or not at all."

Ludwik Eliezer Zamenhof — The Hopeful Linguist

Ludwik Zamenhof
(1859-1917)

Ludwik Zamenhof was an idealist and innovator of the highest order. His approach to the world and its problems was representative of the sentiment of much of pre-war Polish Jewry. He embraced both the traditional Jewish ideal of uniting humanity under a banner of peace and the Maskil notion of cultural universalism. However, unlike most, he saw linguistic rather than ideological barriers as the primary hindrance to Jewish (and global) cultural integration. To his credit, unlike so many who pay lip service to peace but do precious little to advance the cause, Zamenhof attempted the impossible.

Zamenhof was born in the town of Bialystok which was under Russian control at the time. (See Part 3 for more on Bialystok.) The population of Bialystok was made up of Jews, Poles, Germans and Belarusians. Equal measures of discord and dislike were to be found amongst these distinct groups. Zamenhof believed that the primary cause of prejudice was the absence of a common mode of communication that could foster understanding. He therefore set to work to create a universal language, which he hoped could serve as the bridge to overcome cultural differences.

Cover of 1888 English translation of Unua Libro

In 1887, he published his first booklet on the new language, entitled *Unua Libro* (First Book) under the pseudonym, Doktoro Esperanto (Doctor Hopeful). The language, which became known as "Esperanto," was designed to be linguistically intuitive, using a synthesis of the most common grammatical rules and structures of the world's major languages. Zamenhof hoped that Esperanto would promote world peace between different peoples and cultures. Estimates range widely, but today there are probably about a million Esperanto speakers worldwide.

Earlier in his life, after a wave of pogroms had swept through the Russian empire, Zamenhof joined a branch of the Zionist movement in the hope that a Jewish state would put an end to anti-Semitism. A few years later, however, he renounced Zionism, concluding that it could not solve the problem of global anti-Semitism that had plagued the Jewish people for millennia. He soon came to strongly oppose all nationalism, including Judaism (which he viewed as a form of nationalism), believing that nationalism was the greatest cause of oppression and hatred in history.

Zamenhof's grave in Warsaw's Okopowa Street cemetery

He also published a book of religious philosophy called *Homaranismo* (loosely translated as "humanitarianism"). It was based on the teaching of the Talmudic sage Hillel, who said that the golden rule of the Torah is: That which is hateful to you, do not do to your fellow. Zamenhof believed that Judaism should become "Hillelism," by promoting "pure monotheism" and abolishing all of the Torah's laws except for the loving of one's neighbour.

In 1910, Zamenhof was nominated for the Nobel Peace Prize. Hundreds of city streets, parks and bridges worldwide have since been named after him. Regrettably, his hopes for world peace did not materialize in his lifetime. He died in Warsaw during World War I and is buried in the Okopowa Street Jewish Cemetery. (See section on Warsaw in Part 3 for more about the Okopowa Street cemetery.)

Like many of the other idealistic and universalistic notions of secular pre-war Polish Jewry, neither "humanitarianism" nor Esperanto has fared well in the crucible of history.

Sarah Schenirer — The Woman Who Changed the Jewish World

Sarah Schenirer (1883-1935), a Polish seamstress with a passion for Judaism, developed the world's first school system for Orthodox Jewish girls. By the eve of World War II, the "Bais Yaakov" network—as it came to be known—encompassed over 250 schools with more than 40,000. Pictured here is the second graduating class of the Bais Yaakov in Lodz, Poland in 1934.

 Sarah Schenirer was born in Krakow in 1883 to Hassidic parents. She attended a Polish elementary school for eight years. Though a diligent pupil, she was unassuming and withdrawn and never dreamed of taking on leadership of any kind. As poverty prevented her from continuing her studies, at the age of 13, she became a seamstress. Working in an industry prone to vanity, she once wrote in her diary, "People are such perfectionists when it comes to clothing their bodies. Are they so particular when they address themselves to the needs of their souls?"[62]

In the late 19th century, Jewish education for women was extremely limited. While boys were educated in the "*cheder*" system (formalized schooling with local Torah teachers), girls did not receive a formal Jewish education at all. Girls like Sarah often attended secular schools, creating a huge gap between their knowledge of secular subjects and their understanding of Judaism. This system created a further disparity between boys and girls; the boys were generally well versed in Judaism and therefore often more committed to Jewish observance than their female counterparts.

Schenirer made it her mission to address this religious and social problem by creating a formal educational system for young Jewish women. She singlehandedly changed the course of Jewish history, and according to many rabbis, did more to advance Judaism than anyone in the previous hundred years.

Though it would eventually grow into an influential and decisive movement, the beginnings of Sarah Schenirer's school, known as Bais Yaakov, were quite humble. As a revolutionary thinker in an ultraconservative society, Sarah initially received little support for her ideas. Not discouraged, she invested her last cent to travel to Czechoslovakia for a meeting with one of the leading Hassidic rabbis of the time, the Belzer Rebbe. The farsighted Hassidic master encouraged her to pursue her worthy cause and blessed her to have success.

In 1917, with just 25 pupils—all daughters of her customers—Sarah converted the back room of her seamstress shop into a warm and vibrant haven for girls to learn about Torah and Judaism. Her campaign to strengthen women and Jewish society quickly gained momentum. It wasn't long before burgeoning enrolment necessitated renting more rooms and eventually an entire building.

Sarah's work came to the attention of the leading religious authority of the generation, Rabbi Yisrael Meir Kagan (also known by the name of his famous work, *Chofetz Chayim*). He encouraged Jewish communities throughout Poland to take part in Schenirer's dream. He insisted that young Jewish women, as the future guardians of Jewish homes, needed an education that would inspire them to remain committed Jews in the face of the time's dramatically increasing rate of assimilation.

The word spread. Parents clamoured for similar schools for their daughters. Sarah's early students became the teachers in satellite Bais Yaakov schools throughout Poland. Eventually, Sarah opened a seminary dedicated to training young women to become teachers in the Bais Yaakov system, and by the time she died in 1935, Poland alone was home to several hundred Bais Yaakov schools. She was buried in the cemetery that would later be converted into the site of the Plaszow concentration camp, and the memorial to her grave can be found there.

Memorial to Sarah Schenirer, at site of Plaszow labour camp, just outside Krakow.

233

Profiles in Activism: Jewish Resistance to the Nazi Regime

Szmul Zygielbojm — Polish Jewry's Spokesman and Tragic Hero

Szmul Zygielbojm escaped the Warsaw ghetto in 1939, and never returned to Nazi-occupied territory; yet, it was the pain of his brethren in Warsaw and his inability to save them that killed him. From his tragic story we can learn much about the mindset of Jews inside Poland before the war and of Jews outside Poland during it.

Szmul Zygielbojm
(1895-1943)

At the age of 10, dire poverty pushed Szmul Zygielbojm out of the classroom and into the factory. Ever sensitive to the oppression and grim economic conditions Jews faced in Eastern Europe, Zygielbojm became involved in the Jewish Labour Movement in his early 20s. At the age of 22, he was a representative at the first Bundist convention in Poland. So impressive were his oratory skills, that Zygielbojm was soon elected to the Bund's Central Committee—a position he held until his death.

The Bund ("Union" in German) was a socialist movement that sought to advance society in the spirit of Marxism. The movement hoped to achieve minority-nation status for the Jews of Russia by proposing a socialist state in Russian territory. The Bund came to strongly oppose Zionism, arguing that emigration to Palestine was a form of escapism. It also promoted the use of Yiddish as a Jewish national language, and to some extent, opposed the Zionist project of reviving Hebrew.

Many mistakenly believe that the majority of Jews of pre-war Poland were Hassidim. This was hardly the case. In fact, it was Bundism that best represented the largest segment of pre-war Polish Jewry. In December 1938 and January 1939, in the last Polish municipal elections before the start of the World War II, the Bund received the largest segment of the Jewish vote. One-third of the 89 towns with the largest Jewish communities elected Bund majorities. In Warsaw, the Bund took 17 of the 20 municipal council seats won by Jewish parties.

By 1930, Zygielbojm was living in Warsaw, editing the Bund's journal, *Arbeiter Fragen* (Workers' Issues). In 1936, the Central Committee sent him to Lodz to lead the Jewish Workers' Movement, and in 1938 he was elected to the Lodz city council.

After Germany invaded Poland in September 1939, Zygielbojm returned to Warsaw, where he participated in the defence of the city during the siege. Once the Nazis occupied Warsaw, they demanded 12 hostages from the population to prevent further resistance. When the city's president proposed that the Jewish labour movement provide a representative and suggested a particular woman, Zygielbojm volunteered to take her place.

Upon his release, Zygielbojm was made a member of the Jewish Council, or Judenrat, that the Nazis had created. The Nazis ordered the Judenrat to begin the creation of a ghetto within Warsaw. Because of Zygielbojm's public opposition to the order, his fellow Bundists feared for his safety and arranged for his escape from Poland. In December 1939, Zygielbojm reached Belgium. The following year, he spoke before a meeting of the Labour and Socialist International in Brussels and described the early stages of the Nazi persecution of Polish Jewry.

When the Nazis invaded Belgium in May 1940, Zygielbojm went to France before moving on to the United States. There, he spent a year and a half trying to convince Americans of how dire the situation facing the Jews in Nazi-occupied Poland truly was. In March 1942, he arrived in London where he continued to speak publicly about the fate of Polish Jews, including at a meeting with the British Labour Party. In a speech broadcast on BBC Radio on 2 June 1942, he said, "It will actually be a shame to go on living if steps are not taken to halt the greatest crime in human history."

On 19 April 1943, the Allied governments of the United Kingdom and the United States met in Bermuda to discuss the fate of the Jews in Nazi-occupied Europe.

This was the same day that the Nazis began their attempt to liquidate the Warsaw ghetto and was met with unexpected resistance. (See Warsaw Ghetto Uprising in Part 3.)

Zygielbojm saw that nothing concrete had come out of the Bermuda Conference. On 12 May 1943, after receiving word of the suppression of the Warsaw Ghetto Uprising and the final liquidation of the remaining Jews, Zygielbojm turned on the gas in his London flat and killed himself. In his suicide note he wrote:

> The responsibility for the crime of the murder of the whole Jewish nationality in Poland rests first of all on those who are carrying it out, but indirectly it falls also upon the whole of humanity, on the peoples of the Allied nations and on their governments, who up to this day have not taken any real steps to halt this crime. By looking on passively upon this murder of defenceless millions, tortured children, women and men, they have become partners to the responsibility.
>
> I am obliged to state that although the Polish government contributed largely to the arousing of public opinion in the world, it still did not do enough. It did not do anything that was not routine, that might have been appropriate to the dimensions of the tragedy taking place in Poland....
>
> I cannot continue to live and to be silent while the remnants of Polish Jewry, whose representative I am, are being murdered. My comrades in the Warsaw ghetto fell with arms in their hands in the last heroic battle. I was not permitted to fall like them, together with them, but I belong with them, to their mass grave.
>
> By my death, I wish to give expression to my most profound protest against the inaction in which the world watches and permits the destruction of the Jewish people.[69]

Janusz Korczak — Unflinching Dedication

Janusz Korczak, educator, pediatrician and children's rights advocate, had a love for children that knew no bounds. During his life, he devoted everything he had to "his children," and in his death he gave them even more.

Henryk Goldzsmit was born into a deeply assimilated Jewish family in Warsaw. An aspiring writer, he entered a literary contest at the age of 21, under the pen-name "Janusz Korczak." It was a pseudonym that he used to conceal his Jewish identity throughout his life. Torn between the identities of Goldzsmit and Korczak, he was determined to live as both a Pole and a Jew. Often, he was too Jewish for the anti-Semites, yet not Jewish enough for his own people.

Henryk Goldzsmit a.k.a. Janusz Korczak (1878-1942)

His formal training was as a medical doctor and then as a pediatric specialist. Over time, he became a recognised expert on childrearing, child development and child psychology. He hosted his own radio show, trained educators and wrote a number of influential books on childhood psychology, including *How to Love a Child* and *The Child's Right to Respect*. Korczak's writings touched a generation of youth who grew up reading his books, including the classic *King Matt the First*, which depicts the adventures and tribulations of a boy king who aspires to reform his subjects. Recurring themes in his works were the importance of giving

Dom Sierot, the orphanage for Jewish children in Warsaw (Krochmalna Street, ca. 1935) designed in 1911 by Janusz Korczak. He lived in a room in the attic.

Janusz Korczak and the children,
memorial at Yad Vashem

children a moral education, autonomy and a sense of self-determination from a very young age. Still during his lifetime, Korczak's innovative ideas on childcare spread far and wide, and have since continued to achieve worldwide acclaim and influence.

He was not, however, just an academic. Korczak was a man who simply loved children and sought to empower them. In 1911, he became director of Dom Sierot, an orphanage of his own design, for Jewish children in Warsaw. There, Korczak's educational theories were put into practice. His orphanage boasted a court and parliament run by the children. He established the first national children's newspaper, which provided a mouthpiece for the orphaned children who were in his care.

In 1939, when World War II erupted, Korczak volunteered for duty in the Polish Army, but was refused due to his age. He witnessed the Wehrmacht overrun Warsaw, and his orphanage was forced to move into the Warsaw ghetto in 1940. Because of his social standing, Korczak was offered sanctuary on the "Aryan side" of Warsaw; but, he opted to move into the ghetto refusing to abandon "his children."

In August 1942, German soldiers came to collect the almost 200 orphans and staff members of Dom Sierot to take them to Treblinka. Korczak again was offered sanctuary and again declined, insisting that he would go with the children.

In his book, *The Pianist*, Wladyslaw Szpilman movingly describes what transpired next:

> One day, around the 5th of August, when I had taken a brief rest from work and was walking down Gesia Street, I happened to see Janusz Korczak and his orphans leaving the ghetto. The evacuation of the Jewish orphanage run by Janusz Korczak had been ordered for that morning. The children were to have been taken away alone. He had the chance to save himself, and it was only with difficulty that he persuaded the Germans to take him too. He had spent long years of his life with the children and now, on this last journey, he could not leave them alone. He wanted to ease things for them. He told the orphans they were going out into the country, so they ought to be cheerful. At last they would be able exchange the horrible suffocating city walls for meadows of flowers, streams where they could bathe, and woods full of berries and mushrooms. He told them to wear their best clothes, and so they came out into the yard, two by two, nicely dressed, and in a happy mood. The little column was lead by an SS man who loved children, as Germans do, even those he was about to see on their way into the next world. He took a special liking to a boy of twelve, a violinist who had his instrument under his arm. The SS man told him to go to the head of the procession of children and play—and so they set off. When I met them in Gesia Street, the smiling children were singing in chorus, the little violinist was playing for them, and Korczak was carrying two of the smallest infants, who were beaming too, and he was telling them some amusing story.

Joshua Perle, an eyewitness, described the procession of Korczak and the children through the ghetto to the Umschlagplatz:

> A miracle occurred. Two hundred children did not cry out. Two hundred pure souls, condemned to death, did not weep. Not one of them ran away. None tried to hide. Like stricken swallows they clung to their teacher and mentor, to their father and brother, Janusz Korczak, so that he might protect and preserve them. Janusz Korczak was marching, his head bent forward, holding the hand of a child, without a hat, a leather belt around his waist, and wearing high boots. A few nurses were followed by two hundred children, dressed in clean and meticulously cared for clothes, as they were being carried to the altar.... On

Korczak's orphanage, still in operation today

> all sides, the children were surrounded by Germans, Ukrainians and this time also Jewish policemen. They whipped and fired shots at them. The very stones of the street wept at the sight of the procession.

According to a popular legend, when the group of orphans finally reached the Umschlagplatz, an SS officer recognised Korczak as the author of one of his favourite children's books and offered to help him escape. Korczak once again refused. He boarded the trains with the children and was never heard from again.

Szpilman surmised what happened next:

> I am sure that even in the gas chamber, as the Zyklon B gas was stifling childish throats and striking terror instead of hope into the orphans' hearts, the Old Doctor must have whispered with one last effort, "It's all right, children, it will be all right." So that at least he could spare his little charges the fear of passing from life to death.

Adam Czerniakow — Between a Rock and a Hard Place

Adam Czerniaków (1880–1942)

As head of the Warsaw ghetto Judenrat, Adam Czerniakow was forced to play G-d on a daily basis. Like Mordechai Chaim Rumkowski of the Lodz ghetto (see section on Lodz in Part 3), his impossible decisions garnered him as many friends as enemies. When Czerniakow received the order to liquidate the ghetto, he was forced to make the most difficult decision of all. What would you have done?

Born in Warsaw and an engineer by training, Czerniakow became a local politician. From 1927 until 1934, he served as a member of the Warsaw Municipal Council, and in 1931 he was elected to the Polish Senate. On 4 October 1939, a few days after the city's surrender to the Nazis, Czerniakow was made head of the city's 24-member Judenrat (Jewish Council), responsible for implementing German orders in the Jewish community.

He oversaw the creation of the Warsaw ghetto in October 1940. There, Jews were sequestered in the worst conditions. Even before the Nazis began massive deportations, over 100,000 of the residents died from disease and starvation. As Judenrat chairman, Czerniakow struggled to meet the demands of the Germans while still advocating on behalf of the Jews, whose living conditions grew more wretched by the day. (For more on the Warsaw ghetto see Part 3.)

Czerniakow himself had several opportunities to flee to safety, but repeatedly chose to remain with the people he had once been elected to represent. Despite the unbearable conditions in the ghetto, he urged the many hundreds of thousands of Jews living there to avoid armed resistance, a principle that earned him a great deal of criticism. He supported underground educational and cultural activities, including technical and medical training, and he assisted in smuggling food and other raw materials to the residents of the ghetto. Moreover, he constantly pleaded for better living conditions and tried to ease the effects of Nazi brutality by providing the Jews with whatever meagre resources were at his disposal.

On Tisha B'av 5702 (22 July 1942), the day on which Jews commemorate all the tragedies in their history, the Judenrat was instructed to begin the process of deporting Warsaw's Jews to Treblinka. The Germans demanded a minimum of 6,000 souls per day. Failure to comply would result in immediate execution of some 100 hostages, including employees of the Judenrat and Czerniakow's own wife.

On the first day after receiving the order, Czerniakow was able to obtain exemptions for a handful of individuals. Realising that deportation meant death, Czerniakow pleaded on behalf of the orphans, but his efforts were futile. For almost three years, he had tried to fulfill every German command, hoping that by compliance, the Jews would make themselves indispensable to the Nazis' war effort. He had compromised more than one principle for the sake of the ghetto, but he drew the line at deprting its children. He rang for the night clerk and asked for a glass of water. Attempting a smile, he dismissed her with a simple Thank you, his last words before swallowing a cyanide capsule he had been saving for such an occasion.

Adam Czerniakow left a suicide note to his wife, reading, "They demand me to kill children of my nation with my own hands. I have nothing to do but to die." A second note for the public read, "I can no longer bear all this. My act will prove to everyone what the right thing to do is."

*Adam Czerniakóws grave in
Warsaw's Okopowa Street Cemetery*

Mordechai Anielewicz — Warsaw's Little Angel

Mordechai Anielewicz, the leader of the Warsaw Ghetto Uprising, was a Jew of humble origins. Born to a poor family, he rose to lead a life of valour and bravery. He proved himself committed to the Jewish people, to their survival and to their future. Nicknamed Aniolek (little angel), Anielewicz was not yet 20 years old when the Germans invaded Poland. Despite his youth, he was a strong leader who inspired his fellow Jews to hope and fight for their future.

As a young man, Anielewicz was a leader of the Socialist-Zionist youth movement, Hashomer Ha'tza'ir (The Youth Guard). As the German threat increased, he became an underground freedom fighter for the Jews in Poland. He was arrested by the Soviets early in the war when he attempted to open an escape route for Jews to flee to Palestine. Following his release, Anielewicz had numerous opportunities to escape Nazi Poland; but the "little angel" returned to Warsaw to help his fellow Jews and encouraged others to do so as well.

From his return to the Warsaw ghetto in 1940 until the summer of 1942, Anielewicz was instrumental in organising armed resistance both in Warsaw and throughout Poland. After the first major deportation of the Warsaw ghetto Jews to the death camps in July 1942, Anielewicz joined the ghetto's Zydowska Organizacja Bojowa (Jewish Fighting Organization), or "ZOB." Within a few months, he was appointed its chief commander.

When the second round of deportations began in January of 1943, members of the ZOB fought back under Anielewicz's command. Anielewicz and his comrades, armed with little more than handguns, joined the group of Jews selected for deportation and opened fire on the German soldiers. Taken by surprise, the Germans succumbed to the small group of youths, and the deportation was averted as the Germans were driven out of the ghetto.

Three months later, the Germans announced the final deportation of Jews from the Warsaw ghetto. Anielewicz led the courageous Jews of the ghetto in their final resistance. Ukrainian and Latvian SS soldiers marched into the ghetto on 19 April 1943. As before, the vastly outnumbered Jews were armed with little more than pistols and Molotov cocktails. Nevertheless, it was not until 16 May that the SS was able to defeat the handful of resistors. Remarkably, the Jews held out longer than did, the Polish army when German and Russians invaded Poland in September 1939. Ultimately, the Germans prevailed only by burning down the ghetto, building by building.

Photo from SS General Jürgen Stroop's report to Heinrich Himmler regarding the Warsaw ghetto liquidation. Stroop is at centre left (looking up). On the left is the burning balcony of the townhouse at Nowolipie 66, and the ghetto wall is visible in the more distant background.

For their last stand, Anielewicz and his fellow fighters had retreated to 18 Mila Street, the headquarters of the uprising. They were inside the headquarters' bunker when the Nazis destroyed it. Anielewicz was likely killed in the fighting. He died at the age of 24, having lived a life dedicated to and sacrificed for the freedom of his fellow Jews.

Anielewicz's bunker in Warsaw, Mila 18

Profiles in Altruism: Righteous Amongst the Nations

Raoul Wallenberg — Paradigm of Courage

Raoul Wallenberg was a non-Jewish, Swedish diplomat living in Budapest, Hungary at the time of the Holocaust. He performed great acts of heroism and humanitarianism on behalf of the Jewish People. As a diplomat, Wallenberg provided tens of thousands of Jews with Swedish passports and immunity, saving them from death at the hands of the Nazis.

Raoul Wallenberg (1912-1947)

On 9 July 1944, Wallenberg, a businessman, was sent to Budapest as the First Secretary to the Swedish delegation, whose mission was to coordinate a rescue operation for the Jews of Hungary. While in Budapest he arranged countless "protective passports" (German: *Schutz-Pass*), which identified the bearers as Swedish subjects awaiting repatriation (thus preventing their deportation). The Swedish delegation also convinced the Germans that, as Swedish citizens, the holders of the protective passes were exempt from wearing the yellow Star of David on their clothing.

Wallenberg and his associates also raised funds to rent 32 buildings in Budapest and used their diplomatic powers to protect the buildings' diplomatic immunity. He put up signs such as "The Swedish Library" and "The Swedish Research Institute" on their doors, and hung oversized Swedish flags on the front of the buildings to bolster the deception. These buildings eventually housed almost 10,000 people.

These historical facts, however, fail to capture Wallenberg's unimaginable courage and self-sacrifice. To get a glimpse of his personal greatness, consider the account of Sandor Ardai, one of the drivers working for Wallenberg. Here he retells what Wallenberg did when he intercepted a trainload of Jews about to leave for Auschwitz:

> He climbed up on the roof of the train and began handing out protective passes through the doors which were not yet sealed. He ignored orders from the Germans for him to get down. Then the Arrow Cross men began shooting and shouting at him to go away. He ignored them and calmly continued handing out passports to the hands that were reaching out for them. I believe the Arrow Cross men deliberately aimed over his head, as not one shot hit him, which would have been impossible otherwise. I think this is what they did because they were so impressed by his courage. After Wallenberg had handed over the last of the passports, he ordered all those who had one to leave the train and walk to the caravan of cars parked nearby, all marked in Swedish colours. I don't remember exactly how many, but he saved dozens off that train, and the Germans and Arrow Cross were so dumbfounded they let him get away with it. [70]

On 17 January 1945, when the Soviets wrested control of Hungary away from the Nazis, they arrested Wallenberg and charged him as a United States spy. He died as a prisoner in the Soviet Union. To this day, the time and cause of his death remain a mystery.

Raoul Wallenberg memorial in Linköping, Sweden

Raoul Wallenberg saved so many, and yet he himself could not be saved. Cities around the world have named streets and monuments after Wallenberg—the epitome of humanitarian diplomacy and self-sacrifice.

Wallenberg was honoured at Yad Vashem in Israel and has been posthumously awarded honorary American, Canadian and Hungarian citizenship. In 1981, the Raoul Wallenberg Committee of the United States was created to further his ideals and to honour the memory of his non-violent resistance. The Committee awards the Raoul Wallenberg Award to individuals, organisations, and communities who exemplify Wallenberg's humanitarian spirit, personal courage and non-violent action in the face of enormous odds.

Oscar Schindler — The Power to Change

Oscar Schindler, an unlikely hero of the Holocaust and saviour of close to 1,200 Jewish lives, is the only member of the Nazi party buried in Jerusalem. Schindler has been recognised as a Righteous Gentile, a title granted to non-Jews who endangered their own lives in order to save Jews during the Holocaust. He has been honoured by Yad Vashem, Pope Paul VI and the Polish government. His story is retold in Steven Spielberg's movie *Schindler's List*, based on the book *Schindler's Ark* by Thomas Keneally.

Oscar Schindler (1908–1974)

Soon after the German invasion of Poland, Oscar Schindler, an ethnic German born in Czechoslovakia and a member of the Nazi Party, acquired a Polish enamel and ammunitions factory in Krakow. It should be noted that the factory had formerly been owned by Jews and its appropriation was less than equitable. However, given his ultimate good deeds, it is unseemly to recount his ignoble character at the start of the war. Suffice it to say, that at the outset of the war his actions were motivated by a thirst for fortune and vice. He saw an opportunity for cheap labour in the degraded Jewish population and requested that Jewish workers be assigned to work in his factory.

As the war progressed, Schindler became appalled as he witnessed the horrors of the Nazi ghettoes, deportations and concentration camps. He began to relate to the Jews in his factory as "his Jews." As efforts increased to exterminate the Jews, so did Schindler's efforts to protect them. It is hard to determine exactly when the "self-serving" Schindler became "self-sacrificing," but it is clear, that by the end of the war he was a largely transformed human being.

Schindler relocated his factory several times in order to avoid the deportation of his Jewish workers. He claimed that his workers were indispensible to the war

247

effort, even though they included children and people with disabilities. Schindler did everything in his power to ensure his workers' safety and to smuggle others out of the ghetto. His connections and charm, originally tools for furthering his own interests, were utilised in his attempts to save as many Jews as possible.

On several occasions, Schindler was required to present a list of his Jewish workers in order to exempt them from deportation. Years after the war, two authentic lists were discovered.

Schindler is quoted as saying, "I knew the people who worked for me ... When you know people, you have to behave toward them like human beings." Upon examination of his background, Schindler's noble efforts become especially noteworthy. He personified the opportunity every individual has to choose good over evil. Schindler chose good at a time when evil was prevalent and glorified.

While he succeeded in making a fortune during the first part of the war, he had nothing left by the time the war was over. He had expended his all of his assets on bribes and on other attempts to protect "his Jews."

Schindler's enamel factory in Krakow, photographed in 2004, before major renovations. In 2009, the building began its conversion into a museum of modern art.

In a fascinating twist of fate, though he seemed a highly adept businessman during the war, ultimately, his only successful business ventures were the ones which saved Jews. He died penniless, supported by the people he had saved. Many of the descendants of Schindler's Jews live in Israel, where Schindler was rewarded with his final resting place.

Irena Sendler – An Angel of Mercy in Warsaw

Irena Sendler was a Polish Catholic social worker who served in the underground "Zegota" (Polish Council to Aid Jews) during World War II. As head of the organisation's children's division, she helped to smuggle 2,500 Jewish children out of the Warsaw ghetto, finding them shelter in Christian homes and orphanages for the duration of the war.

Irena Sendler
(1910-2008)

Sendler was born in Otwock, a town outside of Warsaw. Her father, a physician and one of the first Polish socialists, raised her to respect and love people regardless of their ethnicity or social status. During World War I he aided victims of a typhus epidemic. At one point, the area in which he was working was evacuated of all medical personnel. He alone stayed behind to provide care to those who had no other hope—many of them Jews. Tragically, he contracted typhus. On his deathbed, he told the seven-year-old Irena that "if you see someone drowning, no matter what their religion, race or creed, you must jump in and try to rescue them, even if you don't know how to swim." This was the motto by which Irena lived her entire life.

In 1939, when Germany invaded Poland and began its campaign of murder and destruction, many Poles were quick to side with the Nazis in order to save themselves. Sendler, however, was prepared to risk her life to save Jews. As a social worker, Irena obtained a pass to enter the ghetto; thus, she was able to smuggle in valuable medical supplies and food. There were over 450,000 people forced into the small 16 block area of the ghetto. Some 5,000 people died there each month. Upon reflection, Irena realized that her limited supplies could only help to prolong their suffering, and she decided that the best thing she could do would be to ensure the survival of the next generation by saving the children.

Sendler smuggled 2,500 children out of the Warsaw ghetto during the last three months before its liquidation. She marshalled a team of 25 rescuers: 10 of them smuggled the children out using secret tunnels, sewers, ambulances and workmen; 10 others helped find families to take them and 5 obtained false documents for the children. Although the challenge of successfully smuggling out children was immense, the most difficult part was convincing parents to part with their children. The only guarantee she could provide the parents was that in the ghetto, their children had no hope. "You shouldn't trust me," she would say, "but there's nothing else you can do." Often she would leave the ghetto empty-handed, because parents were unwilling to give their children to a complete stranger. A few days later, they would be gone.

In October of 1943, after two years of clandestine operations, Sendler was arrested by the Gestapo and tortured. After both her legs were broken, she was sentenced to death by firing squad. She escaped at the last moment, just before her scheduled execution; but by then, the Warsaw ghetto had been liquidated. "I could have done more," she said. "This regret will follow me to my death."

One of her great accomplishments was that Sendler kept a record of every child she rescued, placing the names into a jar which she buried in the ground. She wanted to make sure that every child could be returned to living family members after the war. Although she had made gentile clergymen promise to return the Jewish children after the war, her wishes were not always respected, and she spent years trying to track down missing children. Between 400 and 500 children were never located, and today are believed to be assimilated somewhere in Poland.

Memorial coins issued in 2009 by the National Bank of Poland for Zegota (The underground Polish Council to Aid Jews) and for Irena Sendler (bottom left of silver coin) along with Righteous Gentiles Zofia Kossak, and sister Matylda Getter.

THE MOURNER'S KADDISH / קדיש יתום

יִתְגַּדַּל וְיִתְקַדַּשׁ שְׁמֵהּ רַבָּא. (אָמֵן. –Cong.) בְּעָלְמָא
‹ Grow exalted › and be sanctified › may His Name › that is great! « (Amen.) « in the world

דִּי בְרָא כִרְעוּתֵהּ, וְיַמְלִיךְ מַלְכוּתֵהּ, בְּחַיֵּיכוֹן וּבְיוֹמֵיכוֹן
‹ that He created › according to His will, « and may He give reign › to His kingship, « in your lifetimes › and in your days,

וּבְחַיֵּי דְכָל בֵּית יִשְׂרָאֵל, בַּעֲגָלָא וּבִזְמַן קָרִיב. וְאִמְרוּ:
‹ and in the lifetimes › of the entire › Family › of Israel, « swiftly › and at a time › that comes soon. « Now respond:

אָמֵן.
« Amen.

CONGREGATION RESPONDS:

אָמֵן. יְהֵא שְׁמֵהּ רַבָּא מְבָרַךְ לְעָלַם וּלְעָלְמֵי עָלְמַיָּא.
« Amen. « May › His Name › that is great ‹ be blessed › forever ‹ and for all eternity. «

MOURNER CONTINUES:

יְהֵא שְׁמֵהּ רַבָּא מְבָרַךְ לְעָלַם וּלְעָלְמֵי עָלְמַיָּא.
‹ May › His Name › that is great ‹ be blessed ‹ for ever ‹ and for all eternity. «

יִתְבָּרַךְ וְיִשְׁתַּבַּח וְיִתְפָּאַר וְיִתְרוֹמַם וְיִתְנַשֵּׂא וְיִתְהַדָּר
‹ Blessed, › praised, › glorified, › exalted, › upraised, › honored,

וְיִתְעַלֶּה וְיִתְהַלָּל שְׁמֵהּ דְּקֻדְשָׁא בְּרִיךְ הוּא (בְּרִיךְ –Cong.)
‹ elevated, › and lauded › be the Name › of the Holy One, ‹ Blessed « is He › (Blessed

ROSH HASHANAH TO YOM KIPPUR SUBSTITUTE:

הוּא) —°לְעֵלָּא מִן כָּל [°לְעֵלָּא (וּ)לְעֵלָּא מִכָּל]
« is He) ‹ beyond › any ‹ exceedingly beyond › any ‹

בִּרְכָתָא וְשִׁירָתָא, תֻּשְׁבְּחָתָא וְנֶחֱמָתָא דַּאֲמִירָן
‹ blessing « and song, « praise ‹ and consolation ‹ that are uttered

בְּעָלְמָא. וְאִמְרוּ: אָמֵן. (אָמֵן. –Cong.)
« in the world. ‹ Now respond: « Amen. « (Amen.)

יְהֵא שְׁלָמָא רַבָּא מִן שְׁמַיָּא וְחַיִּים עָלֵינוּ וְעַל כָּל

‹ all ‹ and ‹ upon ‹‹ and life, ‹ Heaven ‹ from ‹ that is ‹ peace ‹ May
upon us abundant there be

יִשְׂרָאֵל. וְאִמְרוּ: אָמֵן. (Cong. – אָמֵן.)

‹‹ (Amen.) ‹‹ Amen. ‹ Now ‹‹ Israel.
respond:

MOURNER BOWS; TAKES THREE STEPS BACK. BOWS LEFT AND SAYS "... עֹשֶׂה שָׁלוֹם, HE WHO MAKES PEACE ...", BOWS RIGHT AND SAYS "... הוּא, MAY HE ...", BOWS FORWARD AND SAYS "... וְעַל כָּל יִשְׂרָאֵל, AND UPON ALL ISRAEL ...", REMAINS IN PLACE FOR A FEW MOMENTS, THEN TAKES THREE STEPS FORWARD.

עֹשֶׂה שָׁלוֹם בִּמְרוֹמָיו, הוּא יַעֲשֶׂה שָׁלוֹם עָלֵינוּ, וְעַל

‹ and ‹ upon us, ‹ peace ‹ make ‹ may ‹‹ in His heights, ‹ peace ‹ He Who
upon He makes

כָּל יִשְׂרָאֵל. וְאִמְרוּ: אָמֵן. (Cong. – אָמֵן.)

‹‹ (Amen.) ‹‹ Amen. ‹ Now ‹ Israel. ‹ all
respond:

KEIL MALEI RACHAMIM / אל מלא רחמים

אֵל מָלֵא רַחֲמִים, שׁוֹכֵן בַּמְּרוֹמִים, הַמְצֵא מְנוּחָה

‹ rest ‹ grant ‹‹ on high, ‹‹ Who dwells ‹ of mercy, ‹ full ‹ O God,

נְכוֹנָה עַל כַּנְפֵי הַשְּׁכִינָה, בְּמַעֲלוֹת קְדוֹשִׁים

‹ of the holy ‹ in the lofty ‹‹ of the Divine ‹ the ‹ on ‹ that is
levels Presence, wings proper

וּטְהוֹרִים כְּזֹהַר הָרָקִיעַ מַזְהִירִים, אֶת נִשְׁמוֹת

‹ – for the souls of ‹‹ shine ‹ of the ‹ who like ‹‹ and pure ones,
firmament the glow

(כָּל קְרוֹבַי וּקְרוֹבוֹתַי, הֵן מִצַּד אָבִי, הֵן מִצַּד אִמִּי)

‹‹ on my ‹ whether ‹ on my ‹ whether ‹ and my female ‹ my male ‹ (all
mother's side,) father's side, relatives relatives

הַקְּדוֹשִׁים וְהַטְּהוֹרִים שֶׁהוּמְתוּ וְשֶׁנֶּהֶרְגוּ וְשֶׁנִּשְׁחֲטוּ

‹ slaughtered, ‹ murdered, ‹ who were killed, ‹ and pure ones ‹ the holy

וְשֶׁנִּשְׂרְפוּ וְשֶׁנִּטְבְּעוּ וְשֶׁנֶּחְנְקוּ עַל קִדּוּשׁ הַשֵּׁם (עַל

‹ (at ‹‹ of [God's] ‹ the sanc- ‹ for ‹ and strangled ‹ drowned, ‹ burned,
Name tification

יְדֵי הַצוֹרְרִים הַגֶּרְמָנִים, יִמַּח שְׁמָם וְזִכְרָם), בַּעֲבוּר

‹ because, ‹‹ and ‹ may their ‹ obliterated ‹ of the German oppressors, ‹ the
memory be) name hands

© Copyright 2001, 2002, 2012, ArtScroll/Mesorah Publications, Ltd.
Reprinted in the JRoots guidebook with permission from the publisher.

שֶׁבְּלִי נֶדֶר אֶתֵּן צְדָקָה בְּעַד הַזְכָּרַת נִשְׁמוֹתֵיהֶם,

《 of their souls. 〈 the remembrance 〈 for 〈 to contribute 〈 charity 〈 I will 〈 [intending] 《 without a vow,

בְּגַן עֵדֶן תְּהֵא מְנוּחָתָם, לָכֵן בַּעַל הָרַחֲמִים יַסְתִּירֵם

〈 shelter them 〈 of mercy 〈 may the Master 《 There-fore 《 their resting place. 〈 should be 〈 of 〈 In the Eden Garden

בְּסֵתֶר כְּנָפָיו לְעוֹלָמִים, וְיִצְרוֹר בִּצְרוֹר הַחַיִּים

〈 of Life 〈 in the Bond 〈 and may He bind 〈 for eternity; 〈 of His wings 〈 in the shelter

אֶת נִשְׁמוֹתֵיהֶם, יהוה הוּא נַחֲלָתָם, וְיָנוּחוּ בְשָׁלוֹם עַל

〈 in 〈 in peace 〈 and may they repose 《 their heritage, 〈 is 〈 HASHEM 《 their souls.

מִשְׁכְּבוֹתֵיהֶם. וְנֹאמַר: אָמֵן.

《 Amen. 《 Now let us respond: 《 their resting places.

שִׁיר לַמַּעֲלוֹת; אֶשָּׂא עֵינַי אֶל הֶהָרִים, מֵאַיִן יָבֹא

〈 will come 〈 from whence 〈 the mountains; 〈 to 〈 my eyes 〈 I raise 《 to the ascents. 〈 A song 1

עֶזְרִי. עֶזְרִי מֵעִם יהוה, עֹשֵׂה שָׁמַיִם וָאָרֶץ. אַל יִתֵּן

〈 He will not allow 3 《 and earth. 〈 of heaven 〈 Maker 《 HASHEM, 〈 is from 〈 My help 2 《 my help?

לַמּוֹט רַגְלֶךָ, אַל יָנוּם שֹׁמְרֶךָ. הִנֵּה לֹא יָנוּם וְלֹא

〈 nor 〈 slumbers 〈 [He] neither 〈 It is so, that 4 《 will your Guardian. 〈 not slumber 《 of your foot; 〈 the faltering

יִישָׁן, שׁוֹמֵר יִשְׂרָאֵל. יהוה שֹׁמְרֶךָ, יהוה צִלְּךָ עַל

〈 at 〈 is your protective Shade 《 HASHEM 《 is your Guardian; 〈 HASHEM 5 《 of Israel. 〈 — the Guardian 《 sleeps

יַד יְמִינֶךָ. יוֹמָם הַשֶּׁמֶשׁ לֹא יַכֶּכָּה, וְיָרֵחַ בַּלָּיְלָה.

《 by night. 〈 nor the moon 《 harm you, 〈 will not 〈 the sun 〈 By day 6 《 your right hand.

יהוה יִשְׁמָרְךָ מִכָּל רָע, יִשְׁמֹר אֶת נַפְשֶׁךָ. יהוה

〈 HASHEM 8 《 your soul. 〈 He will guard 《 evil; 〈 from every 〈 will protect you 《 HASHEM 7

יִשְׁמָר־צֵאתְךָ וּבוֹאֶךָ, מֵעַתָּה וְעַד עוֹלָם.

《 eternity. 〈 until 〈 from this time 〈 and your arrival, 〈 your departure 〈 will guard

תהלים קל / PSALM 130

שִׁיר הַמַּעֲלוֹת; מִמַּעֲמַקִּים קְרָאתִיךָ, יהוה. א

《HASHEM. 〈 I called You, 〈 From the depths 《 of ascents. 〈 A song 1

אֲדֹנָי, שִׁמְעָה בְקוֹלִי, תִּהְיֶינָה אָזְנֶיךָ קַשֻּׁבוֹת לְקוֹל ב

〈 to the sound 〈 attentive 《 — Your ears — 《 may they be 《 my voice; 〈 hear 〈 O Lord, 2

תַּחֲנוּנָי. אִם עֲוֹנוֹת תִּשְׁמָר, יָהּ; אֲדֹנָי, מִי יַעֲמֹד. ד כִּי

〈 For 4 《 could who 〈 O Lord, 《 O God, 〈 You preserve, 〈 iniquities 〈 If 3 《 of my pleas. could survive?

עִמְּךָ הַסְּלִיחָה, לְמַעַן תִּוָּרֵא. ה קִוִּיתִי יהוה, קִוְּתָה

〈 placed 《 in hope 〈 I placed 5 《 You may be feared. 〈 so that 《 is forgiveness, 〈 with You my hope HASHEM,

נַפְשִׁי, וְלִדְבָרוֹ הוֹחָלְתִּי. ו נַפְשִׁי לַאדֹנָי, מִשֹּׁמְרִים

〈 among those longing 《 [yearns] for the Lord, 〈 My soul 6 《 I yearned. 〈 and for His word 《 did my soul

לַבֹּקֶר, שֹׁמְרִים לַבֹּקֶר. ז יַחֵל יִשְׂרָאֵל אֶל יהוה; כִּי

〈 for 《 HASHEM, 〈 for 〈 shall Israel 〈 Yearn 7 《 for the dawn. 〈 those longing 《 for the dawn,

עִם יהוה הַחֶסֶד, וְהַרְבֵּה עִמּוֹ פְדוּת. ח וְהוּא יִפְדֶּה

〈 shall redeem 〈 And He 8 《 is redemption. 〈 with Him 〈 and abundant 《 is kindness, 〈 HASHEM 〈 with

אֶת יִשְׂרָאֵל, מִכֹּל עֲוֹנוֹתָיו.

《 its iniquities. 〈 from all 〈 Israel

Acknowledgements, Sources and References

Acknowledgements

This book would not have been possible without the generous support of Bernhard and Pearl Lazarus who dedicated its publication in honour of Pearl's 85th birthday, and by the Arnold Lee Family of London who funded its research and initial production in memory of Helen Lee. Support for the printing of previous editions was generously provided by the Rothschild Foundation (Europe), the Bill and Judith Rubinstein Family Foundation, Laurence "Benji" Roberts, C. Daniel Chill and Esther Kaplan. Thank you very much. May your kindness be a merit to you and your loved ones.

Thank you to (alphabetically) Raquel Amit, Adam Bell, Hannah Davidson, Gila Green, Michael Gros, Jessica Hod, Gabriel Horan, Miriam Kaplan, Renato Kopstein, Bernhard Lazarus, Yehoshua Levinson, Shelly Padowitz, Elisheva Rosenblatt, Elisheva Rosenblum, Rabbi Daniel Rowe, Pam Russ, Rabbi Naftali Schiff, Tzvi Sperber, Rena Siev and Ruthie Zimberg for your assistance with copy, editing and proofreading; and to Daniella Keene, Eric Olason, Shelly Padowitz, Luke Simons, Joel Southern, and Shana Wasosky for your assistance with graphics and layout.

The top left image on the cover is courtesy of Mayer Kirshenblatt and Barbara Kirshenblatt-Gimlbett, *They Called Me Mayer July: Painted Memories of a Jewish Childhood in Poland Before the Holocaust.* (http://www.mayerjuly.com).

Materially all the images in the book were drawn from Wikimedia commons (http://commons.wikimedia.org/) and were free of copyright restrictions.

Many other historical maps are from the Routledge Companion Website for Judaism: History, Belief, & Practice at www.routledge-ny.com/textbooks/0415236614/resources/indi.asp.

The outline of Przemysl's history is based on the work of JewishGen's ShtetLinks (http://www.shtetlinks.jewishgen.org/Przemysl/history.shtml).

The sections *Shabbetai Zvi* and *Life under the Russians* relied heavily on the work of historian Ken Spiro. Many paragraphs are materially his original work which can be found at www.aish.com.

Much of the history from the Chmielnicki Massacres until the World War I was drawn from Rabbi Berel Wein's excellent work, *Triumph of Survival: The Story of the Jews in the Modern Era (1650-1990)*.

The *Timeline of the Holocaust* is an adaptation of the timeline created by Aish HaTorah, available at www.aish.com/ho.

The *Frequently Asked Questions* section is based on the Simon Wiesenthal Centre's 36 Questions about the Holocaust, which is available on many websites, though apparently not on the Wiesenthal Centre's own website.

The images of Krasnik come from the Foundation for the Preservation of Jewish Heritage in Poland.

The content on R' Elimelech of Lizhensk was drawn largely from R' Tal Zwecker's work, *Mipeninei Noam Elimelech*. The final story of R' Elimelech of Lizhensk comes from www.chabad.org.

The story of Irena Sendler was originally written by Gabriel Horan who subsequently edited it specifically for inclusion here.

Bibliography

Bender, Sara. *The Jews of Bialystok During World War II and the Holocaust* (Brandeis University Press, 2008).

Ben-Sasson, H. H. *A History of the Jewish People* (Harvard University Press, 1997).

Carroll, James. *Constantine's Sword* (Houghton Mifflin, 2001).

Clay, Catrine & Leapman, Michael. *Master Race: The Lebensborn Experiment in Nazi Germany* (Hodder & Stoughton, 1995).

Fishman, David E. *The Rise of Modern Yiddish Culture* (University of Pittsburgh Press, 2005), p. 49.

Dubnow, Simon. *History of the Jews in Russia and Poland* (Varda Books, 2001), Vol. 1, p. 42.

Elazar, Daniel J. *Can Sephardic Judaism be Reconstructed?* Jerusalem Center for Public Affairs. http://www.jcpa.org/dje/articles3/sephardic.htm.

Encyclopaedia Judaica. (Jerusalem: Keter, 1971).

Frischauer, Willi. *Himmler, the Evil Genius of the Third Reich* (London: Odhams, 1953), pp. 85-88.

Geary, Patrick J., ed. *Readings in Medieval History* (Toronto: Broadview Press, 2003).

Gilbert, Martin. *The Holocaust: The Jewish Tragedy.* 2nd Ed. (Fontana/Collins, Great Britain, 1986).

Goldhagen, D. J. *Hitler's Willing Executioners: Ordinary Germans and the Holocaust.* 2nd Ed. (Vintage Books, New York, 1997).

Goldwurm, Hersh. *The Early Acharonim* (Mesorah Publications, 1989).

Hameln, Gluckel of. Lowenthal, Marvin, Trans. *The Memoirs of Gluckel of Hameln* (Schocken Books, 1977).

Harnack, Adolf. *Ausbreitung des Christentums* (Leipzig, 1902).

Henes, R. & Zigelboim, Mordekhai (Arthur). *Commemoration Book Chelm* (Translation of Yisker-bukh Chelm, published in Yiddish in Johannesburg, 1954), pp. 287-294.

Hughes, John Jay. *A Mass Murderer Repents: The Case of Rudolf Hoess, Commandant of Auschwitz.* Archbishop Gerety Lecture at Seton Hall University, 25 March 1998.

Johnson, Paul. *A History of the Jews* (Harper Perennial, 1998).

Jospe, Raphael, ed. *Great Schisms in Jewish History* (Ktav Publishing House, 1981), p. 129.

Katsch, Abraham I. *The Biblical Heritage of American Democracy* (New York: Ktav Publishing House, 1977), p. 133.

Kunich, John C. & Lester, Richard I. *"Profile of a Leader: The Wallenberg Effect."* The Journal of Leadership Studies, 1997, Vol. 4, No. 3.

Laqueur, Walter. *A History of Zionism* (Tauris Parke Paperbacks, 2003), p. 273.

Laqueur, Walter. *The Changing Face of Antisemitism: From Ancient Times to the Present Day* (Oxford University Press, 2006), p.56.

Levy, Richard S. *Antisemitism: A Historical Encyclopedia of Prejudice and Persecution.* (ABC-CLIO, 2005).

Marcus, Jacob Rader, ed. *The Jew in the Medieval World: A Sourcebook* (Hebrew Union College Press, 1905) pp. 167-169.

Meggs, Philip B. *A History of Graphic Design* (John Wiley & Sons, Inc. 1998).

Mendes-Flohr, Paul, ed. & Reinharz, Jehuda, ed. *The Jew in the Modern World* (Oxford University Press, 1995).

Niewyk, Donald L.; Nicosia, Francis R. *The Columbia Guide to the Holocaust* (Columbia University Press, 2000).

Polonsky, Antony. *"The Bund in Polish Political Life, 1935-1939"* in Mendelsohn, Ezra, *Essential Papers on Jews and the Left* (New York University Press, 1997), pp. 194-5.

Rabinowicz, Harry M. *The Legacy of Polish Jewry: A history of Polish Jews in the Inter-War Years, 1919-1939* (New York: Thomas Yoseloff, 1965), pp. 118-125.

Repa, Jan. *"Warsaw's Jewish Heritage Remembered"*, BBC News, 30 June 2005.

Riley-Smith, Jonathan. *The First Crusade and the Idea of Crusading* (University of Pennsylvania Press, 1991), p. 50.

Roth, Cecil. *The Jewish Contribution to Civilization* (Hebrew Publishing Company, 1978), pp. 9–10.

Sanford, George. *Historical Dictionary of Poland.* 2nd edition. (Oxford: The Scarecrow Press, 2003), p. 79.

Schreiber, Mordecai; Schiff, Alvin I; Klenicki, Leon. *The Shengold Jewish Encyclopaedia* (Schreiber Pub., 2003), p. 56.

Spiro, Ken. *Crash Course in Jewish History* (aish.com)

Stachura, Peter D. *Poland, 1918-1945: An Interpretive and Documentary History of the Second Republic* (Routledge 2004), p. 84.

Stevens, Payson R. *Meshuggenary: Celebrating the World of Yiddish* (Simon & Schuster, 2002).

Szpilman, Wladyslaw. *The Pianist: The Extraordinary True Story of One Man's Survival in Warsaw, 1939-1945,* (Picador, 2000).

Teluda, Benjamin of. *The Itinerary of Benjamin of Tudela: Travels in the Middle Ages* (NightinGale Resources, 2004).

Wein, Berel. *Triumph of Survival: The Story of the Jews in the Modern Era (1650-1990),* 2nd edition, (Shaar Press, 1999).

Weinrich, Max. *Yiddish, Knaanic, Slavic: The basic relationships* (1956).

Wexler, Paul. *Two-Tiered Relexification in Yiddish: The Jews, Sorbs, Khazars and the Kiev-Polessian dialects (Berlin: Mouton de Gruyter, 2002).*

William V. Harris. *Ancient Literacy* (Harvard University Press, 1989).

www.hashkedim.com

www.holocaustresearchproject.org

www.jewishvirtuallibrary.org

www.jewishvirtuallibrary.org

www.moreorless.au.com/killers

www.nazism.net

www.nizkor.org

www.ou.org

www.rarenewspapers.com

www.shtetlinks.jewishgen.org
www.simpletoremember.com
www.ushmm.org
www.wikipedia.com
www.yadvashem.org

1   Jan Repa, "Warsaw's Jewish Heritage Remembered," BBC News, 30 June 2005.

2   http://www.shtetlinks.jewishgen.org/Przemysl/history.shtml

3   Martin Gilbert, The Holocaust Fontana Press, 1987, 732-3.

4   James Carroll. Constantine's Sword (Houghton Mifflin, 2001).

5   Teluda, Benjamin, The Itinerary of Benjamin of Tudela: Travels in the Middle Ages. Gives the number 1,049,565 in the year 1170, though his estimates for Persia, India, Arabia, and the unexplained "Thanaim" are probably overestimated.

6   Second chant at Vespers and after the sixth Gospel reading.

7   Patrick J. Geary, ed., Readings in Medieval History (Toronto: Broadview Press, 2003).

8   "In Poland, a Jewish Revival Thrives—Minus Jews.," New York Times 12 July 2007).

9   Reported originally by Jan Dlugosz (1415-1480), a famous Polish historian, in The Annals of Jan Dlugosz.

10 S. Barry and N. Gualde, "The Biggest Epidemics of History: (La plus grande épidémie de l'histoire)" L'Histoire n°310, (2006), 45-6, says "between one-third and two-thirds"; R. Gottfried, "Black Death" in Dictionary of the Middle Ages, Vol. 2, (1983). 257-67, says "between 25 and 45 percent."

11 "Omnes judaei ... fere in tota Polonia deleti sunt." Stanislas of Olivia in his Chronica Olivska, for the year 1349.

12 The year of St. John Capistrano's canonization is variously given as 1690, by Pope Alexander VIII or 1724 by Pope Benedict XIII.

13 Paul Johnson, A History of the Jews (Harper Perennial, 1998).

14 Philip B. Meggs, A History of Graphic Design (John Wiley & Sons, Inc., 1998).

15 Richard S. Levy. Antisemitism: A historical encyclopedia of prejudice and persecution. Vol. 1, 701.

16 William V. Harris. Ancient Literacy (Harvard University Press, 1989). Roth, The Jewish Contribution to Civilization, pp. 9-10; Katsch, Abraham I. The

Biblical *Heritage of American Democracy*, 133 (New York: Ktav Publishing House, 1977).

17 *Zohar* (2:161b).

18 Daniel J. Elazar, *Can Sephardic Judaism be Reconstructed?* Jerusalem Center for Public Affairs. http://www.jcpa.org/dje/articles3/sephardic.htm.

19 This paragraph was taken largely verbatim from Rabbi Berel Wein's *Triumph of Survival*.

20 *The Memoirs of Gluckel of Hameln*, (Schocken Books, 1977), 46-47.

21 Raphael Jospe, ed. *Great Schisms in Jewish History* (Ktav Publishing House, 1981), 129.

22 See William McGuire and R. F. C. Hull, Eds., *C.G. Jung Speaking*, 271-272.

23 Paul Mendes-Flohr & Yehuda Reinharz ed. *The Jew in the Modern World* (Oxford University Press, 1995), p. 390.

24 Berel Wein, *Triumph of Survival*, 173.

25 Peter D. Stachura, *Poland, 1918-1945: An Interpretive and Documentary History of the Second Republic* (Routledge 2004), 84.

26 Martin Luther, "Concerning the Jews and Their Lies," 1543, in *The Jew in the Medieval World*, 167-169.

27 *Time Magazine*, 16 June 1947.

28 Willi Frischauer, *Himmler, the Evil Genius of the Third Reich* (London: Odhams, 1953), 85-88.

29 Catrine Clay & Michael Leapman, *Master Race: The Lebensborn Experiment in Nazi Germany* (Hodder & Stoughton, 1995).

30 John Jay Hughes, *A Mass Murderer Repents: The Case of Rudolf Hoess, Commandant of Auschwitz*. Archbishop Gerety Lecture at Seton Hall University, 25 March 1998.

31 Testimony of Kazimierz Albin, who escaped from Auschwitz 1943. www.auschwitz.info

32 As retold on www.chabad.org

33 http://www.tzemachdovid.org/gedolim/jo/tworld/schenirer.html

in Mendelsohn, Ezra, Essential Papers on Jews and the Left (New York: New York University Press 1997, 194-5.

34 http://www1.yadvashem.org/odot_pdf/Microsoft%20Word%20-%20603.pdf

35 John C. Kunich and Richard I. Lester, "Profile of a Leader: The Wallenberg Effect," *The Journal of Leadership Studies,* 1997, Vol. 4, No. 3.

Space for Personal Reflections

Space for Personal Reflections

Space for Personal Reflections

Space for Personal Reflections

Space for Personal Reflections

Space for Personal Reflections

first-time parents

Dr Miriam Stoppard

LONDON, NEW YORK,
MELBOURNE, MUNICH, DELHI

For Ed and Amie

Medical consultant
Dr Tim Wickham BSc (hons)
MBBS MRCP FRCPCH

Produced for Dorling Kindersley by
Cooling Brown
Designer Tish Jones
Editor Jemima Dunne
Creative Director Arthur Brown
Technical Support Peter Cooling

Dorling Kindersley
Consultant Editor Jinny Johnson
Managing Editor Esther Ripley
Senior Editor Emma Woolf
Managing Art Editor Marianne Markham
Senior Art Editor Nicola Rodway
Senior Production Editor Jenny Woodcock
Creative Technical Support Sonia Charbonnier
Production Controller Hema Gohil
Jacket Design Charlotte Seymour
Special Photography Vanessa Davies
Art Direction for Photography Anne Fisher

First published by Dorling Kindersley in 1998
This revised edition published in
Great Britain in 2009 by
Dorling Kindersley Limited,
80 Strand, London WC2R 0RL
A Penguin Company

Copyright © 1998, 2006, 2009
Dorling Kindersley Limited
Text Copyright © 1998, 2006,
2009 Miriam Stoppard

A CIP catalogue record for this book is
available from the British Library.

ISBN: 978 1 4053 3516 4

Printed and bound in Singapore by
Tien Wah Press

Discover more at
www.dk.com

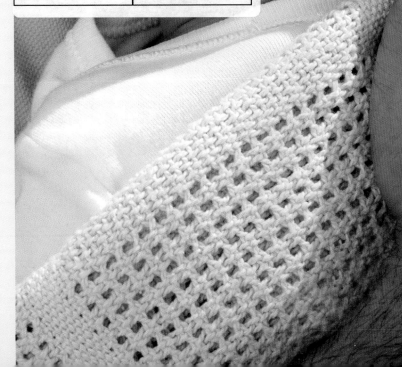

Contents

Introduction

Today's new parents have many advantages over their predecessors, but they also face many new challenges. Knowledge of the way babies grow and develop both before and after birth has increased enormously in the past few years. This knowledge in itself creates new pressures, worries, and anxieties for parents. If you are a couple thinking of starting a family, how do you know where to turn? I hope that this book will help you to find out what best suits you and will make you feel comfortable and confident enough to follow your own instincts.

There's much evidence to indicate that the unborn baby benefits from having a relaxed, calm mother who can take obstacles in her stride. Other research demonstrates that the most important factor in determining whether a pregnant woman is tranquil or not, is a caring, interested, supportive partner. And here we have come to the reason for my writing this book. It is not just for first-time mothers, but for couples – mothers and fathers. I've included basic advice on caring for your baby during his first year of life, but it's just as important to emphasize how a baby will affect your relationship.

The impact on your relationship

Few couples think about the impact their new baby will have on their lives, their work, their emotions, and their feelings for one another. With the care of their baby a top priority, parents can easily give too little consideration to themselves.

Both new mothers and new fathers will find their world turned upside down by the arrival of a baby. This may create tensions and strains, which, if unspoken and unresolved, could drive a wedge between them. It's a huge leap from being a couple to becoming a family. A man is very different from a father, and different things are expected of him.

If they're honest, most men admit to experiencing difficulties in making the transition to fatherhood. By the same token, a mother is a very different person from a woman, who was probably self-confident and independent before she became pregnant. Now she may be apprehensive and come to feel isolated. She has to cope with a baby who is completely dependent upon her, which can bring with it a perceived loss of identity. This in turn may lead to confusion, resentment, and irritation towards her partner.

The good news is that it's possible for both of you to pick your way through this minefield of new feelings and responsibilities. But it isn't always easy and it requires a lot of give and take to smooth the path. Perhaps now, more than at any other time, each of you has to be aware of and sensitive to the needs of the other and actively look for ways of showing you care.

Advice and reassurance

While my main aim is to give new parents the confidence to follow their own instincts in fashioning their particular brand of family life, and to be open and loving with one another so that their relationship is enriched by their new baby, there's no doubt that first-time parents find bits of advice quite useful. So I've tried to be helpful in matters with which most young families have problems.

Issues such as how to stay healthy during pregnancy, where to have your baby, what to expect during labour, how to establish breastfeeding and cope with broken nights or an inconsolably fretful baby are all covered. While love for your baby can begin from the moment of birth, his care is a skill that you'll be learning throughout his first year, and understanding how he develops is a crucial part of it. All new parents feel anxious and inept to begin with, but if you share the worries as well as the joys, you're less likely to strain your relationship.

Making room for fathers

Throughout the book, I approach pregnancy, birth, and babycare as a joint venture. Fathers figure on every page because mothers and babies need involved, active fathers. Men are as good at fathering as women are at mothering; there's no qualitative difference between the two. Fathering instincts are strong and need only a little encouragement to flower. Babies love being nurtured by fathers as well as mothers; it follows that parenting should be equal and shared.

On the face of it, following this principle may seem fraught with obstacles, but it need not be so. Parents can share all the elements of babycare with a little planning and a generous heart. After all, babycare means loving and encouraging your baby, teaching your baby, watching your baby grow and develop, and establishing bonds with your baby that in all probability will be the strongest you ever make with anyone. Who in their right mind would miss out on it?

Men should try not to allow themselves to be deprived of this unique relationship. And when they're fully involved with their baby, a little miracle occurs along the way: their relationship with their baby's mother flourishes, too.

Making parenting a partnership

To help both parents become fully involved, I've included special panels that give the mother's point of view on one side of the page and the father's point of view on the other. Arranging information in this way has a special purpose: it can help you gain insight into what your partner may be feeling about a particular topic, or might want to say, but is reluctant to make demands. Looking at this information together may help you to get a discussion going. Communication is the key to a successful relationship. I hope the panels will enable you to talk things through and be generous about different ways of looking at things.

Above all, couples whose relationship is on a sound footing and who enter into parenthood as a true partnership are doing the best for their baby, who will grow up secure in the love of both parents. Shared care means there'll be time for your baby, time for yourselves, and time when, as well as being a family, you're just a couple – but with the knowledge that together you have produced and nurtured a wonderful baby.

Dr. Miriam Stoppard

Deciding on parenthood

When you decide to have a baby, you're also making the decision to become a parent. This is probably the most important step you'll ever take in your life, because bringing a child into the world isn't something that you can simply add on to your current lifestyle. You're creating a completely new person, and taking on a responsibility that is lifelong. You're also creating a new unit – from being two individuals, you're becoming a family – something that both cements and puts strains on your existing relationships, with each other, your friends, and your family. This is equally true if you're a lone parent and, even if you have children from a previous relationship, your new baby is going to create a new family grouping. So it's well worth looking at all the implications of parenthood and the different forms that the modern family takes, and to ask yourselves some searching questions about how you see parenting, and how it's going to affect your everyday needs as well as your emotions.

The changing family

How roles are changing

At their most basic, the terms "mother" and "father" describe a range of biological facts. A mother produces eggs and gives birth to children. A father's sperm fertilize the eggs and contribute half his children's genes. But these are obviously not the only differences. Human beings belong to a species with clear distinctions between male and female. Traditionally, the physical differences between men and women meant that men (being bigger and stronger) were seen as protectors of women.

No need for brute strength

For thousands of years, men used their biological role to claim authority over women, but today, the traditional roles of mother and father are no longer relevant. Modern technology has done away with the need for brute strength, and nowadays women and children generally don't need men to protect them.

Involving men in parenting

Since the 1970s, it has been increasingly recognized that men should be more involved in the upbringing of their children. This is sometimes seen as a spin-off from the women's movement, but this misses the point. The equal sharing between men and women in the care of their children isn't just the result of women's changing thoughts, but also the outcome of men's need to be involved in the nurture, guidance, and raising of their children.

Having a baby creates a whole new social unit. Instead of being just two people, you become a family. Families give babies constant care and protection and, though family groupings may vary, babies know only the quality of care, interest, and love that they receive.

How it used to be

Until two or three generations ago, the family was usually based on the extended model. People were part of a large grouping of three or four generations, extending outwards to include cousins. When people's lives were less mobile, and they lived and worked in one small area, face-to-face contact was possible on a daily basis. This larger family unit could act as a support group for its members, particularly in the case of child rearing.

The family today

In the past 50 years, the extended family has largely broken down. Rapid technological change produced a labour market that demanded mobility; people wanted to go where the jobs were, or were forced to do so through economic necessity. Leaving home meant leaving the extended family network and possibly settling where there were no relations at all to lean on for financial and emotional support. At the same time, increased prosperity allowed people to set up their own homes, whereas in the past they may have remained in the family home, even when married. This broad social movement saw the rapid spread of the isolated nuclear family – just mother, father, and children. Even when embedded within an extended family, this unit can be a hothouse of troubled emotions; on its own, its long-term survival is more likely to be precarious.

New family groupings

Since the 1960s, women have increasingly developed a degree of financial independence that has made them less likely to hang on to the last remnant of a marriage just because they didn't think they could provide for themselves and their children on their own. Liberal attitudes to welfare have also played their part in the transformation of the traditional family; as the nuclear family – detached from its older members or more tenuous branches – became the norm rather than the exception, so the divorce rate increased, giving rise to less orthodox family structures.

Divorce and remarriage

Many divorced or separated people haven't turned their backs on marriage or partnership as such, but only on the one they found intolerable, and there are a growing number of families in which one partner or even both partners, has children from a previous relationship. As with the nuclear family, the stepfamily has been around for a long time (and hasn't always had a good press), but its recent growth in numbers has been dramatic.

Single parents

The one-parent family is a much maligned institution. It's true that it has often grown out of unhappy situations and the pressures, not least financial, on the lone parent are great. But many single-parent families are thriving, vigorous units that are bound by particularly close ties and offer the children involved continuity, stability, and happiness (see p.140).

A new kind of parenting

Fathers used to be seen as protectors, having little direct involvement in day-to-day childcare, but their importance as equal partners is now recognized – side by side with women's increasing role as equal or even primary financial provider. And in some families the father cares for home and family by choice, while his partner earns the daily bread (see p.176). One reason why such families are often strong and successful units is that they take account of both partners' talents and, generally, are a result of careful discussion and planning. But whatever the practicalities of any individual family unit, providing a stable, loving, and open environment in which to bring up children is probably the only important constant.

BABY IN THE FAMILY If your partner has a child from a previous relationship, a new baby can cause tensions. Encourage your stepchild to develop a relationship with the baby. Reassure her that you still love her and there is time and space for everyone.

What is a father?

No one has a problem defining a mother's role. A mother's role is to care for children: mothers feed, comfort, and dress; they encourage, teach, carry, undress, and put to bed. We know this because it's what we experienced as children. Defining the father's role can be more difficult.

Finding a role model

Much as you may love your father, you may want your relationship with your own children to be different to the one that you had with your father. Men are constantly encouraged to become fully involved in nurturing their children, but few have any role model to demonstrate what this actually means. What we really need is for fathers to be more like mothers.

Babies don't mind

Babies and young children don't mind whether they are cared for by their mother or father. They experience comfort, warmth, and security from their parents and, though they soon learn to tell them apart, they don't make value judgments based on what mothers and fathers ought to do. Apart from breastfeeding, there's nothing a man can't do for his baby.

The need for parenting

Babies don't need mothering and fathering, they need parenting. They need the most important adults in their lives to be models of what parents do for their children. A child will only separate her expectations of each parent if this is what she learns from her experiences.

Why be a parent?

It's worth questioning your own ideas about parenthood, and whether what you think of as a mother's role isn't just as applicable to fathers.

Attitudes to fathering

✳ Traditionally, fathers came home from work expecting the home to be clean, the children ready for bed, and a meal on the table. Today, it's hard to believe that many modern mothers would entertain this.

✳ At one time women expected their partners to handle all of the family finances, sometimes to their disadvantage. Nowadays most couples find a fair way to share their financial burdens between them.

✳ It's often assumed that men do all the heavy work. However, while a man must do this when his partner is pregnant and the baby is young, women are fitter and stronger than they used to be and these tasks can be shared.

✳ Women still tend to take on the chores while their partners play with the baby, even when both parents work. It's much better, though, if both of you play with your baby, and share the housework equally.

✳ Try to agree attitudes to discipline for your family and make sure you both apply them consistently (see p.181).

You may never do anything more important than bring up a child. However satisfying your career, whatever sporting or leisure goals you've achieved, you'll find parenthood is a role that is rewarding in a way that is unlike anything else.

Following your instincts

The instinct to bear children is a strong one, and luckily the joy and fulfilment felt by most parents far outweigh some of the inconveniences and compromises that they may have to accept. Although this isn't always so, making the decision to have a child usually comes from within a close, loving relationship between two people who decide that they would like to express their mutual affection in having a baby. This is just as well – you're unlikely to make the decision because you're attracted by the idea of reduced free time, never being able to put yourself first, sleeplessness, and forking out for designer infant trainers! If you think carefully about the changes brought about by parenthood, you'll realize that it's your genes that are pushing you relentlessly towards recreating yourselves in the form of children. Nowadays, people don't like to admit that they might be at the beck and call of basic urges and tend to dress them up as something more refined. That's fine, so long as we remember that we can also push back and say no to parenthood. For some, that can be the best decision, because having a baby is a commitment like no other.

More than just nature

Aside from biological reasons, people also want to have a baby for fulfilment and personal achievement. Human beings are social animals, and the way they think and act always has a social element. This is shown most clearly in human parenthood in the case of adoption where (usually) two people voluntarily make a commitment to assume all the rights and duties of natural parents, while being genetically unrelated to the child (see p.142). Adoption also illustrates the depth of the emotional need that people feel to nurture, educate, and, above all, love a child. What you give to your children in time, love, understanding, and example will constantly be repaid as you watch them grow and develop over the years. Every child is genetically the sum of his parents, but he is also a unique personality in his own right, and knowing that you have been the primary influences and educators in allowing that personality to take shape and mature is deeply enriching as well as being a major achievement.

Social and economic pressures

In a society where everyone goes to school, everyone expects to go to school. Similarly, when everyone except a small minority has children, people expect to have children. It's as though a person has to have a reason for remaining childless, rather than the opposite. In the past, when families tended to live close together, in the same street or village if not actually in the same house (see p.10), there were quite important economic reasons for having children. As soon as they were old enough to work, children made a vital contribution to the family's economic welfare, and parenthood was also a guarantee of being cared for in old age.

Changing demands

In the much more fragmented society in which we live today, children aren't expected to contribute to the family income (at least not until they have finished their education), and the state has taken over some of the basic responsibilities for the elderly, or people make their own provision for old age. As a result, the economic demands of the family are now directed downwards, from parents to children, instead of the other way round. Bringing up children today can be a costly business, and not just financially. For the first time in history, large numbers of women can achieve a whole range of satisfactions outside parenthood and the home; and with safe methods of contraception, they can also choose whether and when they want to have children. This doesn't mean that large numbers of women are opting out of motherhood, though some are; but what they are doing is fitting having and bringing up children into lives in which work and a career are also seen as theirs by right.

A question of upbringing

Having begun to consider parenthood seriously, the first thing to realize before you go further is that having a baby is just the overture to bringing up a child. It isn't too difficult to imagine having a baby – the excitement, the celebrations, the delighted grandparents, the supportive friends and family. It's almost impossible to visualize bringing up a child if you haven't done it. The demands in time, energy, and emotion are almost limitless, unless of course the first thing you're going to teach your toddler is how to use the remote control for the TV and video. This isn't an option for most people because, even before you become parents, you'll have some idea of the kind of people you hope your children will grow up to be, and of the upbringing that will make this idea a reality.

A firm foundation

Upbringing begins from the moment of birth. For a baby or young child, everything is a learning experience, so how you care for your baby is influential from day one. It's worth looking at the background of someone you know who is independent but has a large capacity to love and interrelate with others, who is effective and confident, who recognizes that there is such a thing as the general good, and wants to contribute to it. You'll probably discover that person found the world an accepting, loving, encouraging, reasonable, and respectful place from birth. His parents made him feel that way, and the foundation for everything he has become was provided by them in his first year of life.

✳ JUST FOR DAD

It's a good idea to be clear about your own attitude to parenting to make sure it doesn't reinforce traditional stereotypes about mothers and fathers. What you may think of as a mother's role can be just as applicable to fathers.

Attitudes to mothering

✳ While it's still true that it's mostly women who stay at home, many are now returning to work within months of their baby's birth. Also, more and more men are becoming stay-at-home dads (see p.176).

✳ Recent surveys show that women, even full-time working mothers, still do most of the chores in the home. Ask yourself if this is fair – there's no reason why cooking and cleaning can't be shared.

✳ Tasks such as dealing with carers and teachers and taking and fetching from school used to be seen as a mother's responsibility. But more fathers are fitting daily activities like the school run or taking their child to the doctor into their working day.

✳ It used to be thought that mothers put children to bed, but most fathers enjoy the bedtime routine, especially if they've been away from their children all day.

✳ The idea – prevalent not so long ago – that it was somehow demeaning for a man to push a pram is now laughable. Men are pleased to be seen doing this and are also more than happy to take their children out without their partners.

Timing it right

Your attitude to parenting

Parenting is not an exact science. However right the decision to have a child may seem at the time, it may be helpful to ask yourselves the following questions. If you answer "yes" to more than five, you may need to think more about your attitude to parenting:

✳ Do you already have ambitions for your child's future?

✳ Are you uncertain about how parental actions affect children?

✳ Have you still got to work out some of your views on parenting?

✳ Do you think that after the birth, instinct will take over and you'll know exactly how to behave towards your child?

✳ Are you worried that you and your partner have different ideas about parenting?

✳ Do you believe in a strict routine for a newborn baby?

✳ Do you think a baby would benefit from such a routine?

✳ Can you spoil a young baby?

✳ Do you believe that babies cry for no reason?

✳ Will you leave investigating childcare until after the birth?

✳ Are your views on babycare at odds with those of your partner?

✳ Will you find it hard to tolerate all the disorder of a new baby?

✳ Do you foresee any conflict with family members about the way you intend to care for your baby?

It's rare for a couple to feel that everything is just right and that the perfect moment has arrived to have a child, but now that we have control over our fertility, it gives time for all the options to be considered carefully.

Making the decision

For many people, finance and accommodation may be the most pressing issues when making the decision whether or not to become parents. Others may look at their personal freedom, and how having a child may affect it. In today's society, where more and more women are finding satisfaction in the progress of their careers, making the decision to break off and have a child can be extraordinarily difficult. Although many companies – and countries – are providing increasingly generous maternity leave and benefits, this may not compensate for the fact that having a baby could delay your career prospects, especially if you want to spend more than just a few months at home with your baby. This is one reason why many women, particularly those with satisfying or high-powered jobs, are waiting to start a family at least until their 30s, when they feel that they've reached a level of achievement that enables them to stand back from their careers for a time with confidence.

Making space for parenthood

Men also need to think about how their work commitments may impact upon their relationship with their children. Many older men who become parents for a second time in a new relationship have acknowledged that they regretted having missed out on their first family's childhood because pressures of work effectively separated them from their children. Childhood passes quickly and you only have one chance with any child, so think about how much time you will be able to give to her.

Practical considerations

You can bring up a child in anything upwards from a two-room apartment – if there's a separate space for the baby, that's ideal. If you're thinking of moving into a larger home to accommodate future children, try to move before you become pregnant; otherwise it's best to wait until after your baby is born. You don't want the double pressure of a new baby and moving house. No one pretends there isn't a financial implication in parenthood, but the cost of having a baby is largely dependent on what a couple sees as essential. Be assured that no baby in a carrycot with one or two loving parents ever lay awake wondering why she didn't have a smart crib with Brahms' lullaby wafting from the attached electronic musical box. Nevertheless, it makes good sense to make the best of what's on offer. Look at your likely overall income and expenditure once the baby is born, taking account of benefits available (see p.184), and plan accordingly. Whenever your purse allows you to shop, invest in the basic minimum (see p.74); leave luxuries until you can really afford them.

Partnership or marriage

If you're in a long-term stable relationship, but are unmarried, you probably had good reason for choosing this kind of partnership. Now that you're considering parenthood, is there a case for reconsidering your position? Has either or both of you anything to gain from marrying and, more importantly, has your prospective child? One of the reasons most commonly given by prospective parents for marrying before the birth of a baby used to be to ensure the father was the legal parent of his child, but in the UK the law is now that if the father is on the birth certificate he has equal parental rights, even if not married to the mother. Clearly neither of you would want to encounter problems in gaining access to your child in the event of your relationship breaking down. However unlikely this may seem at present, no one can see into the future and most couples would want to guarantee that their baby always has the equal benefit of both parents, even if at some time they may not live together any more.

Changing relationships

Sometimes new parents haven't bargained for the fact that their relationships with family and friends will change. More importantly perhaps, the dynamics of their own relationship will also change. No time is better spent before you even start trying for a baby than in exploring together what these differences might be (see p.128).

Grandparents You both know the personalities of the grandparents and you may see difficulties ahead because their views may not be the same as yours. You'll find later that agreement with grandparents about how you're going to set limits for your child is invaluable. It's also a good idea to agree that you'll both gently but firmly resist any attempt by them to dictate methods of parenting to you. You can, however, ask them to help you to implement yours. But it's also wise to listen to their views or you may be passing up good advice based on real experience.

Your friends Once you have children you may not be available to your friends as much as you were before, so they'll appreciate it if you retain your identity as a friend rather than a parent while you're with them. Bear in mind also that you'll meet other people with babies with whom you'll forge friendships, based on the shared experience of new parenthood.

The impact at work Try also to rehearse in advance what difference the advent of the baby may have at work. You may never have clock-watched in your life before now, but it's difficult not to when you're aching to get back to your baby – and this is just as true for fathers as it is for mothers. However, your colleagues, no matter how sympathetic, have the right to assume that you'll be as good value as you were before. If you can see possible pitfalls, be upfront and negotiate; you won't always be a new parent and lost trust is difficult to re-establish.

Questioning your reasons

Even if you think you both really want a baby, it's still sensible to think about all the issues. The following questions don't have right or wrong answers, but provide what I hope will be a useful starting point for you:

✳ Does the idea of having a baby seem to be the instinctive next step for you both?

✳ Have you always taken it for granted that you would have children?

✳ Do you just want a child, or do you want a child specifically with your partner?

✳ Does one of you want this baby more than the other? If so, what effect has this had on your relationship?

✳ Do you want to have a baby because you think it will strengthen your relationship with your partner?

✳ What images do you see when thinking about life with your baby? Do they include sleepless nights and dirty nappies?

✳ What will you miss most about being a couple rather than a trio?

✳ Have you any firm personal ambitions that could be compromised by having a baby?

✳ Do you want a baby to make up for areas in your life that you find unsatisfactory?

✳ Is any part of your motivation to please family members, such as grandparents?

✳ Are you and your partner quite clear about the commitment each of you will make to the baby?

Preparing for parenthood

Pregnancy is an exciting time for you both, but your
excitement can also be tinged with apprehension,
uncertainty, and – if the pregnancy is a surprise – even
dismay. Each person's reaction to the knowledge that
he or she is going to become a parent is different, but
luckily nature has made sure that there is plenty of
time to get used to the idea during the 40 or so weeks
from conception to birth. Pregnancy is not an illness,
but it does put a lot of strain on a woman's body. So if
you're planning to become parents it makes sense to
think about your fitness well before you conceive and
to look after yourselves during the pregnancy. Once
the pregnancy is confirmed, you will both feel happier
if you follow its progress by attending antenatal
checks together and finding out as much as possible
about how your baby develops in the womb. It will
help you both to understand the minor discomforts
and emotional ups and downs that a pregnant
woman sometimes feels, and to face up to the slight
possibility of something unexpected happening.

Plan for pregnancy

JUST FOR MUM

Your due date will be calculated as 40 weeks from the first day of your last period, so you need to take that into account when planning your pre-pregnancy fitness.

Why fitness is important

There are a number of physical changes during pregnancy. Here are a few: the womb increases in volume (muscle) 1,000 times; the womb increases in weight (protein) 30 times; the work done by a mother's heart increases 50 per cent; the volume of her blood increases by one-third; her kidneys filter 50 per cent more blood.

Preventing anaemia

If you're anaemic, your heart is overworked, which can affect your baby. A blood test would reveal anaemia and it may be necessary to take iron supplements.

Avoiding birth defects

Folic acid reduces the risk of some birth defects like spina bifida. It's a good idea to start increasing folic acid intake three months before you stop contraception, and for three months after you conceive. Good food sources are green leafy vegetables, cereals, and bread, or you can take supplements.

Pre-existing medical problems

If you regularly take drugs for a medical condition, let your doctor know before you try for a baby, as the dose may have to be changed once you're pregnant.

When you decide to become parents, it makes sense to prepare yourselves in advance. To have a healthy baby, research shows that by far the most important factors are your own and your partner's fitness and nutrition.

Timing of the birth

Ideally you should begin to think about it at least a year before the time you'd like your baby to be born. It's a good idea to allow at least three months to get your bodies to peak pre-conception fitness (see opposite). There are other issues you may want to take into account as well. If you're planning to move house, or know that work commitments are going to take you away from home at a specific time of year, you'll want to avoid allowing these to clash with the possible arrival of your baby. Some parents may want to take account of whether their baby is born in winter or summer. Most education systems involve an autumn start to the academic year and there is evidence to suggest that some children born in the summer, the youngest in their school year group, may not achieve as well academically as the older and more mature children who are born in the winter.

✳ Routine health precautions

What to look at	What to do
Smoking	Smoking reduces fertility, especially in men as it lowers their sperm count. Give up before you try for a baby; smoking during pregnancy – direct or passive – harms your unborn child.
Alcohol	Alcohol can damage both sperm and the egg (ovum), so prospective parents should consume no more than five units a week for women, ten for men. (One unit = one small glass of wine or a half pint of beer.)
Drugs and medication	Many medicinal and street drugs affect fertility. In particular, cannabis reduces sperm production; the effects can take months to wear off. Consult your doctor if you're taking regular medication.
Pre-pregnancy screening	Well before trying for a baby, have a blood test for rubella (German measles) immunity and get immunized if necessary; have a cervical smear test and any treatment; check for sexually transmitted diseases.
Environmental factors	Make sure you avoid X-rays, hot saunas, and pollutants such as dioxins and PCBs in household products.

Delaying parenthood

More women are now delaying childbearing into their 30s or even early 40s.
A pregnant woman over 35 will be monitored more closely, but women's
general health and fitness have improved so much that the older pregnant
mother is no longer likely to have the same risks of earlier generations.
In addition, couples starting a family in their 30s are more likely to have
planned the baby, be in a stable relationship, and be financially secure.
But leaving conception until later does increase the time you might have
to wait to conceive – an average of six months when you're 35, as opposed
to four months when you're 25 (see p.20).

When to stop contraception

If you've been using straightforward barrier methods, such as the condom
or diaphragm, you can safely conceive as soon as you stop using them.
However, most doctors recommend at least one normal period after
ceasing other forms of contraception before you try to conceive.
The pill It's best to stop the pill three months beforehand, but a month
would do, so long as you have one normal period before conceiving.
Intra-uterine device (IUD) The same timescale would apply to an IUD,
so have it removed three months before you intend to get pregnant. Have
at least one normal period before stopping all contraception – use a barrier
method in the meantime.

How fitness helps you both

As a prospective mother, your body undergoes a great deal of physical
change (see box opposite). The fitter you are, the more easily your body
will cope. But fitness and lifestyle may also change a man's ability to
father a child, by affecting sperm production (see box above). Think about
your health and lifestyle at least three months before you plan to stop
contraception. As well as improving your fitness, it will increase your
chances of conceiving without delay and of having a healthy baby.

A healthy diet

Adjusting your diet shouldn't require uncomfortable changes. Include
good-quality carbohydrates, such as wholewheat bread, rice, and potatoes.
Keep your animal fat intake down and use olive or sunflower oil for
cooking. Eat lots of fresh fruit and vegetables every day (see p.36). Don't
skip meals, avoid processed foods, outlaw the liquid lunch, and eat a
hearty breakfast, though not a fried one. Start taking folic acid at least
three months before you're planning to conceive.

Taking exercise

Exercise makes a contribution to becoming a healthy potential parent,
so if you don't already do so, start a gentle exercise programme together,
such as jogging, swimming, or gym sessions. Try for 20 minutes' exercise
that increases your heart rate at least three times a week. However, bear
in mind that very strenuous training or dieting may reduce fertility.

✳ JUST FOR DAD

Your partner's fitness and lifestyle
obviously have a bearing on her ability
to conceive, but your own fitness is
also a crucial factor. If you aren't fit,
you may not donate the best genetic
material to your child in your sperm.

Why your lifestyle matters
Male fertility not only depends on
the number of sperm produced, but
also on the health of that sperm.
This is affected by all sorts of lifestyle
factors, such as smoking, alcohol, and
drugs (see left), and also stress. Try to
re-order your life if it's stressful, and
look at your diet and fitness.

Genetic counselling

Seek advice and have tests in
advance if a genetic disorder, such
as cystic fibrosis, muscular dystrophy,
thalassaemia, or haemophilia, runs in
your family.

What happens in counselling
The counsellor explains the condition
and your family background and
shows you the pattern of inheritance
through past generations. Not all
carriers of a defective gene get the
condition. If it's recessive it can be
masked by a healthy version, whereas
a dominant gene will always show up.
With a dominant gene, the chances
of your baby being affected are one
in two; with a recessive gene they
are one in four.

Conception

Increasing chances of conception

The following tips might help you conceive more quickly:

✱ Try to have intercourse during your most fertile period (see right). This period is signalled by the texture of your cervical mucus, which becomes clear, thin, and slippery, making it easier for the sperm to swim up through your cervix. Ovulation usually occurs 24 hours after this type of mucus is at its most profuse.

✱ Avoid lovemaking for a couple of days before your fertile period to help build up sperm numbers.

✱ The "missionary position" (man on top) may be most effective for conception, particularly if the woman lies down for half an hour afterwards.

✱ Cut down on caffeine. It may interfere with the embryo's ability to implant in the wall of the uterus.

Conceiving a baby is the ultimate expression of a loving sexual relationship between partners. You could conceive within a few months of deciding to have a baby, especially if you have intercourse when you're most fertile.

When you're fertile

A woman is fertile only when she is ovulating – when an egg has been released from her ovary. This is nearly always 14 days after the first day of the last menstrual period. You can therefore predict ovulation by tracking your periods in a diary, or you can do an ovulation test on your urine, which may be helpful if you don't have a regular 28-day cycle. Three-quarters of all couples who have unprotected intercourse will conceive within nine months, and 90 per cent in 18 months, but from the age of about 25, the fertility of both men and women does start to wane.

What happens when you conceive

As the egg can survive for 36 hours and sperm for 48 hours, your fertile period can last for about three days. When ovulation and intercourse overlap, sperm swim up through the cervix and uterus to meet the egg, and fertilization with one sperm usually happens in the upper end of the Fallopian tube. It then takes three to four days for the fertilized cell (called a zygote) to reach the uterus and implant in the endometrium – the specially prepared uterine lining. The process of implantation is called nidation; the fertilized egg, now called a blastocyst, burrows into the lining and quickly forms a primitive placenta; seven days after fertilization, the blastocyst is embedded and growing.

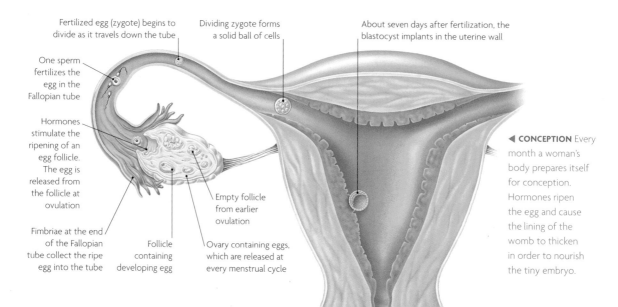

Fertilized egg (zygote) begins to divide as it travels down the tube

Dividing zygote forms a solid ball of cells

About seven days after fertilization, the blastocyst implants in the uterine wall

One sperm fertilizes the egg in the Fallopian tube

Hormones stimulate the ripening of an egg follicle. The egg is released from the follicle at ovulation

Fimbriae at the end of the Fallopian tube collect the ripe egg into the tube

Follicle containing developing egg

Ovary containing eggs, which are released at every menstrual cycle

Empty follicle from earlier ovulation

◀ **CONCEPTION** Every month a woman's body prepares itself for conception. Hormones ripen the egg and cause the lining of the womb to thicken in order to nourish the tiny embryo.

Finding out if you're pregnant

Many women suspect that they are pregnant within days of conception, but the single most obvious indicator is a missed period, and anyone who has a regular menstrual cycle will realize something has happened once they are three or four days late. Other women may not realize for two or three weeks, especially if they continue to have so-called "withdrawal" bleeding, where pre-pregnancy hormones still present in the body cause a weak menstrual bleed. They may, however, suspect that they are pregnant from other physical signs (see below). Either way, you'll probably want to confirm it as soon as possible with a pregnancy test. You can buy pregnancy test kits that confirm whether or not you are pregnant from the day your period is due. If you can wait a day or two longer, you'll get a more reliable result; you may wrongly test negative if you try too early. You can also ask your doctor to do the test.

Other signs of pregnancy

✳ Tender, heavy breasts that may tingle a little. Your bra may seem a touch too tight, the veins on your breasts more prominent than usual, and your nipples and areolae may seem redder than usual.
✳ A feeling of nausea. Although often called "morning sickness", it may happen at any time of the day.
✳ A super-sensitive sense of smell, and a metallic taste in your mouth.
✳ The need to pass urine more frequently than usual.
✳ Feeling incredibly tired, especially in the evening.

Waiting a long time to conceive

If you've been trying to conceive for 12 months without success (or eight months if you're over 35), you could approach your doctor to talk about being referred for investigations into your fertility. Finding out that you are unable to conceive without help can be very stressful, but many couples discover that taking this first step is in itself an antidote to stress and they may go on to conceive before talking to the specialist.

Preparing yourselves for fertility investigations
The test process can be long and difficult, so both partners must enter willingly into the investigation. Before you embark on it, you should think carefully about the strain (including

perhaps financial) of what you are about to do. Many relationships have crumbled under the stress of infertility investigations, and living with the uncertainty, and the unpleasant and invasive tests, can be extremely hard.

Sharing the responsibility
Be aware that your ability as a couple to conceive – your fertility – is the sum of both your fertilities. Investigations may indicate a problem that will probably be treatable, and it's worth remembering that in as many as half of infertile couples, the problem lies with the man. Infertility is nobody's fault, you share the problem. Don't apportion blame, feel resentment or guilt, or you'll drive a wedge between you that may make conception even more elusive.

Boy or girl?

Nature does well in maintaining a balance of about 103 boys to 100 girls and I'm not in favour of trying to interfere with that. With ultrasound and fetal cell investigations, you may be able to find out the sex of your baby during pregnancy – if you want to.

What determines a baby's sex?
Men produce sperm with 22 chromosomes plus either one X (female) or one Y (male) sex chromosome. Women's eggs also have 22 corresponding chromosomes, but they produce only an X sex chromosome. A zygote fertilized by an X sperm will be a girl; a Y sperm results in a boy.

Is it possible to influence a baby's sex?
Although no method with any scientific validity has been developed, by noting the different characteristics of X and Y sperm, it's possible to suggest a way of increasing your chances of conceiving the gender you want:

✱ X sperm are larger and slower than Y sperm and X sperm live longer than Y sperm.

✱ To increase the chances of a girl, intercourse should be two to three days before ovulation, as only X sperm survive long enough to meet the egg when it's finally released.

✱ There's a higher chance that a Y sperm will fertilize an egg on the day of ovulation because it will reach the egg more quickly, and the baby will be a boy.

✱ Frequent ejaculation lowers the proportion of Y sperm, so a girl is likely. Infrequent sex increases the proportion of Y sperm and the chances of a boy.

Adjusting to pregnancy

Pregnancy after loss of a baby

A miscarriage, stillbirth (see p.35), or even a termination in the past, can affect how you both feel about your current pregnancy.

Rekindling grief

Even if your earlier pregnancy or pregnancies were some time ago, being pregnant again may rekindle your grief. Talk things over with your partner or a close friend.

Reliving the past

If you had a miscarriage, you'll both find it difficult to be relaxed about the new pregnancy. Take heart from the fact that most women who miscarry go on to have a healthy child the next time.

After a termination

If you had a termination due to abnormality, you're likely to be offered diagnostic tests in this pregnancy as soon as practically possible. Again, take heart from the fact that many such problems are extremely unlikely to recur. If your termination was for other reasons, you may suffer feelings of guilt that you're going ahead with this pregnancy. It's important to talk about this rather than bottling up feelings that may affect your relationship with your new baby.

After a stillbirth

If you had a stillbirth, you'll probably be wondering whether or not this baby is alive and find the end of your new pregnancy almost unbearable. Although you'll be monitored carefully, talk to your consultant – you may be able to have the baby days or even weeks before the due date.

Becoming a parent is one of the most profound experiences you'll ever have. It's an essentially positive and deeply satisfying experience – but you're going to find it shattering, exhausting, and incredibly hard work too.

Thinking ahead

Your pregnancy is a time to ponder on the changes ahead – for each of you as individuals and for you as a couple. In many ways it's impossible to describe exactly what's ahead in pregnancy until you're there, but it's certainly true that you can be as prepared as it's possible to be by asking questions, reading, and talking to friends who've already gone through it.

Your differing reactions

Men and women often respond differently to the news of pregnancy; elation may fade into fear, anxiety, or depression at the thought of the responsibilities looming, and the changes that are unavoidable. Changes in relationships can be threatening at the best of times. Those that take place in early pregnancy are particularly taxing because they have to be played out when the mother is feeling tired and possibly anxious, and the father may be feeling ambivalent about the new situation (see p.24). Use the months ahead to prepare, as much as possible, for what's in store, but try to enjoy your pregnancy, too. Life will, after all, never be the same again. If you can, go away for a weekend or have a holiday when you're between four and seven months pregnant – it will give you plenty of time and space to share your feelings together.

Feelings about pregnancy

At first, the physical changes common to most pregnant women may colour your view of the pregnancy. Many women find the physical discomforts of the first three months – tiredness, nausea, tender breasts – begin almost as soon as the pregnancy has been confirmed, sometimes within a few days of missing a period (see p.21). This can take couples by surprise, turning initial delight into apprehension and uncertainty. However, this reaction is usually temporary, lasting about 12 weeks; after this you'll suddenly realize that you're not waking up with nausea and a fuzzy head, that you're full of energy, and that instead of just looking thicker around the waist, you're developing a recognizable "bump" that announces your pregnancy to the world, and of which you can be proud!

Planned or unplanned

Whether the pregnancy was planned or not has a bearing on your attitude to it. An unplanned pregnancy may be welcomed by one partner more than the other (and this is often the father rather than the mother), or both of you could be ambivalent about it, especially if you have financial worries. Whether your pregnancy is planned or unplanned, there may well be implications for your career, especially if you work for a company that doesn't have a sympathetic attitude to parenthood, even though they have to stand by their legal obligations. This is more important for working women than men, but experience shows that it is possible to resume a career even when you've had a long break for birth and childcare (see p.170). Once you know you're pregnant, talk to your employer about the options as soon as possible to find out what maternity leave is on offer (see p.184). This will help to allay any fears you have about your career.

If your pregnancy was assisted

Your attitude to your pregnancy is bound to be affected if you've had to wait a long time to conceive, and perhaps had treatment to assist conception. You'll feel an enormous sense of relief that your longed-for baby is at last on the way, but may worry about doing anything that may lead to miscarriage, so there may be a tendency to treat the pregnancy like an illness. Try to avoid this; most specialists in assisted conception will hand their patients over to the normal maternity services once the pregnancy is established – if anything is going to go wrong, it is most likely to happen in the first eight to ten weeks, and you'll have been warned about this. Even if you've had to endure quite lengthy and invasive treatments to achieve the pregnancy, try not to dwell on them and look forward instead to the birth of your healthy baby.

Giving the news

You might want to tell everyone straight away that you're having a baby; on the other hand, you might want to hug your secret to yourself for a while. You may surprise yourself at how it comes out, depending on who you're telling, because many people find admitting they are about to become parents to a third party seems to make it real for the first time. The support of friends and family can help to overcome any feelings of doubt; alternatively you may find yourself confessing to your closest friend your ambivalence to the whole thing, even though on the surface you appear to be delighted. Bear in mind that in the event of a miscarriage, the more people you've told, the more distressing it may be for you if you have to explain that you've lost the baby (see p.35).

Pre-birth bonding

Although it's wonderful to be able to see your baby moving when you have your first scan (see p.29), many women feel that the bonding process really begins once they feel it. Though this may not happen until about 20 weeks in a first pregnancy, it's an advantage you have which your partner lacks – so share your feelings as much as possible and encourage him to feel your tummy. First sensations of movement often coincide with a change in energy levels, so you'll probably be feeling better about yourself and the baby than you ever thought possible to start with.

JUST FOR DAD

The physical changes of pregnancy can affect how your partner feels about it. Preparing for this should help you deal with any low moments she may have.

Your partner's feelings

✳ Exhaustion is common in early pregnancy – it's probably caused by all the hormones that her body suddenly has to deal with. Encourage your partner to take things easy, and look forward to the middle months when she'll probably feel incredibly energetic and wide awake. The "bloom" of pregnancy at this time will make your partner look wonderful – so make sure you tell her!

✳ The effect of pregnancy hormones combined with the whole idea of becoming a parent could make her much more emotional than usual. Be supportive and sympathetic.

✳ She may worry about the fact that she'll inevitably be gaining weight. Don't draw attention to this. Be positive about how she looks and compliment her. It's a very bad idea to diet in pregnancy, but she doesn't need to eat for two either. Encourage her with the fact that most of the fat gained in pregnancy is stored to nourish breastfeeding, and is burned off remarkably quickly once she starts feeding (see p.78).

✳ Your partner may feel that she's lost control of her life because there's always someone else with ideas on what's best for her. Don't add to this – she knows her body best and when it comes to decisions about it, she should have the last word.

The expectant father

Your relationship with your partner will change before the baby is born, so it'll help to be prepared for this.

Understanding your partner

✳ It's very easy for men to feel left out so make sure you involve your partner as much as possible.

✳ Expecting a baby is an external experience for your partner and it may be very difficult for him to empathize with the invisible changes taking place within you. Remember, his day-to-day life will stay much the same until after the baby is born.

✳ Talk to your partner about how you're feeling. You may have big mood swings and go through periods of feeling insecure and unattractive. Sit down with your partner and explain how you're feeling.

Affection and sex

✳ Your partner may be anxious about your wellbeing and treat you as if you're ill. This kind of attention can be suffocating, so tell your partner if you don't like it. Also, remind him that you're as keen as he is not to do anything to harm the baby. Equally, if your partner isn't giving you enough attention, tell him.

✳ Your desire to have sex may well change at different stages of your pregnancy. If you don't want intercourse, tell your partner.

✳ Talk candidly to your partner about sex so that it does not become an issue between you.

One of the most exciting moments of your life will probably be when you find out that you're going to be a father. The emotional impact is just as real for you as for your partner, so talk about your feelings and get involved in the pregnancy and birth plans.

Understanding your conflicting emotions

The pregnancy may not seem real for the first couple of months – not least because your partner will physically look the same. Don't worry if you feel differently from her about the pregnancy; it's an internal experience for her and an external one for you, and you don't suddenly become one person with one set of feelings just because you are having a baby together. However, once you see your partner's body begin to change and, later, when you have felt the baby move, the idea of having a baby will become more real. It is at this time that your feelings of joy and excitement may be replaced by fears and worries; whatever your family set-up, it's normal for a man to begin to worry about being able to provide for his family. Be open about your feelings and express your concerns.

Having a child can be an extra financial burden, especially if your partner is going to give up her job, but try not to make life-changing decisions, such as seeking promotion. It's difficult to know whether you'll want that extra responsibility once you are a parent. Remember, as a father, you have more than material possessions to offer your child.

How you can participate

Being an expectant father is the one time in your life when you're quite likely to feel out of control. This feeling of being an outsider will not be helped by the way other people treat you – well-meaning female friends and relatives may unconsciously push you out of what they see as their territory. You may also find that the professionals, such as obstetricians and midwives, direct their conversations at your partner more than you.

Take the initiative

Don't step back and allow your female relatives and friends to be more involved than you. Tell your friends and colleagues your news – you may be subject to a certain amount of teasing, but people may also view you as more responsible. Try to find out as much as you can about the pregnancy so that you can understand the changes taking place in your partner's body.

Plan for the birth together

You will need to discuss with your partner the type of birth that she wants (see p.26) and decide what your involvement will be. Be involved in all arrangements and plans for the birth. Go to antenatal appointments so that you can hear your baby's heartbeat. If possible go to antenatal classes

Taking an active role

What to do	How it can help you
Talk to your partner	The best way to understand how your partner is feeling, and what is going on in her body, is to talk to her. Ask her what it feels like to feel the baby move; discuss your plans for the birth together; find out if she's got particular discomforts. She'll appreciate your interest.
Go to antenatal classes	If you go to antenatal classes (especially the father-only sessions), you'll have an opportunity to learn about the birth and talk through your own concerns. This will help you to work out the best way to support your partner and enable you to be more involved in birth choices.
Talk to other fathers	Get to know the other expectant fathers at antenatal classes – they will probably be feeling the same as you and be glad of someone to talk to. Talk to friends and colleagues who already have babies; find out what their experiences were like and ask them for advice.
Read about pregnancy and parenting	Read pregnancy and parenting books and any leaflets you're given. The more you understand about what's going on during the pregnancy, the more familiar it will become and it can help you to understand how your partner is feeling. It will also enable you to ask the right questions.
Ask questions	Go to antenatal appointments with your partner so that you can meet the professionals and be present at the examinations. As a first-time parent, there will be things you don't understand and need to know about. If you ask questions of professionals, they are more likely to involve you.

Prenatal bonding

Babies can hear sounds outside the womb by five or six months; if you talk to your baby, he will bond to your voice and, in fact, he can hear your low-pitched voice more clearly than his mother's. To help you to bond with your baby:

✳ Gently massage your partner's tummy and feel your baby move.

✳ Talk to your baby, and nuzzle him through your partner's skin.

✳ Use inner tubes of kitchen towel to listen to the heartbeat.

✳ Go to scans with your partner to see your baby develop (see p.29).

too. Visit the hospital and delivery room with your partner. If possible, go with her to the scans so that you can see your baby developing and watch him move on the ultrasound monitor. Talk about the fact you're going to be a father, and ask as many questions as you want – most of all, enjoy it! You will also need to talk to your employer about taking time off to go to the antenatal appointments as well as the birth.

The birth plan

Contribute to the birth plan. Discuss the issues raised by the birth plan (see p.27) with your partner, but don't impose your views. If your partner feels strongly about issues such as a drug-free labour (see p.43), respect her feelings, but talk about the advantages and disadvantages too. Look forward to being present at the birth. Remember, being at your child's birth is probably one of the most poignant experiences you'll ever have and holding your baby in the first seconds after the birth is proven to help you bond with your child.

▲ **SHARE THE PLANNING** Get as involved as you can in the planning of the birth and give your partner plenty of love and support.

Options for antenatal care

Antenatal classes

Antenatal classes are helpful and supportive for you both.

What classes do

They will help explain a lot of the choices available before, during, and after the birth and will tell you about labour, birth, and babycare. You'll also meet other expectant parents with due dates near yours.

Where to find classes

If you're planning a hospital delivery, hospital-based classes can be useful as they'll help familiarise you with procedures and will include a tour of the labour ward. Community classes may be run by community midwives, providing "shared" care (see right) in your local health or community centre or at your doctor's surgery. Parent education networks or active birth groups (see p.187) are usually run in teachers' own homes and are much more likely to focus on natural childbirth and alternative birth options than classes that are run by hospitals or midwives.

There's now a huge choice in maternity care, although how wide the choice is will depend on what's available in your area. Looking at your antenatal options also means looking at your birth options.

Who can deliver care?

Once you know you're pregnant, your first call will probably be to your family doctor. Your doctor will tell you the different options for antenatal care available in your area and you can also talk through where the baby will be born. Don't feel you have to make your mind up on any of these issues immediately – go away and think before finalizing details.

Shared care Antenatal care may be offered by your doctor, in association with community midwives and the hospital. Routine checks will be done by your doctor and the community midwife, and you'll go to the hospital for specialist checks, such as ultrasound. This type of care is helpful if you live some way from the hospital. However, you may not meet the midwife who delivers your baby in the hospital before the event.

Midwife care In some places, antenatal care is given almost entirely by community or hospital midwives working in teams, or under the "Domino" system (see opposite). They are based at either a local health centre or hospital and can also arrange home births. You'll be able to build up a relationship with the midwives who will also deliver your baby.

▶ **INDEPENDENT MIDWIVES** If you want to be cared for solely by midwives, you might want to consider hiring an independent one. This is expensive, but it does allow you to arrange your care, labour, and birth exactly as you want it.

Hospital care You'll be cared for by hospital-based doctors and midwives. The care may lack the informality of other options, but if you have any complications, have an existing medical condition, or are having twins, it's probably the wisest and safest choice.

Where to have your baby

Thinking about antenatal care also means deciding where you want your baby to be delivered. Whatever type of antenatal care you're having, you'll be booked in to the hospital at the first appointment (see p.28).

Hospital birth

Having a first baby in hospital feels right to many couples. There's plenty of backup on hand and in most hospitals access to the full range of pain relief.

Advantages Having your baby in hospital doesn't necessarily mean opting for high-tech – many hospitals have special low-tech birthing rooms where you'll be free to walk around in labour and where intervention will be kept to a minimum. In some areas, under a scheme known as "Domino", a midwife comes to your home once you're in labour, accompanies you to hospital, delivers your baby, and returns home with you as little as four hours later. If you like the idea of being back home as soon as possible, but want the medical backup for the delivery, this option could be ideal for you.

Disadvantages Having a baby in hospital does mean agreeing to policies that may cramp your style. You may, for example, be given electronic fetal monitoring, at least for a time, which may make it difficult for you to stay active and upright, but this is no longer routine for low-risk mothers.

Home birth

If you feel you'd like a home birth, talk to your midwife. Most midwives are happy to attend a home birth unless there are good reasons why it may not be safe. Alternatively, consult an independent midwife (see opposite).

Advantages Home is a more relaxed place to have a baby than hospital. You're far less likely to need emergency treatment if you remain active as far into labour as you can. Your chances for a straightforward, problem-free delivery at home are good, even if this is your first child.

Disadvantages You don't have immediate access to emergency treatment, so if anything untoward happens or your labour fails to progress, you might need to be transferred to hospital. You also won't have access to pain relief such as an epidural (see p.43), though you can have pethidine.

Delivery in a birth centre

Birth centres are usually sited near or in hospitals, but are self-contained and designed to have a less medical feel. They may be staffed by family doctors and community midwives or run solely by midwives. Staff often wear their own clothes, and you'll probably be given your own room in which to spend your labour, give birth, and then remain after the delivery. These centres can provide an excellent halfway house, giving you the informality of a home birth with the safety net of high-tech care nearby.

Your birth plan

Once you've considered all your antenatal care and birth options, it's worth preparing a simple birth plan in consultation with your doctor and midwife. This should be kept with your hospital notes. Wait until you're about 32–36 weeks pregnant, as by that time you'll probably have discovered whether there are any special factors in your pregnancy that might affect some of your requests. You also need to be prepared to be flexible because things may not go according to plan on the day. Your birth plan might include the following:

✴ Who you want to be present at the birth with you.

✴ Your views on interventions, such as induction, the artificial speeding up of labour (see p.50), and electronic fetal monitoring (see p.44).

✴ Your views on active labour, and whether you would like the possibility of using a birthing pool (see p.43).

✴ Your preferences for pain relief (see p.43), and the use of breathing and relaxation techniques.

✴ Whether you mind student doctors or midwives being present during your labour and birth.

✴ What position you might adopt to deliver your baby (see p.46).

✴ Whether you would prefer not to have an episiotomy (see p.46).

✴ Whether you mind if the delivery of your placenta is speeded up with syntometrine or whether you'd prefer it to be delivered naturally (see p.48).

Your antenatal care

The physical examination

At every antenatal appointment, various checks will always be done to rule out potentially dangerous medical conditions.

Blood pressure

A rise in blood pressure could mean you're at risk of pre-eclampsia (see p.35).

Urine test

Your urine will be tested for the presence of protein, which could mean an infection or, later, pre-eclampsia; glucose or sugar, which could signal diabetes; and ketones, chemicals that indicate you're not eating enough.

Abdominal check

The midwife will feel your abdomen to check the size of your uterus. She'll also listen to your baby's heartbeat, using either a Pinard stethoscope or a sonicaid, an electronic stethoscope that amplifies the baby's heartbeat so you can hear it (see below).

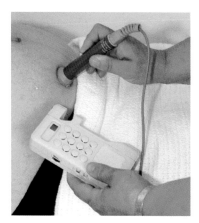

▲ **YOUR BABY'S HEARTBEAT** It's a thrill the first time you hear your baby's heartbeat amplified through a sonicaid.

In general, antenatal checks are to ensure that all is going well with your pregnancy – that you are healthy, and that your baby is growing properly.

Your first appointment

Often known as the booking-in appointment, your first antenatal session may be quite long, lasting as much as an hour. It may be at your home, at the local health centre, or doctor's surgery, or at a hospital clinic. A midwife will take a detailed medical history, and will ask questions about your general health, your family's health, and your gynaecological and obstetric history. She will also ask whether or not this baby was planned, how long ago you stopped using contraceptives or what contraceptive you were using when you got pregnant, and the date of the first day of your last menstrual period. The midwife will also ask you how you feel and talk to you generally about your pregnancy. She'll offer advice on issues like diet, exercise, and maternity benefits. You can discuss what kind of delivery you'd like, though you don't have to decide at this time unless you're absolutely sure (see p.27). You'll probably be asked to bring a urine sample to each appointment.

The blood tests

You'll probably have some blood taken, which will be sent to the laboratory for analysis. Ask the midwife exactly what your blood will be checked for and why; it's routinely checked for iron content, blood group and rhesus status, rubella immunity, blood sugar levels, and sexually transmitted diseases. Most hospitals routinely do an HIV test. Other tests, such as one to check whether you've been exposed to toxoplasmosis (a parasitic disease that may affect your unborn baby) may be available. Blood isn't usually tested at every appointment, but in certain situations you'll be asked to give blood again at later appointments (see opposite), and most hospitals test at 28 weeks for anaemia, blood group antibodies, and diabetes. Your routine antenatal checkups will generally be shorter than your booking-in appointment. Between appointments, it's a good idea to write down any questions you may want to ask your midwife or doctor and keep them with your maternity notes so you remember to ask them.

Ultrasound scans

Ultrasound is now offered routinely to almost all pregnant women, as it enables the baby's age to be measured very accurately and can also detect visible abnormalities. Many hospitals offer two scans, one at about 12 weeks and the other at 16 to 20 weeks. The scans are carried out at the hospital, and your partner should be allowed into the examination room with you; this is a wonderful opportunity for a father to relate to his growing baby as you'll be able to see it moving about.

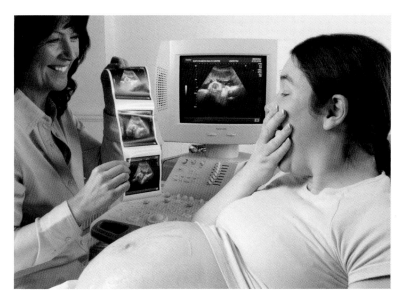

◀ **HAVING AN ULTRASOUND SCAN** The operator slowly scans across your abdomen with a hand-held instrument called a transducer that detects sound waves bounced off your uterus and baby's body. These are transmitted to a computer and monitor for visual interpretation.

✳ Specialist screening and diagnostic tests

If you're offered any of the screening or diagnostic tests for abnormalities (see chart below), it's helpful to ask yourselves what you'd do if you found your baby did have Down's syndrome or spina bifida. If the answer is that you wouldn't do anything, but continue with the pregnancy, it may not be worth having the tests. If you know you would have a termination, or wouldn't be able to decide until you had the information, then you may want to go ahead. Before any test, find out exactly what your baby is being tested for and whether there are any risks. You also need to know how accurate the test is, what information it will actually provide, and whether there's an alternative to having the test.

Test	How it is done	What it can tell you
Nuchal scan	A non-invasive scan at 11–13 weeks, measuring the thickness of the "nuchal pad" in the baby's neck. Often combined with a blood test.	A thick nuchal pad may indicate a higher risk of chromosomal defects, so you'll be offered a test such as CVS or amniocentesis later.
Triple (or Bart's) test	This blood test screens you for the risk of Down's syndrome. It is done at 15–16 weeks along with a scan to confirm dates.	Hormone levels indicate the risk of your baby being affected; if it is greater than one in 250, you'll be offered amniocentesis.
AFP test	A screening blood test that checks the level of alpha-fetoprotein (AFP) at about 15–18 weeks.	A higher or lower level than usual may indicate Down's syndrome or spina bifida.
Chorionic villus sampling (CVS)	A diagnostic test, in which a cannula (tube) is passed through the cervix at about 10–12 weeks to take cells from the developing placenta.	The cells are examined to check the baby's chromosomes for any abnormalities. CVS carries a small risk (about two per cent) of miscarriage.
Amniocentesis	A diagnostic test done at about 15 weeks. Guided by ultrasound, a needle takes a sample of amniotic fluid through the abdominal wall.	Chromosomes in fetal cells can be checked for abnormalities, such as Down's syndrome. There's a small risk (about two per cent) of miscarriage.
Fetal blood test (cordocentesis)	This rare diagnostic test is carried out after about 18–20 weeks. It takes blood from the umbilical cord.	Blood is tested for abnormal chromosomes or infections. There's a miscarriage risk of about one to two per cent.

The progress of pregnancy

Coping with common complaints

❋ Feeling sick is most common in the first three months. It may happen in the morning, but by no means always, and you may also vomit. Eating little but often rather than big meals helps. If you're vomiting incessantly, consult your doctor.

❋ You're more likely to get cramp in your legs or feet. It's not known exactly why, but you can relieve it by pulling your toes up hard towards your knee.

❋ Constipation is a common problem, caused by the presence of hormones that slow down the workings of the large intestine. Eat plenty of fibre, exercise regularly, and drink plenty of water. Iron pills may make it worse.

❋ Later in pregnancy, you may suffer from indigestion or heartburn, because your enlarging womb is pressing on your stomach. Prevent this by eating smaller meals more often, sitting up straight when eating, and avoiding spiced foods. Sipping milk, especially at night, can help if you have heartburn.

❋ Haemorrhoids – swollen varicose veins that protrude from the back passage – can occur in pregnancy due to pressure from the baby, especially if you're constipated. Eat plenty of fibre and avoid standing for long periods. Check with your doctor if they become very painful.

Having a baby growing inside you is like being part of a real-life miracle. Sometimes you'll pat your bump and feel you can hardly believe your child is in there. Take time to ponder on the wonder of what's happening; you'll both be laying the foundations for a baby who feels secure and wanted.

Following your pregnancy

No part of a woman's body escapes when she's carrying a baby, and you both need to keep that in mind. For instance, tender breasts that are getting ready for breastfeeding need to be treated gently by a father when he caresses them; the growing uterus pressing on your internal organs means that you must never be too far from a toilet during the last three months of pregnancy. The guide that follows is only a brief outline of the complex changes going on inside your body.

What's happened by three months

The first three months of pregnancy (the first trimester) are tremendously important in laying the foundations of your baby's healthy development. In spite of this, there are few visible signs of your baby's phenomenal growth, except that you may have been suffering morning sickness (p.21).

You at three months Your pregnancy is well established now:

❋ You'll really start to gain weight regularly; any morning sickness will soon disappear.

❋ The uterus is rising out of the pelvis and can now be felt.

❋ The risk of miscarriage is almost zero by this time.

❋ Your heart is working flat out and will continue to do throughout the rest of your pregnancy.

Your baby at three months She is fully formed, but needs to mature.

❋ She has a fully formed body, complete with fingers, toes, and ears.

❋ Her eyes move, though her eyelids are closed.

❋ Her body is covered with fine hair.

❋ She wriggles if poked – her muscles are growing.

What's happened by six months

The period from about the third to the sixth month (the second trimester) is when pregnancy sickness ends, your baby really grows, and you begin to feel her move. You're brimming with energy, vitality, and wellbeing.

You at six months You'll notice the following signs:

❋ You're putting on about 0.5kg (1lb) in weight per week.

❋ Your uterus is a good 5cm (2in) above the pelvis.

❋ You may have bouts of indigestion.

❋ From about 20 weeks, you'll feel your baby move.

AT SIX MONTHS You'll gain weight regularly each week and will feel healthier and more energetic.

FULL TERM Not long to wait now. Soon you and your partner will meet your new baby for the first time.

Your baby at six months He's well developed and growing:

* His hearing is acute, he can recognize your voice.

* He's becoming better proportioned – his body is now catching up with his head.

* He's well muscled, but thin. He'll start to put on fat now.

* His lungs are growing and maturing fast.

What's happened by nine months (full term)

The final 12 weeks or so of pregnancy, known as the third trimester, are when the baby puts on fat in preparation for birth and the body and lungs mature in preparation for independent life.

You in the last weeks of your pregnancy You may have to visit the antenatal clinic more often and you may notice the following signs:

* You may feel a "lightening" as your baby's head drops into the pelvis.

* It's more difficult to find a comfortable position for sleep.

* Your breasts secrete clear-coloured nutritious colostrum.

Your baby in the last weeks of your pregnancy He's preparing to be born:

* He weighs about 2.7–3.5kg (6–8lb) and he measures 35–38cm (14–15in) from crown to rump.

* His head is "engaged", lying just on top of your cervix.

* The placenta is 20–25cm (8–10in) across, 3cm (1in) thick, and there is 1.1 litres (2 pints) of amniotic fluid.

* His breasts may be swollen due to the action of your hormones.

Pregnancy at a glance

It's useful to be able to visualize what is happening by the end of each of the three phases, or trimesters, of pregnancy, so that you understand what is happening. By the end of the first trimester, your baby is recognizably human but tiny. The second trimester is a period of rapid growth, and during the third the baby gets longer and heavier.

✳ JUST FOR DAD

Although you're experiencing the pregnancy secondhand, following its progress helps you to become emotionally attached to your baby.

The progress of pregnancy

* Accompanying your partner to antenatal appointments (see p.28) enables you to find out together how your baby is growing.

* Remember that the baby is part of you as well as your partner. It's amazing to think that a single cell created from your sperm and your partner's egg (see p.20) can develop so rapidly.

* Understanding and learning about the impact of the growing baby and uterus on your partner's body helps you to be sympathetic when she suffers the inevitable discomforts.

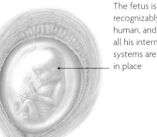

The fetus is recognizably human, and all his internal systems are in place

Hearing is developed; he may respond to noise. Skin is red and thin, with little fat beneath it

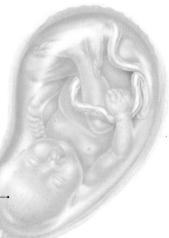

By full term, the baby is usually positioned head downwards

▲ **AT THREE MONTHS** Your uterus is about the size of a grapefruit and can just be felt above the pubic bone. Your baby's organs are formed and are now resistant to potential dangers, such as an infection and medication.

▲ **AT SIX MONTHS** Your baby's organs are fully formed, his face is that of a newborn, and he sucks his thumb. Your uterus is poised for labour. You may notice Braxton Hicks contractions (see p.42).

▲ **AT NINE MONTHS (FULL TERM)** You'll find you get breathless because your baby is now so big. His eyes can open and he's fat and healthy. If your baby is a boy, his testes have descended.

Difficult pregnancies

"Small for dates"

After reviewing the date of your last period and your expected date of delivery, both your heights, and scans of the baby, your pregnancy may be pronounced "small for dates". Don't worry, but doctors will keep an eye on you by:

✱ Giving you scans every two weeks for a while to ensure all's well and to check the placenta.

✱ Checking on the baby's heart rate for any sign of strain.

✱ Discussing with you the possibility of inducing your baby or delivering by Caesarean section (see p.52), to prevent the baby having to go through a vaginal delivery.

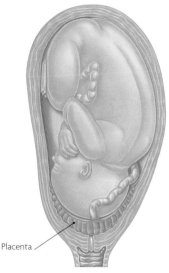

Placenta

▲ **PLACENTA PRAEVIA** The placenta embeds close to or across the cervix. Pressure from the baby may cause bleeding.

Although the majority of pregnancies proceed without incident, occasionally things don't go according to plan. When something unexpected causes concern, you're both going to feel extremely worried about it, especially if all has gone well up to this point. It helps enormously to face what's ahead together and to get as much information as you can.

Pregnancy and pre-existing medical conditions

Any existing long-term medical condition means that your pregnancy will be carefully monitored. Medical conditions like asthma, epilepsy, heart disease, or kidney disease don't in themselves make pregnancy and labour difficult but they may increase the risk of complications. If you take care of yourself, have meticulous antenatal supervision, and prepare yourself for in-patient hospital care in the last ten weeks of pregnancy, the chances are you'll be able to have a normal birth.

Diabetes

Sugar – a sign, but not proof, of gestational diabetes – may appear in your urine at any time in pregnancy. The most common reason for this is a change in the way the kidney handles sugar in pregnancy: no treatment is needed. "Latent" diabetes can do the same thing and can be controlled with diet alone, though you'll be checked more frequently at the antenatal clinic. Pre-existing diabetes needs strict supervision because your insulin needs may change. Babies of diabetic mothers tend to be large so you may be induced early or you may need to have a Caesarean section (see p.52).

Vaginal bleeding

Never ignore vaginal bleeding at any stage of your pregnancy. Although it's always worrying, close medical supervision can help avoid serious problems. **Bleeding in the first three months** Bleeding in early pregnancy doesn't mean you'll lose your baby. You may not yet have high enough hormone levels to subdue your periods. You may have a condition such as cervical erosion or polyps, neither of which are likely to interfere with your pregnancy. Contact your doctor or hospital as soon as possible so you can be referred for a scan; if the heart is beating well, bleeding will probably stop and the pregnancy will continue normally. You'll need to rest and forgo sex for a while.

Bleeding in later pregnancy It's rare to bleed late in pregnancy, but it's serious since it may indicate problems with the placenta, such as placenta praevia or approaching placental abruption. Placenta praevia means the placenta is positioned in the lower part of the womb, possibly across the cervix (see left). Placental abruption means that the placenta is

Multiple pregnancy

Carrying more than one baby will undoubtedly mean you have more professional attention and more antenatal appointments during your pregnancy. The diagnosis of twins, triplets, or more will be confirmed with an ultrasound scan, and the news may take time to get used to, but there's a lot of help and support for you both.

How you may feel

Nausea Multiple pregnancies often cause severe nausea, even vomiting, in the first three months. Eat little and often, and drink plenty of fluids – drinks containing glucose or glucose tablets may boost energy levels if you feel too sick to get calories from food.

Increasing size You get bigger faster than a mother with one baby because, as well as carrying two babies, you produce more amniotic fluid.

Backache Be careful about posture and avoid carrying or lifting heavy weights, because the additional levels of pregnancy hormones mean your pelvic ligaments can soften and stretch, and become painful.

Fatigue You'll tire very easily, and this may be made worse by anaemia. Rest, eat meat, and take folic acid and iron.

Indigestion This may be worse than in a single pregnancy (see p.30) because your stomach is squashed against your diaphragm. Have nourishing drinks and soups and eat frequent small meals.

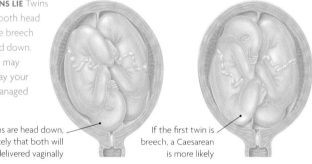

▶ **HOW TWINS LIE** Twins normally lie both head down, or one breech and one head down. How they lie may affect the way your delivery is managed (see p.51).

If both twins are head down, it's more likely that both will be delivered vaginally

If the first twin is breech, a Caesarean is more likely

beginning to separate from the uterine wall. Both conditions can be confirmed by ultrasound scanning, and hospital admission for observation and subsequent Caesarean delivery (see p.52) will be necessary.

Pre-eclampsia

This is a potentially serious condition that affects one in ten women, especially first-time mothers and women carrying more than one baby. It can start at any time in the second half of pregnancy. It's not known precisely what causes it, but it tends to run in families. There are no symptoms, but raised blood pressure and protein in the urine may signal its presence. It affects the placenta and so your baby may grow more slowly than normal. The pregnancy can't be restored to normal, but delivery of the baby and placenta ends the disease; this may need to be arranged as a matter of urgency before serious complications arise. The birth of the baby usually reverses all the effects of pre-eclampsia on the mother.

Losing your baby

No one can imagine the grief of losing a baby. Seek counselling so that you can grieve fully and come to terms with your loss.

Early miscarriage

A miscarriage in the first few weeks is more common than you might think – in fact one in three of first pregnancies. It usually happens because there was something amiss with the fetus or perhaps it had not implanted correctly. Early miscarriage may not be accompanied by much pain, although you may suffer severe period-like cramps. You'll both feel let down, and a woman has to deal with sudden hormonal changes that can make her very emotional.

Late miscarriage

This occurs between 13 and 24 weeks, usually because of placental problems or a weakened cervix that opens due to the weight of the growing fetus. It can also be the result of infection. You have a mini-labour to expel the fetus with whatever pain relief you choose.

Stillbirth

Losing your baby at or close to full term is very hard to bear. Holding and naming your baby and having a funeral can help you come to terms with what's happened.

Dealing with your loss

Your distress needs careful handling: it's a bereavement that may be complicated by feelings of guilt and blame. Talk about your feelings to each other and to your doctor; ask her to explain the reasons for your loss, but accept that no one may know exactly why your baby died. Above all, look forward to the future; most couples who have lost a baby go on to become proud parents of healthy babies.

Taking care of yourself

Balancing your diet

Try to follow these tips:

✽ Eat complex carbohydrates, such as pasta, potatoes, and pulses, for energy.

✽ Eat fish, poultry, dairy products, wholegrain cereals, seeds, pulses for protein. Don't eat tuna more than once a week and avoid shark or marlin as they contain traces of mercury.

✽ Don't cut out fats altogether, but don't eat too much either.

✽ Get vitamin C daily from raw fruit and vegetables, and the B vitamins from wholegrains, nuts, pulses, green vegetables, dairy products, eggs, oily fish, and meat.

✽ Eat lean red meat, fish, egg yolks, apricots, and cereals for iron.

Food safety

Take extra care with food hygiene:

✽ Listeria is a rare bacterium found in foods made with unpasteurized milk (especially some soft cheeses), liver, undercooked meat, and some pre-cooked meals; avoid these as infection may result in miscarriage or stillbirth.

✽ Salmonella is a bacterial infection found in eggs and chicken that causes fever, severe diarrhoea, and abdominal pain. Cook food well to destroy it.

✽ Toxoplasmosis is caused by a parasite found in cat and dog faeces, and in raw meat. It can cause birth defects. Cook meat thoroughly, wash hands after handling raw meat or pets, and wear gloves when gardening.

Pregnancy is natural and women's bodies are designed to accommodate it. However, your body does have to work hard, so it's important to eat well and keep active to help it to cope.

Weight and diet

Your body uses up a lot of energy during pregnancy and you need to eat well to fuel your requirements and those of your growing baby. You could reasonably increase your intake of food by 200–300 calories a day and expect to put on 9–15kg (20–30lb) in weight, much of which is accounted for by the baby, uterus, and amniotic fluid. Pregnancy is not a time to go on a diet, but you should also forget the myth about "eating for two"; the rule is to eat to satisfy your hunger, and no more. Later in pregnancy you may find you simply can't take in much food at any one time, so eat little and often. Keep healthy snacks, such as dried fruit, rice cakes, crispbreads, and hard fruits, in your bag, car, or office.

Body maintenance

The pregnancy hormones have profound effects on teeth, hair, nails, and skin, so don't be surprised by some temporary changes.

Teeth Progesterone makes the gums soft so they may bleed more easily. Take care of your teeth and gums, and visit your dentist at the start of your pregnancy. Make sure you tell him you are pregnant in case he wants to take X-rays, as these may be dangerous to the developing embryo.

Hair and nails Straight hair can become curly, and vice versa. Hair grows and falls in phases – pregnancy often prolongs the growth phase, making thin hair thick and glossy, whereas thick hair may become dry and unmanageable. The downside is that you'll experience hair loss after the birth, although it'll grow back eventually. Although they grow faster, nails also become brittle. Keep them short and use creams to keep them moist.

Skin Oestrogen gives your skin the legendary bloom of pregnancy, but dry skin may become drier and greasy skin more oily. Patches of brown pigment (chloasma) may appear on your face and neck but will eventually fade. All skins deepen in colour with browning of the nipples and a line down the abdomen. Tiny dilated capillaries (spider naevi) on the face are common but disappear later. Stretch marks on the breasts, thighs, and abdomen are very common; they're related to the breakdown of protein in the skin by the high levels of pregnancy hormones. Most marks will fade after the birth.

Dealing with fatigue

Fatigue is a periodic problem during pregnancy, especially during the first three months and the last six to eight weeks. Its extent may take you by surprise, especially during the first few weeks – it's the kind of tiredness when you feel you don't even have the energy to blink. You're sleepy in the early stages of pregnancy because you're sedated by the high levels of progesterone. Your metabolism speeds up to deal with the demands of your baby and the extra work all your organs are called on to do. Later on in pregnancy you're tired because your whole body is working flat out 24 hours a day, and you're having to carry extra weight around that puts a strain on your heart, lungs, and muscles.

Ways of coping

* Never stand when you can sit, never sit when you can lie.

* If possible, put your feet up whenever you sit – if you're in the office invert a wastebin or box under the desk.

* Sleep anywhere: put your head down on your desk during your lunch break; close your eyes on the bus or train home after work.

* When you're at home, plan specific rest times and let nothing interfere with them; some people like to lie down after lunch, others find they need to rest in the late afternoon or early evening.

* Lie in every weekend.

* Go to bed early at least three times a week.

* Find ways to help you drop off, such as watching TV or reading.

* Lie down and listen to music – not too loud as your baby can hear it.

* Find different comfortable resting positions for instant relief of tiredness. Try lying on the floor on cushions with your feet on a bed, sofa, or chair and your knees at right angles, or take up the first-aid recovery position with cushions under your knees and upper body (see below).

Relaxation Use whatever technique you can to relax – you're going to need at least 30 minutes a day from now on and it will be so refreshing if you teach yourself to let go in seconds. Close your eyes and aim to clear your mind of any stressful thoughts and worries. Breathe in and out slowly and regularly and think about your breathing. As you do so, let only pleasant, relaxing thoughts flow through your head. You'll probably be taught some more relaxation techniques at your antenatal classes (see p.26), and there are plenty of books and CDs to guide you.

▼ **POSITION FOR RELAXATION** This position takes the weight off your back and allows free blood circulation, increasing oxygen supply to your baby. Support your head with pillows and put pillows between your legs to support the upper knee.

On your own

Some women decide to have a baby on their own without the baby's father. However, most women on their own didn't make that choice. If being on your own wasn't your choice, you need to allow yourself to work through your feelings of disappointment and even anger.

Coping with your feelings

At a time when women naturally expect support, comfort, and the shared pleasure of contemplating parenthood, you are experiencing the very opposite. Ideally, explore your feelings with a friend or, even better, a professional counsellor who will help you to isolate each issue and deal with it.

Being positive

Avoid those people who may not take a positive view of either you or your condition. Since you don't have the most obvious form of support – a partner – the last thing you need is negativity from others.

Looking after yourself

When you're on your own, it's only too easy to skip meals or opt for easy snacks. Make sure you go to all your antenatal checkups. The health professionals are there to help you and if you need extra support, they will help you find it.

Pelvic floor exercises

The pelvic floor consists of muscles and fibrous tissue suspended like a funnel from the pelvic bones. The layers of muscle are thickest at the perineum, where there are openings for the urethra, vagina, and anus, which the pelvic floor muscles also support. To locate your pelvic floor muscles, stop your urine flow in midstream – the muscles used here are pelvic floor muscles.

Exercising your pelvic floor

The pelvic floor is put under strain by pregnancy, when the presence of hormones causes it to soften and relax. Keep it toned by doing the following exercises five times a day. Restart them after your baby is born to minimize the risk of prolapse.

✳ Pull in your pelvic floor muscles, then let them go quickly; do this five times.

✳ Pull the muscles in and hold for a count of five, then let them go slowly; repeat this five times.

✳ Finally, do the first, quick exercise five more times.

Precautions

Do some gentle stretches to warm up before exercising and to cool down again afterwards. Keep your back straight, breathe evenly, and flex your feet. As your ligaments are softer than normal, take it easy and don't twist suddenly. Stop exercising immediately if you become breathless, dizzy, overheated, or feel pain. Avoid dehydration by drinking lots of water.

Exercise in pregnancy

Both you and your baby benefit from exercise: your blood starts circulating freely; there's a blast of oxygen to your baby's brain; exercise hormones, such as endorphins, give you both a wonderful high; and your baby loves the swaying motion. Exercise increases your strength, suppleness, and stamina, which will make pregnancy easier and equip you for the rigours of labour. Exercise also helps you to understand your body, to believe in its power, and it gives you the key to relaxation so that you can cope with fatigue and prepare yourself for the actual birth.

Whole-body exercise

Try to do some form of exercise every day, beginning gradually, at a pace that is comfortable. Always stop immediately if you get out of breath or feel any pain. Whole-body exercise is best as it tones up your heart and lungs, so walking and swimming are excellent. Dancing is good too as long as it's not too energetic. Yoga is ideal because it stretches tight muscles and joints and also helps relieve tension. Yoga methods will help later on with labour and pain relief. It's worth going to a special antenatal yoga class.

Exercise to avoid

Pregnancy is not a time to start learning an energetic contact sport; however, you can continue sporting activities for a while if you're already fit and play often. Don't engage in sports like skiing, cycling, or horse riding in the third trimester as your balance will be thrown because of the extra weight in front. Take it easy on very energetic sports such as tennis or squash and don't do heavy workouts at the gym.

Preparing for labour and birth

Help yourself to prepare for labour and birth by introducing your body to some exercises and postures that will help when the baby is coming. You'll be taught different techniques at your antenatal classes (see p.26), but it's a great help if both of you can learn the exercises so that your partner can help and encourage you to practise at home. Be especially careful with your posture during pregnancy to protect your back. The hormones of pregnancy soften your ligaments in preparation for the birth; the problem is that this also makes them more susceptible to strain during pregnancy, and your back is the most vulnerable.

Tailor sitting Sit up with your back straight (lean against a wall if you like), with the soles of your feet together. This opens up the hip joints.

Squatting Squat down on your haunches as low as possible, supporting your back against a wall or sofa – or lean against your partner while he is sitting in a chair. Squatting stretches and relaxes the birth canal, and when it comes to the delivery you may well find that this is the position that you adopt naturally, since it will help you to bear down (see p.46).

All fours Getting down onto all fours is very helpful during pregnancy when you have a bad back, especially if you combine it with a few gentle pelvic floor exercises (see above left). Put a pile of cushions in front of you so you can rest on them with your head on your arms, and ask your partner to massage your back. Many women also find this a comfortable position for backache during labour, and for the actual delivery (see p.46).

Standing and sitting correctly

As pregnancy progresses, good posture becomes increasingly important. You may have a tendency to bend your spine to balance the bump in front, which leads to an arched back and slumped shoulders. Try to avoid this by keeping a straight back, tucking your buttocks under, and tilting your pelvis forward. Try to drop your shoulders to avoid tension in your neck.

Sitting badly can be as bad for your back as poor posture when standing. If you have to sit for a long time, make sure you use a firm, straight-backed chair and sit well back with your feet raised slightly on a footstool or flat on the floor. Sitting badly, slumped in your chair, forces your baby up against your diaphragm and stomach, constricts your lungs, and causes breathlessness and indigestion.

Carrying and lifting

Avoid carrying a heavy bag for long periods; this can put a strain on your shoulders and neck. If you need to lift something from floor level, always bend your knees and keep a straight back, lifting the object high against your chest, and hold it close. Never bend down or twist from the waist; you could damage your lower back.

Getting up without strain

1 **TURN ONTO YOUR SIDE** when you first get up from lying down, for example after exercise. Keeping your back straight, push yourself up into a sitting position with your hands.

2 **GET INTO A KNEELING POSITION** before you stand up from the floor (or swing your legs over the edge of the bed). Still keeping your back straight, use your thigh muscles to push yourself up.

✳ JUST FOR DAD

Looking after your partner's wellbeing during pregnancy is good for your unborn baby, good for your relationship, and essential to your partner's long-term physical and emotional health. Try the suggestions below to help her, but don't treat her like an invalid:

How you can help

✳ Your partner's hair and skin will look marvellous, especially during the middle trimester, from four to seven months. Tell her how good she looks to boost her self-esteem. Towards the end of the pregnancy she may begin to get very bored and feel uncomfortable and unattractive; encourage her to go out and treat herself at this time.

✳ Encourage your partner to eat and drink well. Get involved in the shopping and cooking, if you haven't done so before. You can both follow the basic advice on diet (see p.36) – you'll both benefit.

✳ Give your partner opportunities to rest: bring her breakfast in bed at weekends; make sure visitors aren't invited when she normally likes to rest, whether it's after lunch or early evening. Put a television in the bedroom, if there isn't one there already, so she can watch in bed.

✳ Do the heavy lifting so that your partner doesn't strain her back or other muscles softened by pregnancy hormones (see left). If she does lift something, make sure she bends her legs, rather than bending from the waist. Carry the shopping and other heavy items for her.

Your new baby, your new life

The birth of your first baby is one of the most amazing moments of your whole life. It's the sort of event that parents remember in minute detail years later, even when other memories have faded. Although no birth experience is exactly like another, your first is special simply because you have never done it before. But just because you can't predict exactly what it will feel like either physically or emotionally, it doesn't mean that you can't be prepared for most eventualities. Knowing how a normal labour progresses, what your pain relief options are, and what can be done if things don't go according to plan, means that together you can approach labour and birth positively. The importance of how you experience the birth and the first few precious moments you spend together with your baby cannot be overestimated. At this time, the bonds of interdependence and love begin to form and tie you together as a family. Don't be perturbed if it doesn't happen immediately. Rest assured the bonds will strengthen gradually as your body recovers and your confidence builds during the first few days after the birth.

Countdown to birth

✳ JUST FOR MUM

Labour can start any time from 36 weeks, so be prepared. Keep telephone numbers of your partner, your midwife, and hospital delivery ward to hand. Have your bag (see below) or everything for a home delivery ready (see p.46).

What you need for hospital:

✳ Your hospital notes.

✳ A large T-shirt or short, loose nightdress for labour.

✳ You may also want to take a hot-water bottle for backache, a bottle of water and a natural sponge to suck, a water-spray bottle to cool you, and even a hand mirror so that you can see your baby's head as it appears.

✳ Socks in case you're chilly during or after delivery.

✳ Two front-opening nightdresses or pyjamas, a dressing gown, and slippers.

✳ Two packets of super-strength sanitary pads and several pairs of cotton pants. Some disposable pants can also be very useful in the early days of heavy blood loss.

✳ Properly fitted nursing bras and disposable breast pads.

✳ Toiletries, flannel or sponge, and a couple of bath towels.

✳ For your baby you'll need stretchsuits or nighties and vests (see p.96), nappies, and nappy-changing equipment (see pp.86–88). You may need a blanket or shawl for your baby.

As your due date approaches, the days may seem to drag by and you probably feel uncomfortably large. As the expectant father, you'll be waiting for the telephone to ring with the call you've been waiting for.

Getting ready

Although pregnancy is said to last 40 weeks, this is only a convenient method of calculation – it's normal for a baby to be born anything between 36 and 42 weeks. If your baby hasn't been born by the official due date, don't worry. Most doctors aren't in a hurry to induce a baby if the mother is healthy and there are no obvious problems, such as raised blood pressure. Keep active and arrange some outings and visits. It's better for both of you – and the baby – instead of hanging around the house feeling apprehensive.

Packing your hospital bag

It's a good idea to have everything ready for your baby's arrival and your bag packed for hospital three to four weeks before the due date, so that you are prepared for any eventuality. Your midwife will give you a list of what you need to take with you in the way of toiletries and other items, such as sanitary pads, and nappies, bedding, and clothes for your baby (see left). Your tour of the labour ward (see p.26) will help you decide which bulkier items you might need, such as extra pillows or cushions.

Getting near labour

In the few days before labour begins properly, you may notice some signs that indicate you haven't got much longer to wait.

Feeling pre-menstrual You may experience similar feelings to those before your period, such as a low, nagging backache.

Braxton Hicks You may become more aware of the painless tightenings of the uterine wall. These are Braxton Hicks contractions, which can begin at around six months, and occur on and off during the last few weeks.

Mild diarrhoea You may have looser bowel movements as your system is affected by the increasing uterine activity.

Abdominal lightening There may be an easing of discomfort under your ribs – a feeling of lightening – as your baby's head engages in your pelvis. This may happen a week or two before the birth with a first baby, but just as often it doesn't happen until labour.

Burst of energy Many women experience a sudden burst of energy even if they have been very tired and sluggish for several weeks previously. You may find you want to rush around making sure everything is ready for your baby's homecoming; this is known as the "nesting instinct".

Irritability Understandably, you may become short-tempered and impatient, with a definite sense that it's time pregnancy was over!

The stages of labour

Labour has three distinct stages. The first stage is when the uterine contractions pull the cervix open; the second stage, from full dilatation to when the baby is born; and the third stage, until the placenta is delivered.

The first stage This is the stage when contractions are established, gradually becoming stronger and longer; this can last up to 12 hours, or longer with a first baby. There are three phases: the latent phase, which lasts around eight hours when the cervix thins;. the active phase, when the cervix is opened up wide; and the transitional phase, when it reaches full dilatation. You're most likely to need pain relief during the active phase, and you're likely to feel a burst of energy towards the end.

The second stage During the second stage of labour, your baby leaves the uterus and is pushed through the birth canal. This can take anything from a few minutes to two hours with a first baby, and can be exhausting.

The third stage The delivery of the placenta is the final stage of labour; it is almost painless, although you may feel some cramping like a severe period pain. It happens within half an hour of your baby's birth, sooner if helped by an injection of syntometrine (see p.48).

Thinking about pain relief

Consider options for pain relief before labour starts; discuss what is available with your midwife. Many women like the idea of a birth without the need for drugs, but it's good to be prepared, as you can't predict how you'll react when you're in labour.

Gas and air (Entonox)

A mixture of oxygen and nitrous oxide is breathed in through a mouthpiece during a contraction. You start using it when you feel a contraction starting as it takes about 20 seconds to work. The baby is not affected.

Pethidine

This is a form of pain relief given by injection. It is quite strong and you may feel sick or woozy. It can affect a baby's breathing at delivery (though this can be treated), and makes him drowsy, so it isn't given late in labour.

Epidural anaesthetic

Anaesthetic is injected into the spinal canal that numbs the body from the top of the abdomen down to the toes, but you remain awake and alert. A hollow needle is inserted into the spinal canal and a catheter (tube) is passed through it. Once the tube is in place, the needle is removed, and the tube is taped to your back so that the anaesthetic can be topped up. If you want an epidural, it's best to let the hospital know in advance.

TENS

Transcutaneous electrical nerve stimulation (TENS) involves having electrodes taped to your back that connect to a stimulator. You trigger small, safe amounts of electrical current to stimulate the production of your natural painkillers – endorphins.

Birth pool

Buoyancy helps reduce the pressure on the abdomen, making your contractions more efficient, and being in water enables you to change positions easily. Many hospitals now have pools for use during labour. Check early in pregnancy to make sure that one will be available.

Sudden birth – the father's role

Occasionally labour comes on with such speed that your partner could be overwhelmed by the desire to push before you can get professional help, let alone reach hospital! Although the second stage can take a couple of hours, it may not, and babies have been known to be born after a couple of pushes. If this happens, don't panic – babies who come quickly are almost always strong and vigorous, and most births are perfectly straightforward.

What to do

✴ On no account leave your partner alone for more than a minute or two. Help her into a comfortable position.

✴ Telephone the doctor or midwife and explain the situation. If it's difficult to get hold of them, call an ambulance.

✴ Wash your hands well and have some clean towels ready. Put one aside for the baby. If you have time, find some old sheets or plastic sheeting to cover the floor.

✴ When you see the top of the baby's head at the vaginal opening, ask your partner to stop pushing and just pant. This gives the vagina a chance to stretch fully without tearing.

✴ Once the head has been born, feel around the neck to see if the cord is looped around it. If it is, hook your finger under the cord and draw it over the baby's head.

✴ Hold the baby firmly as he emerges – he'll be slippery – and give him to his mother to hold. Wrap him in the spare towel so that he doesn't get cold.

✴ Don't touch the cord. If the placenta is delivered before help arrives, put it in a bowl so that it can be checked by the midwife or doctor.

What happens in labour

How labour starts

The "show"

This is a brownish/pink discharge that indicates that the mucus plug that has sealed the cervix during pregnancy has now come away in readiness for labour.

Your waters break

Sometimes the amniotic sac ruptures before labour starts, causing fluid to leak slowly or in a gush from your vagina. This is painless. If your waters break, put on a clean sanitary pad and call your midwife for advice. Most doctors would prefer labour to start within 24 hours because of the risk of infection to the baby.

Contractions start

The muscular tightenings of the uterus – contractions – gradually start to pull open the cervix. At first they are sharp, cramping pains in the lower abdomen or back that last a few seconds. If they're coming regularly, every 10–15 minutes, you're in labour.

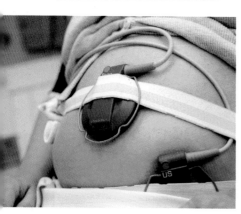

▲ **ELECTRONIC FETAL MONITORING** When you first arrive at hospital, your baby's heartbeat may be measured during contractions through electrodes attached to your abdomen.

When you go into labour for the first time, it's natural to feel both excited and apprehensive. In spite of all the preparations you've made over the last months, for first-time parents labour is a journey into the unknown.

Keeping active

When you realize you're in labour your first reaction may be to rush off to hospital. Try to resist this because the most important thing for a mother in early labour is to keep active. Moving around is a great help in getting and keeping labour established, and most people find it easier to cope with contractions if they're upright. If your partner isn't with you, telephone him so he can join you as soon as possible. The best thing is to potter around at home for as long as possible, trying to behave normally; if you have a contraction, just stop and breathe through it. You might like to have a shower or bath to relax you. However, it's best to avoid having a bath if your waters have already broken (see left), unless your midwife advises it. Try to eat and drink quite often in small quantities. Have high-energy snacks and warm drinks to keep your strength up.

When to go to hospital

There's usually no reason to rush into hospital. The first stage usually lasts at least eight hours for a first baby and you'll be more comfortable at home. Telephone the hospital when you think labour is established, but unless the hospital is far away, stay at home until contractions are coming every five to ten minutes and lasting for about a minute. However, bear in mind that you've got a journey ahead of you, so don't wait until the idea of getting into a car is beginning to sound like agony. If your partner can't get home in time, don't try to drive yourself; call an ambulance or a taxi.

When you're in hospital

It's now accepted that childbirth is not an illness and most delivery rooms are designed to be as homely as possible. You'll be assigned a midwife when you arrive, and she'll check how far the cervix has dilated, and listen to your baby's heart, repeating these checks throughout your labour. You'll only need to be near the equipment while your baby's heart rate is being monitored, then you can move around. Some medical interventions require constant monitoring, however, so you'll have to stay on the bed.

Managing contractions

There are several ways of managing labour pains. Discuss the options with your midwife, including deciding when and if you want to use any pain relief (see p.43). She'll try to accommodate your wishes and she'll support you both in finding ways of coping with contractions.

Positions for labour

Keeping upright as much as possible helps labour to progress as the contractions work with, not against, gravity. Standing or squatting supported by your partner allows you to control the pain and provides warmth and loving reassurance.

Coping without pain relief

If you want to use natural pain relief, make sure you know as much as possible about the methods you prefer and practise them with your birth partner beforehand. If you need any special equipment, check it will be available at home or in hospital.

✱ Relax as much as possible, especially between contractions – concentrate on the out-breath as you exhale, and drop your shoulders. You'll learn breathing and relaxation techniques at your childbirth classes, but make sure you practise them before the big day.

✱ Keep moving about between contractions, then get into the position that feels right for you. These may include a supported squat, leaning against your partner, on all fours, or kneeling down and leaning forwards on a pillow placed on a chair.

✱ Try counting backwards from 100 through a contraction – the concentration needed to do this takes your mind off the pain. Keep your eyes open to externalize the pain; focus on something in the room.

✱ Take sips of still water from a sponge if your mouth is dry and ask your partner to massage or knead your back during a contraction.

✱ Don't be afraid to say – or shout – anything you like; no one's going to hold it against you afterwards.

✱ JUST FOR DAD

Just being with your partner is a huge comfort for her. Trust your intuition as to what's needed, but ask her what she needs too.

How you can help

✱ Be loving and intimate: slow and gentle, quiet and reassuring.

✱ Be there for her when she wants you, and give her space when she doesn't.

✱ Be positive and never criticize; she needs lots of praise, encouragement, and sympathy.

✱ Offer practical help, such as a hot-water bottle if she has backache, sprays of water if she's too hot, water to sip if her mouth is dry.

✱ If your partner doesn't want pain relief, encourage her while it seems reasonable, but if she asks for it, don't put her off.

✱ Talk to the midwife or doctor if you don't understand what's happening, or if you're worried. They are there to help you both, but remember that they are professionals who have your partner's and baby's best interests at heart. At the same time, don't let the hospital staff and their machines become your focus.

✱ If your partner shouts or swears at you, seems to get angry or overwrought, take it in your stride. It's her way of coping with a very stressful situation. This is particularly likely to happen at the transitional phase of the first stage of labour (see p.43), so be positive, as it's a sign that the second stage isn't far off.

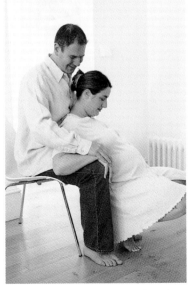

▲ **SQUATTING SUPPORTED** Squat between your partner's knees while he sits on a chair, taking your weight on his legs.

▲ **STANDING UPRIGHT** Stand with knees bent, if necessary, letting your partner take your weight.

The birth of your baby

Who's who at the birth

For a normal vaginal delivery, you'll probably have one midwife and an assistant. Sometimes, though, the delivery room may seem crowded with people – they may include:

✳ Your assigned midwife.

✳ An assistant midwife.

✳ The obstetric doctor on duty.

✳ A paediatrician if there is a potential problem.

✳ A paediatric nurse if your baby is premature.

The early stages of your journey to parenthood are now complete. Ahead of you is a shorter, but not necessarily easier, stage: that of pushing the baby out. Together, at last you'll meet your new baby.

Coping with second stage

As your baby is gradually pushed down your birth canal, you should try to use gravity as much as possible to help, so keep as upright as you can. Get into whatever position feels most comfortable – it may be sitting up on the bed, squatting on a mat with the support of your partner, leaning against a chair, being on all fours, or using a birthing stool – your partner and midwife can follow your lead. Between contractions use your breathing techniques; in particular, let your pelvic floor, rectum, and anus relax.

Crowning

Your midwife will tell you when your baby's head appears at the vaginal opening – this is called crowning. Listen to your midwife; she'll tell you when to push and when to relax. If you take your time and let your vagina stretch slowly, you may avoid a tear. Once the baby's head crowns, your partner can show you by holding a mirror – this is a great encouragement because you know that your baby will soon be born.

Episiotomy

An episiotomy is a surgical cut in the perineum that helps to allow the baby's head to pass through. Given time, you may not need one, but if it's felt you should have one, the midwife or doctor will ask your permission to do this procedure as your baby's head crowns (see above). It's more common to have an episiotomy with a first baby because the vaginal opening may be less elastic and you are more likely to tear. Episiotomies are also performed if your baby is very large, is in the breech position, or you need assistance with forceps or ventouse (see p.51). If you haven't had an epidural, the pelvic floor muscles will be numbed first with an injection of local anaesthetic. Then the

◀ THE MOMENT OF BIRTH
You'll never forget the experience of holding your baby for the first time, immediately after he's emerged. It's so emotional that you may well find yourselves weeping with joy and relief.

Birth at home

More and more women are giving birth at home, though birth in hospital remains the norm.

Practical preparations

About a month before your due date, the midwife will let you know what equipment you need readily available, such as buckets, rubber gloves, and polythene sheeting to cover furniture and carpets. She'll provide all the medical equipment. Decide where in your home you want to have your baby and try to work out your expectations so you can discuss them with your midwife.

When you're in labour

✳ Call the midwife, who will come as soon as possible. She'll probably have an assistant.

✳ For pain relief, your midwife will provide gas and air and pethidine (obtained on prescription beforehand), so you're likely to try drug-free ways

of managing the pain first (see p.45). You'll probably be better able to cope at home, anyway.

✳ You're more likely to feel in control of events as the midwife is on your territory, and that's an important psychological difference for everyone.

If there's a problem

Talk to your midwife beforehand about when and why she'd recommend a move to hospital. If that were to happen, you would go in an ambulance. In most instances, the same midwives who had attended to you at home would look after you in hospital.

After the birth

The midwife will stay for a couple of hours to make sure that you and your baby are comfortable and healthy, and will return later. You, your partner, and your baby can spend your first hours as a family together in your own home.

✳ JUST FOR DAD

Helping your partner and watching your baby being born is an overwhelming experience. The second stage is hard work for mothers – it's a real effort, but there are ways you can help and be involved.

How you can help

✳ Help your partner to get into the position she feels is best, and support her there.

✳ Talk to and encourage her all the time. Keep in physical contact so she knows you're with her.

✳ If you can see your baby's head as it crowns, describe it to your partner or hold a mirror for her to see – this will be a huge encouragement for her. However, don't get in the midwife's way as she'll need to monitor the baby's progress second by second, and to check the birth of the head.

✳ Announce that you have a son or daughter, not just a boy or girl. The words "son" and "daughter" express family feelings.

✳ If the midwife agrees, clamp and cut your baby's cord; he's now become an individual being.

✳ If you feel like weeping, don't hold back. It's one of the most emotional moments of your life.

✳ When the baby is born, share the first minutes of your child's life with your partner.

✳ Photograph or video your partner and baby if you like, but don't do this to the exclusion of helping them. They are more important than anything else.

vaginal tissues, plus underlying muscle, are cut at the height of a contraction to extend the opening. The incision is stitched after the placenta has been delivered (see p.48).

The delivery

The head is the widest part of your baby – it will slowly emerge, and the midwife will check that the cord isn't around the neck. The midwife will ask you to pant, not push at this stage, then with the next contractions she will gently turn the baby so that the shoulders can be born one at a time and the rest of your baby's body will slide out; the pushing contractions stop immediately and you'll feel a wonderful sense of release. Your baby may or may not cry out.

Meeting your baby

This is the moment that will make everything you've just gone through worthwhile. Your midwife will probably lay your baby on your tummy or give him to you to hold while the cord is clamped and cut; let your baby feel your skin, hold him close to your face, and let him look up into yours. This is when you can claim your new status as parents. Share this moment – you're both his parents – and savour it.

After the birth

Bonding

Most newborn animals have an instinct to bond – research has shown that human babies are similarly programmed.

What happens at birth

Your baby can recognize your voice at birth and can focus on your face at 20–25cm (8–10in) away. You will be hyper-sensitive to your baby in the minutes after birth. You can bond with your baby for life almost instantly, if you are left alone together without interference – if this private time isn't offered, ask for it. But don't worry if you don't bond at once – you might be exhausted after the delivery. Falling in love will have to wait.

▲ **GETTING TO KNOW YOUR BABY** Your relationship with your baby begins the second she is born. As you both learn to care for her, your love will deepen and grow.

The first hour or so after your baby's birth is a very precious time for all three of you. Although there will be various medical and administrative procedures that need to be carried out, you'll still have time to enjoy your baby. You and your family might like to be left in peace to cuddle up together and start getting to know one another properly.

Your baby after delivery

The midwife will check your baby's condition immediately after the birth by assessing her "Apgar score" (see opposite). Providing she is breathing without difficulty from the start, your baby will probably remain in your arms for the first minutes after birth. If she needs help to start breathing, she'll be put on the delivery room resuscitation table, which has an oxygen mask and a heater to keep the baby warm. Usually she'll soon be pink enough to be handed back to you, but in a few cases she may need to be taken to the special care baby unit for a while (see p.62). Some time in the first couple of hours your baby will be weighed and measured and every part of her thoroughly examined by a midwife or paediatrician.

Delivery of the placenta

The placenta is usually delivered with the help of an injection of a drug called syntometrine given as the baby's body emerges. The cord is cut and the midwife will then press gently on your abdomen and pull the cord slowly to draw out the placenta. Once the placenta is delivered, the midwife will check to make sure that none has remained inside you. If you'd like the placenta to be delivered naturally, without syntometrine, it will take about half an hour and putting your baby to the breast will help the process.

How you will feel

Immediately after the birth, your body temperature drops a few degrees and you may shiver and shake quite violently as your thermostat resets. You'll need to be wrapped in a blanket, and may need to put on a pair of warm socks. The shivering usually passes in about half an hour, by which time your body temperature will be back up to normal. If you are famished after labour, ask for a small, easily digestible snack – a cup of tea and a piece of toast perhaps – and drink plenty if you want to.

If you need stitches

The midwife will examine your perineum and assess whether or not you need stitches. Research shows that minor tears heal better on their own, so it's not necessarily true that any tear will inevitably mean stitches; however, an episiotomy (see p.46) must be stitched. Depending on the

The Apgar score

This a standard method of making sure your newborn baby is healthy and well, and to determine whether she needs special attention. At one minute, five minutes, and ten minutes after the birth, the midwife or doctor does five checks on your baby's heartbeat, breathing, muscle tone, reflexes, and skin colour, and gives them a score of 0, 1, or 2, with a possible total of 10. A score of 7 or more is normal, and a low first score improving to a normal second or third score is also fine. This may happen if you had a long second stage, or your baby has been affected by pethidine given during labour (see p.43). The assessment is named after Dr Virginia Apgar, who devised it.

How the score works

✱ Heart rate over 100 scores 2; below 100 is 1; no heartbeat is 0.

✱ Regular breathing or crying scores 2; slow or irregular breathing scores 1; absence of breathing scores 0.

✱ If your baby is active (good muscle tone), the score is 2; if hands and feet only are moving, the score is 1; if the baby is limp, the score is 0.

✱ Strong reflexes score 2; weak reflexes score 1; no reflexes score 0.

✱ Pink colouring scores 2; body pink but extremities blue scores 1; blue or pale colouring scores 0. Skin colour shows how well a baby's lungs are working.

✱ JUST FOR DAD

You may feel as emotionally exhausted as your partner, but it's important not to underestimate the physical impact of labour and birth on a woman.

How you can help

✱ You'll probably experience a wave of euphoria now that your baby is born, but if labour has been long and hard, your partner may be too exhausted to experience this same "buzz" immediately. It doesn't mean that she isn't as delighted as you are, but after labour, it's not surprising if she finds it difficult to express immediate enthusiasm. Just hold her close and let her know how proud you are of her and of your new son or daughter. Stay with them both for as long as possible after the birth, including settling them into the postnatal ward.

✱ Congratulate your partner on her achievement, and let her know how much you appreciate her. Don't belittle your own contribution. You may think you haven't really been much help – this is common for fathers who have seen their partners in labour. However, most mothers will say how beneficial it was to have their partners' emotional support and encouragement.

✱ Hold your baby while your partner is being stitched, or checked. Go into a quiet corner of the room and get to know your baby. Let her look into your eyes – if you hold her close so that she's just 20–25cm (8–10in) away from your face, she can see you and smell you, and she'll learn to recognize you (see p.156).

length of the cut or tear, stitching will be done either by a senior midwife or the doctor on duty and you may be given a local anaesthetic. You may be able to cuddle your baby while you're being stitched if you want to, but this is also a good chance for your partner to have time with his baby so that you both get a chance to bond individually.

The first breastfeed

Putting your baby to the breast within an hour of the delivery increases your chances of breastfeeding successfully; many women feel able to put their babies to the breast immediately after the birth, although not all babies want to suck then. Ask your midwife to help you get your baby to latch on, but don't worry if she doesn't want to suck immediately. It doesn't mean she isn't able to breastfeed, just that at this point she doesn't feel like sucking, or she may be tired. She may also be affected by painkillers used during labour, such as pethidine, which leave her rather drowsy and may take a few hours to wear off (see p.43).

The importance of colostrum

You won't produce milk for three or four days after the birth (see p.65), but it is very beneficial for your baby to have the high-protein "pre-milk" called colostrum that is produced in your breasts at this time. As well as water, protein, sugar, vitamins, and minerals, colostrum contains important antibodies from your body that protect a newborn baby from infections, plus a substance called lactoferrin, which acts like a natural antibiotic. Putting your baby to the breast also helps the uterus to contract.

Special labours

It's okay to feel disheartened if something happens that means you need an assisted delivery, or even an emergency Caesarean section (see p.52). Being prepared for the fact that intervention may be needed can help to avoid too much heart-searching after the birth.

Coping with a special labour

✳ The medical staff will always tell you why a particular course of action is recommended, whether it's before or during labour. Ask questions or for repeat explanations if you need to.

✳ If you're in labour, it may be difficult to concentrate; ask your partner to make sure that all the reasons for certain procedures are clarified so that he can relay the information to you. Remember, unless you're actually unconscious, staff must ask your permission to proceed; they won't accept your partner's opinion.

✳ At the end of the day, the most important thing will be that your baby has been born safely. But that doesn't mean your feelings don't matter, and many women can't shake off the idea – however illogical – that they were in some way to blame because things didn't go to plan. If you find yourself in this position, talk to your partner or your midwives or doctor. Having a baby can unleash deep emotions and you may need to work through them before you can enjoy new motherhood fully.

There are many different procedures if labour proves difficult. If a particular procedure is suggested, ask the midwife or doctor to explain why it's necessary, what the risks are, and what would happen if you waited a while before it was started.

When labour is induced

Sometimes labour may need to be induced, which means it is started artificially. If you haven't gone into labour spontaneously by 42–43 weeks, or if there are worries about your own or your baby's health in the last few weeks of pregnancy, induction may be suggested. Similar procedures will be needed if your labour is not proceeding as it should. Don't worry if you do have to be induced. Induction is fine provided it's done strictly for medical reasons and either for your wellbeing or the baby's – although contractions will be stronger.

How labour may be induced

Induction is often introduced gradually, first with pessaries; then, if necessary, ARM; finally, a syntocinon drip if things are going too slowly.

✳ You may be given vaginal pessaries containing prostaglandin, a hormone that should trigger labour.

✳ Your membranes may be ruptured artificially (ARM), which can either start or strengthen contractions.

✳ You may be given an artificial hormone (syntocinon) into a vein to induce contractions. Syntocinon is started at a low rate and increased gradually so that contractions build up slowly. It may also used to speed up labour.

If you're having twins

Twins or higher multiples are exciting for everyone, although you're bound to be apprehensive. Twin deliveries are much safer than they used to be because the exact position and acondition of the second baby can be determined by ultrasound and fetal monitors. Medical interest in the birth is likely to be greater if you're expecting more than one baby, and intervention is more likely to be recommended. Often this becomes necessary, but there's no need to think it's inevitable; many twins, and even triplets, are born vaginally after a normal labour. But continuous electronic fetal monitoring is much more common, and, as with breech birth, you'll probably be offered an epidural because of the likelihood of intervention being needed. This means it's in place in case there are problems with the delivery of the second twin and you have to have assistance with forceps or even a Caesarean. If the first twin is known to be breech, your doctors will probably advise you to have both babies delivered by elective Caesarean.

Breech birth

Instead of being born head first, a breech baby is born buttocks first, usually followed by the legs and lastly the head. Breech babies often need to be delivered with the help of forceps or by Caesarean section for the baby's safety, although a natural breech delivery is occasionally possible with the help of an experienced midwife and obstetrician. A breech baby is almost always delivered in hospital; because of the likelihood of intervention, you'll probably be offered an epidural, so that you're already anaesthetized if your doctor needs to apply forceps or do a Caesarean (see p.52). You're more likely to have an episiotomy (see p.46), because your baby's buttocks may not stretch the vagina enough to let the head out safely, or to allow forceps to be inserted to help lift the head out.

Assistance with ventouse or forceps

Even if you have a normal vaginal delivery, there may be times when you need help, particularly in pushing the baby out during the second stage. Depending on the circumstances, your hospital will provide assistance with forceps or ventouse (vacuum extraction). You'll need to have an episiotomy for either of these procedures.

Ventouse, or vacuum, extraction This is a more gentle procedure than using forceps and is used in similar circumstances. Your cervix has to be fully dilated and the baby's head must be in the birth canal. The vacuum plate leaves a bruise on your baby's head where the suction was applied, but this will fade within the first two to three weeks.

Forceps The two blades of forceps cradle your baby's head and pull it safely through the birth canal without too much compression. Forceps can normally only be used once the baby's head is engaged in the pelvic bones.

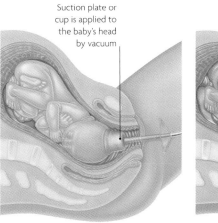

Suction plate or cup is applied to the baby's head by vacuum

▲ **VENTOUSE OR VACUUM EXTRACTION**
With ventouse assistance, a small suction plate or cup is applied by vacuum to the lowest part of your baby's head. The doctor will gradually help your baby to be born by applying gentle traction.

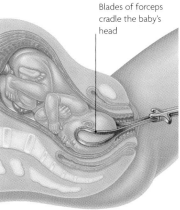

Blades of forceps cradle the baby's head

▲ **FORCEPS DELIVERY** Forceps are instruments that look like the two halves of very large sugar tongs. The blades are inserted one at a time and the baby is drawn out with a few gentle pulls during contractions.

✳ JUST FOR DAD

A labour that doesn't go to plan can be very scary for you as well as for your partner. Be prepared for any unexpected interventions.

How you can help

✳ Well before your baby is due, talk to your partner and make sure you know her views and preferences for any eventuality. Bear in mind, though, that she may change her mind when the time comes.

✳ Unless it's an absolute emergency, make sure that any interventions suggested are talked through properly with your partner, and either or both of you ask questions if anything isn't clear. Remember that the medical team must have your partner's consent for any intervention.

✳ If something is suggested that you know your partner wants to avoid, try to buy time. For instance, if labour has slowed, suggest a change of position before procedures to accelerate labour are introduced.

✳ If the medical team decide the labour needs monitoring with high-tech equipment, try not to be distracted by it. Concentrate on your partner, not the technology.

✳ Remember that if something unexpected happens, and intervention is needed, it's never your partner's fault. Everyone will be working in the very best interests of your partner and the baby.

✳ Whatever happens, talk about it afterwards, especially with your partner, but also with friends and, if necessary, health professionals.

Why you might need a Caesarean

There are several reasons for a Caesarean delivery:

✳ Baby's head is too large for your pelvis (disproportion).

✳ Baby is breech (bottom first).

✳ Baby takes up a cross-wise position (persistent horizontal lie).

✳ You have a medical condition, such as pre-eclampsia or diabetes.

✳ Any problems with the placenta.

✳ Your labour is progressing too slowly or has stopped, which might cause fetal distress.

✳ If there is fetal distress, even if labour hasn't slowed or stopped.

Caesarean section

In many countries, Caesarean sections are currently on the increase, partly because this procedure in expert hands may be safer than, say, a difficult forceps delivery. Sometimes, however, interventions earlier in labour, such as induction or epidural anaesthetic, may lead to a situation in which a Caesarean becomes more likely. If a Caesarean is recommended, your doctor is obliged to give you clear reasons why, even in an emergency. If it was something you had wanted to avoid, ask whether you could wait or if there is anything else you could try first.

Elective Caesarean

If a Caesarean operation is planned in advance it is known as "elective". This means the reason for it has become apparent before labour started – for example, your blood pressure may have shot up, or your pelvis is so small that delivery is likely to be difficult, or your baby is breech (see p.50). Your obstetrician will discuss this with you two to three weeks before your due date, and a date will be booked for you to come into hospital, so you'll know well in advance exactly when your baby is going to be born.

Emergency Caesarean

An emergency (unplanned) Caesarean happens when events during labour make it preferable to a vaginal delivery. For example, your baby may show distress (measured by heart rate and movements); the labour may not progress despite the use of drugs to speed things up; or your own condition may deteriorate. If you haven't had an epidural anaesthetic, the Caesarean will take place under general or spinal anaesthetic.

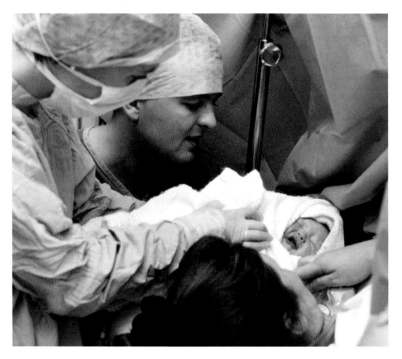

▶ **DELIVERY OF YOUR BABY** If you have a Caesarean under epidural anaesthesia, you'll both be able to share your baby's first moments after delivery.

What happens during the operation

Before a Caesarean, some of your pubic hair may be shaved and a catheter inserted into your bladder. You'll probably be given a saline drip.

The anaesthetic Most elective, and some emergency, Caesareans are performed under epidural or spinal anaesthesia, because women recover more quickly afterwards. You'll be awake during the operation, but you won't feel anything, and your partner can be with you throughout. You won't be able to see anything because the operating team will be masked by a surgical sheet draped across your chest. Spinal anaesthesia takes effect in five to ten minutes and so it can be used in some emergency situations. If, however, you have a general anaesthetic your partner won't usually be allowed into the operating theatre, but will be able to hold the baby afterwards while you recover.

The operation Your abdomen is opened through a small horizontal incision along the line of the top of your pubic hair, and your baby delivered through a similar cut in the uterus. The amniotic fluid is drained off by suction before the baby is gently lifted out. You may feel some tugs as the operation proceeds. Your surgeon will tell you when the moment approaches when she will lift your baby from your uterus.

After the birth It takes about ten minutes to deliver the baby. You or your partner can then hold your baby while the placenta is removed and you are stitched. A baby born by Caesarean is likely to need help in starting to breathe, but a paediatrician will be on hand to help. Closing the wound can take as long as 45 minutes. You'll be encouraged to get up and walk around a few hours afterwards to stimulate your circulation.

The birth partner's role

Even an elective Caesarean can be worrying, because it's quite a major operation. If it's an emergency, your partner may be feeling distressed, but there's much you can do to help her.

✳ If an emergency Caesarean is recommended, and your partner is finding it difficult to talk to the doctors, make sure you ask why it is suggested. Even though she has to give her permission, your partner may still not be quite clear afterwards why it was necessary, and it's important that you're able to help her understand.

✳ Unless your partner really wants a general anaesthetic or the operation is too urgent, see if it can be done under epidural or spinal anaesthesia. This means you can share the experience and meet your new baby together.

✳ During the operation, sit by your partner's head and reassure her that all is well.

✳ You don't have to watch, but if you do and you find it distressing or you feel faint – and many people do – leave the room quickly. Don't hang on; you may cause further difficulties for the medical staff.

✳ If the Caesarean is being done under general anaesthetic, your partner may not regain consciousness for an hour or more, and you'll probably be given your baby to hold. Cherish this time. Father–child bonding can be at its best after a Caesarean, because this early time together is so precious.

✳ JUST FOR MUM

You're bound to feel apprehensive about having a Caesarean, and you may feel disappointed if you have an emergency Caesarean after going into labour naturally.

Concerns about Caesareans

✳ You may worry about being able to deliver a subsequent baby vaginally, but about 75 per cent of women who have a Caesarean can deliver normally the next time.

✳ If you have a general anaesthetic, you'll need longer to recover, so it may be a little while before you feel close to your baby. Don't worry, you will bond with your baby in time, especially when you start breastfeeding (see pp.48–49).

✳ You'll be left with a scar on your "bikini line", but it will fade.

The first day

Some aspects of the hospital routine can be tiresome, though you may enjoy talking to other mothers.

Keeping your baby close
Almost all hospitals now expect babies to remain in their cots beside their mothers' beds at all times.

Food and drink
The food may be bland, so ask your partner to bring fresh fruit as this will help prevent constipation. Drink plenty of water.

Visits from staff
The midwives will check your stitches, lochia, and uterus (see p.64). They'll also give advice on cleaning your baby's umbilicus and on breastfeeding. At some point, an obstetrician and a paediatrician will check you and your baby, and a physiotherapist may visit to advise you on postnatal exercise.

You have both been looking forward to this moment for the best part of a year; your baby is safely delivered and you've experienced a heady brew of strong emotions: relief, pride, elation, excitement, and triumph. Now your baby is lying quietly in her cot by your bed and you both have a chance to take stock.

Your reactions to the birth

Unlikely as it may seem, this could be an awkward moment for you both. It could be passing through either or both of your minds that there is something missing. Where is the rush of love for your baby? It isn't a subject that gets much attention, but it is, nevertheless, a fact that large numbers of parents, quite possibly the majority, don't feel an overpowering attachment to their baby straight after the birth. Most highs, because of their intensity, are followed, not necessarily by a low, but by a diminution of emotion that leaves you feeling somewhat flat in comparison. Having a baby is no exception. It may have been a momentous event for you both, but the hospital routine has to proceed as normal and, anyway, a hospital ward isn't conducive to the kind of closeness that you would like to feel for each other on this shared birthday, especially if you're both exhausted.

Looking forward

When you go to the postnatal ward – and this may be two or three hours after the birth – the father goes back to an empty home and the mother is left wondering what her first night as the mother of a baby is going to be like. If it isn't quite what either of you envisaged, don't worry, be philosophical. In a very real sense, life with your baby will actually begin on the day you take her home.

After a Caesarean

A Caesarean section involves major abdominal surgery and you're likely to feel quite sore once the anaesthetic wears off. As well as asking for pain relief, there are other ways of coping:

✳ Holding and feeding your baby may be difficult as pressure on your scar may be painful. Try laying her next to you on the bed (see p.79) or supporting her on pillows in the so-called "football position" (see left).

✳ Mobility helps you recover, so you'll be encouraged to get up and move around as soon as possible after the birth. Support your wound as you walk about. Be very careful how you move, especially when you're getting up from sitting or lying down. Be careful not to strain your abdominal muscles.

✳ Your dressing will be taken off after a couple of days. Keep the wound dry. Most stitches are absorbable; if not, they'll be removed after about a week.

▲ **COMFORTABLE FEEDING** Put your baby on a pillow and tuck her body under your arm.

Handling your new baby

It's natural to be nervous about holding and handling your baby for the first time; although she may seem vulnerable, remember that she is really very robust. The main problem is that she has no neck control so her head is very floppy, and her joints are very soft so you need to be gentle when putting on her clothes (see p.96). Support your baby's head at all times and pick her up as shown here.

◀ **LIFTING YOUR BABY** Slide one hand under her rump and cradle her head with the other. Lift her gently but firmly towards you, using a smooth upward movement so that she isn't startled. Then hold her close to you. Talk to her all the time and make eye contact with her as you chat.

▲ **HOLD HER ALONG YOUR FOREARM** Some babies like to be held face down on your arms so that they can see out. Hold her so that her cheek rests on your forearm and she can feel your skin against her face.

First discomforts

You'll feel a little shaky in the first 24 hours, and there may be some specific discomforts, although these do pass quite quickly:

✽ Your perineum will feel bruised and tender, especially if you had stitches. Don't stay in the bath too long as water can harm scar tissue and soften stitches.

✽ You may find it difficult or even painful to pass urine. Take a jug of tepid water to the toilet to pour over your vulva as you pass urine.

✽ A sore perineum plus stitches may deter you from opening your bowels. Support your vulva with a pad of tissues as you bear down.

✽ Sitting upright can be awkward when your abdominal muscles are weak and your vulva and perineum are sore. Prop yourself up with plenty of pillows and half sit and half lie on your side to reduce pressure.

◀ **CRADLE HER IN YOUR ARMS** You baby will feel safe and secure cradled in your arms, or on the crook of your elbow. Remember she can see you clearly if you hold her so that she is about 20–25cm (8–10in) from your face. Support her head throughout.

Preparing for going home

New fathers

If you leave your partner and baby in hospital, you are likely to feel a bit lonely when you go home. Use the time to telephone everyone as you'll probably have a huge urge to talk through all that's happened.

Fathers need sleep too

Although you may feel too excited to start with, make sure you catch up on sleep. You've had an exhausting time too during the labour and you can't support your partner when she comes home if you're tired as well.

Prepare for the home coming

Use your time at home alone to do the washing and cleaning and stock up on groceries and other household items. Work out how to strap the baby seat into the car, if you haven't already done this, so that everything is ready for when your new baby comes home.

When the family comes home

Some hospitals encourage mothers to go home as soon as four or five hours after a normal delivery. It may seem very soon, but you're likely to be more relaxed in your own environment. You'll be visited twice on the first day by a midwife. Remember, though, that going home doesn't mean everything is back to normal. Childbirth leaves a mother exhausted, so try to keep the first day or two virtually visitor-free.

▶ **RESPONDING TO YOUR BABY** A newborn has only three states he can be in: awake and quiet, awake and crying, or asleep. Crying is his way of communication. He may be hungry, uncomfortable, tired, or just cry for no apparent reason.

Your baby's first day

There's a lot to learn on your baby's first day, and you may feel awkward and anxious about looking after him. On top of trying to get him to feed, you'll have to get to grips with changing a nappy, "topping and tailing" (see p.90), and dressing your baby. (Most hospitals and midwives leave the first bath for three or four days.) Don't worry though, no-one expects you to be an instant expert. A midwife will show you both what to do; if you're uncertain about anything, don't be afraid to ask.

Reluctance to feed

You may be concerned if your baby is reluctant to feed for the whole of the first day, but this is no cause for worry. Express colostrum (see p.83) if your breasts feel uncomfortable, so that you'll find it easier to feed him as soon as he is ready. Once your baby feels the need to feed, you may find you are putting him to the breast as often as every two hours.

Your sleepy baby

Your baby will probably have been wide awake and alert for the first hour or two after the birth, but then he may well sleep on and off for much of the first day. Take it in turns to hold him and just look at him rather than simply leaving him in his cot.

Your baby's cries

Unless he is very sleepy, you'll probably experience your baby crying several times during this first day and you may be astonished by its force. Just as amazing is the fact that you'll recognize it immediately. Neither of these things is accidental. Newborn babies are programmed to signal their needs vociferously and adults are programmed to respond to these needs with a feeling of urgency. Pick your baby up straight away when he cries; sit and cuddle him in bed with you unless you want to sleep. Over the next few weeks, you will gradually learn exactly what his cries mean.

ENJOY YOUR NEW BABY Take it in turns to hold your new baby and talk to him, or just let him sleep in your arms. You can't spoil a baby by giving him lots of attention in the precious early days.

Adjusting to parenthood

Even though you're longing to be home, use your time in hospital to regain your strength and lean on the professional staff for advice. If you're back home within a couple of days of the birth, accept offers of help from friends and relations.

How you can adjust

✱ When your partner visits you both in hospital, share anything you've learned about your baby's care with him. If you learn how to care for your baby together, you'll start out on an equal footing and he'll be more likely to take the initiative once you're back home.

✱ Use these first few days to build on the network of support systems that you will hopefully have set up through antenatal classes before the baby was born. Prepare for time on your own when your partner has gone back to work and friends and family aren't around as much.

✱ At some point during the first few days, you may experience tearful moments – it often happens just as your milk comes in, three or four days after the birth. The so-called "baby blues" (see p.132) are a normal reaction to the sudden withdrawal of pregnancy hormones and to the enormity of your new situation. They usually subside in a week to ten days. You'll probably be very tired too, especially if you had a fairly long labour. Be open and share your feelings with your partner.

The first few days of parenthood can be bewildering as you seesaw between intense periods of close attention from health professionals and moments of isolation, when you just have to get on with things by yourselves. You may feel that caring for your new baby leaves little room for your own relationship as a couple, but it will help if you concentrate initially on sharing the simple practicalities of your baby's care and acknowledge rather than hide your natural nervousness and apprehension.

Taking care of each other

When a baby comes to first-time parents, three new relationships begin: mother–baby, father–baby, mother–father. The last is the most complex. Of course a relationship has existed between the parents that predates the baby, but you will not have related to each other before in the roles of mother and father. You have to start thinking of each other in an entirely new way. You have to "redesign" your relationship in the light of your new roles – being more understanding, more patient, more flexible, more long-suffering than you were before. Most of all, you have to be more generous and less self-centred. This can put a strain on your relationship, so you need to be ready to respond to each other (see p.128).

Help and advice

Use your time in hospital, or when you are in the daily care of a midwife or doctor, to get the advice you need. Don't feel shy about asking, even if it seems trivial; most health professionals recognize that it's vital to provide reassurance. However, in hospital they may not have enough time to advise you exactly when you need it, particularly with breastfeeding problems, so it may be helpful to contact a breastfeeding counsellor when you get home. Most counsellors are themselves mothers who have been trained to provide support in a non-medical way and will continue their support for some months. This helps to alleviate the nervousness many mothers feel when they are finally discharged by the midwife, ending a close relationship with the midwifery service that's built up over months.

Advice from family and friends

In the early days of parenthood, your friends and relations may be keen to offer advice. Although it can be irritating if delivered in an overbearing way, the advice that other parents give you reflects their own experience and can be very reassuring. However, if the advice goes against your own beliefs, simply ignore it and do things the way you know is best. If you're confused about what to do for the best, try talking things through with your health visitor or midwife, who'll be able to help clear up any worries.

Feeling isolated

After the intense activity of labour and birth, when you were fully involved and couldn't think about anything else, you may both feel quite isolated, disorientated, and lonely for a few days; this could affect how you relate to each other when you do have time together. The new mother may feel bewildered in hospital. Even though she's surrounded by other people, she suddenly finds herself in sole charge of the needs of her tiny new dependant when she's feeling exhausted and possibly in pain. The new father, too, may feel very odd and detached from his new situation when he has to come and go from an empty home.

Talk to each other

When you're together, try hard to talk about how you feel and make sure you tell each other what you have been doing while you're apart. Most hospitals now have unrestricted day and evening visiting for new fathers, so it should be possible to spend quite a lot of time together supporting each other through this short but significant period of separation. It may be difficult to find time alone to articulate your feelings, but it is important for all of you that you do.

✳ JUST FOR DAD

As a new father you may feel rather cut off from your partner, particularly while she's in hospital. At the same time, you may feel an intense elation that you want to share with your partner, but she may seem a bit distant as her body recovers from the birth and she tries to establish breastfeeding.

What you can do to help

✳ Take the initiative – learn how to do all the practical things your baby needs while your partner is still in hospital.

✳ Get to know your baby. Use these early days to establish a close relationship. Even if your partner is in hospital, change your baby, learn to handle her, talk to her, hold her close so that she can focus on your face if she's awake, or simply hold her if she's asleep. Bring her to your partner when she needs to be fed, carry her around, try to be there for her first bath.

✳ Be ready for your partner's mood swings. At some point during the first week your partner will probably experience the so-called "baby blues" that come as a reaction to the sudden withdrawal of the pregnancy hormones as well as to new responsibilities. She may also be very tired if the labour was prolonged. The "baby blues" subside after a week to ten days. Your partner may try to hide her feelings from you so as not to worry you or because she fears that you won't take her seriously. Be sensitive to her needs and talk to her about them (see p.128).

▲ **FAMILY TOGETHERNESS** A period of peace and relaxation in the days following the birth of your baby is vital. It gives you both a chance to celebrate the birth, welcome and bond with your new baby, and get used to being a family.

Your newborn baby

A newborn's reflexes

A newborn has a set of inbuilt reflexes that help him to survive. They disappear within a few weeks as he develops (see p.156).

Grasp

He grasps anything put into his fist; the reflex is so strong that he can take his own weight. The reflex is lost in a couple of weeks.

Step

If his feet touch a firm surface, he will take a step – this has nothing to do with real walking.

"Moro" response

If startled, your baby throws out his arms and legs in a star shape to stop himself falling.

Rooting

If you stroke his cheek, he automatically turns his head ("roots") to find the nipple.

Few newborn babies are conventionally pretty, but even though everything is perfectly normal, your baby's appearance may make you slightly apprehensive, so you'll find it hard to resist going over him with a fine-tooth comb, just to make sure.

What your baby looks like

The size of a newborn baby varies enormously – a perfectly normal birth weight could be anything from 2.5 to 4.5kg (5½lb to 10lb). But even a 4–5kg (9–11lb) baby will seem tiny and vulnerable when newborn. Your baby may look slightly battered and bruised after the birth, and his head may be rather elongated because of moulding in the birth canal, but it will return to a normal rounded shape in a week or so. There may be the odd bruise here and there on his head, especially if your birth was assisted (see p.50), or there may be a small scar if a fetal monitor was attached to his scalp. Until he has his first bath, his hair may be a bit matted with dried blood and fluid from the birth.

Hands Your baby's hands will be curled into fists most of the time. Nails may be long and sometimes stained with meconium (see opposite).

Legs His legs may be so tightly flexed that you can't easily straighten them, but don't apply force. His feet may be rounded and toes curled.

Genitals These will look large because of the action of pregnancy hormones. For the same reason, both girls and boys may have pronounced breasts, which will shrink, and girls may also have a slight vaginal discharge for a day or two.

Umbilical cord The stump usually dries and shrivels within a few days, and your healthcare provider will remove the clamp. The rest drops off.

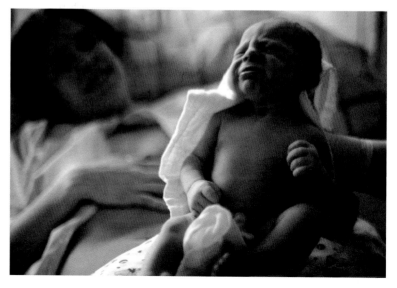

▶ **YOUR BABY'S HEAD** Your baby's head may look quite large compared to the rest of him. There may also be a bump on one side where the skull bones have been moulded during birth – the skull bones are soft and can override one another to protect the brain. The skull bones don't fuse completely for a few months, leaving a diamond-shaped soft spot on the top of the head, called the fontanelle, covered by a tough membrane. You may notice a pulse beating there.

What your newborn baby can do

Sight Babies like looking at faces more than anything else. He can see you clearly if your face is 20–25cm (8–10in) from his. He's wired to respond – his heart rate rises when he focuses on your face, so talk and smile. He'll react with body jerks and fish-feeding movements of his mouth – that's his first attempt at a conversation.

Hearing His hearing is acute – he knows both your voices from having heard them in the womb and he'll respond instantly to pleasure in your voice. Start talking and singing from the moment of birth and never stop.

Movement He loves physical movement – after all, he's been jogging and swaying in the womb for nine months – so carry him around as much as possible. Slings allow you to carry your baby close while keeping both hands free. Move his limbs gently while changing him, clap his hands gently, do gentle knee bends. But avoid sudden movements that startle him.

✳ Concerns about your newborn baby

Your concerns	What it is and how it is treated
Birthmarks	Many babies have birthmarks, most of which fade within a few months. Some, such as the strawberry mark, which is raised, may take much longer and usually become bigger and redder before fading. The Mongolian blue spot, a blueish birthmark on the lower back of babies with dark skin tones, is sometimes mistaken for bruising.
Milk spots	Tiny white spots on the bridge of the nose. These disappear after a few weeks.
Neonatal urticaria	A blotchy rash, a bit like a nettle rash; there may also be small yellow spots. It only lasts a couple of days.
Meconium	At birth your baby's bowel contains a dark green or almost black, sticky substance called meconium, which is usually passed into the nappy during the first 2–3 days.
Jaundice	Neonatal jaundice is quite common due to a baby's immature liver. It makes the skin yellowish and the urine dark. Your baby may be sleepy, so he'll need to be wakened for feeds to ensure he has enough fluid. Persistent cases may be treated with ultraviolet light.
Breathing	Babies snuffle and sneeze a lot, and get hiccups. They may even stop breathing for a second or two, but breathing soon becomes strong and regular.
Lip blisters	Some babies develop a white sucking blister on the lips. It doesn't cause discomfort and will fade in a few days.
Scalp swelling	Some babies develop a swelling on the scalp due to bleeding under the skin during the birth. This is quite normal, but it does take a few weeks to disperse.

✳ Newborn baby check

Your baby is given a top-to-toe check by a doctor before you leave hospital.

Vision
The doctor will shine a light into your baby's eyes and will note if they move on hearing her voice. She will also check for cataracts.

Heart and lungs
She'll listen to your baby's heart and check his lungs and breathing.

Ability to suck
She'll put her finger into his mouth to check the palate and that he can suck properly.

Internal organs
She'll gently feel his abdomen and check his anus.

Spine
She'll feel his spine to make sure the vertebrae are in place.

Hip manipulation
She'll remove his nappy and check his legs and hips for any sign of congenital hip dislocation.

The Guthrie test
On about the sixth day, a tiny drop of blood will be taken from his heel to test for thyroid function and for phenylketonuria, a rare disorder that may cause mental retardation if undetected. It may also be tested for a number of other conditions, including cystic fibrosis.

Hearing
In addition to the top-to-toe check, all new babies are now also given a special hearing screening test in the days after the birth. It's quick and doesn't hurt. If the response is not clear, your baby may be given a second test.

The special care baby

How a pre-term baby may look

If your baby is born prematurely, she may look a little different from what you expect:

✴ Her skin will be loose, wrinkled, and red because she hasn't had time to fill out with fat.

✴ She'll be covered in downy hair called lanugo hair.

✴ Her head will seem very large.

✴ She'll be very thin and bony, especially her ribs and buttocks, with stick-like limbs.

✴ Her breathing may seem laboured and uneven.

✴ Her movements may be jerky.

Feeding special care babies

At first your baby may need to be fed glucose intravenously, or have milk fed through a tube in her nose, but hopefully she will soon be able to try sucking. Breastmilk is especially good for a premature baby as your body will make milk suited to your baby's gestation. You can express your milk so your baby can be tube-fed.

Introducing breastfeeding

It may take time to get your baby used to breastfeeding, when she's ready. Avoid bottles as far as possible if you want to breastfeed fully, as weaker babies can get used to bottles and may reject your nipple.

If your baby does need some specialist care, you'll be understandably anxious. However, it will only be done for the best of reasons – to increase your baby's chances of thriving as a normal, healthy baby.

Why do babies need special care?

Although many people think special care only applies to premature births, in fact about one in ten babies needs some sort of special attention, and by no means are they all born before term. There are several possible reasons.

Prematurity A baby born before 37 weeks is pre-term or premature, and may need close monitoring, as well as help with breathing and feeding.

Low birth weight Any baby who weighs 2.5kg (5½lb) or less at birth is considered to have a low birth weight. Low birth weight babies may be either pre-term, or full term but "small for dates" (see p.34), and may need to spend a short time in a special care unit.

A health risk A baby who may have had difficulties with breathing during the birth, or have picked up an infection, may need special attention for a while. Alternatively, there may be birth defects, such as a "hole in the heart", that may have been diagnosed before or at the birth.

What special care means

If your baby needs special care, her needs can be catered for in a special care baby unit (SCBU) or a special section of the unit called a neonatal intensive care unit (NICU). This may mean she has to be moved to a different hospital. If she was premature or of a low birth weight, she could have difficulty with breathing, be prone to infections, be unable to regulate body temperature, or feed properly. Without support, low blood sugar levels can cause brain damage and she may lack iron and calcium. For these reasons, she may need the protection and constant monitoring of incubator care, with intravenous or tubal feeding (see left), until she catches up on growing and learns to feed and breathe without help.

Getting through it

Having a baby in special care is a bit like feeling you've lost a leg. Something is missing; your baby is born, but isn't yet able to be where she should be – in your arms. If she was born early, you may feel cheated on having missed out on the end of your pregnancy. Another common reaction is to feel that your baby isn't really yours – while she's in the SCBU, it may seem as though she belongs to the medical staff. Try to remind yourself that this is your child, and that soon she will be home where she belongs. Be as involved as possible in discussions about her condition and in her care, and try to look forward to the day when she'll be truly yours, and you can take her home.

Helping to care for your baby

All special care baby units welcome parents and actively encourage them to help with feeding, washing, and nappy changing. There may be rooms where you can stay overnight from time to time, and many units provide space for parents for a day or two before your baby is discharged so that you can get used to the normal care routine of a small baby – this is particularly important if you had a multiple birth.

Making contact

Just because your baby is in an incubator doesn't mean you can't touch, kiss, and cuddle her. This sort of contact is vitally important because it actually helps your baby to develop and become strong. If it's a closed incubator, you can reach into her through hand-holes to play and fondle, and you should talk and sing to her as much as you can so that she hears your voice. Open special care cots enable you to stroke and fondle directly. All this will keep her contented and help her to thrive – love is an essential vitamin for premature babies.

If it's practical, give your baby as much skin-to-skin contact as you can. When you hold your baby to your skin, her body temperature rises if she is cold, and then falls once she has warmed up. A successful experiment has also revealed that babies who are born prematurely thrive if they are nursed continuously between their mother's breasts – ask if you can try it. Skin to skin contact is essential for your baby, but it's essential for you, too, in fostering the bonding process. It will especially help you if you're nervous; you may feel this way because your baby is so small and you're finding it difficult to relate to her because she's in a special care unit. It's also very important for your partner to have skin-to-skin contact with his baby to help his bonding process.

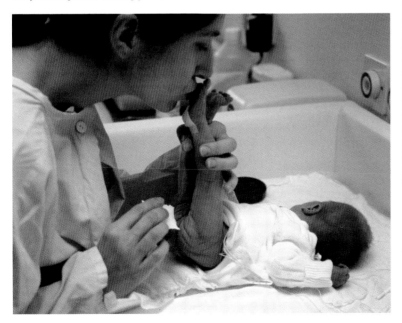

Coping with the technology

Many parents are worried by special care technology. Share your feelings with the staff in the unit and ask them to explain what the equipment does:

✳ An incubator provides a warm, humid environment for the baby.

✳ A ventilator takes over the baby's breathing, getting air into and out of the lungs.

✳ A humidifier ensures air in the ventilator is warm and moist before it goes into the lungs.

✳ The apnoea alarm alerts the staff if a baby stops breathing.

✳ The saturation monitor and blood gas analyzer measure levels of oxygen and carbon dioxide in the blood.

✳ The blood pressure gauge measures a baby's blood pressure.

✳ A perspex head box may be used to provide extra oxygen when the baby is breathing on her own.

✳ The glucose monitor records the baby's glucose levels.

✳ The electro-cardiogram (ECG) monitor measures heart rate.

✳ The bilirubinometer measures the risk of jaundice.

✳ A phototherapy lamp treats jaundice with ultraviolet light. A shield protects the baby's eyes.

✳ A heat shield keeps the baby warm in an open cot.

◀ **SPENDING TIME WITH YOUR BABY** It's important to spend as much time as possible in the special care baby unit with your baby. It will help to demystify the technology and allow you to bond with your baby.

You and your body

Postnatal check

Your family doctor or hospital obstetrician will examine you about six weeks after the birth. Your baby will also be checked at about this time, and it may happen at the same appointment (see p.155). This check will make sure that your body has fully returned to its pre-pregnant state. Your doctor will examine your uterus, heart, and blood pressure, your breasts, and any scarring if you had stitches. This is an ideal time to discuss contraception or anything that concerns you. At the checkup your doctor may:

✱ Test your blood pressure.

✱ Check your heart rate.

✱ Check your weight.

✱ Examine your abdomen to make sure the uterus has contracted down.

✱ Look at your breasts and nipples.

✱ Do an internal examination to assess the size and position of your uterus and the state of your vaginal muscles.

✱ Check on the site of perineal stitches. Tell your doctor if it's still sore, especially during sex.

✱ Carefully check your scar and abdomen if you had a Caesarean.

✱ Give you advice about contraception. During the internal examination, an IUD or Mirena device can be inserted or a cap fitted.

It takes a woman's body more than nine months to recover completely from pregnancy and childbirth. For the first week or so, you'll be weak and unable to walk any distance or carry anything heavy. Even if you feel well, try not to overdo it, or you'll prolong your recovery period.

Getting back to normal

The medical term for the immediate period of recovery after the birth of your baby is the puerperium. It's defined as the first four weeks, but most women are physically back to normal well before that, even if their emotional adjustment takes much longer. However, you may well be concerned about what is happening to your body during the first week or two after the birth, when changes are rapid but often accompanied by a certain amount of discomfort. When this is your first experience of childbirth, it's important to realize that vaginal discharge, painfully engorged breasts, and unexpected abdominal cramps are quite normal!

How your body recovers

Cervix and vagina Because both were stretched during delivery, they will take at least seven to ten days to regain their former elasticity and close up. Doing your pelvic floor exercises (see p.38) will help your vagina to tighten again. Start immediately after the birth.

Placental site (lochis) As the placental site heals, it may bleed for up to six weeks. This discharge (lochia) has three colour phases: red (four to five days), pink to brown (six to eight days), yellow to white (seven to ten days). If you over-exert yourself, you may start to bleed, making the lochia red and copious again. If this happens, tell your doctor and rest with your feet up.

Uterus Immediately after the birth, your uterus shrinks down to the size it was at about the fourth month of pregnancy. By about the tenth day it can no longer be felt in your abdomen – your midwife will check daily to make sure that it is shrinking normally. It takes about six weeks to revert to its normal pre-pregnant size.

Ovulation If you're not breastfeeding, you may begin to ovulate within six to 14 weeks of the birth; menstruation will follow in between eight and 16 weeks. Breastfeeding hormones can suppress menstruation, but don't rely on breastfeeding as a contraceptive. Use contraception as soon as you want to start penetrative sex again (see p.137).

Postnatal sex

You can have non-penetrative sex whenever you both feel like it after the birth, but you'd be wise to abstain from penetrative sex until after the lochia has stopped (see p.136). However, neither of you will probably feel like it for

Postnatal discomforts

Discomfort	How to relieve it
Coping with stitches	Discomfort from stitches can last up to a couple of weeks. Don't stand for long periods and have daily baths to prevent infection. Dry stitches with a hairdryer rather than a towel. Keep a bottle of witch hazel in the fridge and apply cold on a sterile pad to soothe the stitches. Occasionally stitches may not dissolve and need to be removed by your midwife or doctor.
Stress incontinence	Leaking urine when coughing, sneezing, taking exercise, or even laughing is a common though embarrassing problem for many women after childbirth. It's the result of stretched and weakened perineal muscles, so once again it's important to concentrate on doing your pelvic floor exercises (see p.38).
Breast engorgement	Three or four days after birth lactation begins; your breasts become engorged with milk, making them uncomfortably large, hard, and tender. Relieve this by expressing, putting your baby to the breast as often as he wants, and having warm baths or laying hot flannels on your breasts. Always wear a supportive nursing bra.
Afterpains	As your uterus shrinks back, you may continue to experience quite severe cramps, similar to menstrual pain, especially during breastfeeding. This is due to the action of the hormone oxytocin, which controls the "let down" of milk in your breasts (see p.78), and also causes the uterine muscles to contract (see p.49).
Headaches	In a very few cases (less than one per cent), some women experience a severe headache after an epidural anaesthetic. It's caused by a minute puncture in the membrane of the spinal column, made when the needle was inserted. If you experience this sort of headache, you'll be advised to lie down flat and drink plenty of fluids, and you'll be given painkillers, such as paracetamol, until the hole has healed and the headache lifts. This usually takes a couple of days.

a while. Nature has seen to it that most men have a low sex drive for some time after the delivery of their baby, especially if they are present at the birth. Not surprisingly, low libido lasts longer in women who have just had babies. No one who has vaginal bruises, painful stitches, and enlarged, tender breasts finds it easy to feel sexy; your need for rest and recuperation is much more important. If you've had stitches, make sure your partner feels your scar when it's healed – he'll be much more understanding and compassionate about sex after he's felt the extent of it (see p.46). It's best to be philosophical about these things, and discuss them openly and lovingly. This will stop them developing into long-term difficulties.

After a Caesarean

If you've had a Caesarean delivery, you'll be monitored more closely while you're in hospital, and your stay will be longer than after a normal delivery. The doctors will want to be sure that you and your baby are progressing well. Even so, your stay in hospital is likely only to be about five days.

Stitches

Stitches are usually dissolvable and do not need to be removed.

Time for recovery

It may only be when you get home that you realize how much the Caesarean has affected you. This won't last for long, but you won't feel completely back to normal for at least a month.

Help in the home

You need to avoid exertion while the wound is healing, so it's a good idea if your partner can take extra time off work, or if a friend or relation can stay for a while. You won't be able to lift heavy things, and you'll probably be warned not to drive for several weeks.

Your healing scar

At first your scar just needs to be kept dry and well ventilated, and you can bathe once the dressing is removed. If the wound becomes red or inflamed, consult your doctor as there may be a slight infection that can be treated with antibiotics. Your scar will feel less sore gradually, but may itch as the pubic hair grows back. As the scar is on your "bikini line", it's a good idea to wear pants that come up to your waistline to avoid irritation.

Resuming sport

Even if you were taking part in a regular sporting activity before you were pregnant, it's best to avoid strenuous aerobic exercise for at least nine months after the birth. Your body has just completed nine months of extra work ending in the huge effort of labour and needs time to recover. Avoid anything that puts a strain on your abdominal muscles, and don't resume working out in the gym until your doctor advises it. Ask a qualified fitness trainer or sports instructor to give you a graded programme, take it very easy, but don't expect to be back to your previous level of fitness or stamina for at least a year.

▲ **GET OUT AND ABOUT** Simply taking your baby for a walk is a good way to get some exercise. Your baby will also enjoy the fresh air and change of scene.

Looking after your body

Pregnancy and childbirth aren't illnesses, and your body is designed to recover naturally. However, this doesn't mean it couldn't do with a little help. Gone are the days when women were literally "confined" for several weeks, but you'll need to conserve your energy during the first few weeks to help the healing process and to enable you to get breastfeeding successfully established (see p.78). The fat laid down in your body during pregnancy specifically to provide the calories for breastfeeding will take a few weeks to be used up, but many women are surprised by how quickly they regain their pre-pregnancy shape and weight when they breastfeed.

Postnatal exercises

Losing weight isn't the same as regaining muscle tone; you'll need to exercise the muscles in your abdomen and perineum to bring them back to normal. But finding the time and energy to do postnatal exercises may seem an impossible dream to you immediately after the birth. While you're in the postnatal ward you may be visited by a physiotherapist within a day of the birth. She will explain exactly what has happened to your body and will show you the best way to start exercising. Your abdominal muscles will have stretched and parted to accommodate your growing baby; this muscle tone can be regained if you find ten minutes a day to do the simple exercises given here. And you can even do things like simple stretches and forward bends while your baby lies kicking on his changing mat. Make sure you warm up properly first (see below).

Getting started

Start gently – your muscles and ligaments are still soft from the action of progesterone – and don't forget your pelvic floor muscles (see p.38); just because you can't see them doesn't mean they aren't important.

Before you exercise

You can start the gentle programme of exercises given here at any time after the birth, but avoid vigorous exercise until the lochia has stopped (see p.64). And if you've had a tear or an episiotomy, don't do any stretching exercises until you've healed.

Warming up Athletes and dancers always warm up before exercise or performing, as they know the damage they could do to their bodies without it. It's equally important for you when doing postnatal exercises. Warming up helps relieve tension and warms up muscles and joints so that they don't overstretch when you begin more demanding exercises. It also helps to avoid cramp and stiffness afterwards.

If you've had a Caesarean You can start doing pelvic floor exercises straight away, but don't attempt any other exercises until you've had your postnatal check.

Taking care Don't exercise if you feel exhausted or unwell, and be careful if you've had back trouble. Avoid sit-ups or straight leg lifts and always stop doing an exercise if it hurts.

How to exercise

Little and often is best; start with one or two repetitions of each, every day, then progress to ten. Remember to exhale on the effort, and inhale as you relax. Always stop if any exercise hurts.

Cat arching

1 **KNEEL ON ALL FOURS** with knees and hands slightly apart. Make sure your back, head, and neck are straight.

2 **TIGHTEN YOUR BUTTOCKS** and slowly arch your back upwards. Keep your arms straight, but don't lock your elbows. This exercise is wonderful for relieving lower backache.

Stomach toner

1 **LIE ON THE FLOOR**, with knees bent and arms straight by your sides. Pull in your tummy muscles and press the small of your back down. Hold the position for four seconds, then relax.

2 **KEEPING YOUR FEET FLAT**, tilt your pelvis up and lift your head off the pillow as far as you can. Don't try to sit up; it's enough just to lift your head and perhaps your shoulders.

Curl-ups (after two weeks)

1 **TRY THIS MORE ADVANCED** abdominal exercise at least two weeks after the birth. Lie down with your legs bent as before. Try to reach your knees by sliding your hands up your thighs.

2 **WITH YOUR HANDS** as close to your knees as possible, as you exhale, pull in your tummy muscles and lift your head for a count of four, then relax.

Leg lifts

1 **STRENGTHEN YOUR THIGHS AND ABDOMINAL** muscles with these simple lifts. Lie on your side comfortably, supporting your head with one hand, and balancing your body by resting the other hand in front of you. Make sure your legs are in line with your hip and shoulder.

2 **KEEPING YOUR KNEE AND FOOT** facing to the front, lift your whole leg straight upwards to shoulder height, hold for a count of two, and then lower. Do this a few times, then turn over and repeat with the other leg.

Side bends

STAND WITH YOUR FEET APART and arms by your sides. Slowly bend sideways at the waist, stretching your leg outwards at the same time. Return to upright, and repeat on the other side.

Caring for your baby

The excitement of the birth is over and now you're back home. But as new parents the chances are you'll feel daunted by the sheer work involved in the day-to-day care of your baby. There are practical details to think about, such as making sure you've got all the equipment and clothes you need, which nappies to use, and how to keep your baby clean. And then there are the more serious questions like how to get breastfeeding established, how to pacify your crying baby, and how to cope with broken nights. As time passes, you'll get to know your baby and her needs will become easier to predict and to cater for. It will still be hard work, but if you share the joys and burdens equally, you'll find the pleasure of watching your baby grow and develop makes everything worthwhile.

The first weeks

✳ JUST FOR MUM

Your baby's first few months of life would be tiring for you even if you hadn't been through the rigours of labour and birth. Spoil yourself and look after your own needs.

How to be kind to yourself

✳ Rest with your baby. Use the time when your baby is asleep to catch up on your own sleep. If he has his longest unbroken sleep in the morning, take advantage of it, or rest in the afternoon when he does.

✳ Share with your partner. If things are getting on top of you, he needs to know, for your sake and for your baby's. Encourage him to look after the baby when he's at home; don't be over-protective and try to do everything yourself.

✳ Ask for help. If you're feeling isolated, don't soldier on alone. Early offers of help may tail off because friends and family don't want to impose, but often they are glad to be asked.

✳ Get out and about (see p.134). Being tied to the house can make you depressed, so try to get out as much as possible. It's helpful if you have friends locally who are also at home with young babies. You'll probably have met like-minded parents at antenatal classes. Having other new parents around you means you can share the good times as well as the worries. In addition, as your baby grows, he'll have a ready-made circle of friends to play with.

After all the months of preparation and the excitement of the birth, you're back home and at last you're a family. Now you can get down to the serious business of learning how to care for your child as he grows and develops from a small, vulnerable baby to a social, communicative one-year-old. It's immensely rewarding, but there's a lot to do and it's a full-time commitment from the start.

Finding a pattern

When you become a new parent, perhaps the most difficult thing to adjust to is the fluidity and unpredictability of your new lifestyle. Most people's lives have very distinct patterns, based on doing roughly the same things at roughly the same times, and they feel discomforted if this structure dissolves. Alternatively, you might be used to doing what you want exactly when you want to do it. But trying to impose this sort of orderliness on a young baby is the equivalent of spitting into the wind. If you can both relax and follow your baby's lead, you'll find that a pattern of some sort will eventually emerge.

Following your baby's lead

Ignore anyone who tells you that you shouldn't pick up your crying baby because "he's only exercising his lungs" or "he'll cry himself back to sleep in a minute" – very young babies shouldn't have to wait. If a baby learns that he has to scream for ten minutes to receive attention, he is laying down a pattern of behaviour that you will not appreciate in the future. So-called "good" babies are either those who are contented because all their needs are met promptly, or those who have been taught by experience that their needs won't be met at once and have become apathetic. You cannot "spoil" a young baby except by imposing a regime that is governed by the clock – and by placing your needs before his. This is what will lead to him becoming discontented and hard to pacify. Helping him to separate his needs from others' needs will come much later on in his development.

Changing your priorities

If you're both following your baby's lead, you'll have to learn to be as relaxed as possible about things like meal times and housework, even if you normally have a set routine and are house-proud. It's much more important for both of you to concentrate on becoming skilled and confident in the practical care of your baby. Initially, there may seem to be a lot to learn and you'll feel clumsy and nervous (everybody does), but you'll soon find that it becomes second nature, and you'll gradually develop a routine that allows you time to fit in household chores at some point in your day.

If you feel low

If either or both of you feels disillusioned or dissatisfied with what you imagined you would be experiencing at this time, you're not necessarily depressed, you're probably just out of sorts. This is natural – you're both tired. If the baby is fractious, a mother may feel that somehow it is her fault and she may also be suffering from the "baby blues" (see p.132), while a new father may feel inadequate if he's unable to help as much as he'd like, because he's at work. Don't worry, you'll both soon begin to adjust to the new situation, but if negative feelings persist, talk to your doctor or health visitor. They'll help you to realize that lots of people feel the same way, but will also be able to tell if you're suffering from the signs of actual postnatal depression, which is easy to treat if recognized early on (see p.133).

Reassure each other

If you both start out in the knowledge that these first few months can seem like hard work, you'll be able to reassure each other that you're coping extremely well. If you accept the validity of each other's feelings, and hold on to the fact that any difficulties are temporary, you'll discover that parenthood really is as pleasurable as you expected.

❋ Coping with the night shift

What to do	How it helps
Prepare yourselves for broken nights	Many babies continue to wake once or twice during the night well beyond 12 months of age. If you're both prepared for this, you'll find it much easier to adjust.
Share the burden	Taking turns to get up is important. You may have followed the traditional pattern of father going to work, while mother stays at home, but remember, looking after a baby is also a full-time job.
Change your sleep pattern	Broken nights are not necessarily sleepless nights. By developing a new sleep pattern, you'll find that you're able to wake, attend to your baby, and then go back to sleep immediately.
Keep your baby close	If your baby's cot is by the side of your bed, you don't have to disturb yourselves too much when he wakes for a feed. Put him back in his cot when you're ready to go back to sleep (see p.102).
Stay together	Sleeping separately could undermine your relationship as a couple and with your baby. Only sleep in separate rooms as a last resort – for example, because of illness or extreme fatigue.
Avoid sleep deprivation	Long-term sleep deprivation can have serious consequences, so it's better that you both lose some sleep than for one parent alone to take all the burden and become completely exhausted.

❋ JUST FOR DAD

The first few weeks with your baby are important in helping you get used to your new role as a father.

How you can help

❋ Support your partner. She will be very tired to start with as a result of going through labour and birth, and from the physical and emotional responsibility of breastfeeding. Provide her with the time and space to meet your baby's nutritional needs, and reassure her constantly that she's doing a difficult job well. Your support can make all the difference.

❋ Find time to help. If you're back at work, relish the opportunity to do as much as you can for your partner and your baby when you're at home.

❋ Give your baby love. Babies need as much love as they can get, and there's no difference between the love of a father and a mother. If your baby is being breastfed, then obviously he'll need his mother when he's hungry, but at all other times he'll benefit just as much from your closeness and attention. This closeness from you will mean that your baby learns to be secure with both of you, which will help him to settle and take the pressure off your partner.

❋ Build a relationship with your baby from the start. Your own feelings as a parent will be strengthened if you spend as much time as possible with him. Being an equal partner in your baby's care will be rewarding and beneficial to you and to your family.

Equipment

Safety measures

You'll need to have safety checked all equipment throughout your home. Before your baby becomes mobile, check you have the following:

✳ Covers for all electric sockets.

✳ Corner protectors for furniture.

✳ Locks and catches for video and DVD players, doors, cupboards and drawers (especially in the kitchen), and the refrigerator.

✳ A cooker guard.

✳ Retractable flex for electrical goods, such as the kettle, iron, and toaster.

✳ A stair gate at the bottom of stairs and across the kitchen door.

Providing for your new baby is exciting and rewarding, and you naturally want the best. However, as you set out to plan the nursery, do bear in mind that at first your new arrival will need very little in the way of essentials.

The basics

Manufacturers of nursery "hardware" have recognized that couples expecting their first child are among the biggest spenders around, but you don't need to break the bank to provide for your newborn baby if you stick to the basics shown here.

▶ **HIGH CHAIR** Choose a sturdy chair with easy-to-clean surfaces and a fitted safety harness. Some have a seat and foot plate that can be adjusted as your baby grows older.

▲ **BABY BATH** For use in the first three to four months, a flat-based bath comes with a stand or can be rested on a firm surface; others fit over the big bath..

▲ **CHANGING MAT** A changing mat is a comfortable and practical way to avoid mess when nappy changing and at bath time.

BABY CHAIR A rigid or bouncing baby chair with back support is useful for young babies before they can sit. Always place the chair on the floor.

▲ **FULL-SIZE COT** When your baby outgrows her Moses basket, you'll need a cot. Choose one with two mattress positions and a drop-side to protect your back when lifting her.

◀ **MOSES BASKET** A Moses basket is useful for a newborn as it is portable. You could make linings and trimmings yourself. Use a baby sleeping bag instead of bedding, but make sure it's the right size.

BABY CARRIERS There are several types of carrying sling suitable for young babies; try them on to see which is most comfortable. A backpack may be more comfortable once your baby can sit up.

Out and about

Your baby won't be walking until he's at least a year old, and even then he'll need transporting in a buggy or car seat for safety. It's worth looking ahead to future needs when you're thinking about buying any of these larger, more expensive items.

▲ **INFANT CAR SEAT** All babies under 10kg (22lb) should be put in a rear-facing seat in the car. The seat must be fixed in position. These seats can be used in the front seat (only if the airbag can be disabled) or the rear seat; your baby is safest in the rear seat. Rear-facing seats provide better protection for a young baby's head, neck, and spine.

◀ **PRAM AND BUGGY** A pram/buggy combination is ideal. Check ease of folding, and that the height of the handle doesn't make you stoop. This carrycot can be used for babies up to six months or until your baby can sit up by himself. The cot can then be replaced with a seat to make a buggy.

Buying secondhand

If there's a secondhand shop in your area, it's well worth a visit. You can also try shopping at charity shops, car boot sales, and internet sites. Check all equipment carefully, and avoid certain items (see below). .

Good secondhand buys

✳ Clothes, especially newborn baby clothes and outerwear.

✳ Bedclothes (except duvets), but always wash before use.

✳ Moses basket, but you may want to buy a new mattress.

✳ Plastic or wood toys only, but check carefully for cracks or splinters. Avoid anything that has metal or moving parts; even soft toys or dolls may contain hidden metal parts.

✳ Large plastic items, such as sterilizing equipment.

Possible secondhand buys

✳ Pram or buggy, but check brakes, folding mechanism, and all of the accessories.

✳ Cot, but check drop-side mechanism is safe, and you may also want to buy a new mattress.

✳ Travel cot, though always check the folding mechanism and carrying case. Buy a new mattress if necessary.

✳ High chair, but make sure that all screws are really secure and check crevices for food remains.

✳ Safety items, such as baby monitors or stair gates, but check that they work properly.

Bad secondhand buy

✳ Never buy a secondhand car seat, as the seat may have been weakened in an accident.

Breastfeeding

Breastmilk is the most suitable food for your baby, providing all her nutritional needs during her first six months. As a father, you can be involved by supporting your partner.

Advantages of breastfeeding

Here are some of the many advantages of breastfeeding.

* Baby and mother bond closely.

* Helps burn off fat laid down in a mother's body during pregnancy.

* Milk is readily available, sterile, and is the correct temperature.

* Milk is easy for a baby to digest.

* Milk has a perfect balance of protein, carbohydrate, fat, salt, and other minerals, vitamins, and iron.

* Milk protects against infection.

* Milk may protect against allergies.

* Breastfed babies have fewer nappy rashes and their stools are softer and inoffensive.

Getting started

You don't need any specialist equipment, but you will need two or three nursing bras and some breast pads. Some people have no difficulty with breastfeeding; but for many others it doesn't go smoothly at first. Don't feel demoralized: follow my step-by-step guide (see p.80) and discuss any problems with your midwife, health visitor, and/or breastfeeding counsellor, who will be happy to give advice. Don't give up without consulting one of them first. Remember, your baby is learning too, so you have to be patient.

Ensuring a good milk supply

When your baby feeds, the milk she drinks first – the foremilk – is thin, watery, and thirst-quenching; the hindmilk that follows is richer in fat and protein, so your baby gets all her nutritional needs at one feed. To ensure that you provide a good milk supply, make sure you are eating a good diet and drinking lots of fluids, especially in hot weather when your baby will be thirsty too. Feed on demand, when your baby is hungry; your body will automatically produce enough. If your baby feeds slowly in the first few

▶ **SITTING IN A CHAIR** Sit with both feet firmly on the ground. Support your back and arms with pillows and place an extra pillow on your lap to raise and support your baby if necessary.

days, you may have to express milk (see p.83) in order for more to be produced. If she feeds often, you will keep pace, no matter how small your breasts are; breast size is irrelevant to the amount of milk you make. However, it is important to rest between feeds, so that your metabolism can catch up. Many women find the mid-evening feed the most difficult as the milk supply is often lower because they are tired, and so the baby may be fretful at this time of day. Try resting in the afternoon, preparing an evening meal earlier in the day, or better still, leaving the cooking to your partner.

Frequency of feeds

Be prepared to feed often – your baby could feed ten or 11 times in 24 hours for the first few weeks. Feeding will take over your life to start with, but you'll find that your baby is contented, goes to sleep easily, and by the time she's six to eight weeks, she'll be feeding more efficiently, and less often. Don't try to impose a rigid routine – your baby will get upset and the stress will affect your ability to feed. During the first few weeks, use alternate breasts for feeds. This helps to balance the milk supply and prevents either breast becoming sore. Many babies find one side easier than the other; if this happens with your baby, put her to the less favoured breast first.

Breastfeeding positions

It's important to be in a comfortable position before you start feeding as you're likely to be there for some time. Make sure you have a glass of water with you too. Whether sitting or lying, make sure your baby's whole body is angled towards you; in this position she's more likely to latch on first time. Lying down is ideal for night feeds; when your baby is very small you may need to lay her on her pillow so that she can reach your nipple. You may also find the lying position the most suitable if you've had an episiotomy and sitting is uncomfortable. If you've had a Caesarean section and your stomach is still tender, try tucking your baby's feet under your arm.

The "let-down" reflex

When your baby suckles at your breast, she needs to latch on properly with her gums firmly gripping the areola and the nipple so far into her mouth that the milk can be squeezed right into her throat for her to swallow. As she sucks, nerves in the areola stimulate the hypothalamus in the brain, which in turn stimulates the pituitary gland to secrete oxytocin. This causes the breast to release (or "let down") milk.

▼ **FEEDING WHILE LYING DOWN** This is a good position when you're tired or if you need to keep your baby's weight off a Caesarean wound. Lie down on your side and lay your baby alongside you so she can reach your lower breast.

Latching on

1 **SUPPORT YOUR BABY** along the length of his back with your arm. Support the back of his neck and bring him up to your breast. Line up your nipple with your baby's nose. As soon as he smells your milk, he'll open his mouth. While your baby is very young, you can gently stroke the cheek nearest the breast; when you do this, he'll turn towards your breast as a reflex action.

2 **YOUR BABY SHOULD** "latch on" to your nipple at once. If not, support your breast with your hand and guide him on to it so that he has a mouthful of nipple. Your breasts are stimulated to produce milk by your baby's sucking, so the more eagerly he feeds, the more milk your breasts will produce. You supply what your baby needs and you won't run out.

3 **RELEASING** – a breastfeeding baby creates a strong vacuum on the breast, so when he has finished, you may need to release his grip on the nipple by gently easing your little finger into the corner of his mouth. Never pull your nipple away from your baby; this is a sure way to make it sore, and sore nipples (see opposite) may deter you from breastfeeding.

Latching on

The key is getting your baby's mouth correctly fixed or latched on to your breast, with your nipple well inside his mouth. Your baby stimulates milk flow by pressing the tip of his tongue against your areola. Then he presses the back of his tongue up towards his palate to squeeze milk from your nipple into his throat.

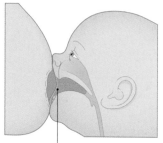

Baby's gums should
encircle the areola

Being determined

Few women breastfeed without encountering problems at least once, and sometimes several times. So while you shouldn't necessarily expect to find it difficult, neither should you be surprised if you seem to have a run of problems. The important thing to bear in mind is that most breastfeeding difficulties can be put right – provided you have support and the commitment and confidence to continue.

Taking care of your breasts

Your breasts need special care when you start breastfeeding. Buy at least two maternity bras – the best you can afford. A good bra will minimize discomfort if your breasts become sore. A few weeks before the birth get advice from an in-store expert who will help you try some on. Look for a bra with front fastenings and wide straps that won't cut into your shoulders. Drop-front or zip-fastening bras are easy to undo with one hand while you hold your baby. Wear your bra all the time, even at night, as you'll need lots of support.

Take great care of your breasts and nipples. Bathe them every day with water – don't use soap because it dehydrates the skin and encourages sore or cracked nipples – and gently pat them dry. Dry them gently after feeding, too. If you can, leave your nipples open to the air for a time when you've finished feeding. Breast pads and shields do help you keep your nipples clean and dry, although not everyone finds them essential.

Concerns about breastfeeding

Your concern	What you can do
How long on each breast	Your baby takes 80 per cent of the feed in the first five minutes, five minutes more and he's sucked out the creamy aftermilk, so as a rough guide, expect him to spend about ten minutes feeding per breast. Breastfed babies are rarely underfed, though they may only feed for a short time. Do not restrict feeds at each breast. If your baby is feeding happily, allow him to take his time.
Slow feeding	Many babies take a few days to get the hang of latching on and may be slow to feed. If this becomes a problem, seek advice. A baby who sucks for a long time isn't necessarily feeding. He may just love sucking. If your baby tends to fall asleep at the breast, let him take all he wants from one side, then offer the other breast first next time.
Baby's weight gain	Don't weigh your baby before and after feeding. Weight gain in breastfed babies should always be calculated over a two-to-three-week period, as weight is often gained unevenly. The very rare instances of underfeeding usually occur because the baby isn't properly latched on.
If you're ill	Common infections such as colds needn't interrupt breastfeeding. Stay in bed and let your partner bring your baby to you just to feed. You could also express milk so your partner can feed your baby instead. If you need medication of any sort, make sure your doctor knows you are breastfeeding as some medicines are not recommended for breastfeeding mothers. If you go into hospital, breastfeeding is usually still possible if you take your baby in with you.
Breastfeeding in public	Breastfeeding is the most convenient way to feed your baby, and you should be able to breastfeed any time, anywhere. It's possible to feed discreetly if you use a nursing bra that undoes easily in front with one hand, and a big shawl or cardigan to screen yourself. A baggy T-shirt or sweatshirt also works – you can tuck your baby up underneath it.

Sore nipples

Painful nipples are the most common reason for women giving up breastfeeding. However, there are ways to avoid them. Make sure your baby is correctly positioned and properly latched on and never pull your baby off the nipple (see opposite). Keep your nipples dry with disposable or cotton washable breast pads or clean cotton hankies. Don't use tissues as they will fall apart. Let the nipples dry naturally at the end of each feed whenever possible. If they become cracked, ointment such as chamomile or calendula cream may be helpful. If your nipples become very sore, feed your baby before he is desperate as he will be calmer and treat you more gently. Try to get the milk flowing before the feed starts by expressing a little first.

Blocked ducts and mastitis

Tight clothing or engorgement can cause a blocked milk duct, resulting in a hard red patch on the outside of the breast where the duct lies. You can prevent this by feeding often and encouraging your baby to empty your breasts, and by making sure that your bra fits properly. A blocked duct can lead to an acute infection known as mastitis. The breast will be inflamed and a red patch will appear on the outside, as with a blocked duct. Continue to breastfeed because you need to empty the breast. Your doctor may prescribe antibiotics to clear up the infection.

▲ **FEEDING AWAY FROM HOME** One of the advantages of breastfeeding is that it's possible to feed at any time and anywhere while you are out and about.

Your support is essential.

What you can do to help

✱ Be gently encouraging.

✱ Don't leave your partner to feed the baby alone unless she asks you to – she could feel isolated and you'll feel neglected.

✱ Your partner may like to express milk that you can give in a bottle at night. Undo your shirt and hold your baby against your skin to mimic breastfeeding.

✱ Be aware that your partner's breasts may be tense, sore, and very sensitive for the first few weeks of breastfeeding.

What if it's twins?

Don't be put off by people who say you can't breastfeed twins. Lots of mothers prove otherwise and, like all babies, twins benefit enormously from breastmilk. All the usual advantages of breastfeeding apply, but especially the protection against infection – it's important to twins because prematurity is more common than with single babies. It may be slightly more difficult to establish breastfeeding for twins, but once it's established you can feed them at the same time, though it's not quite as easy to feed both babies together when you're away from home.

Get advice Confidence is a crucial factor in breastfeeding twins. Try to talk to other mothers who've done it successfully – there are support groups to help you (see p.187).

One at a time to start with Concentrate on latching on with one baby at a time at first. Feeding singly may be easier in the early days, and it gives you a chance to get to know each baby individually, each of whom has the

▶ **FEEDING YOUR TWINS** Once breastfeeding is established, you can try feeding your babies together.

same need to bond with her parents. However, feeding one at a time does take much longer than feeding them together.

Feeding together To feed your babies at the same time, lay them on their backs, one under each arm with their heads forward, supported on pillows.

There's plenty of milk Human breasts are quite capable of nourishing two babies. Breastfeeding is always controlled by demand, so your breasts will produce as much milk as your babies need. If one feeds more readily than the other, put the slower baby to the breast first; the stronger baby will stimulate more milk.

Look after yourself Eat heartily, have lots to drink, and rest when you can. Although twins' practical needs are the same, there are two of them to look after, and you'll tire more easily. Accept any offers of help you get.

Expressing milk

When you're breastfeeding, you can express milk so that your partner can feed your baby; it also helps to relieve overfull breasts in the first days. If your baby is in a special care unit (see p.62), you can express milk for her. Few women find expressing milk easy, so don't be disheartened – it's a knack. If you "leak" milk while feeding, place a breast shell against the other breast, and keep the milk in a sterile container.

Using a breast pump

You can express milk more quickly using a pump, which applies a rhythmical suction to the breast. A funnel is fitted over your areola, you then operate the lever or plunger to express the milk (see right). Electric pumps are more expensive than hand pumps, but they imitate the baby's sucking cycle more closely. An electric pump is best if you need to express often – for example, if you're going back to work before weaning. You can get pumps that allow you to express from both breasts at the same time.

▲**USING A MANUAL PUMP** Start by fitting the funnel of the pump over your areola carefully to form an airtight seal. You then operate the lever or plunger of the pump to express your milk.

Expressing milk by hand

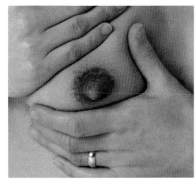

1 **MASSAGE YOUR BREASTS** with flat hands, beginning at your ribs and working towards your areola, gradually going over the whole breast.

2 **THEN ROLL YOUR** fingers and thumb together below and above your areola so that you press on the wider milk ducts behind the nipple.

3 **COLLECT THE MILK** in a sterile bowl, transfer it to a sterile container, and keep it in the refrigerator for a few hours. Freeze it for longer storage.

Bottle-feeding

I'm not going to pretend that bottle-feeding is as good for your baby as breastfeeding, but I don't want you to feel guilty, either. If you're undecided, look back to the sections on breastfeeding so that you're aware of its positive advantages. Bottle-feeding does, however, mean that both of you can share all of your baby's care equally.

Sterilizing and preparing bottles

Hygiene and making up feeds correctly are important if you are bottle-feeding to avoid health problems with your baby. To ensure your baby thrives and to avoid infection:

✳ Buy equipment well in advance and practise cleaning and sterilizing bottles and teats.

✳ Always wash your hands thoroughly before handling bottles and feeding your baby.

✳ Always follow the manufacturer's instructions carefully when you are sterilizing bottles.

✳ If using a chemical sterilizer, bottles and teats should be fully immersed in sterilizing fluid and left for at least two hours, or according to the manufacturer's instructions.

✳ With six or seven feeds to make in 24 hours for the first few weeks, change the sterilizing fluid twice a day. Later you can do this once a day.

✳ Make bottles one at a time; don't make feeds in advance and store them in the refrigerator.

✳ Never add extra scoops of formula, sugar, or baby cereal to a bottle.

✳ When a feed is over, pour away leftover milk, clean and rinse the bottle, cover it and place to one side until you are ready to sterilize it.

✳ Never give a baby leftover milk from a bottle because it may be contaminated with bacteria.

✳ Keep a couple of cartons of ready-made formula for emergencies.

Feeding your baby

Either of you can bottle-feed your baby, but bottle-feeding really allows a father to come into his own. When you are giving your baby a bottle, you can mimic the closeness of breastfeeding by cradling him close in the crook of your arm. Hold him so his face is 20–25cm (8–10in) away from yours, in a position where he can make eye contact with you (see p.61). If possible, open your shirt and hold him against your bare skin.

Giving your baby a bottle

Before you start, check also that the flow from the teat is neither too fast nor too slow – before giving the bottle, tip it up to make sure the teat produces a flow of several drops a second. Your baby may break naturally for a burp halfway through the feed, but it isn't necessary to force him to burp by rubbing his back; if he's still hungry, he'll just get upset. If he seems comfortable, let him feed without a break until he's had enough.

BOTTLE-FEEDING YOUR BABY
Cradle your baby close enough to have eye contact throughout, and talk to her while you feed. She'll soon learn to associate the pleasure of feeding with the sight of your face.

Making up a feed

1 **FILL A BOTTLE** with freshly boiled water. Using the scoop provided, level the powder with the back of a knife.

2 **ADD THE SCOOPS OF FORMULA** to the boiled water. Add it one scoop at a time; never add extra.

3 **CHECK THAT YOU'VE ADDED** the right amount of formula. Put the teat on the bottle.

4 **SHAKE THE BOTTLE** to make sure the formula mixes thoroughly. Cool the bottle in a bowl of cold water.

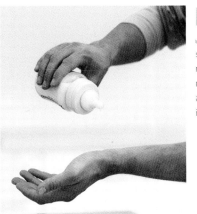

5 **CHECK THE TEMPERATURE** Always check that the milk is not too hot before offering it to your baby by shaking a few drops on to your wrist. The milk should be blood temperature, which means it should feel neither hot nor cold against your skin. If necessary put it back into the cold water to cool it down.

You will need

* Steam or chemical sterilizing unit

* Freshly boiled water

* Powdered formula
with measuring scoop

* Straight-backed knife
for levelling powdered formula

* Bottles, teats, and covers

Keeping bottles clean

Scrupulous hygiene is essential if you are bottle-feeding. Milk can be a rich breeding ground for the bacteria that cause diseases such as gastroenteritis, so sterilize bottles, teats and all other equipment used for feeding until your baby is six months old. Clean bottles and teats thoroughly as described below before sterilizing. Once your baby is over 12 months you can wash the equipment in a dishwasher.

* Scrub bottles and teats with a bottle brush and hot, soapy water to remove all traces of milk, then rinse well in cold water.

* Wash the teats thoroughly, paying attention to the inside rim and making sure that the holes are also clear. Then rinse in cold water.

Your baby's nappies

You'll have to use nappies for at least two and a half years, until your baby gains full bladder and bowel control, so it's worth familiarizing yourself with the most efficient way to change your baby. Give some thought, too, to which type of nappy best suits your circumstances – there's certainly plenty of choice nowadays.

Nappy rash

Nappy rash is preventable if you always change your baby's nappy promptly, particularly after she's had a bowel movement; bacteria in faeces breaks down the urine to release ammonia, which can irritate and ulcerate the skin. Always keep your baby's skin clean and well aired. Use barrier cream only as a preventive measure. If your baby does become sore, leave her nappy off whenever possible and let her kick on her changing mat. Apply nappy cream at every change. Check with your doctor if the rash persists for more than two to three days.

Which nappies to use

Your first choice in nappies will be between fabric and disposable types. Many parents prefer disposables, although an increasing debate on environmental issues has led other parents to consider fabric nappies. Yet the issue is not clear cut: the detergents required to clean fabric nappies can be viewed as pollutants to the water supply, and the energy required to wash them might also be regarded as wasteful. You need to consider the increased electricity bills for frequent washing and the cost in your time, although there are laundry services in many areas. Another option is to use "green" disposable nappies, which are produced with fewer chemicals, biodegrade, and have less impact on the environment.

Nappies, liners, and fasteners

Here is a selection of nappies. Provided your baby is changed as often as necessary, she will be happy in whatever style you choose.

Disposable nappies

Plastic pants

Shaped fabric nappy

Fabric nappy with Velcro fastener

Fabric nappy liner

Liners and safety pins

Reusable nappies

Traditional terry towelling squares are bulky, and can be uncomfortable for your baby when she's mobile. Modern reusables are usually shaped, and many types have strong Velcro fastenings or poppers, or you could use pinless fasteners, so you don't have to worry about using safety pins. If you're using these, it's a good idea to also use disposable or reusable liners (see box left) to avoid heavy soiling with faeces.

Nappies for boys or girls

Some manufacturers of disposables have taken the differences between the sexes into account: boys tend to wet the front of their nappies so boys' disposables have extra padding in the front. Girls tend to wet the back of nappies, and this is also accounted for in the design of girls' disposables.

Cleaning your baby

Change your baby's nappy whenever you notice that it is soiled or wet. The number of times the nappy needs to be changed will vary from baby to baby and from day to day.

LIFT YOUR BABY'S LEGS by holding her feet or ankles. Use cotton wool or baby wipes to clean the labia on the outside only.

Cleaning girls

Always clean your baby's vulva and anus from front to back to avoid spreading bacteria from the anus to your baby's vagina. Don't clean inside the labia; just rinse away faeces gently with damp cotton wool.

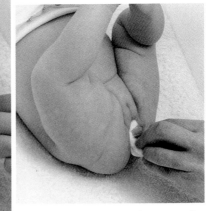

USE A CLEAN PIECE of cotton wool or baby wipe to clean the vulva, wiping from front to back.

Cleaning boys

Cover a boy's penis with a tissue as you take off his nappy in case he passes urine. Clean around the penis and scrotum with damp cotton wool. Don't try to pull back the foreskin as this remains fixed until your son is much older.

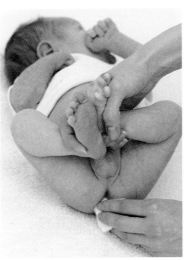

LIFT HIS LEGS by holding both ankles as shown. Clean around genital area with water. Use a different piece of cotton wool each time you wipe.

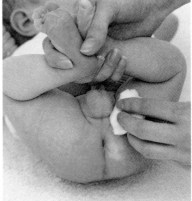

MAKE SURE ALL soiling is removed. Work from the leg creases in towards the penis.

Changing your baby's nappy

Always change your baby on a firm flat surface, covered with a changing mat or towel. Protect your back by using a changing table of the correct height, or kneel beside the bed. Never leave your baby alone on the changing mat if it's on a surface above floor level. Even a newborn baby can wriggle off a mat, particularly if he's upset or angry. Collect together all the equipment you need before you start. Dispose of faeces in the toilet if possible; but don't flush disposable nappies or fabric nappy liners down the toilet. Put dirty nappies in nappy sacks, preferably placing them in a covered bin.

1 **REMOVE THE SOILED NAPPY** and clean carefully as shown on p.87. Make sure all creases are clean and dry if you used water to clean. Slide the clean nappy under your baby, lifting her buttocks gently into position.

You will need

* Changing mat
* Tissues
* Clean nappy
* Bowl of warm water
* Cotton wool or baby wipes
* Barrier cream
* Bin with lid or nappy sacks

2 **USING BOTH HANDS**, bring the front of the nappy up between your baby's legs, as high as it will go. Tuck in the corners securely around her waist, ready for fastening.

3 **HOLDING THE NAPPY** in place with one hand, fix the adhesive tabs firmly on to the front flap of the nappy.

Changing a reusable nappy

The technique for changing reusables is the same as for disposables, but there are few more layers to deal with. You need to soak dirty nappies in a bucket of water containing nappy solution before you wash them.

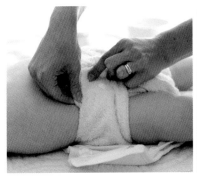

1 **CLEAN YOUR BABY CAREFULLY** as decribed on p.87. Put a clean liner inside the main nappy. Slide the prepared nappy and the waterproof outer wrap under your baby's bottom. Bring the front of the nappy up as far as it will go and secure it using the nappy fastenings.

2 **PULL THE OUTER WRAP** up over the main nappy and secure it using the adjustable poppers. Make sure it is comfortable and that the outer wrap fits snuggly over the nappy to prevent leaks.

▶ **FREE TO MOVE** Shaped resuable nappies are far less bulky than the traditional terry towelling nappies. Your baby will be just as comfortable when she is crawling and learning to to walk as she would be in disposable nappies.

Keeping your baby clean

Bathing tips

To bath your baby as quickly and as safely as possible:

❋ **Wash or bath her** in a room that is warm and draught free; it doesn't have to be the bathroom. Use a bucket to carry the water and to fill and empty the bath.

❋ **If you use a sponge** and face cloth, make sure they are reserved strictly for your baby's use and wash them frequently.

❋ **Never poke about** inside your baby's ears with a cotton bud as you could easily damage her delicate eardrum. Only remove ear wax that is visible at the opening.

Very young babies don't get dirty, so they don't need frequent bathing – but bath time provides a perfect opportunity for cuddling and playing that infants come to relish. It also gives fathers a chance to spend time with their babies. Later, bath time will be part of your baby's bedtime routine, a signal that it's time to wind down.

While your baby is young

Many parents are understandably nervous of bathing their newborn baby while she's still tiny and seems so vulnerable. It is, however, worth remembering that a baby is quite resilient provided she's handled gently but firmly, so try to be as confident as possible. You'll be shown the safest and easiest methods for bathing your baby a few days after the birth by a midwife at the hospital or when she visits you at home. As with all aspects of caring for your baby, bathing her will soon become second nature once you've given yourselves time to get used to it. The first few times, your baby may get quite distressed when she's being bathed, so don't feel you have to bath her every day. Thorough cleansing using the "topping and tailing" method outlined below is quite sufficient.

Topping and tailing

"Topping and tailing" means cleaning your baby thoroughly by washing her face, hands, and nappy area, without undressing her completely. You can do this most days as part of your baby's nappy-changing and dressing routine and then just give her a bath every two or three days. This will save you time and is less distressing for your baby.

1 **UNDRESS YOUR BABY** on a changing mat or towel. Leave her vest on or wrap her in a towel. Gently wipe her face, ears, and neck folds with cotton wool moistened with warm water. Pat her dry, making sure that you have dried thoroughly between her neck folds.

2 **TAKE TWO MORE CLEAN PIECES** of cotton wool and moisten them with cooled, boiled water. Using separate pieces of cotton wool for each stroke, to avoid the risk of cross infection, carefully wipe your baby's eyes from the inner corners outwards.

3 **USE ANOTHER PIECE OF COTTON WOOL** moistened with cooled, boiled water to clean her hands and feet. Dry them with a towel.

4 **TAKE OFF HER NAPPY** and clean the nappy area (see p.86), then wipe with cotton wool moistened with warm water, especially around the folds in your baby's thighs. Wash the genital area front to back. Pat dry and put on a fresh nappy, then dress her in clean clothes.

You will need

✱ **Cotton wool**
for face, eyes, and nappy area

✱ **Cooled, boiled water**
for washing the eyes

✱ **Bowl of warm water**
for washing face and body

✱ **Soft towel**
for wrapping and drying

✱ **Nappy-changing equipment**
(see p.88)

✱ **Clean clothes**

Bathing your baby

Choose a bath time that suits you and your baby; it doesn't always have to be in the evening, especially if your baby tends to be fretful at that time of day. However, if you're working parents, bathing your baby in the evening is often a good way for you to spend time with him; you can even have a bath with him when he's older (see p.95) to make it more fun! Make sure you've got all of the items you need within easy reach before you start.

1 UNDRESS YOUR BABY down to his vest and wash his face and neck. Wrap him firmly in a towel, then, holding him under your arm and supporting his head over the bath, gently wash and rinse his hair with water from the bath. Pat his hair dry with a towel.

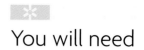

You will need

* Baby bath and baby bath solution

* Two towels

* Cotton wool for face, eyes, and nappy area

* Cooled, boiled water for washing the eyes

* Nappy-changing equipment (see p.88)

* Clean clothes

2 LEAVE A DRY TOWEL ready for after the bath. Unwrap the first towel, remove the nappy, and lift your baby into the bath, supporting his head and shoulders firmly with one hand, and his bottom and legs with your other hand.

3 SUPPORTING YOUR BABY'S HEAD and upper body with one arm, gently wash his body with your free hand, and encourage him to kick and splash.

4 **TO LIFT YOUR BABY** out of the bath, support his head and shoulders with one hand and slide your free hand under his bottom. Lift him out of the bath and on to the dry towel. Wrap him up immediately so he doesn't get cold. Pat him dry all over, paying particular attention to the folds of his neck, bottom, thighs, and underarms, then put on his nappy and dress him.

Bathing an older baby

Safety first

When you use the big bath, bear in mind that your baby could drown in just an inch of water (see p.123). Take the following precautions to avoid accidents:

✱ Put all equipment on the floor beside the bath and change your baby there. It's safer than carrying a wet slippery baby to a chair.

✱ Put a non-slip mat in the bath.

✱ Kneel on the floor to support your baby, and to prevent straining your back.

✱ Never leave your baby alone in the bath, even if she can sit up.

You will need

✱ Non-slip bath mat

✱ Sponge or face cloth

✱ Baby bath solution and shampoo

✱ Towel

✱ Nappy and clean clothes

✱ Face shield can also be useful to protect her eyes from shampoo

Once your baby is three to four months old and has good head control, you could start using the big bath. Once she has got used to it, she will appreciate the extra room to play in the water. The same principles apply – keep your baby warm before and after the bath, don't over-fill the bath, and check that the water isn't too hot before you put her in.

Using the big bath

Making the transition from the baby bath to the big bath can cause some babies distress, while others love it. It's a good idea to begin by putting the baby bath into the big bath the first few times so that the change is gradual and less frightening. Once your baby has got used to it and can sit up in the bath by herself, she'll begin to look forward to it as part of her routine, and enjoy bath-time games and play (see opposite). You'll find bath time can become a riotous affair with lots of shouts and splashing, but the problems may come when you want to get her out! It's advisable to make bath time a part of your baby's overall bedtime routine (see p.103) so that it acts as a clear signal to her that the day is over.

Having fun at bath time

Older babies really enjoy bath time and it's an excellent time to catch up on your baby's developing personality and skills if you aren't able to be with her during the day. Bath time is a wonderful opportunity for creative play and you can use it to help stimulate her development in a variety of ways. Babies love the freedom to sit in the warm water and you'll find that your baby will be endlessly fascinated by filling things, pouring, and splashing

BATH TIME SAFETY Give your baby toys that float to play with in her bath. But, however much she is enjoying playing, watch her all the time; don't leave her on her own, even for a second.

Giving your baby a towel bath

Cleaning your baby by towel bathing her is a halfway house between topping and tailing (see p.90) and a proper bath. It's useful if your baby isn't feeling well or if she doesn't like having a bath. As it's much quicker too it's useful for those times when she needs a wash, but you're short of time.

Your baby will grow to love bath time, particularly if it is her special time with you. Encourage this bonding by handling her with confidence; the more often you do it, the less nervous she (and you) will be. Giving a bath is a positive way of contributing to your baby's care, and it helps her to see that you're an equal partner in her life with her mother.

Make the most of bath time

✳ When you have a bath with your baby, lay her on your chest half in and half out of the water. Smile and talk to her all the time as you clean her.

✳ Splash water gently over her body carefully, avoiding her face. This way your baby will learn to enjoy, and be unafraid of, water.

✳ Allow plenty of time; a bath is not much fun for either of you if you have to rush. Remember, sharing a bath with your baby is also a good and enjoyable way for you to wind down after a stressful day at work.

1 TOP HALF FIRST Collect the same equipment as for topping and tailing (see p.90). Undress her to her nappy and wrap her lower half in a towel. Wash her face, neck, and upper body and pat dry.

2 LOWER HALF Put a clean vest on your baby. Remove the nappy. Wash her legs and feet, followed by her nappy area. Dry your baby thoroughly, then put on a clean nappy and clothes.

water. This really is learning through play – your baby is finding out about the properties of water and other liquids. Help your baby to do this by:
✳ Using household items like plastic cups, spoons, and sieves to show her what holds water and what doesn't, and how it can be poured and stirred.
✳ Introducing floating toys such as boats or traditional bath ducks that your baby will enjoy handling.
✳ Having fun with your baby by taking her into the bath with you; have a lovely skin to skin soak together. Keep the water at an even temperature with a slow trickle from the tap.

Hairwashing

Even though your baby may love her bath, hairwashing can be difficult if she hates having water poured on to her head or over her face, especially if it goes in her eyes. Don't worry; this is very common. Take your time in getting your baby used to water on her head and face; make a game of it by dripping tiny amounts over her head from time to time. Until she's more confident, you can simply sponge her hair clean or wipe it with a face cloth.

Some babies love having water on their faces and don't even mind it in their eyes. If your baby likes water, use the shower attachment or a cup to rinse her hair and make a game of it. But even mild baby shampoo will sting your baby's eyes a little. Use a face shield to keep the soap and water out of her eyes until she's old enough to keep them shut or to hold her head back for you. Towel dry her hair and brush it with a soft brush.

Dressing your baby

Choosing clothes

Look for clothes that are simple to put on and take off, and quick to wash and dry:

✳ Choose roomy garments, with loose elastic at the cuffs.

✳ Snap fasteners are better than buttons. Avoid ribbons as they may be difficult to undo.

✳ Avoid pure wool, which may irritate skin. Choose non-irritating fabrics, such as cotton.

✳ Only get machine-washable, colour-fast clothing.

✳ Always look for labels that indicate clothes are inflammable.

✳ Clothes can safely be bought secondhand, but check for inflammability, shrinkage, and the condition of fastenings.

✳ Nightdresses are quick to put on and allow easy access to the nappy.

✳ Buy adequate protective clothing to avoid sun damage (see p.118).

Babies grow out of clothes very quickly in the early months so don't spend a lot of money on first-size babywear. Many of the presents you will be given for your baby will be tiny outfits that will only fit your child for the first few weeks, so you should concentrate on buying a few practical, simple items for the first four months.

How to dress and undress your baby

Many parents are nervous of dressing their very young baby, particularly when it involves handling his "wobbly" head with its soft fontanelle (see p.55). Lay him down on his back on a changing mat or towel to dress and undress him; it's safer and you'll both feel more secure. Although your baby doesn't know day from night, nightdresses may be easier to use when he's tiny.

Putting on your baby's vest

Vests are probably the most awkward items of clothing to put on a tiny baby, because they have to be put on over his head, which is the biggest yet least manageable part of his body. Most vests are now designed with wide, "envelope" necks or shoulder fastenings to make it easier for you to slide the vest over his head. By the time your baby is three or four months old, he will have developed some head control, and you can safely dress and undress him on your lap, if you haven't had the confidence to do so previously.

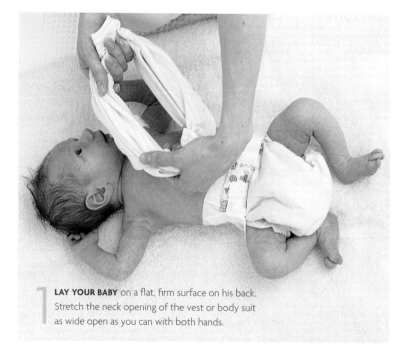

1 **LAY YOUR BABY** on a flat, firm surface on his back. Stretch the neck opening of the vest or body suit as wide open as you can with both hands.

2 **SLIDE THE VEST** over your baby's head, gently lifting his head up to bring it over to the back of his neck.

3 **WIDEN EACH SLEEVE** or armhole with your fingers and bring your baby's arms through, fist first, one at a time. Draw the vest down over his body.

You will need

Basics for a new baby
* 6–8 vests or body suits

* 6–8 stretchsuits

* 2–3 cardigans

* 2–3 pairs of socks

* Blanket or shawl

Useful extras
* 2 pairs of scratch mittens

* 2 nightdresses

* **All-in-one pram suit** for a winter baby or protective clothing and a sunhat for a summer baby

Practical clothes for older babies

Once your baby is sitting up, and especially when she becomes mobile, clothes have to be robust and comfortable, as well as machine-washable. Look for:

✱ Bigger sizes, especially with outdoor clothes, so movement isn't restricted and she doesn't grow out of them too quickly.

✱ Clothes that have easy access to the nappy area, such as dungarees or all-in-one suits with snap fasteners, or tights.

✱ Lightweight clothing to protect your baby's skin from the sun. Use a wide-brimmed sunhat and shirts with sleeves and collars.

✱ Soft boots or socks with non-slip soles for when she starts to pull herself up to stand.

Putting on a stretchsuit

Stretchsuits are very practical and economical items of clothing for you to buy for your baby. They're particularly useful at first because they allow freedom of movement, easy access to the nappy area, keep your baby warm, but not too hot, and they are simple to put on even the tiniest baby. They are ideal for all-day use for the first three to four months and can also be used as sleepwear when your baby is older. To put on a stretchsuit, follow the steps illustrated here; to take it off, reverse all the steps, beginning by undoing all the fastenings.

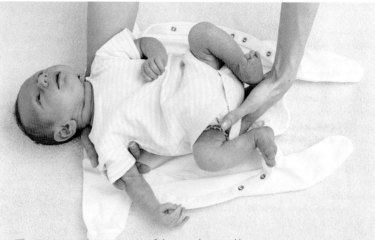

1 **UNDO ALL THE FASTENINGS** of the stretchsuit and lay it on a flat surface. Then, lay your baby on top of the suit so that her neck lines up with the neck of the suit.

2 **PUT YOUR BABY'S LEGS** into the legs of the suit feet first, one at a time. Fasten the suit under the nappy area so that she can't kick it off.

3 **TO PUT HER ARMS** in, roll back one arm of the stretchsuit, holding it open with one hand. Then guide your baby's arm, fist first, into the arm of the suit and roll the sleeve down into place. Repeat with the other arm and do up the rest of the fastenings.

DRESSING OLDER BABIES Once your baby can sit up, you'll find she's a lot easier to dress. But she may also wriggle and protest when you want to put on her clothes, so hold her firmly while you dress her. You could make a game of it to keep her occupied.

When your baby sleeps

If you're always struggling to get your baby to sleep, ask yourself why.

Does your baby need to sleep?
Trying to get your baby to sleep when he doesn't need to is pointless. If he's longing for your company, talk and play with him instead, or put him in a baby chair so that he can watch you. Research has shown that even young babies are receptive to interaction with their parents, and with increased stimulation, your baby is more likely to sleep more soundly and for longer.

You need rest too
You may become overwrought if you're suffering from lack of sleep. Being over-tired builds resentment, makes you irritable and liable to get things out of proportion. If you're exhausted, express breastmilk (see p.83) so your partner can do the night-time feeds for a couple of days.

✳

You will need

For the first three months:

✳ 4 small cellular cot blankets as cotton is better than wool

✳ 6 flat cotton top sheets

✳ 6 fitted cotton mattress sheets

✳ Spare mattress (optional)

✳ Portable Moses basket, cradle, or carrycot (see p.75)

Young babies spend up to 14 hours of any 24-hour period asleep. Unfortunately, this doesn't often coincide with their parents' sleeping pattern, because it takes a few months for babies to learn the difference between night and day.

How babies sleep
The way babies fall asleep differs from adults; adults can crash suddenly, whereas babies sleep lightly for about 20 minutes, then go through a transitional stage before reaching deep sleep. Nothing will wake them, until they've had enough sleep. This means that babies who are simply "put down" will not necessarily go to sleep peacefully. You may need to nurse your baby to sleep for quite a while, so try to be patient, particularly at night, when you're longing to go back to bed yourself.

Where should a baby sleep?
Where a baby sleeps isn't important to him to start with. He won't automatically fall asleep when put into a darkened bedroom; light doesn't bother him at all. He's much more likely to be disturbed by being too hot or too cold. Your baby will be happiest going to sleep hearing your voices and the household noises that he is used to in the background so let him sleep in a Moses basket or carrycot in whichever room you happen to be.

Using a baby monitor
If you leave your baby in another room, set up a baby monitor so that you can hear him as soon as he wakes. He may feel disturbed by the silence when you leave the room, and this could make him more fretful; leave the door open so he can hear you moving around – unless you have a cat that may climb into the cot. Avoid going back into the room once your baby is asleep; your smell could wake him, so resist the temptation to check him too frequently.

Encouraging longer sleeps at night
A young baby needs food at regular intervals, so he'll wake for a feed when his body tells him to. The way to encourage your baby to sleep for a stretch (four, then rising to five or six, hours) during the night is to make sure he's taken in sufficient calories to last that long. This means feeding him whenever he shows he's hungry during the day. As he steadily gains weight, he can go longer between feeds and by about six weeks he could be sleeping for at least one period of about six hours – hopefully during the night. When he wakes for a night feed make as little fuss as possible – feed him in bed; if he needs changing, do it quickly in a dim light. Don't make this a time for chatting and games and he'll learn that waking at night doesn't bring any special privileges.

Understanding the way your baby's sleep patterns work will help you to tune into his and your partner's needs.

Being realistic

Your new baby will probably sleep less than you think. He spends 50–80 percent of the time in light sleep, when he wakes very easily. His sleep cycle – light sleep, deep sleep, light sleep – is shorter than an adult's sleep cycle, so he's vulnerable to waking each time he passes from one sleep state to another. He is programmed to wake up for all kinds of reasons – when he is wet, hot, cold, unwell – because his survival depends on it. It's good to know that light sleep is likely to make your baby more intelligent because the brain remains active and this enhances brain development.

Having a sleep routine

Your baby has to be deeply asleep before he'll settle, so try a tranquillizing sleep routine – gentle rocking, quiet songs, and talking. Or lay him down and gently pat his shoulder at about 60 beats a minute for a few minutes. He's deeply asleep when his eyelids don't twitch and his limbs feel limp.

Getting home late

If your baby is asleep when you get home from work, ask your partner if your baby can nap in the afternoon so that he's awake later. Be patient if this isn't possible. Try getting up earlier and spending time with your baby before work.

▲ **USE A MOSES BASKET** While your baby is very young, put him to bed in a Moses basket or carrycot. You can then put the basket in the room with you while he sleeps.

Rescue package for a sleepless baby

Night after night of broken sleep is wearing for parents, and a young baby who perhaps only "catnaps" during the day makes it hard to catch up. Use this checklist of strategies to reduce unnecessary fatigue.

Be aware of background noise Don't shield your baby from the sounds of your home. They won't disturb his sleep; in fact some babies are soothed by the rhythmic noise of household appliances!

Keep him close to you At night, put your baby's cot next to your bed so that you can take him into your bed to feed him. Then put him back in his cot afterwards with minimum disturbance.

Play music Babies respond well to soothing music (classical is best). Keep certain pieces for when your baby shows signs of tiredness.

Carry him in a sling Rhythmic movement can hasten sleep, but your baby may wake up when you stop moving. Carry him around in a sling when you're in the house, whenever possible. As well as being relaxed by the constant movement, your baby will be comforted by your body and your smell when he is close to you.

Rock him in his buggy Take him for a walk in his buggy, or you can simply rock him backwards gently over a slightly uneven floor to get him to sleep – again, he may wake when you stop.

Give him plenty of fresh air Fresh air is said to tire babies out. In fact, it's probably the stimulation they receive from the sounds and sights outside, or simply the movement of trees or branches, that makes them sleepy.

Safe sleeping

The way babies are put to bed can affect the likelihood of sudden infant death syndrome, also known as "cot death". The number of babies dying has halved due to better awareness:

✱ Stop smoking – and NEVER let anyone smoke in the same room as your baby or in your home at all.

✱ Always lay your baby on her back to sleep so that her breathing is unimpeded and she can lose heat from her front, face, and head.

✱ Don't let your baby get too hot, as she isn't very efficient at controlling her temperature. If the air temperature is hot to you, it's very hot for her.

✱ Never over-wrap your baby. Cover her with a cotton sheet and cellular blankets according to the room temperature (see right). Don't increase the bedding when your baby is unwell.

✱ Lay your baby in the "feet-to-foot" position at the end of the cot so that she can't wriggle down under the blankets and get too hot (see below), or put her in a baby sleeping bag.

▲ **FEET TO FOOT** Lay your baby with her feet touching the foot of the cot, even if it means her head is halfway down the mattress.

Wakeful babies

Most babies develop a napping routine of sleeping for perhaps two hours in the morning and again in the afternoon, but there are always exceptions. While wakeful babies can be trying, they reward you in the end as they're usually very bright and affectionate, so don't be downhearted. Your baby is wakeful because she loves you and craves your friendship; she doesn't mean to starve you of sleep, she just wants to learn and be sociable. Every minute spent awake with you, she'll be forging new links with the world and developing many skills. Think about this, too, when she's awake during the day; if she isn't tired, why should she sleep? From her point of view, it's much better for her to stay with you, so don't be surprised if she cries when you leave her in her cot.

What you can try

✳ Keep her temperature even; touch her skin to check that she isn't too cold or hot, add or remove blankets if necessary (see below). Check the room temperature; a temperature of about 18°C (65°F) is comfortable.

✳ Change her nappy if it's wet or soiled and soothe the nappy area with a bland nappy cream (zinc oxide), if necessary.

✳ Use a rocking cradle or push her rhythmically in her pram.

✳ Play her a tape of the human heartbeat, the sound she heard in the womb.

✳ Play her music you listened to during pregnancy, or an old-fashioned musical box with a simple repetitive melody can be really effective.

✳ Play her a tape of you and your partner quietly talking.

✳ Put the cot on alternate sides of the bed each night so that you can take it in turns to see to her. Talk to her and rock her back to sleep; you don't need to actually pick her up.

✳ If she's obviously reluctant to sleep, get her up, and put her in her baby chair where she can see you.

✳ Hang a mobile over her cot so she's got something interesting to watch when she wakes up. A mobile that plays music is ideal.

✳ Fix a "baby gym", with different noises and textures, across her cot or attach it to the bars so she can reach for it when she's bored. Remove when she can sit up though as she could use it to climb out of her cot.

Which bedding to use

Temperature	What to use
14°C (57°F)	A sheet and four blankets or more
16°C (60°F)	A sheet and three blankets
18°C (65°F)	A sheet and two blankets
20°C (68°F)	A sheet and one blanket
24°C (75°F)	A sheet only

Blankets and bedding

Use enough bedding to keep her comfortably warm (see opposite). When your baby is under 12 months, don't give her a pillow, and don't use quilts, duvets, or baby nests because they also prevent loss of heat.

Sleep and your older baby

As your baby grows, her sleep pattern will gradually change; she'll begin to stay awake and alert for longer periods during the day, even after feeds. When she's being stimulated with play and talk from you, she'll start needing longer periods of sleep. The trick is to persuade her that these longer sleep periods should be at night, to align with your own.

Establishing a bedtime routine

Your baby may well get upset at bedtime – she could be anxious about being separated from you (see p.162), or she may simply want to continue playing, so establishing a bedtime routine is essential to build her confidence and to help her learn that there is a time when playtime has to stop. Set up your own routine at a time to suit all of you – for example, if you're working you may want it to be a little later – but try not to vary the routine, whatever time you do it. A suggested routine might be as follows:
* Give her the final meal of the day – not her main meal though (see p.113).
* Give her a calming bath, and change her into her nightclothes.
* Spend a quiet time in your baby's room; sing gentle songs, or read a story (depending on her age and stage of development).
* Give her the last breastfeed (unless your baby still wakes at night).
* Lay her in her cot, with any security object she is attached to, turn the dimmer switch down low, then sit quietly with her for a few minutes.
* Go out of the room quietly, saying good night, but leave the door open.

You will need

For 3–12 months:
* 4 cellular cot blankets
* 6 flat cotton top sheets
* 6 fitted cotton bottom sheets
* Full-size cot (see p.75)

Nursery extras:
* Dimmer switch for the nursery light
* Baby monitor
* Cot toys (see below)
* CD or tape of soothing music

Daytime naps for your older baby

As babies grow older they sleep less, but up to 12 months your baby will still nap in the day. Many children still rest up to the age of three:

* To help your baby relax and drop off, put her in her favourite place, which may not be her room. Make sure she has any special comforter with her. Play calming music, let her have toys and books, and keep her within earshot so she can hear you. If she calls out to you, it's probably only for reassurance, so calmly call back.

* If she doesn't want to sleep, that's okay; just make it a quiet time when she can sit in her cot and play. But never let her cry for more than a few minutes without going to her.

* If your baby falls asleep in the car, or her pram, never wake her suddenly. Like you, she'll need time to adjust. Never leave her asleep alone in the car or in her pram outside a shop.

▲ **THE BEDTIME ROUTINE** Allow your baby to play quietly. Put some books and toys in her cot or hang a mobile above it. Remove hard objects from the cot when you lay her down.

When your baby cries

Why you should respond promptly

* Your baby is longing to communicate with you, but his repertoire is limited to start with. Crying is the only way he can convey his feelings so don't just ignore him.

* Your baby will develop good communication skills and outgoing, friendly behaviour.

* It will make him feel secure and self-confident.

* It will not "spoil" your baby or teach him "bad habits"; you can't spoil a baby this way, only love him.

What happens if you don't respond

* Not responding to your baby's cries is a form of rejection, and your baby will soon sense this.

* If you don't respond, he will cry for longer, continuing until he gets the attention he needs.

* He will be driven to create a pattern of frequent crying.

All young babies cry at some time during the day. Whether it's a subdued grizzle or a full-throated roar, a baby's cries are his only means of communicating his needs. Having said that, there is no doubt that a persistently fretful baby can be a strain for parents, so it's worth thinking about the underlying causes. Look upon crying as conversation rather than an irritant designed to upset you.

What makes a newborn cry

The circumstances of your baby's birth may affect the amount that he cries. It helps if you understand the possible underlying causes of a fretful baby's behaviour. Try not to become impatient with him as it will be out of his control. He'll begin to settle as he gets older. Your baby may cry more:

* If you had a general anaesthetic.
* If you had a forceps delivery.
* If he was born after a long labour, after which babies tend to sleep in short bursts.
* If he is a boy. Boys may cry more than girls in new situations. Try not to make the mistake of some parents of boys who have been known to attend to them less, in the mistaken belief that it will "toughen them up".

Responding to your baby's cries

Research shows that babies do better if you respond promptly when they cry. It's a mistake to think of a baby as "good" if he doesn't cry much and

▶ **GIVING YOUR BABY ATTENTION** All babies thrive on the company of their parents, and will cry because they miss the comfort of your presence. Try to give your baby as much contact as you can.

one who does as "naughty", because a baby's cries have nothing to do with good or bad behaviour. Responding to your baby's cries is a crucial part of bonding – your attitude to your baby in the first few weeks forms the blueprint for your future relationship with him, and for all his future relationships. He'll learn kindness and sympathy from you, which is why you should always answer his cry, whatever anyone else tells you.

A loved baby will be secure and when the time comes he will be able to take separations in his stride if he's learned that you will answer his needs. A baby who's left to cry is more likely to grow up clingy and attention-seeking because he's learned that he has to work harder to make you respond to him.

Persistent crying

Some young babies have prolonged bouts of crying, which typically occur in the late afternoon and evening, and can last for anything between two and four hours. Babies often begin this pattern of persistent crying at about three weeks of age, and will usually have grown out of it by about three months. This pattern of crying has become known as "colic", because as the baby becomes increasingly upset and difficult to soothe, he may often pull his legs up and arch his back as if experiencing abdominal pain. In fact, it's probably misleading to give it any special name, because there doesn't seem to be any known cause for this pattern. A treatable condition known as gastro-oesophageal reflux often presents as colic, especially in a small baby who vomits a lot. Talk to your doctor if your baby fits this description.

▲ **SOOTHING "COLIC"** If your baby cries persistently, you may find that laying him across your lap makes him more comfortable. Support his head and then gently massage his back and legs.

✳ What to do when your baby cries

Problem	Description	What you should do
Hunger	If your baby has been asleep for two or three hours and begins to cry insistently, he is probably ready for a feed.	Give him a feed. If he cries afterwards, he may not have had enough so offer more. If it's very hot, offer him a drink of water.
Discomfort	A cold, wet, or soiled nappy could be uncomfortable enough to cause your baby to cry. Your baby may also be too hot or too cold.	Check and change his nappy if necessary. Treat nappy rash (see p.86). Check bedding and air temperature (see p.102).
Insecurity	A jerky movement, bright light, or sudden noise can startle a young baby. Many babies are also upset by being undressed and bathed.	Cuddle your baby to promote security. Handle your baby as gently and firmly as possible when dressing or bathing.
Fatigue	Your baby will cry when he is tired, and may become quite upset when over-tired, which can make it doubly difficult to soothe him.	Create a soothing bedtime ritual (see p.103) of rocking or stroking when you lay him in his cot, or push him in his pram.
Boredom	As your baby grows, he is more aware of people and cries because he wants company.	Cuddle him; at four to six weeks, sit him in a baby chair where he can see and hear you.
Pain	Your baby may have earache, abdominal pain, or persistent nappy rash.	Contact your doctor if he's hard to soothe, off his feed, or appears unwell (see p.120).

Soothing your crying baby

A baby who is persistently fretful may cry readily at other times, not just in the evening (see p.105). However, the evening pattern of crying can be a particular strain for parents, especially if one or both of you has been out at work during the day. It may be that your baby senses and reacts to your tiredness at this time. Although the crying pattern may only last three months, this period can seem never-ending to new parents who have to deal with their baby's distress day after day. Trying some of the suggestions for soothing your baby given below and on p.105 should help you through this difficult time.

▶ **USE A DUMMY** Encourage your baby to find his thumb or give him a dummy. There is no stigma attached to a baby sucking a dummy, but make sure it is sterilized and never sweeten it with honey or juice. However, it may only be a temporary relief so it's probably better to look for the underlying cause of the crying, keeping the dummy as a last resort.

▼ **LAY YOUR BABY ON YOUR CHEST** Lie on the bed or sofa, well supported by cushions. Lay your baby on your chest and gently rub her back. It will relax both of you, but never fall asleep with your baby like this because it puts your baby at risk of cot death.

CARRY YOUR BABY IN A SLING Put your baby in a sling and carry him around with you. Your baby will love being close to you and will enjoy the movement as you walk around.

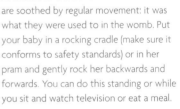

▲ **COMFORT WITH MOVEMENT** Most babies are soothed by regular movement: it was what they were used to in the womb. Put your baby in a rocking cradle (make sure it conforms to safety standards) or in her pram and gently rock her backwards and forwards. You can do this standing or while you sit and watch television or eat a meal.

▲ **HOLD UPRIGHT** Bring your baby up against your shoulder and gently rub her back. (Put a cloth on your shoulder to protect your clothes from any regurgitated milk.) Walk around, gently singing or talking to your baby.

HELPFUL GRANDPARENTS
Grandparents know you need a break and will enjoy developing their own relationship with their grandchild.

Accepting help from others

Sometimes a crying baby can make parents who are already tired from broken nights feel quite desperate: this is the time to seek help. Don't ever feel that you are failing as parents if you accept assistance; countless other parents will have felt as frustrated and exhausted as you because their babies have cried a lot and have been difficult to soothe. Jump at the chance if your baby's grandparents or other friends or relations offer to look after your baby for a while so you can get out on your own for a couple of hours' break, or enjoy some unbroken sleep. If they don't offer any help, don't be afraid to ask them. There's no need to feel guilty – they'll be glad to have the chance to relieve you, they can get to know your baby, and it will help you to get things back into perspective. It's a great help, too, to talk to health or babycare professionals, who are there to support you. You are not the first parents to experience this; it happens all the time.

Comforting your older baby

As your baby grows and becomes more aware of her surroundings, her pattern of crying will change because it's not the only way she can communicate with you now. Her reasons for crying will also be easier for you to both predict and interpret. You'll learn to distinguish between frustration, hunger, pain, or loneliness. Even when your baby is beginning to become more mobile and independent, the best way to comfort her if she's unhappy is with your company, hugs, and cuddles.

Comforters

Towards their first birthday, many babies will have become attached to a particular comforter – a favourite soft toy, a cloth, or blanket – that probably helps them sleep and that may be grabbed when they're feeling a bit insecure and upset. Other babies become attached to a dummy or suck their thumbs (see p.106). This is perfectly normal and there's no point in distressing your baby by removing a comforter on the grounds that it is a "bad habit"; it isn't. As your baby's confidence and independence develop after her first birthday, she'll gradually become less dependent on her comforter, although it may take a year or so. It's also a good idea to have some spares to hand in case the main one needs a wash.

Teething and crying

Your baby's teeth will normally start to come through from about the age of six months (see p.154), although it can be later or even earlier than this. When this happens, you will notice that she dribbles a lot and her gums will occasionally be sore. Your baby may become rather grizzly when she's teething and it's usually quite obvious if she's uncomfortable; she'll want to chew a lot and may have a hot, red area on her cheek. She may also become more wakeful than usual.

However, it isn't a good idea to blame persistent crying on "teething" too readily. It may in fact be that your baby is bored (see right), or even unwell (see p.120); teething does not cause a fever, for example.

Troubleshooting

There are lots of reasons why an older baby may cry.

She's bored

Your baby may cry from boredom if left alone, unable to hear your voice and with nothing to look at or play with. You are her favourite playmate so keep her where she can see you and you can talk to her, and don't leave her alone in her cot for long periods if she's crying. Some babies do play happily in their cots for a while after waking, so leave toys and books within reach.

She's frustrated

As your baby grows, her desire to do things outstrips her ability to do them and so she gets frustrated and often starts to cry as a result. She may also cry if you don't let her have something she wants. Change her toys frequently – her attention span is still short. Find time to sit down and play with her (see p.174).

She's frightened

At about six months, your baby will cry when she's separated from you and she'll be nervous of other people, even when she knows them well. Right from the start, get her used to seeing you leave the room and come back in again. This way she'll gradually learn that she can trust you always to return to her. Make sure she meets lots of other people before she reaches this stage and learns that even if you leave her with someone else for a while, that you always come back.

She's ill or has hurt herself

If your baby hurts herself, you'll know at once from her cry, but it may be more difficult to tell when she's ill. See pages 120–123 for what you should do if your baby is ill or has an accident.

Touch and massage

Massage tips

Babies love massage as much as you do and it's a good way to calm an unsettled baby. It's also an expression of love and your baby knows it. Always prepare carefully for massage:

✳ Make sure the room is warm. Lay your baby on a soft blanket or towel.

✳ Play his favourite music or a recording of a heartbeat. Talk in a low, gentle voice or sing a song quietly.

✳ Although massaging your baby's skin directly is best, many younger babies don't like being undressed. If your baby is one of these, dress him in a cotton vest or similar garment, through which you can easily feel his body.

✳ Work around his body, massaging both sides with slow even strokes. Keep your face close to your baby's and look into his eyes as you massage him.

Being touched is an essential part of the bonding process that helps young creatures to thrive. Premature babies are known to gain more weight on lambswool blankets than cotton ones because it feels as if they're being stroked when they move and they feel contented.

The importance of touch

Your baby is born sociable and he craves physical affection. This is best communicated through touch, cuddles, being gently held, kissed, and nuzzled. It's important, therefore, that you're both completely free with your physical affection from the start. Your baby longs to be close to you and to be carried, and he will cry less and be more easily comforted if you carry him. Remember also that being carried in a sling close to your body feels like being cuddled to a baby (see p.106), and allows you to do other things at the same time. Small babies are much stronger than you think so be firm, but avoid sudden jerky movements – your baby may think he's falling and he'll be startled rather than comforted.

As your baby gets older you can be more robust with him; he'll enjoy tickling and rolling about on the floor with you, but don't overdo it if he becomes at all distressed, and don't blame him if he pulls your hair or scratches you – under a year old he won't know that it hurts. And as children grow up, they need the reassuring and loving embrace of caring parents more, not less as some parents may think.

Giving your baby a massage

1 **NECK AND SHOULDERS** Lay your baby on her back. Gently massage her neck from her ears to her shoulders and from her chin to her chest. Then stroke her shoulders from her neck outwards.

2 **ARMS** Stroke down each arm using your fingertips, first from wrist to elbow, then from elbow to shoulder. Gently squeeze all along her arm, starting from the top.

3 **CHEST AND ABDOMEN** Gently stroke down your baby's chest following the line of her ribs. Massage her abdomen in a circular motion with one hand, working outwards from the navel.

Physical affection

Children should be encouraged to express their emotions – boys just as much as girls. Indeed, a child's ability to achieve some kind of emotional stability is more or less determined before the age of 12 months – a sobering thought, but true.

Emotional feedback

A child learns to master his emotions by getting sympathetic feedback from adults that mirrors the emotions he's feeling. If your baby holds out a hurt hand, what helps most – as any parent knows – is lots of sympathy, "kissing better", and cuddles. Physical affection is necessary for emotional growth. If you deprive a child of physical affection, you deprive him of an essential "growth vitamin".

Your baby needs you both

This applies equally to both parents, and continues through babyhood, childhood, and, in some cases, into adolescence. Nothing should be allowed to discourage loving parents – mothers and fathers – from doing what their child needs them to do.

4 **HEAD** Using both hands, lightly massage the crown of your baby's head using a circular motion, then stroke down the sides of her face. With your fingertips, massage her forehead and cheeks, working from the centre outwards. This is particularly calming for a fretful baby.

5 **FEET AND TOES** Rub your baby's ankles and feet, stroking from heel to toe, and then concentrate on each toe individually. Your baby may kick her legs and curl her toes while you're doing this. If she's less than four months old, show her her toes – it will help her to realize they're part of herself (see p.159).

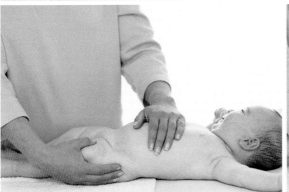

6 **LEGS** Massage your baby's legs one at a time. Work from her thigh down to her knee. Stroke down her shin, and move round to her calf and ankle. Place your free hand on her tummy, then gently squeeze her leg from the thigh down to the ankle. Then work on the other leg.

7 **BACK** Once you've massaged your baby on her front, gently turn her over on to her tummy and massage her back. Using both hands, run your palms down her back from under her arms to her buttocks, pressing gently against her spine with your thumbs. Talk to her all the time, as she can't see your face.

Weaning your baby

Trouble-free weaning

Knowing what food to give and when to give it, will help you to introduce it with confidence.

What age to start

Don't start weaning until at least six months; before that, a baby's digestive system can't cope.

What to offer

Offer a simple, semi-liquid food once a day. Give her one taste at a time. Start with a non-wheat cereal mixed with her normal milk, as it's closest to what she's used to, then gradually offer puréed fruit or vegetables. Introduce food at a second meal when she happily takes the first. Milk is still her main food. Try new foods 10–12 times; don't assume she doesn't like it after a couple of tries.

How much to give

Start with a teaspoonful a day for a week, as her digestive system needs time to adapt, then go on to two spoons. Use the suggested weaning schedule (see opposite) as a guide.

You will need

To start weaning:
* 2–3 fabric plastic-backed bibs
* 2–3 feeding spoons and a beaker

For the older baby:
* 2–3 moulded plastic bibs
* 2 non-spill plastic bowls
* Two-handled training beaker

Weaning may seem like a huge step. There are so many questions: when to start, what to give, how much to give, but it needn't feel so daunting if you try to think positively and see it as encouraging your baby's independence rather than as an obstacle.

Introducing solids

Weaning is rarely a problem from the baby's point of view, but some babies take longer than others to get used to having solid food as well as their normal milk feeds. It really doesn't matter – until six months, milk is enough for many babies' complete nutritional needs. However, after that time they will need the extra calories, vitamins, and minerals in solid food, as there won't be enough for them in milk alone (look at the weaning chart opposite for a suggested pattern of feeding).

When you introduce her first solids, choose a feed when you know she's usually alert and awake – for instance, at midday, halfway through her milk

▲ **FIRST FEEDS** Choose a time when your baby will be relaxed. Hold her firmly on your lap as you offer the spoon. She may take a while to get used to taking food from a spoon, and may push out more than she takes in to begin with.

Weaning schedule from six months

Feeds	Week 1–2	Week 3–5	Week 6
1st feed	Milk feed	Milk feed	Milk feed
2nd feed	Half milk feed 1 tsp cereal Finish milk feed	Half milk feed 1–2 tsps cereal Finish milk feed	3–4 tsps cereal Milk feed
3rd feed	Milk feed	Half milk feed 1–2 tsps puréed fruit or veg Finish milk feed	2–3 tsps puréed chicken and veg 2–3 tsps puréed fruit Water
4th feed	Milk feed	Milk feed	2–3 tsps puréed fruit or veg Milk feed
5th feed	Milk feed	Milk feed	Milk feed

feed. Sit your baby on your lap or in her baby chair and offer her tiny amounts at first on the tip of a sterilized plastic spoon. Don't force it into her mouth; brush her upper lip with the spoon and let her suck it off. She might splutter and dribble a bit the first few times, but keep trying. When she has had a few tastes, finish off her milk feed. She will gradually take more solids before wanting the rest of her milk. Once she is used to solids she'll want it before her milk feed.

Extra fluid

Remember milk is a food, it isn't a drink, and so from the moment mixed feeding is introduced, your baby will also need another fluid to drink. Cooled, boiled water is best. Start by giving your baby 15ml (½fl oz) of fluids between feeds, increasing it gradually according to her needs. It's a good idea to take this opportunity to introduce a trainer cup, or if she prefers it, give the water in a bottle.

Trouble-free meal times

Just as it was important not to get hung up about how much milk your baby drank when you were establishing breastfeeding, try not to worry now about how much she is eating, or about how much is going on the floor! It's going to be messy – until the age of five or six all children are messy eaters – so be philosophical, put newspaper under the high chair, and clear up afterwards. As long as meal times are happy and relaxed, don't worry. It's important that you don't allow them to become battlefields. You can't win – your baby will simply refuse to eat (you can't force her) and the battle is lost. She's cute enough to learn that food is a weapon she can use to manipulate you, so don't join in the struggle.

Starting self-feeding

Self-feeding is an important step to your baby's independence, so be patient with her:

✳ Use shaped plastic bibs that catch spilled food, and put a plastic sheet under the high chair.

✳ Give your baby her own spoon and offer food that is of a stiff consistency, such as mashed potato or other puréed vegetables, in a non-spill bowl. Never mind that she gets very little at first, she'll have a lot of fun. Have a spare spoon handy so that you can feed her, if need be.

✳ Even if she finds a spoon difficult, she'll love feeding herself with finger foods (see p.117). Finger foods can keep her busy if the meal isn't ready.

✳ Above all be flexible; if one food doesn't suit, try another – no single food is essential.

✳ Introduce a trainer cup for drinks as soon as your baby can manage it. Some breastfed babies never accept a bottle and go straight to a cup for water; others like a bottle.

▲ **RELAXED SELF-FEEDING** While your baby feeds herself, have your own spoon to feed her at the same time.

Best food for your baby

Do's and don'ts

Foods to give

Vary your baby's diet so that he learns to like different tastes and textures. Make sure you include:

* Fruit and vegetables: wash them thoroughly in cold running water, and peel potatoes, carrots, apples, and peaches to avoid the risk of pesticide residues. Aim to give some vitamin C at each meal, whether as fruit, vegetables, or juice, as it helps your baby's body to absorb iron.

* Milk: from seven months use full-fat cow's milk in cooking. From one year, give it as a drink.

* Meat and fish: try to offer at least one serving every day of lean meat or boneless fish.

* Protein in the form of low fibre foods such as cheese or tofu, if your baby has a vegetarian diet.

Foods to avoid

Don't worry too much, but do take some sensible precautions:

* Don't give foods containing wheat flour or gluten before your baby is seven months old as he may find them difficult to digest.

* Don't add sugar or salt – sugar encourages bad habits and bad teeth; salt is too much for your young baby's kidneys to cope with.

* Avoid giving your baby soft-boiled eggs until he is about one year old.

* Very high-fibre breakfast cereals have little place in your baby's diet as they are too difficult to digest.

* Avoid unpasteurized cheese until your baby is at least two.

To grow and develop well, babies need as varied a diet as possible; research shows that babies who are offered a wide menu to choose from invariably choose a healthy diet and accept varied tastes. On the other hand, if they're only given fast foods and sweet things, they'll inevitably want chips and ketchup with everything.

What your baby needs

To provide for your baby's needs for healthy growth and development you need to give him with foods in the right proportions from all the different food groups. He needs most foods from the complex carbohydrates group. These include sugar-free cereals, wholemeal bread, potatoes (not fried or roast though), rice, and pasta. Secondly, he needs the vitamins and minerals contained in fresh fruit and vegetables – at least five portions a day. He needs protein, which he'll get from lean white meat, fish, and pulses such as beans, and, after he's about seven to nine months, eggs and cheese. Offer the vegetables first, then follow with proteins to make sure that he has enough vegetables. Your baby needs some fat, but he should be able to get enough for his nutritional needs from the other foods you give

Suggested menus for an older baby

Time	Day 1	Day 2	Day 3
Breakfast	Rice cakes Chopped hard-boiled egg Milk	Mashed banana Wholemeal toast fingers Milk	Cottage cheese or yogurt Wholemeal toast Milk
Lunch	Vegetable or chicken casserole Stewed apple Diluted fruit juice	Mashed potato and cheese Pear slices Diluted fruit juice	Strained lentils and mixed vegetables Banana and yogurt Diluted fruit juice
Snack	Toast fingers Peeled peach slices Milk	Rice cakes Peeled apple pieces Milk	Rusks Peeled seedless grapes Milk
Supper	Cauliflower cheese Semolina and fruit purée Diluted fruit juice	Pasta with sauce Yogurt and fruit purée Diluted fruit juice	Tuna, mashed potato, courgettes Rice pudding Diluted fruit juice

him, especially milk. You can use cow's milk in cooking now and he should have full-fat milk until he's about two years old. Use very little oil or fat in cooking and don't add salt to foods. Avoid giving him the "empty" calories of sweet foods like biscuits and sugary cereal.

Preparing your baby's food

At first your baby's food needs to be puréed, but this stage doesn't last for long. As your baby gets used to solid foods, introduce him to coarser mashed or minced foods so that he learns about different textures. Use a variety of liquids to thin down home-prepared foods: the water used to steam vegetables is ideal as it contains the minerals. You can thicken foods with wholegrain cereals, cottage cheese, yogurt, or mashed potato.

Enough to eat?

Even if you think your baby isn't taking enough food, he is. Don't make the mistake of forcing adult standards on him. Think of a balanced diet in terms of what you offer your baby over a period of time, such as a week, and make sure it's varied. Accept that there will be a certain amount of waste and don't force him to finish everything if he does not want to. Don't worry about fads either; he's eating what his body needs.

Food hygiene

Once your baby is on solids you don't need to sterilise his feeding utensils. But bacterial infections picked up from badly prepared food can be dangerous for babies and children.

✳ Wash your hands thoroughly before handling any food and after you've handled raw meat.

✳ Store raw meat away from other foods in the refrigerator and keep fish in the coldest part.

✳ Clean the spout holes of your baby's feeding cup regularly.

✳ Throw away leftover baby food; don't reheat it. If you're using ready-prepared baby food, spoon it into a bowl; don't feed from the pot.

✳ To avoid waste, prepare small amounts and freeze it in individual containers.

✳ If you use a microwave, stir the food thoroughly to ensure the heat is evenly distributed.

▼ **HAPPY MEAL TIMES** Once your baby happily takes one or two different solids, it's important to introduce him to a variety of textures and tastes. Never force him to eat more than he wants.

Finger foods

Once your baby is more than seven or eight months and has been weaned onto solid foods, she'll want to try feeding herself so give her easy-to-hold finger foods. Try:

✽ Any fresh fruit that's easy to hold, such as a banana or peach: remember to peel and remove pips.

✽ Vegetables, particularly carrots, cut into a shape that's easy to grasp. Don't cut them too small.

✽ Pieces of dry, sugar-free cereal.

✽ Wholemeal bread or rusks (without grains), toast fingers, bread sticks, or rice cakes.

✽ Cooked pasta shapes.

Make meal times fun

It's frustrating to find that good food is being thrown on the floor or wiped over the high chair, but remember that your baby will eat if she's hungry. If she starts to throw food about, she's probably bored with eating because she's had enough so she's moving on to experiment with the textures instead. Try tempting your older baby to try new tastes with fun food, and she'll learn to see meal times as enjoyable occasions.

Remember, a baby's stomach can't hold very much and she'll need to eat more often than an adult. Encourage her to have regular meal times, but don't insist she finishes everything in her bowl if she's had enough. Give her healthy snacks between meals if she is hungry.

Joining family meals

As soon as your baby is sitting in her high chair to eat, she'll enjoy joining you at the table for meals too. The sooner you can include your baby in this, the sooner she'll learn by example what is and isn't acceptable behaviour at the table.

You may find it easier occasionally to feed your baby before you sit down to a family meal, then give her some finger foods to eat and play with while you eat. That way she can learn about tastes as well as join in the "conversation" at the table with the family.

▲ **FUN FOODS** You can encourage your baby to eat by making her meals look fun and attractive. Make her vegetables into a friendly face, for example.

▶ **TEETHING FOODS** When your baby is teething she'll like to chew and suck to soothe her gums. Any piece of raw vegetable or fruit that's large enough to hold easily and can be sucked or chewed makes a good teething food.

FINGER FOODS If your baby has difficulty using a spoon, she'll enjoy having some finger foods, which are easier to handle; vegetables are idea for this. Don't give her very small things that she might choke on and never leave her alone with finger foods.

Out and about

Baby-friendly activities

There are lots of activities on offer for new parents and their babies:

✳ Coffee mornings and parent-and-toddler groups (see p.138).

✳ Music groups for babies.

✳ Swimming – ask if your local pool has parent-and-baby sessions.

✳ Baby movement classes may be run at leisure centres.

✳ Baby massage classes, probably run by a natural health centre or local yoga teacher.

Try to get out and about with your baby as soon as you feel up to it. It's good for both of you – it helps get him used to travel, new places, and people, while giving you a change of scene and keeping you in touch with the world outside your home.

First outings

The first few outings that involve more than pushing the pram around to the local shops may seem daunting, and you'll probably be a bit nervous and unsure about how your baby will react. Keep calm and try to relax – your baby will pick up on any anxieties you have. You'll soon become a family of seasoned travellers. The easiest time to be out and about with your baby is while he's small and portable. Make the most of it because when he's toddling and needing constant supervision, the range of outings will become more limited for a while. Don't be too ambitious on your first outings – go to the park, or for coffee at a friend's house. Make sure you're confident about being away from home with your baby before you go further afield. Travel at off-peak times when there's less congestion, especially if you're travelling by bus or train.

Going shopping

There's no need to leave your baby at home when you go shopping as most supermarkets and department stores now provide facilities to help parents with babies (see chart opposite) and some even have crèche facilities. Shopping malls can be more difficult if they are on more than one level, but most have lifts as well as escalators. When you are in the supermarket:
✳ Always use a supermarket trolley that is appropriate to your baby's size and weight and strap him into the seat with a harness. Be aware that he may try to grab items off the shelves.
✳ Shopping tends to make children hungry and therefore fretful. Avoid this by taking a snack and drink with you. These will provide refreshment for your baby and also keep him occupied.

Travelling by car

Rear-facing car seats (see p.76) make travelling by car with a young baby relatively trouble-free, but the car seat must be correctly fitted. An older baby or toddler should sit in a front-facing car seat. Car seats for babies and young children should be put in the back seats of the car. You can only use a child seat in the front passenger seat if there is no airbag or the airbag has been switched off. Keep a few nappies, wipes, and nappy sacks in the car for emergencies. The sun can be a problem for babies, so place a detachable blind on your car window to provide shade. After any accident, do replace your seat belts, your child's car seat, and the anchorage kits, as they will have been badly strained and may be damaged.

▲ **TRAVEL SAFELY** Your baby must travel in a special car seat. By law, you must have a car seat for each child under the age of 12, correctly fitted and with a safety harness.

Shopping with your baby

Facility	What to look for
Parking spaces	Most stores have dedicated parent and baby parking spaces close to the entrance.
Wider checkouts	Many supermarkets have at least two wider than average checkouts to accommodate prams.
Special discounts	Some stores offer discounts for parents with a baby under 12 months.
Babycare	Supervised crèches are available at some stores, as long as you're there to be called if necessary.
Changing and feeding	Many stores have a baby changing area in their toilets, and some have a room where you can breastfeed – but if you're happy just to sit out of the way to feed your baby, don't feel you have to do it in private. Just ask an assistant.

Holidays

If you're going away with a very young baby, you may feel more comfortable not going abroad in case you need medical help. Having said this, young babies – especially breastfed ones – often travel abroad very well, but it's sensible to take out adequate medical insurance. Whatever the age of your baby, when you're away you should:

✳ Check how far you'll be from a doctor's surgery, medical centre, or hospital while you're away.

✳ Make sure the cot in your holiday accommodation conforms with safety standards – the tour operator, travel agent, or Tourist Information Office should be able to reassure you on this. Alternatively, take your own travel cot – modern designs are very compact.

✳ Always make sure your baby is protected from the sun (see below): use adequate sunscreen, dress your baby in protective clothing, and keep him in the shade.

Sun protection

Babies have very little skin pigment so they have much less protection from the sun's ultraviolet rays than adults. Direct sunlight can cause skin damage and skin cancer later in life. If your baby is under six months, never expose his skin to direct, strong sunlight. Keep him as cool as possible, with light cotton clothing that covers almost all his body. When he's in his buggy, shield him with a sunshade. For older babies and children, use a sunscreen with a protection factor (SPF) of at least 30. Apply the sunscreen 30 minutes before going out in the sun and then every two hours, or after swimming. Keep your child out of the sun between 11am and 3pm when the heat is at its strongest. There are also now special T-shirts and sun suits that filter UVA and UVB rays for additional protection.

Public transport tips

Planning ahead is the secret to trouble-free travel by public transport:

✳ If you're travelling alone, make sure you can manage everything yourself.

✳ Allow plenty of time to reach the station or airport to avoid the extra stress of worrying about missing a train or aeroplane.

✳ On an aeroplane, feed your baby during takeoff and landing as sucking reduces the risk of earache caused by changing air pressure.

✳ If you're flying long-haul, try to book a seat with a bassinet so that your baby can sleep in mid-flight.

✳ A portable car seat is invaluable, though for air travel you may have to pay for an extra seat on busy flights if you want to use one just for your baby.

▲ **USING A BACKPACK** A backpack is more convenient for an older baby than a buggy if you like to do a lot of walking.

Caring for your sick baby

If you suspect that your baby isn't well, don't hesitate to get medical advice if you're worried. You're the best judge of when your baby is unwell because you know and understand her moods and personality so will be aware of changes.

Medication

The doctor may prescribe a medicine, such as liquid paracetamol for your baby's high temperature and/or an antibiotic for infection. Give her the medicine in her mouth using a sterile syringe or dropper. Always give the dosage recommended by the doctor or instructed on the bottle.

Taking your baby's temperature

A raised temperature usually means your baby is fighting off an infection. Take her temperature with a digital thermometer. Hold it firmly under her bare armpit for three minutes. Bear in mind that the temperature in the armpit is about 0.6°C (1°F) less than actual body temperature. You can also use a temperature strip, although these are less accurate. Don't put the thermometer in your child's mouth. Alternatively use an ear thermometer.

▲ **CHECKING THE TEMPERATURE** Place the thermometer under your baby's bare armpit and hold her arm across her chest to keep it in place.

Nursing your baby

When babies are ill they are often grizzly and fretful, probably waking more frequently at night and needing constant attention and cuddles. However, a very ill baby will become listless and unresponsive. If your baby has a cold, it might make feeding difficult as she won't be able to breathe properly through her nose. Be patient and let her come up for air when feeding, but if this becomes a real problem ask your doctor or pharmacist for nose drops.

Recognizing a fever

A fever is a temperature over 37°C (98.6°F). The best way to recognize it is to lay your hand on your baby's forehead. If her skin is hot, red, and clammy, she has a fever. If the temperature is very high, she may also shiver.

Lowering temperature

If your baby has a very high fever, you should try to lower it to prevent overheating. Remove all her clothing, but don't let her get too cold. If your baby is over three months, you may also give her liquid paracetamol (see above left).

Preventing dehydration

Dehydration in babies under 12 months can be dangerous, and steps must be taken to replace lost fluids. Signs of dehydration in babies are general listlessness and a sunken fontanelle (the soft area of skin on the top of the skull). Your baby may

▶ **COOLING BABY** Undress your baby if she has a fever, but check she's not getting too cold.

also wet her nappy less frequently. When your baby has a temperature, or when the weather is hot, make sure she doesn't become dehydrated by offering the breast more frequently or giving her cooled, boiled water in a bottle or on a sterile spoon.

If your baby suffers from vomiting and diarrhoea for more than 24 hours, always consult your doctor. If you are bottle-feeding, try giving half-strength milk and encourage your baby to drink water with or without rehydration salts (available from your doctor or pharmacist). If your baby has been weaned, stick to a bland diet. Breastfed babies should continue with their normal milk feeds. If you're breastfeeding, give water containing rehydration salts in a bottle before the feed if you can. If your baby won't take a bottle, you'll need to breastfeed more often to maintain fluid intake.

Mild diarrhoea can sometimes occur when you introduce new types of solid food (see p.112) – if you suspect this is happening, stop giving your baby that particular food and then try again after a couple of weeks.

Recognizing an illness

Ailment	When to call the doctor
High or low temperature	* If your baby's temperature rises above 38°C (100°F) and she's obviously ill, or if it rises above 39.4°C (103°F), and she doesn't seem ill. * When your baby's temperature goes up and down. * If your baby is unusually quiet and limp and her skin is cold, though her hands and feet are pink (see p.123).
Breathing difficulties	* If your baby's breathing becomes difficult. * The rate of breathing speeds up and you notice her ribs being drawn sharply in with each breath.
Loss of appetite	* If your baby is under six months and refuses to feed either at the breast or from a bottle. * If your older baby refuses food and drink.
Vomiting	* If your baby is burping up whole feeds or the vomiting is violent, prolonged, or excessive, it can cause rapid dehydration and medical help should be sought straight away. However, all babies regurgitate a little milk from time to time after feeds.
Diarrhoea	* If the stools are watery, possibly greenish in colour, foul smelling, and are abnormally frequent. * If diarrhoea is accompanied by a raised temperature, you should always consult a doctor.
Rashes	* If you notice an unusual rash it can be a sign of infection, especially if it's accompanied by a raised temperature, or it might be an allergic reaction. Your baby's doctor will want to examine the rash. * One type of rash caused by meningitis is very serious and should be treated as an emergency (see above right).

Meningitis

This is an inflammation of the membranes that cover the brain, resulting from an infection. Viral meningitis is usually relatively mild; bacterial meningitis is life-threatening and requires immediate action. The main symptoms can develop over a matter of hours.

Symptoms
In a baby under 12 months, the main symptoms are irritability, a slightly tense and bulging fontanelle (see p.60), fever, and a rash of flat, pink, or purple spots that don't disappear when you press them. There may be listlessness, vomiting, loss of appetite, and pain in the eyes from light.

What to do
Press a glass to her skin to see if the rash remains visible through it. If you think she has meningitis, get her to a hospital immediately.

Febrile seizures

These can happen when children have a rapid increase in temperature due to infection. This causes the brain cells to discharge impulses to muscles, which contract jerkily. Although frightening to see, they are fairly common and rarely serious. The risk of epilepsy developing is very small.

Symptoms
Loss of consciousness and uncontrollable twitching of limbs. There may also be frothing at the mouth and the eyes may roll back.

What to do
Clear a space and remove her clothing to lower her temperature (see opposite). Call an ambulance.

Emergency first aid

Is your baby unconscious?

Gently tap or flick the bottom of your baby's foot. Try calling his name to see if there's any response – never shake your baby.

✳ If there is no reaction, he is unconscious. Tilt his head back gently to open his airway and check to see if he is breathing, right, before you call an ambulance.

✳ If he responds he is conscious; check him for other injuries. Get medical advice if you are concerned.

The following isn't a substitute for first-aid training, but it's a good idea to familiarize yourself with the information so that you are prepared. The British Red Cross, St John Ambulance and St. Andrew's Ambulance run first-aid courses (see p.187).

Unconscious baby

Check whether or not he is breathing. Place one hand on your baby's forehead and one finger on his chin, then tilt his head back gently to open the airway to the lungs. Remove anything obvious from his mouth, but don't put your finger in his mouth to look for anything. Put your ear near his mouth and look along his chest. Look for any movement and listen and feel for breathing for no longer than ten seconds.

If your baby is not breathing

Ask someone to call an ambulance while you begin CPR (cardiopulmonary resuscitation) – a combination of rescue breaths and chest compressions. If you're on your own, give CPR for one minute before you call an ambulance.

If your baby is breathing

KEEPING THE AIRWAY OPEN If the unconscious baby is breathing, cradle him in your arms, with his head lower than his body, and take him to the phone with you while you call an ambulance. If possible, ask someone else to phone for you while you look after the baby.

GIVING RESCUE BREATHS
✳ Tilt the baby's head and lift the chin to make sure that the airway is still open.
✳ Take a breath. Place your mouth over the baby's mouth and nose and blow steadily into his lungs until you see the chest rise. Take your mouth away from the baby's and watch the chest fall. If the chest rises and falls you have given a rescue breath.
✳ Repeat to give him FIVE rescue breaths.
✳ If the chest does not rise: adjust the baby's head; re-check his mouth and remove anything that is obviously blocking the airway; check that the seal is airtight.
✳ Make no more than five attempts to give rescue breaths before you start giving chest compressions, see right.
✳ Don't stop to check signs of circulation.

GIVING CHEST COMPRESSIONS
✳ Put the index and middle finger of one hand on the centre of the baby's chest.
✳ Press down vertically on the breastbone, depressing it by about one third of its depth. Release the pressure and let the chest come back up again, but leave your fingers on the chest.
✳ Repeat to give 30 compressions at a rate of about 100 per minute.

COMBINE CHEST COMPRESSIONS AND RESCUE BREATHS Alternate 30 compressions followed by TWO rescue breaths for one minute, then call an ambulance if this has not already been done. Continue until help arrives, the baby starts breathing normally, or you are too tired to continue.

First aid for accidents

Injury	What happens	What you should do
Severe bleeding	If your child has an accident that causes severe bleeding, you must act quickly to stop the bleeding before seeking help.	Press firmly on the wound and raise the injured part. Keep it higher than the baby's heart. Cover the wound with a sterile dressing and bandage the dressing in place. Call an ambulance.
Head injury	If a baby bumps his head he may be concussed, which causes a brief loss of consciousness, or there may be a more serious injury.	if your baby is unconscious, see opposite. If he is conscious, treat any wound (see above) and take him to hospital, even if he appears to recover.
Electric shock	Your baby may get an electric shock if he plays with electrical sockets or flex. This can cause his breathing and heart to stop and cause burns to his body.	Immediately switch off the current at the mains. Or, stand on dry, insulating material, such as a telephone directory, and push the source away from the baby with a broom. Call an ambulance.
Drowning	Just 2.5cm (1in) of water is enough to drown a baby if he falls forward. Never leave him in a bath alone, even if he can sit unaided.	Carry him with his head lower than his chest to allow water to drain. If he is unconscious, treat as described opposite and call an ambulance.
Bites	Bites can range from minor insect stings to animal bites and the treatment will differ accordingly.	For an insect bite soothe it a with cold pad, then cover it with a plaster. For an animal bite, follow the procedure for severe bleeding (see above).
Burns and scalds	If your baby is burned or scalded, you need to act quickly to cool the burn and remove any clothing from the area before it begins to swell.	Cool the burn under cold running water for ten minutes. Cover it with kitchen film or a plastic bag and take him to hospital or call an ambulance.

Choking baby

If your baby is choking, he may turn blue and make strange noises because he is trying to cry, or he is unable to make any sound at all. Don't turn him upside down or shake him. Try to clear any blockage in his throat.

Clearing a blockage

* Lay the baby face down along one forearm and keeping your hand flat, give him up to five sharp slaps between his shoulders (see right).
* Turn him face up along your other forearm and check his mouth. If the blockage has not cleared, supporting his head, place two fingers on the lower part of the breastbone. Press down and forward up to five times (chest thrusts). Check the mouth each time.
* If he is still choking, repeat the back slaps and chest thrusts three times, then call an ambulance. Continue until help arrives or the baby becomes unconscious.
* If the baby becomes unconscious, treat as described opposite.

Hypothermia

Hypothermia occurs when the body temperature falls below 35°C (95°F). The temperature-regulating mechanism in babies is immature, so they can lose body heat rapidly in a cold place.

Symptoms

He will look misleadingly healthy because his skin will have a pink glow, but it will feel cold. He may refuse to feed, be limp, and quiet.

What to do

Call a doctor. Warm him gradually. Take him into a warm room and wrap him in blankets. Put a hat on him and hold him close to your body.

Your special baby

Early signs

Although the rate of normal development is enormously varied (see p.147), it may become apparent that your baby's development is delayed. Don't leap to conclusions, but as parents, you're likely to be the first to recognize some of the signs.

Hand awareness

A baby becomes aware of her hands at about eight weeks (see p.158). At 12–16 weeks this interest wanes, but may last up to 20 weeks in a baby whose development is delayed.

Grasp reflex

From birth to about six weeks, a baby wraps her fingers tightly around anything placed in her palm, then the reflex fades as she begins to gain control of her hand movements. This reflex may last longer in a developmentally delayed baby.

Exploration with the mouth

At about four months, a baby puts everything in her mouth. Most stop at one, but a developmentally slow child may go on longer.

"Casting"

From 8–16 months, all babies go through the stage of "casting" – dropping things to see where they fall. This may last longer in a baby whose development is delayed.

Dribbling

Most babies achieve mouth control at 12 months; delayed babies may dribble for much longer.

Chewing

Most babies develop the ability to chew, even without teeth, by about seven months. A developmentally delayed baby may take longer.

Fortunately, few parents ever have to learn that their baby has a problem. This doesn't make it any easier for those parents who have to face the fact that their baby has a condition that is going to affect, and perhaps dominate, her life, and theirs too.

Diagnosis

Your baby will be examined by the midwife at birth and by a paediatrician or a specially trained midwife before you leave the hospital (see p.61). They may find something that requires further investigation at this point. If not, you may be the first to spot that something isn't quite right (see left). Talk to your family doctor who should refer your baby for an expert assessment – insist that this happens if you're concerned. Among the first things to exclude are impaired hearing or vision; these should be tested at your baby's developmental checks (see p.155).

Coming to terms with the news

Whenever you find out about your baby's disability, you'll need time to adjust to the shock and pain. Every new parent has expectations and hopes for their child, and it's as though all of these are dashed in the space of a few minutes. In many ways, it is like a bereavement; you need to mourn for the baby you thought you were expecting, the perfect, able-bodied child you longed for, and come to terms with the special baby you have. In time, of course, this child will be your perfect child, and you'll feel ashamed that you ever thought her second-best, but in the early days, it's almost impossible not to feel a sense of loss.

Talk to others

Many of the congenital conditions that affect children and babies are extremely rare, but it will help you enormously if you can find other parents to talk to who have a child with exactly the same problem as your own. Your doctor, health centre, or local Social Services department can put you in touch with specialist organizations. Many of these organizations have self-help groups that include other parents who are in the same or a similar position to you (see p.187).

Physical problems that can be corrected

With advances in neonatal paediatric surgery, many of the physical problems babies are born with can be corrected, even in the first months. This is a worrying time because it's distressing to see your baby having to undergo a series of operations. It can also be a strain emotionally (and financially), particularly if the hospital treating your baby is a long way from your home, but it helps to know that there is every chance that your baby will be able to grow up to be a normal healthy child.

Recognizing developmental problems

A baby with a developmental problem is going to reach her milestones (see p.146) at a slower than average rate, and in some cases may not reach them at all. You may notice quite early on that your baby is behind from various signs, such as unusual quietness, lack of alertness, no interest in her surroundings, floppiness (lack of muscle tone), docility, and sleeping for long periods. Sometimes a baby who's been termed "good" turns out to be a baby with a problem, because this kind of baby cries rarely, makes little noise, and doesn't interact well with her environment.

Later signs

As your baby grows older, at around seven or eight months you may notice that her attention span is very short and she'll spend time moving quickly from one toy to another instead of examining one slowly and carefully as most babies do. Later still, she may be over-active and have difficulty in concentrating on a single activity. She may also be reserved and unresponsive to people, even when she knows them very well.

Avoid comparisons

Comparing one baby with another is never a good idea, but if you have a baby with delayed development it's doubly important to see your baby for herself, rather than against the standard of other people's children. With perseverance, the support of specialists, and encouragement from you, your baby will reach some of her milestones (see p.146) eventually, and the reward of seeing her do so will give you huge satisfaction.

Other people's attitudes

Most people don't have direct experience of a disability, and have little idea of how to react to a disabled person or child. Indeed, this may have been your own position until recently. Almost inevitably there will be those who will say the wrong thing, make a crass comment or remark without thinking. You'll just have to remind yourself that their insensitivity comes from ignorance and embarrassment, and they probably don't mean to be offensive. Try not to let this get you down; be open about your baby's disability so that it doesn't become a taboo subject.

Giving a lead

What you'll find is that many of your family and friends will take their lead from you in learning how to relate to your child. Make it clear that although her disability may be permanent, she is in no way inferior to anyone else and has the same right to love, understanding, and support as any child. You'll need courage, but you'll discover, like many other parents of disabled children, that you've got an inner strength that you never thought you would have. If you can be positive and hopeful about your child, and show by example how much you value her individuality and personality, other people will learn to do the same. It can be helpful and comforting to talk to people in similar situations, so contact any relevant national agencies.

How you can help

If and when your baby is diagnosed with developmental delay, disability, or learning difficulty, you'll be given specialist advice on how to stimulate her both physically and intellectually. Here are some ideas:

✳ Stimulate your child from birth. Do this visually – make sure she can see your face close up as much as possible and hang a picture of a face down the side of the cot. Stimulate her aurally by playing music or a heartbeat, by talking and singing. Use touch with different textures, such as lambskin, cotton, rubber, or plastic.

✳ Talk and sing to your baby in pronounced rhythms and rhymes, such as "Jack and Jill".

✳ Read and talk aloud to her as much as you can.

✳ Make her aware of her body with gentle clapping games and baby massage (see p.110).

✳ Find toys that are educational and enjoyable and show her how to play with them (see p.146).

✳ Introduce her to as many people as possible.

✳ Give her lots of love and make her feel secure. Praise her often.

✳ Give her lots of cuddles and kisses; make sure others do, too.

✳ Never scold or punish her slowness.

✳ Encourage her to be independent – help her to try to do things, even if it's hard.

✳ Be patient when she's frustrated. Life will be a bit more difficult for her, especially when she realizes that she can't do things that other children her age can.

Adapting to parenthood

As well as mastering the practical care of your newborn baby, you need to think about your lifestyle and your relationship so that you're able to get the most out of being parents and a family. Your baby will undoubtedly be your main priority and it's easy to let him soak up all your emotional and physical energy. But to maximize the many joys of parenthood, it's worth ensuring that you have time for each other and time for yourself. You are, after all, still individuals and still in a loving relationship and it would be wrong to think that your baby could fulfil all your needs. How easily you adjust will depend on your individual circumstances: having a good and equal relationship with each other already and an adequate support network can make the transition to parenthood that much easier. If you have difficulty in adjusting at first, don't worry – things will get easier. Parenthood is full of ups and downs, but if you work together to get the balance right, hopefully it will turn out to be all that you wanted it to be.

Helping each other

If you're at home with your baby while your partner is at work, you may begin to feel that you know your baby better than he does. Or, you may feel that you don't get enough help from him. Think about how your attitudes may affect your partner.

Supporting your partner

* Try to avoid thinking that your partner isn't as "good" as you are at caring for your baby. By encouraging him to get involved with your baby's care and to share the work load, you'll all benefit.

* If your partner is tired after work, be patient. Let him unwind, then encourage him to spend time with your baby as a way of relaxing, not as a chore. Bathing the baby is often both a good way for him to look after the baby and to relax (see p.95).

* Tell him about your day. If it's been difficult, don't bottle it up, but, equally, try not to convey it accusingly as if it's his fault.

Building your self-esteem

* Be proud of your achievements. As the main carer, take pride in the upbringing of your baby.

* Keep in touch with work colleagues so that you're up to date with career developments and office gossip! That way it will be less of a shock when you return to work.

* Try to have some time away from your baby, on your own and with your partner (see p.134).

New parenthood is a joyful but testing role, when both of you are faced with a new set of priorities and when expectations come up against hard realities. So spare a thought for each other's needs, as well as those of your baby.

The initial impact of the baby

As first-time parents you may seriously underestimate the amount of work and disruption caring for a baby entails and the extent to which this affects your relationship. Many couples are shocked to find that rather than bringing them closer together, their baby can bring to light differences that drive them apart. This is normal and very much part of your growth into parenthood, when you begin to lay the foundations of your new parental relationship with your baby and with each other.

Different patterns of bonding

While two-thirds of mothers bond with their babies almost immediately or within a few days, many fathers admit that intense paternal feelings take

▲ **SHARING THE CARE** Your child can't have too much attention and love from her parents. Family mealtimes can be a great time for both of you to feed her and talk to her. She'll enjoy the company, and you'll learn to be parents together.

Defusing areas of conflict

What to do	How it helps
Discuss who does what	You probably both have views about what roles men and women should play; this can be a powerful hidden agenda. Discuss how you feel and be prepared to have your views challenged.
Talk about your expectations	Disappointed expectations may produce disillusionment, so it's best to give and take in those areas where your views diverge, even though you won't escape hard choices.
Listen to each other	Try to talk openly about your feelings and think about how to express them. Do this in a way that avoids accusation, sarcasm, or belittling your partner. Give "I" rather than "you" messages.
Resolve conflict immediately	Resolve conflict by determining the cause and coming to a mutually agreed solution. A common area of conflict is when you have differing views on the division of labour (see below).
Put your family first	Self-denial isn't a very popular concept these days, but if you're to turn your trio into a family, you'll each need to forgo some individual pleasures in the interest of building that family.
Learn to cope with stress	Reactions to stress differ from person to person. Try to evolve together a pattern of "stress management" for difficult periods, to minimize any possible damage to your relationship.

JUST FOR DAD

If you're at work and your partner is at home with the baby, try to see her point of view. At work, you'll have the challenges and friendships of working life to stimulate you, while your partner may be missing these if she's stopped work to look after the baby, and she may well be finding the change difficult.

Supporting your partner

* Telephone her at different times of the day – several times a week. If you're near enough, go home for lunch every now and then.

* Let her know what time you're going to be home and stick to it. She'll need a break in the evenings and this is valuable time for you to spend with your baby.

* Share the ups and the downs. If you've had a rotten day at work, talk to her about it, but listen to her and be sympathetic if she's also had a bad day at home.

* Make sure she has time out to relax away from the baby and to see her friends (see p.134).

Becoming more involved

* Even if your partner is at home with the baby most of the time, remember that your role in caring for your baby is vital and will be rewarding for you.

* Find out what happened during the day and what milestones your baby may have reached – then spend time with your baby so that you can experience them too.

* Try to use your weekends and days off to have extended time with your growing baby.

much longer to develop. Many mothers are overwhelmed by the depth of their feelings for their baby. Unfortunately, some fathers view this as an obsession, to which they are not sympathetic, and they resent being excluded from their partner's affection and attention. A man whose partner breastfeeds often feels excused from nurturing as a result, driving a wedge between himself and his baby. Fathers who are involved in their baby's daily care will strengthen their paternal bond in the early weeks and close the gap between how differently fathers and mothers feel about their baby.

Division of labour

By far the biggest bone of contention between new parents is how they should share caring for the baby and the workload that goes with it. Many fathers do their fair share, but others help with the fun tasks, such as bath time and bedtime stories, but are less enthusiastic about changing nappies, washing clothes, and getting up in the middle of the night. This attitude is inappropriate – parenting should be a partnership. Find ways of sharing the drudgery and the delights of caring for your baby. Look positively at her development and how you can stimulate and enjoy it together (see p.146). You and your partner should think of parenthood as one of the most demanding jobs you can have, and reinforce each other's equal responsibility to succeed in this new role.

Learning to cope

Caring for a baby tests all parents. Getting through the difficult times is part of being a parent; you'll learn from every occasion and be a better parent and partner for having come through it.

Minimizing stress

Most family arguments happen at stressful times. Early in the morning when you're only half awake, it's easy to feel clumsy and irritable. If you're in full-time work, you may bring stress home with you, making it more difficult to cope with the demands at home. It's at times like these that you both need to work together to help each other; taking out your stresses on each other or on your baby will probably only make things worse:

✳ Try to find ways of relaxing with each other and by yourselves (see p.134).

✳ Try to be honest about how you're feeling to help prevent any misunderstandings.

✳ Don't try to do too many things at once – you'll only get frustrated and over-tired.

✳ Try not to bring work home with you – physically or mentally.

Negative feelings

Having negative thoughts towards your baby because he's kept you up all night or because he's crying a lot is normal. There's no point in refusing to accept how you feel; it doesn't make you wicked. It's abnormal, however, to use violence as a way of expressing yourself; if your temper is really being pushed to the limit, talk to someone or take time out before you do something you'll regret.

Why anger is normal

If your baby cries for long periods or sleeps only for brief intervals, you're bound to feel concerned and worried. If this worry is then compounded by a feeling of impotence, it often expresses itself as anger. You may sometimes be seized by acute feelings of helplessness, guilt, and inadequacy when nothing you do seems to pacify your baby. At such times it's difficult not to feel victimized and the worry can often quickly escalate to resentment and then anger. You may also feel angry that nothing you do seems to work, and resentful that you're left with little time or energy for your own needs. These are very natural feelings.

Breaking the circle of negativity

The knowledge that your tension and frustration can be communicated to your baby will only increase your anxiety, which will in turn make your baby feel more insecure. It's all too easy to become locked into a vicious circle of negativity. Your baby will express his feelings in the only way he knows, by crying more, and his crying will further unnerve you. This circle must be broken to prevent storing up difficulties.

Talk to someone Telephone someone you can confide in; just getting your feelings out in the open will help to put everything into perspective. Talking to other parents in the same situation is often useful – you'll realize that how you feel is very normal. You should also talk to your partner, but remember he or she may also be feeling exasperated; try to talk to each other when you're able to go out without the baby or when the baby is asleep. If none of the above is possible, speak to your health visitor or doctor.

A change of scene If you're alone with your baby during the day, get out of the house. The change of scene will help to relax you and being driven in a car, wheeled in a pram, or walked in a sling can often soothe a baby. In the short term, if you feel yourself being engulfed by anger, leave the room or put the baby in another room until you feel calmer. When your baby is older, make sure you have adequate time away (see p.134).

If your baby is difficult to love

Just like both of you, your baby has his own personality. He may be happy and smiling all the time, or he may be reserved and seemingly unsociable. He may be independent and not very affectionate, or clingy and easily upset. Remember, your baby doesn't choose to behave in a certain way to spite you – it's just how he's made. As with all relationships, you need to keep the communication channels open with your baby. You have to get to know what makes him tick and accept that you're not going to have an easy relationship with him all the time.

Maintaining affection

Some babies don't like to be handled or cuddled very much; others go through phases of being unsociable. If a baby doesn't want attention, he will tend to stiffen his body and cry when you hold him. Most babies will become more sociable with time, but if you're particularly worried, seek advice from your health visitor. Try to do the following:

✳ Accept that babies are sometimes just difficult and don't blame yourself.
✳ Don't thrust unwelcome attention on him – it may make matters worse.
✳ If your baby is more affectionate with your partner, be grateful! Don't take this personally; babies often go through periods when they prefer or cling to one partner and this will pass with time.
✳ Remember, your baby will respond to you so make sure you're smiling and being affectionate towards him.

When your baby misses you

If you have invested time in your baby and bonded closely, you'll have created a feeling of rightness when you're together that is shattered when you're apart. An upheaval, such as returning to work, the preferred parent being away for a while, or the introduction of a childminder may unsettle your baby. This is most likely to reveal itself in him being fretful, fussy, needing more cuddles than usual, and a change in his eating and sleeping patterns. If your baby appears to be very unhappy, reassess the situation; it could be that he's unhappy with his childminder. If you're away:

✳ Telephone frequently.
✳ Ask your partner or childminder to talk about you to your baby.
✳ Leave an item of your clothing for your baby and some photos of yourself.
✳ Tape yourself singing and talking to your baby.

▶ **KEEP IN TOUCH**
A baby will love to hold the telephone, hear Daddy's voice, and "talk" to him when he's away from home.

A fretful baby

Most parents experience a period when their baby is consistently fretful and demanding for no apparent reason. The inability to communicate what's wrong can be very frustrating for both of you and your baby.

Why he may be fretful

✳ He may not be receiving as much stimulation as he needs. Babies who can sit up and who would like to explore their surroundings, but who can't yet crawl, can become frustrated.

✳ If your baby is teething, he may be experiencing discomfort or even pain (see p.109).

✳ If you're particularly stressed, your baby may be picking up your heightened tension.

Getting through it

✳ Remember, your baby's behaviour is normal. Much of your frustration stems from his inability to communicate. This is natural and not a failing in him or you.

✳ It doesn't mean that you're inadequate if your baby is going through a bad patch. Most parents experience difficult periods.

✳ Try to accept your feelings rather than get angry with yourself and you'll find it easier to keep an overall positive attitude.

✳ Try to keep things in perspective by sharing any negative feelings with each other or a friend.

✳ There are particular ways that a crying baby can be comforted. Try some of the suggestions I've outlined on pp.104–109.

Feeling low

Helping each other

In the days after the birth, when the "baby blues" may be rife, you'll both need to support each other. Just sharing the day-to-day care of your baby and listening and being there for each other will help.

What fathers can do

✳ Encourage your partner to talk about the things that are getting her down. Give her lots of affection.

✳ Boost her self-esteem. She may feel unattractive and dislike her body – tell her how much you love her often and that she's beautiful.

✳ Take her shopping for clothes. Be patient and compliment her. Don't push her to lose weight.

✳ Encourage her to join a mother-and-baby support group and make it easy for her to go.

✳ Encourage people to visit if that's what she wants, but, if not, help to maintain her privacy.

What mothers can do

✳ If you've got the blues, try your best not to take out your tensions on your partner. Try to express how you're feeling. If you need a cuddle, tell your partner.

✳ Remember that your partner also has some big adjustments to make and may be finding it difficult too.

✳ Make sure your partner has time with the baby. It will create problems if he feels left out.

✳ Try to limit visitors. Your partner may feel excluded if your house is full of female friends and family.

The "baby blues" usually last a few days, but in some mothers they go on for months due to postnatal depression. A partner needs to know the difference between the "blues" and depression so that he can help and knows when to seek medical advice.

Baby blues

The "baby blues" are mood swings caused by hormonal changes. In all likelihood this period of feeling low one minute and euphoric the next won't last beyond the first week, but you'll still need a lot of support to get through it. Maybe the "baby blues" are a natural sign to those around you that you need time and space to come to terms with being a mother. That's certainly how a concerned partner, relative, or friend should deal with it; although you'll find that because your hormones are all over the place, you'll also cry when someone's nice to you!

Why you get the blues

Your hormones, progesterone and oestrogen, will have been high during pregnancy. After you have had your baby, these hormone levels drop and your body may find it difficult to adjust. This drop can have a marked effect on your emotions. With this, exhaustion from the labour, and lack of sleep, it's not at all surprising that you may not be feeling on top of the world.

What you can do

✳ Give yourself time. Accept that you'll feel like this for a short time and that what you're going through is incredibly common. Accept offers of help and don't try to do everything yourself.
✳ Try to talk about your feelings and have a good cry if it helps.
✳ Tell your partner you need a lot of love and affection, but remember this is a time of upheaval and change for him, too.

When fathers get the blues

Most fathers feel an anticlimax after the birth. There are so many changes and if your partner is feeling low, you'll be called on to be a tower of strength, which can be a huge strain. Try to think of the first few months as a period of rapid change that is testing for both of you; when you come through it, you'll be closer than you were before. If you get really unhappy, talk things over with your health visitor, doctor, or a close friend.

Postnatal depression (PND)

If symptoms that started out as the common "baby blues" don't go away and, in fact, start to become worse, you could be suffering from postnatal depression. This is a temporary and treatable condition that varies from woman to woman. It can develop slowly and not become obvious until several weeks after the baby's birth, but if it's diagnosed and addressed early enough, there's a good chance of a fast cure. Health visitors are trained to recognize the symptoms, and treatment ranges from something as simple as talking to a friend, health visitor, or doctor about how you feel, to taking medication, such as antidepressants, in more severe cases.

Why PND happens

There are many reasons why postnatal depression occurs. It depends on you as a person, your personal circumstances, and the way your baby behaves. Research shows that the following risk factors may make you more susceptible to postnatal depression:

* If you enjoyed a senior position at work or high-flying career before the birth, it can be difficult to adjust to the status change.
* If you already have difficulties in your relationship, the baby may make them worse; this in itself may lead to disillusionment and low self-esteem.
* If you had an unexpected difficult birth experience (see pp.50–53), you could easily feel demoralized and feel that you've failed in some way.
* If you've had depression in the past.
* A very demanding, sleepless baby can trigger postnatal depression from sheer exhaustion.
* If you have particularly difficult living conditions and no support network, this can make postnatal depression worse.
* If you've bottled up your emotions and not sought help early on.

Seeking help

Many women are too embarrassed to admit how they feel, fearing that it will appear that they've somehow failed. Talking about how you feel is the most important thing you can do. Once you accept that you're not "mad" and that there are things you can do to help yourself, you are one step on the road to recovery. Once you seek help, you'll be guided to:

* Understand how you feel and learn to express this.
* Learn to prioritize, devote more time to yourself, and find ways to relax.
* Visit the health visitor more regularly and seek support.
* Begin taking medication if your postnatal depression is extreme.

What fathers can do

You may feel helpless because you don't understand postnatal depression. Remember, it's temporary and treatable, so try to be patient. You can be a huge help if you make an effort to understand and do the following:

* Talk and listen to your partner. Never tell her to pull herself together – she can't. Don't assume she'll snap out of it – she won't.
* Mother the mother – encourage her to rest and eat and drink properly.
* Encourage her to be with the baby as much as she wants so that she can take things slowly and gradually work out how the baby will fit in.
* Make sure she's not alone too much as she'll fear isolation.
* Go to see the doctor first for advice as your partner may refuse to accept that she's ill. The doctor may arrange to visit her informally at home.

PND signs to look out for

Signs and symptoms may include:

* Anxiety – in particular, a mother may worry about her baby and refuse to be parted from her.

* Irrational fears, for example about being left alone.

* Loss of appetite.

* Insomnia.

* Fatigue.

* Lack of concern with appearance.

* Making mountains out of molehills.

* Withdrawal from social contact.

* Feeling negative and inadequate.

* Growing feelings of despondency and helplessness.

Postnatal psychosis

Postnatal, or puerperal, psychosis is the rarest and most serious form of PND. It affects about one in 1,000 women, usually in the first three months after the birth. Urgent medical help is needed. Symptoms include:

* Sleeping all day.

* Crying for long periods.

* Feeling tense and anxious.

* Being manically jolly and behaving oddly.

* Being paranoid and hallucinating.

* Thinking about harming herself and the baby.

Taking time out

You need time out, but don't forget so does your partner. He needs his own time with your baby, time alone with you, and a chance to relax away from work and home.

How to help your partner

✳ Encourage him to have an occasional night out with friends or time to continue a hobby, even if he's been out at work all day. It's good for anyone who works to relax this way, as long as it doesn't take over his life to the exclusion of you and your baby.

✳ Make the most of your time at home with your partner. He may feel left out, so make the effort to make him feel special, particularly when the baby is asleep.

How your baby gains

Spending short periods away from your baby can make you a better parent, so don't feel guilty:

✳ You'll appreciate your baby more when you see him again.

✳ A break will help you feel relaxed and rested so you cope better.

✳ It's good for your baby to get used to you going out (he'll learn that you always come back). He'll begin to gain confidence and develop his social skills by having to relate to others.

Being a new parent is undoubtedly a tiring and time-consuming experience, but you need to have time out for you and your partner – individually and together. Making time for yourself is not a luxury, it's a necessity. You'll need to be well organized, but it'll be good for your relationship and good for your baby.

Make time for yourself

✳ If you're the primary carer, incorporated into your daily timetable should be at least half an hour devoted entirely to yourself, when you can have a soak in the bath, read a magazine, or see a friend.

✳ When your baby is asleep, take the opportunity to rest; if you're feeling tired, having a catnap is more important than cleaning the house. Don't be hard on yourself – it's okay to sleep in the middle of the day, especially if you're having to get up during the night.

✳ Time away doesn't only mean half an hour away from your baby when he's asleep; it means time away from the home environment. If you arrange to see a friend, suggest that you visit her or meet her somewhere. If you're at home you're more likely to become involved with your baby.

✳ Arrange a "baby swap" with other parents: they look after your baby alongside their own on a particular day or evening, and then you do the same for them. Ask friends and relatives to help out, if they live nearby.

✳ Find out if the local leisure centre or gym has a crèche – and use it!

Be flexible with your daily routine

You can roughly plan your day, but don't be too regimented and inflexible. The needs of a young baby change all the time and if your baby wakes up unexpectedly you may not be able to have the half an hour you wanted. Try to be relaxed about it and take a break later in the day.

Accept help from others

It will be much easier to make time for yourself if you learn to accept offers of help. Don't be stoic and don't feel you're somehow a failure because you let someone else look after your baby. Just say yes, gracefully, and then do your own thing – you deserve it. It's very normal to feel strange about leaving your baby to begin with, but this will pass with time once you've learned to trust your helpers. Your baby will also benefit in many ways by not only being with you all the time (see left).

Spending time together as a couple

An important part of keeping the communication channels open with your partner is to find time when you can be alone together. Doing this is possible, but may require planning. It will seem odd to book a time to see your partner, but if you try to be spontaneous about it, you'll always find an excuse or decide that your baby is more important. Sometimes it may only be possible to spend time together in the house, but try to find times when someone else can look after your baby so that you both have the opportunity to go out and have uninterrupted time as a couple.

At home

❋ Try to continue any rituals you had before your baby was born, such as having a drink together in the evening, sharing a bath, or just doing the crossword. Try not to talk about your baby all the time.

❋ Cuddle up together for half an hour on the sofa; this precious time together will help you to keep some semblance of normality and act as a reminder that you're still a couple, as well as being parents.

Going out

❋ Don't turn down invitations and, if possible, try not to take your baby with you all the time (although it may be easier to do so in the first six to eight weeks). Find a reliable babysitter and, if you're breastfeeding, express milk (see p.83) so that you don't have to cut your evening short.

❋ When your baby is a bit older, find people you can rely on – such as grandparents – to look after him for a longer period of time so that you can take the opportunity to have a weekend away together.

❋ Continue hobbies you enjoyed together before the baby was born, such as playing sports (see p.66). If you can't find a babysitter, go swimming as this is something you can all enjoy together (see p.139).

Grandparents

Your baby's grandparents can loom large in your life both positively and negatively. If they respect your privacy, and your right to bring up your children your way, grandparents are unquestionably the best friends, helpers, and supporters you and your baby will have.

Making the most of grandparents' help

Grandparents are the people most likely to encourage you to have time off, not least because they'll want to spend some time with their grandchild. Make the most of this. Let them be a part of your baby's life and have their own relationship with him – the bond between grandparents and grandchild can be priceless for your child and for them. It is, however, important to get the balance right, as much as anything because you don't want to fall out with the people who are your best helpers:

❋ Don't let bossy parents or parents-in-law take over, pop around every five minutes, or turn up uninvited. If they live nearby, try to get into a routine that suits everyone; for example, choose a particular day of the week for them to look after your baby.

❋ Be clear from the outset about how you want to bring up your baby to prevent any misunderstandings later on. Make sure that grandparents do things the way you like them done, and not the way they think best.

❋ JUST FOR DAD

Sharing the care of your baby will help you understand how your partner feels and how important it is for her to have some time off.

How to help your partner

❋ Take your baby out shopping or just out for a walk at weekends to give your partner some space.

❋ Be fair to your partner – if she has stayed in with the baby while you've been out with friends, offer to do the same for her.

❋ Share the cooking, even if you've been at work. Treat yourselves to a takeaway occasionally.

Babysitters

Use a babysitter who has experience with babies and young children, and preferably one recommended by friends. Don't use someone under 16 years old in case a problem arises that he or she may not be able to handle. The babysitter will need:

❋ Telephone numbers for you and a relative or neighbour.

❋ The location of your first-aid kit as well as an explanation of how to use the baby monitor.

❋ An idea of your baby's routine and what to do if he wakes up.

❋ Feeding equipment and details of what your baby should be fed.

❋ Nappy-changing equipment and a change of clothes.

Sex and parenthood

Given your new responsibilities and possible physical discomforts (see below right), having sex is unlikely to be a high priority.

Your body image
You may feel unattractive if you have stretch marks and feel bloated, but your partner is probably less bothered about these things than you think. However, you do have to start liking yourself again before you can enjoy sex. Consider exercising (see p.66); if nothing else, you'll feel better about yourself. If you're breastfeeding, you may be uncomfortable about your partner touching your breasts. Tell him – he may share your feelings.

Your baby
You're likely to be completely preoccupied with your baby and having sex may be the last thing you want to think about. This is normal, but once you decide to make love again, try to put the baby to the back of your mind.

Your partner
Don't put up with uncomfortable or painful sex because you feel dutiful. Your main priority is your baby and, although your partner needs to feel loved, you can show that in other ways. Remember, although you're preoccupied and fulfilled by your baby, your partner may not be to the same extent. Talk about this and how it affects your feelings about sex.

Your sexual relationship will, for a short time, be one of the many aspects of your partnership that has to adapt. Talk openly to each other about your sexual needs and expectations so this doesn't become a difficult issue.

Your feelings about sex

Don't just have sex because you think it's what your partner wants or expect to have sex after a certain time. It's normal to feel sexually different now that you're in the dual, contradictory roles of being a parent and a lover. You may even feel guilty about wanting or thinking about sex because you feel you should be looking after and thinking about your baby. Don't take sexual rejection personally. Talk to each other and try to understand the reasons for wanting or not wanting to resume intercourse. Sex can only become a problem if you let it, and it should be easily resolved if you keep talking to each other about how you feel.

How sex can help Looking after a baby can cause tensions and problems. Having intercourse at the right time, when you're both ready for it, may be just what you need to reaffirm your desire and affection for each other.

Physical considerations

You can generally resume sex when you both feel ready (unless you have been advised to wait for any reason), but there may be physical problems that will deter you from resuming sex in the first weeks after the birth.

Vaginal discomfort It's normal to feel too sore and tender to resume penetrative sex. The vagina will be bruised, making sex painful, even if the childbirth was free of intervention. If you had an episiotomy (see p.46), you may not be able to tolerate anything rubbing against the site for many months. Also, the glands that normally lubricate the vagina will not function effectively because of hormonal changes, so it's advisable to use a lubricating cream, which is available from your pharmacist.

Lochia (see p.64) Don't resume penetrative sex until this discharge has stopped, which may not be for up to six weeks.

Breastfeeding Your breasts may leak milk during intercourse, especially when you orgasm, which can be a shock unless you're both prepared for it.

Tiredness Given the choice between having sex or sleeping, most new parents would choose the latter. Until you have more of a routine, and have found ways to have time to yourselves, it's difficult to resume a normal sex life. Try to be understanding if either one of you is too tired to make love.

Libido It appears that the sex drive in both new parents is much lower than normal and it returns slowly over a matter of months.

Caesarean Although you won't have any vaginal discomfort, a Caesarean is major abdominal surgery. You're likely to feel very tender for around six weeks and should wait to resume sex until you're fully recovered.

Contraception

The last thing you're likely to want when you're looking after a newborn baby is to find that you're immediately going to be parents all over again! The midwife or family planning adviser will ask you about contraception before you're discharged from hospital, and you will also be asked about this at your six-week check (see p.64). You can become pregnant if your periods have not started and you can be fertile as early as three weeks after the birth of your baby.

Breastfeeding While this does reduce fertility, you have to be feeding very regularly (at least every four hours, and more often for some women) to prevent ovulation. Breastfeeding is not a contraceptive.

Having sex

Without it being an automatic prelude to sex, you should both feel that you can engage in physical contact whenever you feel like it. It's important that you continue to enjoy sex and find what is right for both of you – talk about your preferences and be open to trying new things.

Foreplay It's good to build up your sex drive through foreplay – touch and caress, massage each other with aromatic oils, or take a bath together.

Non-penetrative sex For the first few times, maybe quite soon after the birth, try bringing each other to orgasm through gentle manual and oral sex. Consider being experimental; for example, try using some sex toys, such as a vibrator.

Comfortable positions Once you feel confident enough to try penetrative sex, experiment with different positions to find the ones that put least pressure on the sore areas. Stop at any time if you feel discomfort.

Methods of contraception

Type	Advice
Pill	Those containing oestrogen are not prescribed for women who are breastfeeding because they reduce milk production.
Mini-pill	These contain only progestogen, which does not inhibit milk production, but they may worsen any postnatal depression (see p.132) by inhibiting the natural production of progesterone. The mini-pill must be taken at the same time each day.
Condom (male and female)	These should be used with a contraceptive gel for comfort and security. A female condom may cause discomfort if you're bruised and sore after childbirth.
IUD (inter-uterine device), Mirena, or diaphragm	Your cervix may have enlarged and won't return to its normal size for two to three months. If you used a diaphragm or had an IUD or Mirena device or before you were pregnant, you'll need a new one. Some doctors will fit this at your six-week check (see p.64), although others prefer to wait a bit longer.

JUST FOR DAD

It's quite natural to have a low sex drive (see below) for a short time after your baby is born. It's often a good thing because it allows you to concentrate on your baby. Many men, though, do want to resume sexual activity sooner than their partners.

Reasons for a low sex drive

* Being too tired and preoccupied with the baby.

* Having witnessed the birth.

* Sharing a bedroom with your baby.

* Feeling that your partner's body (especially her breasts) belongs to the baby and finding it difficult to think of her sexually.

* Being frightened of physically hurting your partner.

Understanding your partner

* Start being closer and more affectionate gradually and you'll soon begin to see your partner as your lover again.

* Don't expect too much from your partner too soon. Sex will be much less enjoyable for you if she's not ready or comfortable.

* Your partner may find it difficult to relax during sex as she will be listening for your baby's cry. Be understanding and try to find time when you can be alone without your baby (see p.134).

* If your partner cuddles you or you're just being affectionate with each other, don't assume you will have sex. This will only upset her, disappoint you, and probably cause an argument.

Your new world

Playgroups and crèches

Playgroups and crèches range from informal arrangements between several parents to professionally organized sessions, where a trained supervisor offers a wide variety of play-based activities.

✳ The playgroup gives you a chance to meet other parents, and your baby an opportunity to make friends with other children and adults.

✳ A child of two and a half can be left at a playgroup for a couple of hours, but many also have a mother-and-baby group where parents can go with their babies. You'll need to stay with your baby, though, as the group won't have the resources to look after her.

✳ Many shopping centres, leisure centres, and supermarkets have crèches where babies and children can be left for a couple of hours. You must, however, stay in the vicinity in case you're needed.

Being a parent becomes a huge part of how you see yourself and how others see you. Your priorities change and this takes some getting used to. Caring for your baby is easier and more fun if you meet other parents and use the facilities available to you.

Other parents and children

Being a parent will extend your range of friends to include those who have children. As well as counteracting the demoralizing effect of mid-morning and early-afternoon isolation that can be the curse of solitary childcare, making friends with other parents benefits you in many ways:

✳ You mix with other people who are equally focused on being a parent.

✳ It's a good way to introduce your baby to relationships outside the family, which helps to develop her social skills.

✳ Parenting is a learning process – you'll be breaking new ground every day and be able to exchange tips with the friends you've made.

✳ You'll have people who understand the difficulties you're going through because they're going through them too.

How to meet people

A good way to make friends who have children is to stay in touch with some of the parents you met while pregnant, particularly if you live in a rural area where there may be fewer activities. If you have a spring or summer baby, you'll probably meet people in the park or playground. If your baby is born in the winter, find out about activities from your health visitor or local library.

▶ **MEETING PEOPLE** Forming friendships with other parents and their babies can be hugely beneficial to you and your baby.

When parenthood is not enough

It used to be thought that being at home with a baby was a satisfying way for a woman to spend her most creative and active years; the same would rarely be thought of a man. But nowadays many mothers and fathers are far from fulfilled by simply being a parent. Some who've tried to do it, because they believe that it's the best start they could give their child, have found the experience quite limiting.

Learning to adapt

In a society where the worth and freedom of the individual, the opportunity for self-development, and an obligation to be oneself are constantly cited as legitimate goals, it's not surprising that most people are ill-prepared for the narrowing of horizons that comes with caring for a baby. You and your partner simply won't have as much of yourselves left over as before and this doesn't sit easily with the kind of ambitions bred by modern society.

Finding fulfilment Women who want to take an active part in the wider world, and have been educated and trained to do so, can hardly be expected to substitute an intimate relationship with the washing machine for the stimulation and satisfaction they derived from their work. The thousand joys of nurturing babies and children don't, for some women, compensate for the loss of a life outside the home, as the joys are not the same. You can't make up for a lack of vitamin A by taking large doses of vitamin B. It goes without saying that full-time parenthood is a worthwhile career for a person who is happy in it, but anyone who hankers for more than pure domesticity shouldn't feel ashamed. Just because you have interests beyond day-to-day childcare doesn't mean you don't love your baby.

Avoiding isolation Many people decide to become parents with the view that it will be a temporary – never total – denial of their needs and ambitions. This is why it's important – and, ultimately, in the baby's best interest – that you don't feel trapped by your parenting role. What most of us understand as isolation is the absence of other people and for those who spend their days caring for children, this means other adults. However much you love your baby, it's important to have the stimulation of adult interaction, which is why you need to get out and meet people.

Working from home

To make the transition to being a parent easier and less of a shock, some women try to keep some of their old self by working from home. The information technology revolution has made this more possible than ever before, but it's not as easy as it sounds, especially if it's attempted too soon.
✳ You must have a routine with your baby in order to do justice to your work and to make sure you don't end up working in the evenings.
✳ It's important to make sure you're not just dividing your time between work and your baby; you need time for yourself and with your partner.
✳ You'll still need to organize some form of childcare (see p.172), which could mean that you miss out on time with your baby in her early months.

Activities at home

You'll be at home for some of the time, so getting together with other parents to host activities at home is a good idea. It's also a good way for your baby to get used to different people. Here are some ideas:

✳ **Coffee morning:** this is a good and cheap activity, giving you the chance to chat as your babies play.

✳ **Lunch party:** provide simple snack food, so that you can eat and baby watch at the same time. Ask friends to bring a contribution (especially for their babies) or just take it in turns to host lunch.

✳ **Home-selling party:** this is a good way to be sociable and earn some money. It involves presenting and taking orders for products, such as household goods or books, and earning commission on what you sell. Before you start, always check that the company you're working for is a reputable one.

Leisure centres

A good way of getting out is to join a leisure centre. Find one that has crèche facilities (see opposite) so that you can take your baby with you – some have a "soft room" where your baby can play safely. Most swimming pools offer parent-and-baby sessions and your baby, equipped with suitable buoyancy aids, will enjoy the water as soon as she can hold her head up confidently (at about four months). Remember, you should avoid high-intensity exercise for the first nine months and while breastfeeding.

Single parents

Accepting help

Most couples struggle to bring up a baby without help, so as a single parent don't think you have to do it all yourself. Having guaranteed time on your own during the week is good for both you and your baby:

✳ Try to build up a small network of people you can depend on.

✳ If you have several helpers, spread their time with your baby throughout the week if you can.

✳ Ask a relative or friend who's not working to stay over once a week so that you get a good night's sleep, especially if you're working.

✳ Seek the help of voluntary organizations (see p.187) if you don't have people you can rely on.

✳ Make sure you're getting all your financial benefits and any maintenance payments from the absent parent, if applicable.

✳ If you know other single mothers, "baby swap" with them so that you all get a chance for some time to yourselves.

✳ Don't be embarrassed or too proud to accept gifts – people would probably have given you these even if you weren't single.

Negative reactions

Some people may judge you and your ability to bring up your baby. Dealing with this can have a positive effect – many single parents become determined to prove that they can raise a happy and contented child. Criticism can also put pressure on you, making you feel that you can't ask for help, but you can, so try to remember this.

Being a single parent and being without a good support network can be physically and emotionally exhausting, but the knowledge that you've done it alone can be hugely rewarding for you and good for your baby.

Single parent by choice?

If you've chosen to be a single mother, you may be more prepared emotionally, practically, and financially for looking after a young baby and look forward to the prospect. If you've split with your partner during the pregnancy or soon after the birth, you may have more difficulties. Coping with the emotional problems of separating from someone while looking after a young baby is bound to have an impact on your ability to cope. In this situation, it's more important for you to ask for and to accept help from family and friends.

Lone parenting can be positive

Being a single parent is by no means all doom and gloom. You and your baby can benefit in many ways from the special relationship you'll form:

✳ Single parents tend to develop a very strong bond with their babies; they don't have to share their love between a partner and a child.

✳ Extended family – grandparents, aunts, and uncles – often get more involved when there's only one parent. The baby can greatly benefit from this network of support and love.

✳ Looking after a baby alone is a great achievement. You'll strengthen as a person as you watch your baby develop.

✳ If you're single because your relationship has broken down, you've made the right decision; it's better for the baby to live with one fairly contented person than two people who are at war.

Balancing your relationship with your baby

I believe in showing boundless affection to babies, but you do need to balance your relationship with your baby – some lone parents may invest all their emotions and energies in their baby and use him as an emotional crutch. You don't have to be a mother and father; being a responsive parent is good enough. Your baby has no notion of lacking a second parent; he's happy with you, so you don't need to over-compensate.

You and your baby will have a very close and important one-to-one relationship and no one can take that away from you, but babies need and thrive on exposure to others and should be encouraged to interact with a wide range of people. Introduce him to other adults, and children, so he gets used to being without you now and then. This will make it much easier for you and him if you have to introduce a childminder. As your baby develops new skills (see p.146), don't be afraid to share your joy with your relatives and friends – if they're close to your baby, they'll love to hear about it. Keep your own record of when each milestone occurs; when there is only one of you it will be more difficult to remember them.

Having a social life

All single parents are bound to experience feelings of loneliness and yearn for adult company. It's important for you to have a social life away from your baby and, of course, if you want to build future relationships you have to get out and meet people:

* If it's difficult for you to go out for financial or childcare reasons, invite people to your house for a meal – ask your guests to bring a course.
* Get to know other mothers – they'll probably be glad of the company.
* Ask people if they will babysit – you don't know unless you ask.
* Find hobbies, classes, and events that have crèche facilities.
* Find out about local activities so that you can meet other parents.

The absent parent

Try to keep in touch with your ex-partner and agree on access arrangements and on how you want to raise your child. Ensure that he or she is clear about financial support required. Seek legal advice if necessary. Try to spend time together as a family occasionally, and, if appropriate, encourage the other grandparents to see your baby.

JUST FOR DAD

The single father

There are very few men who are the sole carers of a young baby, but for those who are, the pleasures and most of the problems will be the same as those of a single mother. Remember that fathers can do everything mothers can do except breastfeed.

The benefits

Although being a single father isn't ideal, a single father may benefit in ways that wouldn't have happened had he been sharing the care with his partner. Research has shown that single fathers are more satisfied parents, feel closer to their child, and are more confident and effective than the average father.

The problems

Isolation may be the main problem experienced by the single father. Like a father who stays at home while his partner works (see p.176), a single father may find the female-dominated environments that he is faced with difficult and, sadly, there may be those who question his ability to bring up his baby properly.

Potential difficulties

Problem	How to deal with it
Financial	With only one income, you're more likely to struggle financially and be unable to provide your baby with as many toys and clothes as you would like. Make sure you're getting all the benefits to which you're entitled, especially from your ex-partner. Remember that material possessions are not the most important things you can give to your baby.
Tiredness	If you're looking after your baby alone, the physical and emotional strains will be more of a problem. Catnap whenever your baby does. Try to take proper breaks and ask for and accept offers of help.
Concerns about the baby	If your baby becomes ill, you're unlikely to have someone there to reassure you and keep things in perspective. Look at pp.120–23 and consult your doctor as early as possible to minimize your worries.
Childcare	Affording childcare (see p.172) can be a struggle. You may find that local council-run nurseries make special provision for single parents. Look into sharing a nanny with another parent. If there is a crèche at work, or one could be set up, this can minimize having to transport the baby around.

The instant family

Questions and concerns

Adopting a baby is a big decision. You're bound to have doubts and fears about this new responsibility.

What if I can't cope?

All new parents have days when they can't cope (see p.130). As an adoptive parent, you may have the added pressure of feeling that you're responsible for someone else's child and may have had less time to prepare. Don't be afraid to ask for help; use the adoption services as they're there to help.

What kind of child will I raise?

No one can predict the kind of person any child will turn out to be. Each individual is unique, so even biological parents have no idea whether their children will resemble them physically or in terms of personality.

Will I be a good enough parent?

Your motives for wanting to adopt and your suitability will be analyzed before you're accepted as adoptive parents. It's natural to question whether you'll be good parents, but I think the most important aspects of being parents have nothing to do with whether you are the birth parents. These are:

✱ Your feelings and actions towards your child.

✱ Your sensitivity to your child's individual needs.

✱ Being consistently loving and accepting.

✱ Being fair and firm in setting limits for your child.

An "instant family" may be created through adopting a baby or by joining a ready-made family. A new baby brought into either situation can raise important issues that aren't present for most new parents.

Adopting a young baby

If you're fortunate enough to adopt your baby when she's very young, then everything said about bonding in earlier chapters applies to you. Babies come equipped with a strong urge to bond with their parents, or to anyone who gives them loving care, so you'll be off to the same promising start as everyone else. What may be difficult is that you won't have had the nine-month buildup to the birth and the internal bonding in the same way as a pregnant mother. On the other hand, as an adoptive parent you may have a stronger yearning for a baby than a natural parent. This makes you ideally placed to be a generous and loving parent, so be confident.

Adopting an older baby

If you adopt a baby when she is a few months old, it's really important that you find out as much as possible about the circumstances of her life up to the time when she came to you. This will help you to compensate for any experiences on which she has missed out and for any delay in the developmental stages you would normally expect her to have passed through. Don't, however, worry about her development too much; your baby may not have been affected at all by not being with her natural parents. Even if it has affected her, in the right loving environment your baby will soon be able to catch up.

▼ **BABIES NEED LOVE** Birth children, stepchildren, or adopted – all children need their parents' wholehearted love and support.

Bonding with an older baby

Trust is the basis of all good relationships between babies and their parents. If you have adopted an older baby, you may have to work harder to establish this trust than parents who have had their babies with them from birth. An older baby is likely to have been placed with foster parents for the first few months of her life and will have formed a strong attachment to them. Your baby may not immediately react as you had hoped; she has to learn how to respond to and accept your love and affection, and this takes time. Be reassured, however, that if you are relentless in offering your baby love, comfort, and affection, she will eventually learn to trust you and to accept and reciprocate your feelings.

A new baby in the stepfamily

If partners with a stepfamily decide to have a baby of their own, the dynamics of the family will change. While the baby may act as a uniting force within the family, her arrival may equally provoke some of the anxieties and tensions that were present at the formation of the family.

How stepchildren are affected

Your stepchildren's reaction to your baby will depend on how old they are, their relationship with you, and their past experiences. If their parents have split up recently, it may be more difficult; they're again being asked to adjust because of the actions of their parents.

Insecurities The news of the baby may remind the children of a previous breakup, and feelings such as rejection and fear of losing a parent may resurface. They may worry about the baby being seen as more precious and more desirable because she is a product of the present (your preferred) relationship, rather than of the past (your rejected) union.

Realisation Many children from broken marriages live in hope that their parents will reunite. A new baby is a clear sign of commitment between their parent and stepparent, which often brings the truth home.

Relationship with stepparent If you and your stepchild have already established a good relationship, the arrival of your baby will cause fewer problems. If there are underlying tensions, the new baby may be the catalyst for resentment and anger.

Second time around A man who has a child later in life may change his priorities and be a more devoted father. Older children may resent not getting this attention when they were growing up. It's also common for children to find it distasteful for a parent to start a new family.

How you can help

Once the baby is born, your stepchild may become more accepting. To minimize problems, talk to him as early as possible. Ask him to tell you his concerns and reassure him that you still love him and that there's space and time for everyone to enjoy the baby. Encourage him to develop his own relationship with your baby. He may enjoy some responsibility, but don't abuse this – older stepchildren may resent being used as babysitters.

Deciding to have a baby

A couple may decide to bring a new baby into the stepfamily for a variety of reasons. One partner may be childless and want a baby of his or her own. The other partner, who is already a parent, may feel less of a need. Even if they both have children, they may feel that a baby will make them and also the whole family closer.

Planning ahead

✳ There may be financial obligations to an ex-partner and children from a previous relationship that can make affording another baby more difficult. Also, be aware that stepchildren living with you may resent having to sacrifice new clothes or going out because of the baby.

✳ Do you have room for the baby? If it means that stepchildren will have to move out of, or share, a bedroom. Discuss this as a family rather than just telling the children it will happen. If you have to move house, will it make it more difficult for visiting stepchildren to stay?

Telling an ex-partner

It's always better for your ex-partner to hear that you're having a baby from you rather than from someone else, and he or she definitely shouldn't be told by the children. Some people are shocked at their feelings when they hear the news and worry that their own children will lose out. However, if you have a good relationship with your ex-partner and he or she reacts positively to you having a baby, this could also have an effect on how your children handle the news.

Your baby's development

Your baby is developing from day one and it's one of the most fulfilling aspects of parenthood to watch him grow and learn. You'll become fascinated by his skills and amused by how he tries to copy you. In his first year, he'll change from a tiny helpless newborn into a sturdy and sociable toddler who very much has a mind of his own. Your role as parents is crucial in your baby's development: you are his first teacher and friend, and by being aware of the stages of development you can encourage certain skills at certain times. It's important, however, to remember that your baby's physical and mental development is individual to him, so never push him beyond his capabilities. Your baby mainly learns through play: he'll love it if you're his playmate and, although you should show him how things work, it's essential to his sense of self and independence that he finds out how to do things for himself. He also learns by watching others, so encourage his social skills; getting to know other people is crucial to his development.

How babies develop

New skills

You'll see clear signs when your baby is close to acquiring a skill – a "milestone". Watch for the signs and only then match your efforts to her development and give her games to help. With correct timing, she'll acquire skills at 100 per cent of her potential. If you try her too early or leave it too late, she'll acquire the skill, but not at her full capability. Main milestones are:

* Smiling at a distance (six weeks).

* Discovering her hands and feet (three to four months).

* Blowing bubbles – the first sign of real speech (five months).

* The ability to transfer an object from one hand to the other (six months).

* Knowing her name (six months).

* Sitting unsupported (seven months).

* "Getting" a simple joke like peep-bo (eight months).

* Wanting to feed herself (nine months).

* Crawling (nine months).

* Pointing to an object with her forefinger (10 months).

* Picking up objects with her finger and thumb (10 months).

* Swivelling around while sitting to reach a toy (10 months).

* Putting things into containers and taking them out (11 months).

* Saying her first word with meaning (11–12 months).

* Walking unsupported (12–13 months).

One of the most fulfilling aspects of parenthood is watching and sharing in your baby's development. Encourage her to learn new skills, while allowing her to develop at her own pace.

Newborn babies

Your baby starts to develop from the very second she's born and she'll be longing to learn. She enters the world in a state of "quiet alertness" and this state of intense focus on her surroundings lasts up to an hour. She's a sponge ready to soak up information about her new environment:

* She recognizes your voice – and your partner's – immediately. She's heard these voices for months and switches on to them instantly.

* Your baby's born with her sight at a fixed focus of 20–25cm (8–10in); if you hold her at this distance from your face, she can see you and she'll smile.

* She has an acute sense of smell and will be able to inhale and register the natural scent (pheromones) from your body.

* She'll "mouth" in response to you if she can see your face and your lips moving (at a distance of 20–25cm/8–10in); she's attempting conversation.

Stimulating your baby

Both of you are your baby's first teachers and playmates. You must feed her with all kinds of stimulation, through play and through the way in which you interact with her, if you want to help her develop to her optimal

▲ **BEING A PLAYMATE** Spend time with your child; read books together and play with her – you are her best playmate. She'll enjoy you joining in with her conversations and games.

potential. Your job is to teach her to be imaginative, adventurous, curious, helpful, and generous. There is no limit to the amount of praise and encouragement you should give her as she begins to discover her world.

Rules of development

Your baby develops to her own timetable and it's pointless trying to set a different one. Remember the following:

❋ No two children develop at the same rate so don't compare your baby to other babies – even if they did walk or talk before her.

❋ Development is continuous, although certain skills will be acquired in a spurt while other skills slow down. For example, when a child is mastering walking, she may turn into a sloppy feeder.

❋ Development of the whole body depends on how mature the brain is and whether or not brain, nerve, and muscle connections have grown. Your baby can't learn a skill like walking or talking until all the connections are in place. Bladder control is not possible until 18 months (see p.181). If you expect her to use the potty any earlier, this is likely to lead to failure and could slow down your baby's progress later.

❋ Development proceeds from head to toe (see p.150) so a baby can't sit until she can control her head and she can't stand until she can sit.

❋ Skills gradually become finer; for example, at about five months she "grasps" with her open hand; at eight months she can pick things up with her fingers, and, when all the nerves and muscles have connected, she can pick up an object with her index finger and thumb.

❋ Over-stimulation is as bad as under-stimulation; if there is a constant barrage of noise, your baby may become very confused and gain very little.

Positive discipline

Teaching your baby right from wrong starts at the very beginning, but it's the way you teach her that will affect her physical and emotional wellbeing:

✱ Praise and reward her good behaviour and ignore bad behaviour, especially if it occurs at mealtimes.

✱ Discipline her through love, praise, as well as encouragement. Never use anger and smacking – this can have a damaging effect.

✱ Set useful tasks to help her understand the discipline of a daily routine – for example, encourage her to feed herself and brush her hair.

✱ Hold your finger up and say "no" firmly if she's likely to harm herself, others, or cause damage. She'll begin to understand this from around the age of four months.

Helping your baby to develop happily

What to do	How it helps your baby
Set realistic goals	Set appropriate goals for your baby; for example, don't expect her to be able to play properly with toys designed for older babies. If you do this, it will outstrip her skills and she will become unhappy, frustrated, and demoralized. Always concentrate on accomplishments, not deficiencies, and praise your baby with theatrical gestures.
Be a playmate	You are your baby's first playmate as well as her teacher. Make time to play with her whenever you can – even if it means the washing up has to wait another hour! Babies have to be shown how to do things, so get down there and join in – your baby will love it. But don't interrupt when she's engrossed in something; it's hard enough for her to concentrate and see a job through to completion, without being distracted.
Encourage speech	Encourage your baby to talk – even when she's only gurgling. Keep her eyes 20–25cm (8–10in) from yours when she makes noises, especially when feeding and talking to her. That's her first experience of feeling valued, and a valued baby will grow up to be a child who talks to you about everything – good and bad.
Repeat everything	Repeat and repeat words and actions until you're sick of it. You must tell your baby the same thing over and over again – using the same even tone of voice – and show her how to do things. It will all be worthwhile once she understands and begins to copy.

Boys and girls

Newborn babies

The differences in behaviour and development of boys and girls begin at birth and continue as they grow and develop (see p.182). In newborn babies, the differences are mainly in the way they use their senses to perceive things and in the kinds of things in which they show an interest.

Hearing

Boys' hearing is less acute than in girls, which means they have more difficulty in locating the source of sounds. Girls are more easily calmed by soothing words because of their acute hearing. Whisper close to your baby boy's ear to stimulate his hearing and to help calm him.

Speech

A baby girl uses her voice to get attention earlier and more often than a boy. If a newborn boy hears another baby cry, he'll join in but will stop crying quite quickly, whereas a girl will cry for longer.

Sight

A newborn girl responds enthusiastically to visual things. A boy quickly loses interest in a design or picture and requires much more visual stimulation up to the age of about seven months.

Social skills

Boys are as interested in things as they are in people, while girls show a clear preference for the human face. This female trait continues into later life as an ability to intuitively read facial expression. Encourage your son to develop his social skills by holding him 20–25cm (8–10in) from your face so he can see you clearly.

It's a biological fact that there are differences in behaviour and development between boys and girls from birth. Don't enforce stereotypes, but you can help your baby to develop skills that don't come as naturally, such as language for a boy and spatial skills for a girl.

Differences in brain development

Gender differences stem from the way the brain develops in male and female embryos. For a baby to learn and develop, certain connections have to have taken place between the right and left halves of the brain. Girls grow these connections earlier than boys (many are already in place when girls are born), which enables them to adapt faster to their new environment after birth. Connections form in a boy's brain more slowly and because of this later development, a baby boy will need slightly more help from you to reach his milestones (see p.146).

Avoiding stereotypes

Stereotypes influence children and, worse, they tend to make people label certain qualities as inferior and superior – the latter usually being attributed to males. When children are taught to think, feel, and act in line with a stereotyped model, it can stunt their personal growth. Individuality should be encouraged, regardless of gender.

▲ **SPATIAL SKILLS** Help your daughter to develop her spatial skills by encouraging her to play with practical toys, such as a baby work bench, or beakers or blocks to stack.

▲ **BEING A ROLE MODEL** You can positively influence your son's gentle caring side by actively joining in with pastimes traditionally associated with females.

Gender differences up to age six

What develops	Girls	Boys
Natural ability	Girls are better at language skills like talking, reading, and writing and they tend to keep this ability.	Boys are slower to develop language skills, but from a very early age they show superior spatial skills.
Social skills	Girls are more sociable than boys – they're more interested in people and feelings and display this regard for others even in their first year.	Boys are generally more interested in objects than people and feelings. Unlike girls, they tend to look after themselves rather than play in groups.
Behaviour and personality	Girls cope better with stress and are more conciliatory. They tend to have fewer behavioural problems than boys.	Boys tend to be more aggressive, competitive, and rebellious than girls. They're more likely to develop behavioural problems.
Physical growth	Girls walk earlier than boys. They grow faster and more steadily – they don't tend to have growth spurts. They gain bladder and bowel control earlier.	Boys shoot ahead physically after five years. They develop faster during growth spurts, when many skills tend to emerge over a short time.

Discouraging sexual stereotypes

Stereotypes of male and female roles will inevitably influence our children as they grow up if we're not sensitive to them and don't take appropriate preventative action. Research has shown that we even speak in a different tone of voice to boys and girls, and all too early, our children can become affected by stereotyped concepts of appearance, including body build, facial features, and clothes. There are also stereotyped concepts of behaviour and role-playing. As parents, we all have to be vigilant if we want our children to escape stereotyping. Stereotypes are dangerous; once accepted, they are used as yardsticks against which our children are judged – good and bad, successful and unsuccessful, appropriate and inappropriate. Far better is to encourage individuality and originality.

Worse, stereotypes can be used as guidelines for training children. You need to act carefully from day one if you are to encourage a girl to be adventurous and strong, and a boy to be caring, able to show affection, and act as a peacemaker. Encourage more physical activities associated with boys for your daughter and don't always play over-boisterous games with your son. Traditional stereotypes have little to recommend them, whereas egalitarian gender roles offer massive scope for self-realization. Regardless of gender, each child needs to be able to reach his or her own potential.

JUST FOR DAD

Think about your attitudes and the type of activities you're encouraging, as all of these influence how your child develops and comes to see him- or herself.

Influencing your daughter

As a father, you may consciously or unconsciously reinforce your daughter's femininity. Fathers often involve boys in "rough-and-tumble" games, whereas they'll be more gentle with girls. Expose your daughter to all kinds of activities and let her choose – rather than limiting her to traditionally feminine pastimes like ballet and drama, introduce other activities like football too. Don't fall into the trap of believing some behaviour is acceptable in boys and not in girls – you diminish your daughter if you do this. Try to be aware that your daughter is very likely to feel devalued if she sees you devaluing her mother.

Influencing your son

Research shows that boys learn how to behave from their fathers. You can encourage your son to develop the more attractive male qualities (such as gentleness and a sense of responsibility) rather than the less desirable ones (such as being aggressive, dominant, and confrontational) simply by the way in which you behave. Your son will watch your actions and will imitate you in every respect. The quality of fathering that he receives from you is the most critical factor in how he views himself as a male.

How your baby grows

Concerns about weight gain

A baby's growth is an important indicator of health and wellbeing, but don't become blinkered about weight gain – it isn't the only issue. Any real discrepancies between length and weight should be picked up at your baby's developmental checks (see p.155), but, if you're concerned, talk to your doctor about it.

What if my baby isn't gaining weight?

Some babies remain the same weight for a while and then have a growth spurt. So don't worry if your baby doesn't gain weight over, say, one week or appears to have lost weight. Don't be tempted into switching to bottle-feeding (or add to his bottle) in the hope of improving "slow" weight gain. In fact, if you breastfeed your baby he's likely to grow faster, especially in the first few weeks.

What if my baby is overweight?

Some babies are naturally fatter than others, which may lead to some physical development happening slightly later. If you're concerned that your baby weighs too much for his age, seek medical advice, but don't reduce his intake of food as this could affect growth and development. The aim should be to maintain his weight at the current level until his length catches up. Research does, however, show that the pattern of heart disease and adult obesity can be set very early by being overweight from overfeeding. Never press your baby to finish off the last drops of a feed if he doesn't want it, or add extra formula to his bottle either.

Your baby's physical development will be monitored closely at the developmental checks (see p.155): growth (centile) charts, which show the rate of growth expected for your baby's weight and gestational age at birth, will be used to map his progress. In the first year, your baby will grow faster than at any other time in his life. His physical development starts at the top, which is why his head looks large, and from the inner parts to the extremities, which is why his hands and feet look tiny. Remember, your baby's development is individual to him; don't worry if he appears to be growing faster or slower than other babies. All babies grow at their own rate.

Weight

When a baby is born, the question "How heavy was he?" comes only second in the West to "Is it a boy or a girl?". Although people will place importance on your baby's weight, it is not the only sign of growth and it is important not to use this as the only way to judge his wellbeing (see left). Your baby's weight will be monitored at the developmental checks (see p.155); you can also have him weighed at your local baby clinic or doctor's surgery. Babies are normally weighed naked. One feature all babies have in common is chubby arms and legs; this is due to uneven fat distribution which remains uneven until he begins to use his limbs and becomes active. He may not lose it until he starts crawling, and possibly not until he's walking.

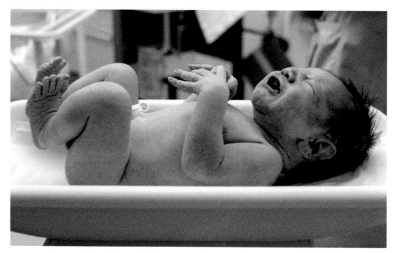

▲ **YOUR NEWBORN** At first, a newborn baby is floppy and has poor head control. As his bones and muscles develop over the next few weeks, your baby will learn to control his head. Amazingly, this is the first step towards his being able to walk.

AT SEVEN MONTHS Once your baby learns to control her head, she will learn to sit. At first she'll need to be propped up with cushions but soon she'll sit unsupported.

12 MONTHS At around one year your baby should be able to stand unsupported and perhaps be ready to take his first steps.

The normal pattern of weight gain

✳ In the first few days it's normal for baby to lose up to ten per cent of her birth weight. By the tenth day, she'll have regained her birth weight.

✳ In the following six months she'll gain weight rapidly, at a rate of about 1kg (2lb) each month.

✳ In the second six months weight gain slows down and she'll put on around 500g (1lb) each month.

Length (height)

Your baby's size is partly due to inheritance – if you're both tall, the chances are you'll have a long baby. The biggest increase in length occurs in the first six months, after which growth slows down. If your child appears well and healthy, there's no reason for you to worry about her growth rate; any pronounced disproportion between length and weight will be investigated at the developmental checks (see p.155).

An approximate guide to a baby's growth rate

✳ A newborn full-term baby is on average 50cm (20in) long.

✳ Her length will increase by 25–30cm (10–12in) in the first year.

✳ On average, boys tend to be taller than girls for the first two years.

Head size

A newborn baby is top-heavy, with a disproportionately large head – this gradually alters over the first four years. Head circumference is monitored at the developmental checks; if the proportions don't even out, it could alert doctors to certain, rare, medical conditions.

✳ A newborn baby's head circumference is about 35cm (14in), which is disproportionately larger than the rest of her body. By the time she is 12 months old, the size of her chest and head should have evened out.

✳ When a baby is born, her head makes up one-quarter of the length of her body, compared to an adult's head, which makes up around one-eighth.

How the senses develop

During the first year, your baby will begin to discover her world through her senses.

Vision

Your newborn has limited, but excellent, vision. At a distance of 20–25cm (8–10in) she sees clearly, so keep your face at this distance from hers when talking or smiling and she'll respond. At six weeks her eyes focus at any distance and both eyes work together. By three months she has full perception of colours; at six months she can see more detail; by one year her vision is well developed.

Hearing

She recognizes your voice and your partner's from birth, and will turn her head when you speak, so talk to her from the very first day.

Touch

Babies begin by "feeling" the shape and texture of objects. Initally they do this with their lips and tongue and then they explore with their hands.

Taste and smell

Newborn babies have a complete set of tastebuds and can recognize their parents' smell. They like only sweet tastes and smells, which is why they love breastmilk, but they gradually accept different tastes and make their likes and dislikes known.

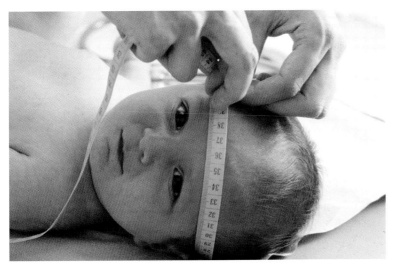

◄ **HEAD CIRCUMFERENCE** Your baby's head circumference will be measured at birth and again at her main health checks. The growth of her head reflects the growth of her brain.

✳ Nerve and muscle development

What develops	How it develops	What it means for your baby
Nerve connections that control limb muscles	Nerves extend from the brain and spine to reach the different muscle groups in the limbs. In a newborn, connections, or pathways, within the the brain that control nerves have not been formed, so a baby's movements are uncontrolled and crude. As the connections are forged, movements become finer and more precise.	Your baby progresses from picking things up with his fist at four months, to being able to pick up objects with his finger and thumb by ten months. As the nerve pathways develop, your baby will achieve head control and then he will sit, crawl, and then stand, before finally he starts walking.
Nerve connections that control bladder muscles	It takes at least 18 months to complete the nerve pathways that affect the bladder. Prior to that your baby can't have any control over how his bladder works – so don't expect it.	Once nerve connections are in place, your baby has to "train" his bladder muscles to hold urine and then let go. This takes several months and can't be hurried.

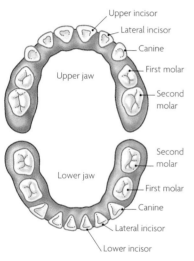

Upper incisor
Lateral incisor
Canine
First molar
Upper jaw
Second molar
Second molar
Lower jaw
First molar
Canine
Lateral incisor
Lower incisor

▲ THE ORDER IN WHICH TEETH APPEAR
The age when teeth are cut varies, but they always come through in the same order: incisors, first molars, canines, and finally second molars.

How your baby's teeth develop

Your baby's first tooth is an exciting milestone. Teeth usually start to come through from six months, but the age varies from baby to baby (a few babies are born with a tooth already through, while others are still toothless on their first birthday). During teething, your baby may be more irritable and more wakeful than usual (see p.109).

How teeth come through

✳ The first tooth to appear is usually a lower incisor, followed straight away by its neighbour.
✳ The next teeth to come are the upper incisors, followed first by the upper lateral incisors, then by the lower lateral incisors. There may be a delay before the first molar appears.
✳ Next come the canines, and finally the second molars appear.

▶ CLEANING HIS TEETH Once your baby has his first tooth, start helping him to clean his teeth. Give him a toothbrush of his own and encourage him to copy you. Get into a routine of brushing his teeth morning and evening, and after mealtimes.

Preventing tooth problems

You can help prevent your baby developing any teething problems. Give him firm-textured foods such as a carrot or a rusk to chew while he is teething. Make sure he has his own small, soft toothbrush and get into the routine of brushing his teeth in the morning, at bedtime, and after meals. Don't give him drinks and snacks that contain added sugar. Give him water to drink instead of juice; try to keep juices to mealtimes. Dilute his fruit juice and never add sugar, and give him juice in a beaker rather than bottle.

Developmental checks

You'll be asked to take your baby for a developmental check periodically, for example at six to eight weeks, and perhaps once again later in your baby's first year. As well as discussing any issues with you, the health worker will weigh your baby, measure his length and head circumference, and then a doctor will check the baby's general health and carry out specific medical checks, see right.

What is the purpose of the checks?

Many health professionals feel that "testing" babies at certain stages to see whether they are "up to the mark", is crude; now they are much more interested in the wellbeing of the whole child. When you're invited to go to a clinic, or perhaps meet a health worker at your home, you'll be asked a series of questions to establish how you're all getting on together, how you are managing, and whether you've noticed any specific problems with your baby. You should think of it as an opportunity to discuss any aspects of your baby's life (not just his development), or of your life with him that seem relevant: baby checks aren't, or at least they're not supposed to be, just about ticks in boxes.

Prepare yourself before you go

Make a list of questions and concerns you'd like to discuss. For example, you may have problems feeding or difficulty coping with sleepless nights. Don't be afraid to highlight problems – being a new parent is not easy for anyone and you should take the opportunity to get expert advice.

What if my baby has a problem?

It's worrying to have doubts cast over your baby's development (see p.124). If you have any concerns or a problem is found:

✳ Ask for time to sit down and talk through exactly what is wrong with your baby. Ask as many questions as necessary, especially if it isn't clear what the doctor is saying. Don't allow yourself to be fobbed off by being told the health worker or doctor hasn't got time at the moment or that you are worrying for no reason.

✳ Don't accept that you should "wait and see" – if there's any question of a problem, your baby should be referred for tests or to see a specialist straight away.

✳ Get a second opinion if you're not satisfied or are still concerned.

Your baby's medical checks

Six- to eight-week check

Heart and lungs The breathing and heart sounds are checked, particularly to rule out a heart murmur.

Palate The palate is checked at birth, and now, for completeness and to test the sucking reflex.

Vision Your baby will be tested to see if he can follow movement and look towards light.

Hearing Your baby will have had his hearing tested before this checkup as part of the newborn hearing-creening programme.

Mobility Your baby's hips are checked for displacement and any correction needed. Head control is checked.

Testes If you have a baby boy, the doctor will check to ensure that his testes have descended.

Later in first year

Speech Your baby should be making a range of sounds by now and his ability to do this will be noted.

Vision Any problem should have become apparent, but your doctor may check for a squint, especially if there is a family history of squints.

Handling The doctor will give your baby a toy to hold so that he can check his handling skills.

Mobility The doctor will check that your baby can sit up and is able to stand supported.

Testes A baby boy's testes may be checked again. If they still haven't descended, an operation may be needed later.

Baby development
0–1 month

✳ What to look out for

What develops	How she progresses	How you can help
Her mind	✳ She can see clearly at a distance of 20–25cm (8–10in). ✳ She will respond to your voice by moving her eyes and turning her head. ✳ She will gaze at you and recognize you. ✳ She will become quiet when you speak soothingly and distressed when you are loud.	✳ When talking to her, hold your face 20–25cm (8–10in) away from hers. ✳ When you speak, let her see your mouth moving. Smile and make eye contact at 20–25cm (8–10in) from her face. ✳ Use your voice: speak in a sing-song voice, sing lullabies, and laugh a lot.
Her mobility	✳ She will turn her head: this control is the first step towards learning to walk. ✳ By the end of the first month, the most she may be able to do is lift her head 1in (2.5cm) off the surface when lying on her tummy.	✳ Do gentle exercises to make her aware of her body (see p.61). ✳ Her neck and back muscles are too weak to lift her head so give her something to look at when she is lying on her back.
Her handling skills	✳ Your baby is born with "the grasp reflex", which means she will keep her fists tightly closed and grasp anything put into her fingers (see above). ✳ If she's startled, she'll spread her arms, fingers, and legs to protect herself.	✳ Your baby can't purposely hold on to anything until she loses the grasp reflex. ✳ Gently open her fingers one at a time. ✳ If she grasps your fingers, she'll take her weight if you pull her up a little way.
Her social skills	✳ Your baby is born ready to love other people and asks for love. She longs for company and takes immediate delight in you. ✳ She'll respond instantly to your voice and your smell. She is upset by a harsh-sounding voice.	✳ Let her have contact with other people from when she's very young. ✳ Be physical: make skin-to-skin contact with your baby; use your body to express love; rock, sway, and dance with her.
Her speech	✳ She "mouths" if you speak to her at a distance of 20–25cm (8–10in) because she's trying to imitate your gestures and expressions. ✳ She's born longing to communicate and makes little burbling noises to show contentment.	✳ Talk to your baby all the time so she gets used to your voice. ✳ Make facial expressions to match what you're saying.

Stimulating play

✳ Stimulate her senses with songs and by talking to her. Hold her where she can see you, ideally at 20–25cm (8–10in).

✳ Move your fingers or a colourful toy through her line of vision so that her eyes and head follow your movements and put a mobile over her cot.

✳ Do gentle knee bends and straighten her legs when you're changing her nappy; this will encourage your baby to straighten out her body.

✳ Place a small mirror or a clear, cartoon-style drawing of a face in her cot where she can see it when she is lying down.

Baby development
1–2 months

✳ What to look out for

What develops	How he progresses	How you can help
His mind	✳ Your baby begins to smile at you from a distance and bobs his head when you talk to him (see above). ✳ He starts to be interested in his surroundings, looking in the direction of sounds and staring at objects as though "grasping" with his eyes.	✳ Prop him up slightly with cushions or put him in a baby chair. Place lots of brightly coloured toys within his view. ✳ Put a mobile over the cot – it's good if it makes a sound or has a musical box.
His mobility	✳ He can raise his head to 45 degrees when he's lying on his tummy. ✳ By the end of this month he can support the weight of his head if you hold him upright with your hands around his chest.	✳ Hold a coloured toy close to his head so that he has to lift his head to see it. ✳ To teach your baby about balance, hold him upright on your knee so his legs take his own weight for a second.
His handling skills	✳ Your baby will no longer have a grasp reflex. ✳ His fingers are open most of the time and he's starting to become aware of them.	✳ Touch, tickle, and massage his hands. ✳ Give him toys and encourage him to bend his fingers over them.
His social skills	✳ He's starting to notice people, but knows you from all others. ✳ He smiles from a distance at six weeks and moves his whole body with excitement when he sees you.	✳ Make sure you give your baby frequent skin-to-skin contact and maintain eye contact when you're talking to him and, more importantly, when feeding.
His speech	✳ He will begin by answering you with small throaty sounds and by the end of two months he'll make grunts, cries, and move his whole body in his desire to communicate with you. ✳ He knows your voice – and your partner's – and turns his head and neck when he hears you.	✳ The more your baby is stimulated to talk by being talked to and encouraged to respond, the earlier he'll learn to talk and the better his quality of speech. ✳ Talk non-stop, be theatrical with your conversations, and ask questions.

Stimulating play
✳ Sing and make eye contact (see right). Sway while you hold him.
✳ Show him his hands and demonstrate how to wiggle his fingers. Play "This little piggy".
✳ Gently rub a soft brush over his hands and fingers, especially at the tips.
✳ Sit him up supported at an angle of 45 degrees – this helps to increase his concentration span. Use cushions or a bouncing baby chair on the floor. Let him touch toys or objects of different textures and shapes. Dangle, kick, or bat small soft toys within striking distance of his hands.
✳ Every day have a special walk, talk, and sing time with your baby. Carry him in a sling (see p.77).

Baby development
2–3 months

❋ What to look out for

What develops	How she progresses	How you can help
Her mind	❋ She's becoming familiar with her own body, staring at her fingers and then moving them. This is her first lesson in cause and effect. ❋ She has a repertoire of responses to you: she smiles, mouths when you speak to her, nods, squeaks, yelps, and blows raspberries.	❋ Show your baby her fingers so that she can study them. ❋ Answer her with responses that are theatrical and larger than life. ❋ Reward her attempts to relate to you with hugs, kisses, and squeals of delight.
Her mobility	❋ She can keep her head up steadily now when in a standing or sitting position or while lying on her front, but not for long (see above). ❋ When she's lying on her tummy, she can hold her head in line with her body.	❋ Encourage her to reach out for soft toys, especially when she's on her tummy. ❋ Teach your baby about balance: hold her in a standing position with your hands around her chest, for a few seconds at a time.
Her handling skills	❋ She begins to discover her hands – she keeps them open and looks at them. ❋ She'll hold a rattle for a few seconds if you place it in her hand.	❋ Encourage her to look at her fingers and to hold a rattle. ❋ Put toys over her cot or give her a baby gym to encourage her to reach out.
Her social skills	❋ She turns her head to your voice and smiles because she is happy to see you. ❋ She expresses her joy in you by waving her arms and kicking her legs.	❋ Keep eye contact with her when feeding – it's heaven for her to have food and your attention at the same time! ❋ Respond positively to her overtures.
Her speech	❋ She will begin to make simple vowel sounds, such as "oh", "ah", and "uh". ❋ She has a repertoire of easily recognized cries to express how she is feeling: hungry, tired, frustrated, lonely, angry, impatient, or just wanting to be left alone.	❋ Imitate all the sounds she makes back to her. ❋ When your baby cries, it's her way of communicating with you – always respond to it (see p.104).

Stimulating play

❋ Introduce her to small toys with different textures and say out loud to your baby how they feel (see left).

❋ Act out nursery rhymes and play pat-a-cake.

❋ Play lots of simple physical games, such as gentle jerks, knee bends, arm pulls, and tickling feet.

❋ Lie on the floor opposite her while she lies on her tummy and looks at you – this will encourage head control.

❋ Encourage her to reach out for soft objects.

❋ Take her into the bath with you and encourage her to kick and splash. Make her aware of her hands by splashing them in the water.

Baby development
3–4 months

✳ What to look out for

What develops	How he progresses	How you can help
His mind	✳ He's curious and wants to join in. ✳ He can recognize places and faces as familiar. ✳ He loves the breast or his bottle and shows it. ✳ He'll laugh by the age of four months.	✳ Offer a wide range of toys. ✳ Explain everything you see and do. ✳ Pin photographs of yourselves in his cot with a safety pin.
His mobility	✳ He loves sitting up now with a little support from you or cushions. ✳ If you gently pull him into a sitting position, he will bring his head up in line with his body. ✳ If he is lying on his tummy, he can look straight at you now.	✳ Sit him up with cushions for support. ✳ Pull him gently up into a sitting position to strengthen his back and neck muscles. ✳ Play games that make your baby swivel from the waist and offer him toys that he is able to reach easily when he turns.
His handling skills	✳ He's starting to control his hands and feet and will start reaching for his toes (see above). ✳ He moves his hands and feet together. ✳ He crosses his feet and puts a foot on the opposite leg.	✳ Put toys in his hands when he reaches for them or he will overshoot. Make him reach for things in every position. ✳ Give him rattles so that he can make noises with his hands.
His social skills	✳ He looks at and smiles at people who talk to him – he hasn't learned shyness yet. ✳ He knows you and your partner and people he sees regularly, such as grandparents. ✳ He loves company and cries when left alone for long. He knows warmth, love, and the opposite.	✳ Encourage his sense of humour. Laugh with him, share the joke, and imitate everything he does. Don't be afraid to over-act all your responses. ✳ Encourage emotional development: laugh when he laughs and cry when he cries.
His speech	✳ He'll squeal with pleasure. ✳ He's learning all the basic tones of voices. ✳ He says "m", "p", and "b" when unhappy and "j" and "k" when happy.	✳ Repeat sounds back at him – "M, m, m you're not happy are you?". Speak in a tone of voice that is appropriate.

Stimulating play

✳ Gently pull your baby up by his arms when he is lying on his back to help his head control (see right).

✳ Play "peep-bo" and hiding-your-face games. When playing "peep-bo" stay slightly to one side so that your baby has to swing his trunk to find you.

✳ Put objects on a string over his cot and pram so that he can examine them – one day he'll reach out and knock one.

✳ Amplify his experiences by talking to him about what you see and do.

✳ Place a rattle in your baby's hand and shake it a few times. He will be intrigued by its texture and by the sound that it makes.

✳ Play tickling games to encourage his laughter.

Baby development
4–5 months

❋ What to look out for

What develops	How she progresses	How you can help
Her mind	❋ Your baby loves games – she learns skills from them by copying what you do. ❋ Her concentration is expanding. She spends a long time examining things. ❋ She smiles at herself in the mirror. ❋ She moves her arms and legs to attract you. ❋ She pats her bottle when feeding.	❋ When she attracts your attention respond to it; this will encourage good behaviour. ❋ Turn your body theatrically towards her. Let her know you're attending to her by focusing on her: move towards her, bend down, and make eye contact. ❋ Call her by her name all the time.
Her mobility	❋ She has now mastered full control of her head. Although it's quite steady, it may wobble if she moves suddenly.	❋ Give her plenty of rocking motion. This will promote head stability and aid her when she begins walking.
Her handling skills	❋ She puts things such as toys, her fist, and her feet into her mouth as it's the most sensitive area (see above). ❋ She grasps large toys with both hands and begins to use the little finger side of her hand to grip things. She sometimes can't let go.	❋ Don't try to stop her putting her hand in her mouth – it's natural. ❋ Play with her toes and guide them to her mouth. ❋ Play give-and-take games with toys.
Her social skills	❋ Your baby is beginning to be shy with strangers (this is the first sign of her emerging "self"), but she still smiles at people she knows.	❋ Introduce her to all visitors so that she gets used to strangers and the concept of friends.
Her speech	❋ Her language is very colourful: she tries to "talk" by blowing, babbling, squealing, laughing, and she says "ka" in an attempt to sound like you. ❋ She uses different facial expressions to communicate with you.	❋ Imitate all her sounds with changes of pitch and volume. If she listens, stimulate her with new sounds and name them.

Stimulating play

❋ Play rocking games while she is sitting on your lap (see left).

❋ Play lots of games with her, especially those that involve clapping.

❋ She loves crumpling paper – give her sheets of old lining paper or lots of tissue paper that crackles.

❋ Hide her face under a towel for a second then whisk it away and say "peep-bo" – she'll squeal with delight.

❋ Look out for your baby holding her hands up and her arms wide – this means that she wants to play.

❋ Encourage her to open her fingers by playing giving and taking away games. Always give her the object when she reaches out.

Baby development
5–6 months

✳ What to look out for

What develops	How he progresses	How you can help
His mind	✳ He gets excited if he hears someone coming. ✳ He expresses his discomfort or insecurity. ✳ He makes lots of attention-seeking sounds and raises his arms to be picked up.	✳ Respond to his call as soon as you hear it. Shout out that you're coming, then go towards him and say his name. Hold out your arms as you approach him. ✳ Keep using his name every time you speak to him.
His mobility	✳ He's now strong enough to take the weight of his upper half on his arms. ✳ He can sit for a few minutes supported on the floor with lots of cushions (see above).	✳ Play bouncing games with your baby. Get a baby bouncer if he likes it. ✳ Lie next to him on the floor and crawl around. It will encourage him to copy.
His handling skills	✳ He now has the ability to transfer objects from one hand to another. ✳ Holding one toy in his hand, he'll drop it to take hold of another. ✳ He'll hold his bottle.	✳ Show him how to let go and drop things and how to pass a toy from hand to hand. ✳ Play give-and-take games – this will also encourage him to share.
His social skills	✳ He starts to make assertive advances: pats your cheek, scratches, and slaps. ✳ He explores your face with his hands – it means "hello", so say "hello" back and smile. ✳ He's possessive of you and may be very wary of people he doesn't know.	✳ Show your baby new gestures, stretch out your arms to him and he'll lift his too. ✳ Make expansive gestures and pitch your voice to match. He will copy you. ✳ Avoid leaving him in a room with strangers.
His speech	✳ He blows bubbles (this is his first real speech). ✳ He now says "ka", "da", and "ma" all the time and a new sound emerges: "ergh". ✳ He seems to understand a bit of what you say.	✳ If he appears to understand you, ask if he does, repeat what you said, and praise him.

Stimulating play

✳ Play weight-bearing games: these encourage him to take more and more weight on his legs, which helps to strengthen them. Hold him on your lap or on the floor, gently bounce him up and down, and you'll feel him push himself off your legs (see right).

✳ Demonstrate cause and effect. Push a ball to him while he's sitting up and say "the ball is rolling".

✳ Blow "raspberries" on his tummy when you're changing his nappy – encourage him to copy the different noises you make.

✳ Reward him for holding out his arms by playing lifting games – squeal with delight as you lift him and swing him around.

Baby development
6–7 months

❋ What to look out for

What develops	How she progresses	How you can help
Her mind	❋ She starts off conversations and you'll understand many of her own sounds. ❋ She knows her name and who she is. ❋ She may want to feed herself. ❋ She anticipates repetition and imitates you.	❋ Encourage her sense of self by showing your baby her reflection in the mirror. When you are looking in the mirror repeat her name over and over "That's Oona, that's you". ❋ Have conversations with her.
Her mobility	❋ She can now bear weight on one hand when she is lying on her tummy (see above). ❋ She can lift her head when lying on her back. ❋ When you hold her up she can take all her own weight on straight legs and hips.	❋ To encourage her to take her weight, play lots of standing games. ❋ Place a toy above her while she's lying on her back and encourage her to lift her head to reach out for it.
Her handling skills	❋ She reaches out for objects using only her fingers now. ❋ She holds on to a toy if she reaches for another. ❋ She bangs the table.	❋ Let her try to feed herself from a dish with her own baby spoon. ❋ Give her plenty of toys that are easy for her to hold.
Her social skills	❋ Your baby loves other babies and stretches out to them in friendship. ❋ She may cry if she's left with anyone other than you or your partner, especially if it's someone whom she doesn't know.	❋ Give her physical affection; she can't be loving to anyone (including herself) if she doesn't have a bank of love to draw on. ❋ Keep introducing her to strangers and give her time to adjust.
Her speech	❋ She now has very clear syllables with actions, "ba", "da", and "ka". ❋ Cries have high and low pitches and a nasal sound has appeared.	❋ Make every sound back to her to make her feel important.

Stimulating play

❋ Play touching games together: use every opportunity to touch your baby and let her touch you. She'll love it if you let her explore your face with her hands (see left).

❋ Encourage her sense of self by playing games with her things and using her name: say "That's Oona's dress," and "Whose teddy is this? It's Oona's".

❋ If she's wary of strangers now, introduce them gradually.

❋ Develop her sense of humour with simple jokes like tickling; play "Round and round the garden, like a teddy bear".

❋ To encourage her to try to pull her tummy off the floor, play at aeroplanes. Lie side by side on your front and lift your arms and body – and your baby's – off the floor.

Baby development
7–8 months

What to look out for

What develops	How he progresses	How you can help
His mind	✳ He's showing signs of determination; he'll keep going after toys he can't quite reach. ✳ He concentrates hard on discovering what he can do with his toys – he's learning all the time about the properties of various objects.	✳ Encourage him to retrieve a toy for which he has to stretch. ✳ Play water games in the bath. ✳ Give him plastic containers to pour, empty, and fill over and over.
His mobility	✳ He'll sit rocking his body backwards and forwards to try to reach a toy. ✳ He loves standing when supported. If you stand him on your lap, he'll jig about. ✳ Lying on his front, he'll try to wriggle forwards.	✳ While he's sitting, sit a little way from him and hold your arms out. He'll try to shuffle along on his bottom to reach you. ✳ Hold him upright as much as possible. ✳ Get him to reach a toy while on his front.
His handling skills	✳ He loves making any noise by banging. ✳ He'll try to copy you if you clap. ✳ He can hold any toy firmly in his fingers. ✳ He'll point to objects – this is the first stage of him learning the finger-thumb grasp (see above).	✳ Give him spoons, pan lids, or a toy drum so that he can use his hands to bang and make a noise. ✳ When he's sitting on the floor or in his cot, make sure that he has lots of toys to reach for, pick up, and explore.
His social skills	✳ He will respond fully to sociable games such as "Pat-a-cake" or "This little piggy". ✳ He doesn't like it when you're angry and will respond accordingly. ✳ He's clear what "no" means and responds to it.	✳ Make him feel valued by using his name in every situation. This will help him to develop a sense of himself. ✳ When you need to say "no", say it firmly and use a different tone of voice.
His speech	✳ He plays games with his mouth and tongue, blowing "raspberries" and smacking his lips. ✳ He may combine two syllables such as "ba-ba" and "da-da", though not with meaning.	✳ Play sound games to convey meaning – "quiet" (whisper) or "loud" (shout).

Stimulating play

✳ Hold a mirror up in front of your baby so she can see herself, and say her name (see right) while she's looking at herself.

✳ Play and sing word games to encourage him to vocalize. Say rhymes over and over again, always with the same emphasis, and move your body; he'll start to copy you and use his.

✳ Play with all kinds of safe household items as toys – for example, plastic or wooden spoons, pans, and brushes. Banging games will be huge fun.

✳ Always answer his needs and cries; this fosters self-confidence and self-esteem in your baby.

✳ Sit with your baby on the floor and encircle your legs around him. Fill the circle with his favourite toys.

Baby development
8–9 months

✳ What to look out for

What develops	How she progresses	How you can help
Her mind	✳ Your baby loves familiar games and rhymes and laughs at the right times. ✳ She can anticipate movements. ✳ She will turn her head to her name and hold out her hands to be reached.	✳ Help her to understand life on a day-to-day basis by explaining all routines. ✳ Use meals and bath times as cues for special activities – "Now it's time for lunch", "Now it's time to have your bath".
Her mobility	✳ She can take her weight on her legs, if supported. ✳ She can sit for ten minutes, lean forwards and sideways, and stay balanced. ✳ She can roll from side to side, but can't get up from a sitting position to stand.	✳ Help her to stand from a sitting position, bend her hips and knees for her. ✳ Help her to cruise round the furniture by putting pieces close together. Encourage her to hold on to a low piece of furniture.
Her handling skills	✳ Her movements are becoming more refined. ✳ Her fingers are used for exploring – she puts things in her mouth much less often. ✳ She has the ability to lean forwards and pick up small things easily (see above).	✳ Show her how to stack bricks on top of one another or side by side – she's learning about volume as well as fine movements. ✳ Give her a soft cooked pea to pick up between her finger and thumb.
Her social skills	✳ She's shy with new faces and may be reluctant to be picked up by people she doesn't know. ✳ She remembers people she has got to know well, even if she hasn't seen them for a few days.	✳ Talk to her on the telephone if you have to be away from home at all. ✳ Get her a toy telephone to play with. ✳ Help her get to know the babysitter.
Her speech	✳ She's understanding more and more of what you say so repeat "Yes, that's what daddy means: it's cold outside, brrrr". ✳ She'll start to add "t", "d", and "w" sounds. ✳ She might make one animal sound if you do.	✳ Repeat words that start with t, d, and w. ✳ Repeat all her sounds back to her. Name everything when you are talking to her. ✳ Read animal stories and make the noises.

Stimulating play

✳ Get lots of noisy toys (wooden spoons, metal pots and pans, or a toy drum). It helps her to understand how to exert some control over things and herself and develops her understanding of cause and effect (see left).

✳ Read a book or magazine. She'll love a commentary from you.

✳ Name parts of your body and ask her to copy.

✳ Crawl alongside your baby and imitate her movements to encourage her to do the same.

✳ Show her how you can put one brick on top of another. It takes great skill and she won't achieve it by herself for at least another month or so, but she'll enjoy knocking the bricks over and scattering them about!

Baby development
9–10 months

✳ What to look out for

What develops	How he progresses	How you can help
His mind	✳ Your baby is getting used to rituals; they order his life and make him feel secure. ✳ He'll wave bye bye. ✳ He'll put his foot out for a sock – he's longing to be helpful! ✳ He knows teddy and dolly. ✳ He'll look around corners for a toy.	✳ Try to keep to some sort of routine so that your baby can get used to it. ✳ Show him how to dress and undress, so that he can begin to understand the concept of a daily routine. ✳ He should have toys such as teddies or dolls that are "like baby".
His mobility	✳ He's discovered mobility. ✳ He moves forward on his hands and knees and loves changing positions (see above). ✳ He can twist his trunk around quite confidently.	✳ Hold out your arms, call his name, and encourage him to crawl to you. ✳ Offer your fingers for him to pull himself up on, then lift his foot on and off the floor.
His handling skills	✳ He reaches for objects with his index finger and will master picking up something small, such as a raisin, with his thumb and index finger. ✳ He'll let go of objects deliberately. ✳ He can build a tower of two bricks.	✳ Point to objects for him. ✳ Put toys on the tray of his high chair and encourage him to throw them over; you can tie them on. ✳ Ask him to roll a ball to you.
His social skills	✳ He shows affection by pressing his face and head against yours and hangs on to you tightly. ✳ He'll give you a toy if you ask him for it, but become angry if you take it away.	✳ Teach about hugs – let's both have a hug together – he's learning reciprocity. ✳ Teach sharing: ask him for a bit of food and show him how nice he is for sharing it.
His speech	✳ He begins to make lots of consonant sounds. ✳ He chatters away in the rhythm of speech, without any meaning.	✳ Name absolutely everything. ✳ Face your baby when you speak to him so that he is able to read your lip movements.

Stimulating play

✳ Read to him each day: read real story books and point out pictures. He'll learn to look at pictures the right way up and begin to recognize pictures of objects (see right).

✳ Rock him on your knee and pretend to drop him – he'll enjoy "falling".

✳ Play hide and seek by hiding yourself or a toy.

✳ Give him bath toys – plastic jugs, beakers, sieves, boats, and ducks.

✳ Show him how to dress and undress a doll or teddy of his own.

✳ Give him squeaky toys, horns, and bells.

✳ Stack blocks or cubes of the same size on top of one another and side by side for him to see.

Baby development
10–11 months

✳ What to look out for

What develops	How she progresses	How you can help
Her mind	✳ Your baby will point things out to you. ✳ She loves dropping toys off her high chair, then looking for them. ✳ She asks to be picked up. ✳ She learns through opposites: keep showing her examples, such as in and out, here and there, and over and under.	✳ Read different kinds of books and magazines to her. ✳ Encourage her concentration span by telling her a simple storyline. ✳ Pick her up if she reaches out to you. ✳ Keep demonstrating cause and effect, by pushing over bricks or splashing water.
Her mobility	✳ She's crawling or shuffling at great speed. ✳ If you support her standing, she'll lift one leg. ✳ She's completely balanced while sitting.	✳ Place a toy right behind her to make her twist around – it's okay, she's got the skill now. ✳ Position her so that she can crawl or shuffle.
Her handling skills	✳ Your baby loves taking things out of containers and putting them back (see above). ✳ She will hold something out to you if you ask her for it.	✳ Play giving things to each other and then taking them away, but don't force her to relinquish something. ✳ Take her hand and point to objects.
Her social skills	✳ She knows her name and knows who Mummy and Daddy are when you use the words. ✳ She's got a wonderful sense of humour: play little jokes all the time and laugh at her attempts to make you laugh.	✳ Use laughter to show your approval and silence to mean the opposite: this is gentle baby discipline and she'll soon catch on. ✳ Demonstrate social rituals, such as kissing and waving goodbye.
Her speech	✳ Your baby is now beginning to imitate real speech sounds. ✳ She may start to attempt to say one word with meaning – "Dada" when Daddy appears is often the first. She will probably understand the word "No".	✳ Keep saying "Mama". ✳ Repeat "Dada". Use association, for example: "Dada has gone to work".

Stimulating play

✳ Play games with bricks: make a tower of bricks and show her cause and effect by knocking them down and saying "all fall down" (see left).
✳ Play games using the hands, such as "Incy-wincy spider" and "Jack and Jill" – buy a book that shows you the movements.
✳ When reading, name several items on each page and go over them in the same order each time you read. Let her turn the pages.
✳ Encourage her to practise putting in and taking out by giving her a wooden spoon and bowl or bricks and a basket.
✳ Encourage her to pull herself up to standing by holding a favourite toy just out of reach.

Baby development
11–12 months

✳ What to look out for

What develops	How he progresses	How you can help
His mind	✳ He loves jokes and will do anything for a positive response like a laugh – this will make him feel good about himself. ✳ He knows about kissing and wants to kiss you.	✳ Laugh when he finds something funny. ✳ Let him kiss you, but don't ask him to kiss strangers. ✳ Talk enthusiastically about your activities.
His mobility	✳ He can walk if you hold one hand. ✳ He'll walk if he pushes a sturdy trolley, or he'll hold on to furniture to steady himself.	✳ While he's cruising, encourage him to launch off by calling him. ✳ Make sure the furniture is steady.
His handling skills	✳ He is getting better at feeding himself (see above). ✳ He can rotate his hand to turn toys over. ✳ He loves throwing things away. ✳ He makes lines with a crayon. ✳ He holds on to two things in one hand.	✳ Keep putting two blocks into his hand. ✳ Encourage self-feeding of soft (but not runny) food with a spoon. Give him his own special dish and spoon. ✳ Give him crayons and paper.
His social skills	✳ He knows who he is. ✳ He becomes quite possessive of his toys and resents them being removed. ✳ He loves social gatherings as long as you or someone he is familiar with carries him. ✳ He'll give you things if you ask for them.	✳ Introduce him to lots of babies. ✳ Encourage him to share. ✳ Encourage affection by cuddling his doll. ✳ Leave him with a babysitter occasionally. ✳ Sit him in his high chair at the table or playpen in the room in which you're sitting.
His speech	✳ He follows conversation and makes sounds in the gaps. ✳ He may say one word, such as "dog", with meaning. ✳ He can make you understand he wants something and what it is.	✳ Teach him "thank you"; he may be able to say "ta". ✳ Congratulate him when you understand what he's saying.

Stimulating play

✳ Give him non-toxic coloured crayons and large sheets of plain paper on the floor, to encourage him to draw (see right).

✳ Read simple stories about animals and their young to encourage his interest in other "babies". All babies love this.

✳ Encourage him to stand unaided by holding him steady, then letting go for a second or two.

✳ Concentrate on the names of objects and name parts of the body. Point to parts of your body and he'll copy you.

✳ If he uses the furniture as support to get around, place it slightly further apart to encourage him to bridge the gap. Be ready to help.

Going back to work

No sooner than you've settled into being a mother and found a routine that's right for all of you, you may find yourself thinking about returning to work. For many women, this is a financial necessity and for some it's a relief after months of nappies and baby talk! Going back to work requires some reorganization and a change of priorities, and it's sensible to consider all the options quite soon after your baby is born. Try to decide as a family which arrangements suit you best. You may, for example, have the option to return part-time or work from home some days, or your partner may decide to give up work to care for your baby, especially if you earn more money. If you both work full-time, you'll have to arrange childcare and accept that on weekdays you're only going to see your baby for a couple of hours in the morning and evening. This is never ideal or easy, but as long as you maintain your baby's routine, and she has your undivided attention while you're with her, she won't suffer from having working parents.

Work and parenting

Make the return to work easier for you all by ensuring you've made good childcare provisions and deciding how you'll adjust your routine. Remember that the changes may be unsettling at first, especially for your baby.

When is the right time?

Aside from legal requirements (see p.184), your baby's needs and your feelings will, to an extent, dictate when you return to work:

✳ If you want to continue breastfeeding, practise expressing enough milk for your baby's needs (see p.80). If you intend to stop breastfeeding, you need to introduce the bottle in good time.

✳ Think carefully about whether you are physically and emotionally ready.

Work options

Look carefully at all your options.

Part-time/job-sharing
Part-time can be the best of both worlds, as you have time with your baby and the stimulation of work, but you also have the pressure of both. If you can job-share, you may be better able to continue to build your career.

Working from home
You need to be self-disciplined and you'll still need some childcare (see p.172), as it's easy to be distracted.

Career break
You may decide to have a break. Make sure this is what you really want and that you've thought about all the implications.

Father at home
If you want to return to work full-time, it may be an option for your partner to be the main carer (see p.176).

Making the decision

You may decide while you're pregnant that you want to return to work at the end of your maternity leave (see p.184). Once the baby is born, however, it's normal to feel unsure about leaving him, especially as this is likely to coincide with the time that you're just settling into being a mother. On the other hand, you may find that you actually miss work and are ready, after a few months, to take a break from the domestic routine and return to an adult environment. Of course, there may simply be no decision for you to make – financially, you may have to work.

What to consider

Whatever you decided while pregnant, it's important to look at your financial and domestic situation once the baby is born and for you and your partner to talk about work options:
✳ What type of childcare can you afford? Have you checked what is available in your area?
✳ After covering the cost of childcare, does your salary leave enough extra to make it worthwhile? (Don't forget to take travel costs into account.)
✳ Is it feasible to return to your old job as it was and also devote enough time to your baby? For example, does your job involve lots of overtime or travel away from home?

Concerns

For the past few months you'll have been focused on preparing for the birth and then looking after your new baby. Once you have to think about returning to work, you're likely to have concerns and mixed feelings.
Feeling guilty You may feel guilty (especially if you can't wait to get back to work), but don't. Just because you're a working mother doesn't imply that you're a bad mother. There's no point in staying at home with your baby if it doesn't fulfil you – it will be more beneficial to him if you're happy and contented when he does see you. Also, don't forget how your baby will benefit from the additional income.
Losing your confidence After a few months at home with your baby, you may doubt your ability to readjust to a working environment. Try to ease yourself back into work mode by catching up on what's been going on and by talking to colleagues. Nearer the time, go into the office (by yourself, if possible) so that it isn't such a shock when you return. You'll soon realize that not much has changed while you've been away.

Making the transition

Area of change	How to make it easier
Preparing your baby	Introduce your baby to the childminder, starting with a couple of mornings each week and gradually building it up, or take him to the nursery for a trial run. You should also start to adapt his feeding routine in good time.
Adapting to a change of routine	Trying to juggle work and looking after your baby can be difficult. Establish a routine in the mornings and evenings so that you are sharing the babycare and chores equally. You'll soon find a routine that works.
Coping with tiredness	No one who is consistently deprived of sleep can be expected to cope adequately with a job, so you must take it in turns to care for your baby during the night. If one of you is in part-time work, you should still organize a pro-rata arrangement.
Focusing on work	It's an acquired skill not to think about your baby while you're at work. If you've made the best arrangements you can for his welfare, any energy you now dispense on worrying is wasted and sells you and your employer short.
Settling your baby	The fact is your baby will have to settle and he will. What you can do is prepare yourselves for his reaction and, when he's with you, be reassuring and comforting. Make sure he has whatever comfort object he loves.

JUST FOR DAD

The routine at home will change if you're both working full-time and it'll help if you prepare yourself for this.

How you can help

✳ Be supportive. Your partner is likely to find going back to work a strain and may be distressed by leaving the baby. Try to plan in advance as much as possible and give her time to adjust.

✳ Share the responsibility. Don't assume that your partner will sort out childcare problems. The carer or nursery needs telephone numbers for both of you (including mobiles), so that you can easily share the responsibility if a problem arises.

✳ Share the chores. Your partner may have been doing most of the chores while she was at home, but now she's back at work this should be more equal. Alternate doing the domestic work, getting up during the night, and collecting your baby from the childminder or nursery.

When you're back at work

It may take a few weeks to settle back into work. You'll just about have worked out a routine with your baby at home and then suddenly have to adapt to a different timetable and concentrate your mind on a different set of priorities. You'll also, for the first time, be doing your job while having to handle added pressures and responsibilities at home.

Career considerations

People often assume that a woman's first priority will be her child and, in some situations, they're right – when push comes to shove, it's quite often the mother's employment that takes the strain and not the father's. If your partnership is different, you're probably going to have to demonstrate this several times before it's recognized.

How your career is affected may also depend on your employer's attitude – set the ground rules early on by talking to your manager and telling him or her that you're committed to your job, but that your responsibilities at home mean you'll need some flexibility. Explain that you need to leave on time (although, ideally, collecting your baby should be shared equally with your partner), but that with sufficient notice you're prepared to work extra hours, if necessary.

Emergencies

Talk about a strategy for emergencies, such as your baby or the childminder being ill. If you don't have an alternative carer, one of you will need to take time off work to care for your child. If either of you feels strongly that your job takes priority, try to agree this in advance. This can save a lot of arguments.

Choosing childcare

Finding and choosing a carer for your baby is mainly dictated by practical and financial considerations, but there are also emotional issues. It's hard to leave your baby with someone new, so you need to be as happy as possible about the care and carer you've chosen.

Trial period

It's worth having a trial period before you return to work, so that you can settle your baby gradually:

* Your baby will have time to become familiar with her new surroundings and her new carer.

* You'll have an idea of the impact on your baby and be able to find ways of soothing her if she becomes unsettled.

* You'll be able to sort out any practical hitches.

* If you introduce your baby to her new carer gradually, the emotional impact should be less once you actually return to work.

If things go wrong

If the childcare doesn't work out, it can be disappointing and problematic, especially if your carer lives with you. Treat the problem professionally:

* It's best if issues are dealt with quickly; ignoring problems will only make matters worse and lead to resentments building up.

* Talk to your carer and try to reach a compromise. Agree to see how things go and, depending on the problem, set a time limit. If, after this period, the matter isn't resolved, it may be better to terminate the employment.

* Decide on a set notice period. This benefits both of you and if your carer decides to leave, you won't be left in the lurch.

What to look for in a carer

Once you've decided on the type of childcare you'd prefer, you need to look around for the best carer. The earlier you plan your childcare, the more choice you'll have. Ask the person or institution that you're considering lots of questions to find out the type of care they provide, and thoroughly check the facilities. If you're not sure, follow your instincts, and look elsewhere.

Qualifications and references A nanny or nursery nurse should have accredited training with a proper qualification (for example, NNEB in the UK). If you're using a childminder or a nursery, check that the person or institution is registered with a local authority. Any nursery worker, nanny, or childminder must also have up-to-date Criminal Records Bureau (CRB) clearance. Au pairs are not professionally trained. Ask a potential au pair for the name of another employer and at least two written references. Talk to any referees on the telephone to get a better idea of a person's suitability.

Level of care With a nursery, crèche, or childminder, check how many babies are looked after at one time and the carer-to-child ratio. Even if your baby will not be receiving individual care, she still needs enough care to be stimulated and to encourage her development. Check the space and resources available, such as the kitchen and sterilizing equipment, the play area, and the types of toys offered. Ask what kinds of activities your baby will be involved in on a day-to-day basis.

Interaction with your baby Always invite a potential carer to spend time with your baby, or take your baby to the nursery. Watch to see what a carer says while holding your baby and how your baby reacts to her.

Commitment It can be confusing and distressing for a baby to have a change of carer. Check that the person or institution will be able to provide relatively long-term care.

Your relationship with your carer

However sure you are about employing your carer, it's advisable to discuss and agree on all aspects of caring for your baby from the outset:
* A trial period before you agree to a full contract is a good idea.
* Write down your requirements so that you can agree some ground rules; especially with regard to telephone use and visitors for live-in carers.
* Find out a carer's thoughts, or an institution's policy, on discipline to make sure they match your own.

The carer's relationship with your baby

Leaving your baby with a carer is likely to come at a time when you've just settled into being a parent and feel particularly close to your son or daughter. Your carer will also form a close relationship with your baby, but this doesn't mean you're any less important and you're by no means replaced. Your baby is capable of being close to – and accepting the attention of – more than one person; in fact it's beneficial to her if this happens because the more love, attention, and stimulation she receives the better she'll develop.

Babies often go through periods of time when they favour certain people (see p.131); if your baby seems closer to her carer, it's probably only a phase. Your baby may also seem unsettled now and then, but don't read too much into this. However, if she continues to be unsettled for more than a week or two, spend time with the carer and your baby together to try to pinpoint any problems.

Hidden costs

When thinking about the cost of childcare, it's worth considering:

* Are there transport costs?
* Are your baby's meals provided?
* What are the additional costs associated with a live-in carer?
* If you have twins, would it be cheaper to employ a nanny?
* Are there hidden emotional costs, such as feeling indebted, if you're using a friend or relative?

Childcare options

Type of care	Description	Advantages	Disadvantages
Relative	You may leave your baby with a family member, such as a grandparent. Encourage him or her to involve your baby in activities, such as a playgroup.	* Usually a cheaper option. * Your baby is with someone who loves her. * You're less likely to have strict time restraints; don't abuse this.	* It can be difficult if there are disagreements. * You may worry about your baby forming a closer relationship with that person.
Registered childminder	A childminder looks after several children at one time in her own home. She is likely to be very experienced, especially if she has her own children.	* You can often pay by the hour to suit your budget. * Your baby will mix with lots of children, which will help to develop her social skills.	* No professional qualification required. * May have limited resources. * You can't take your baby if she's ill.
Nanny	A nanny cares for your baby at home and may live with you. Interview her together – you both have to get on with her and observe her with your baby.	* A nanny is professionally trained and qualified. * Care takes place at home, which helps your baby to settle and is more convenient for you.	* A nanny is expensive (you pay her tax and insurance too), but consider a nanny share. * Beware of domestic tensions if the nanny lives in.
Day nursery or crèche	There are very few local authority nurseries, so you'll probably have to pay for private care. If you're lucky, there may be an all-day nursery at your workplace.	* Your baby is with other babies and care is based around developing skills. * Nurseries must be registered and they often employ qualified carers.	* Can be expensive and there will be limited places. * You'll have to collect your baby by an agreed time. * You can't take your baby if she's ill.
Au pair or mother's help	This is a foreign student who lives with you as part of the family. She'll want to attend language classes and is suitable only if you work part-time or from home.	* Care is provided in the home. * Cheaper than a nanny. * When your baby is older, the au pair may be able to teach her a second language.	* Not professionally qualified, so not suitable for the full-time care of a baby. * Works limited hours. * There will be live-in costs.

Special time with your baby

✳ JUST FOR MUM

Remember, play doesn't have to involve toys; often just being with you is fun for your baby.

What you can do

✳ When you get home from work, make a habit of picking your baby up straight away and holding him as you walk around doing things.

✳ Exaggerate your pleasure at seeing him, talk to him, make eye contact, laugh a lot, and play little jokes.

✳ Try to spend ten to 15 uninterrupted minutes playing with your baby each evening.

✳ Read the paper or a book together so that you both relax. Read out items and show your baby pictures to involve him.

✳ If you're really tired, have a bath together. A skin-to-skin soak is good for both of you.

An hour a day

An hour playing with your baby each day is rewarding and fulfilling for all. A baby who has his parents' undivided attention for an hour a day acquires self-esteem and self-confidence and becomes generous, loving, and well adjusted. It doesn't have to be a solid hour. He won't concentrate for long so it could be in half- or quarter-hours as long as he has all your attention.

If you're working parents, the time spent at home as a family becomes not just important, but precious. Play is essential to your baby's mental and physical development, and he'll love the attention from you both while he plays.

The importance of play

As well as being a parent, you are your baby's playmate and best friend; this is especially true in his first year when he may not have much opportunity to interact with other children. Every game you play with him is magical and every lesson becomes worth learning, so time spent in games, no matter how simple, ensures that your baby is avidly learning and acquiring skills. Don't underestimate how important play is to your baby: it's his full-time job; a job that requires great concentration and expenditure of energy. It's harder than most adult work because everything is new and fresh lessons are learned all the time. These lessons, however, are made easier and are more fun if he can enjoy them with his favourite playmates – his parents.

Why play is essential

Your baby investigates his world through play.
✳ Play stimulates and excites him.
✳ For the first few years of his life, play is the only way he learns.
✳ Play is an integral part of his physical and mental development.

Getting the most out of play

Make the time to join in activities with your baby and encourage him in play that will stimulate his development.

Investing time Formal play isn't necessary, but some planning does reap dividends so try to make play a part of your morning, evening, and weekend routine so that your baby is getting at least an hour of playtime in total from both of you each day (see left). A baby has a very short attention span so don't expect him to sit playing happily while you cook the dinner. Fifteen minutes invested in playing with your baby before you begin a task will pay off; if you only give him five minutes of your time, he's more likely to become attention-seeking when you're busy doing something else.

Stimulating development Babies start acquiring skills from the very moment of birth. These mental and physical milestones (see p.146) emerge at particular stages as your baby's brain and body develop. It follows that these are optimum moments for you to introduce games that encourage particular skills to flourish, so make sure you vary the activities that you play with your baby; for example, physical games encourage mobility; singing helps to develop speech; playing with toys, such as building blocks, helps your baby to become more dextrous.

Maximizing your time

If you work full-time, try to take advantage of any spare moments you have to spend time with your baby. It helps if you're organized and can prioritize. If you're both in high-pressured jobs, it's easy to let work take over and work an extra hour at the beginning or end of the day, but this hour is invaluable time you could be spending with your baby (see box opposite).

Weekends

Don't bring work home with you; if it's not there you can't do it, which means you can spend time with your baby without feeling guilty. Try to get out as a family at least one of the days at the weekend; if you're in the house, you're more likely to get distracted with other things. Keep to your baby's weekly routine as much as possible – at around nine months he'll begin to understand that certain things happen at certain times. If one of you doesn't have much time on weekday mornings to dress or give your baby breakfast, he or she can try to make time to do this at the weekend. Your baby will enjoy the change and it gives your partner a break too.

Mornings

Most babies do wake up early so use this opportunity to spend time together. If you don't have time for proper play, sing and talk to your baby as you change and dress him and get him ready for the day. Sit down and have your breakfast with him.

Evenings

Working full-time will make you tired in the evenings. Try to establish some sort of routine for when you get home because as well as having time with your baby, it's important that you both have time to yourselves and time together as a couple (see p.134).

Leave work on time Try to leave work on time. It's unfair on your partner and the baby if either one of you is always home late. Don't take advantage of the childminder – an extra hour in the evening is a lot when she's been looking after the baby all day.

Divide the chores One of you should cook and the other wash up so that you both have time to spend with your baby.

Choose relaxing activities It will be difficult to get your baby to bed if he's very excited. Give him a bath, then read or sing to him to calm him down before you put him to bed.

Time-saving tips

To give yourself more time with your baby in evenings:

* Try to prepare some weekday meals at the weekend and freeze them.
* Record any early evening TV programmes and watch them once your baby has gone to bed.
* Save any long telephone calls until after your baby's bedtime.
* Eat mid-afternoon sometimes so that it's possible for you to wait later for your evening meal.

✳ JUST FOR DAD

Your baby will look forward to you coming home in the evenings. Shower him with attention and show him how special he is.

What you can do

✳ Develop a special routine for when you get home from work. It could just be holding out your arms for your baby to crawl or to walk you, or picking him up immediately, walking around with him, and telling him about your day.

✳ Try to find time each evening to spend ten or 15 minutes playing a game.

✳ If you read the paper in the evening, read to your baby and give him some paper to crumple.

✳ You and your baby can relax with a bath together (see p.95) before getting him ready for bed.

▲ **RELAXING TOGETHER** Play doesn't always have to be energetic. Settle into a comfortable chair in the evening and read a story to your baby. This is a relaxing and enjoyable activity for both of you.

Fathers at home

✳ JUST FOR MUM

Being the breadwinner while your partner stays at home can lead to conflicting emotions.

How to help yourself
In general, society still pressures women to be the main carer and it's difficult not to be affected by this. You may feel guilty, and envy other women who have more time at home. Try to be confident in your decision or accepting of your predicament and spend as much time as possible with your baby. Being the breadwinner can be stressful, so find ways to relax and try not to feel resentment.

How to help your partner
Make sure he has time out to relax, see his friends, and spend time with you (see p.134). Try not to leave all the chores to him.

✳

Reactions

Full-time dads are more common nowadays, but you may get some flak. Some traditionally minded men find it threatening that a "house-husband" is independent enough to flout the traditional social conventions – they like to hang on to these conventions as it gives them security. But if you're a man who's strong enough to have made the decision to be a full-time parent, you'll no doubt be strong enough to take the flak!

It suits some couples best for the mother to return to work and be the breadwinner, while the father is a stay-at-home dad, caring for the baby and running the home.

Making the decision

For many couples, the decision to reverse roles is made because they feel that their baby will benefit from having a full-time parent at home. If the mother is earning more, it makes sense for the father to be that person – especially if his work is something he can do from home. When a parent stays at home full-time, a couple will be financially worse off than if both work, but this is often compensated for by an improvement in their quality of life and is seen as a worthwhile investment in their child. A man may be forced to stay at home due to a job loss; even if this is only short term, it can often be an invaluable opportunity for him to spend time with his child and take on the role of primary carer.

A learning process

Those people who take a stand on the traditional roles of father and mother as being "natural" are missing the point, and to divide parental labour along the lines of gender is completely redundant. Looking after a baby is a learning process for all new parents, whether they're male or female, so don't let anyone tell you otherwise. Remember the following:
✳ Women are not born with an innate ability to change nappies and dress babies. Possibly, they appear more confident at it because they're made to feel that they should know what to do.
✳ Looking after and nurturing a baby is a learned skill and to begin with it's as difficult for a mother as it is for a father.
✳ Men are not at a disadvantage when it comes to caring for a baby. If you're a father who has decided to stay at home to be the main carer, you have as much chance at being good at it and raising a happy, confident, and intelligent child as your partner.

Parenting

If you're a couple who have chosen the father-at-home option, you are hopefully committed to parenting in general rather than fathering or mothering (see p.11). It's only sensible to base your family set-up on your mutual strengths rather than be captive to stereotypes that may well conflict with your personalities.

The advantages

As a father who chooses to stay at home, you'll form a close bond with your baby and have a chance to watch and enjoy her development at an age that most men miss out on. This role will enable you to express your affection and feelings in ways that are difficult when you're in the more traditional male role. Being the carer lets you change your priorities and releases you from the pressures of being the main provider for your family. This leaves you with more of yourself to offer your baby and partner, which can be hugely beneficial to the family as a whole.

How your child is affected

To a baby, her mother and father are interchangeable. The baby only knows parental love and care – it doesn't matter who is doing the giving. The advantage of a man being the main carer is that he can offer a positive role model to his children free from the commonest kind of stereotyping. A son will grow up feeling comfortable with the emotional side of his personality and he'll follow his father's lead in having an independent spirit unpressured by prevailing social mores. A daughter, of course, will seek out the same well-balanced kind of men as her father – and that's no bad thing.

Being the lone man

The main problem for most full-time parents is isolation and since a large proportion of people are working during the day, adult company is found largely with others looking after children. As these are usually women, this can cause a problem for the full-time father. It's pointless to pretend that people interact with the opposite sex in the same way as with their own, but it's likely that a man with enough flexibility and confidence to become the main carer will move fairly easily into this predominantly female world. While some mothers may be surprised to find their ranks as full-time child carers joined by a man, few will be hostile. The surprise at the "house-husband" is usually a bit of a nine-day wonder whose presence is soon taken for granted. Most men are welcomed, although some are victims of the "let-me-help-you-love" maternalism, which can be as irritating as the "leave-that-to-me-darling" paternalism practised by some men.

An equal share

Some couples decide that they'll both work part-time or one or two days at home, so that they both have a mix of parenting and work. This is possible if the job can be done part-time or at home – new technology has made it even easier to do this. It may mean that both of you put your careers on hold, but many feel that it's the right choice. At least it prevents either person having to give up their career altogether. The advantages include:

∗ Both of you have real quality time with your baby, which will mean you'll form an equally close bond with her.

∗ You'll both have a strong appreciation of the frustrations involved in being in sole charge of your baby and the problems of juggling work and home.

∗ The baby benefits from building a close relationship with you both.

∗ You become a real team by sharing things equally, and prevent the resentments that often build up when one parent is at home.

◀ **BEING ACCEPTED** Over time, a full-time father will stop being the token male and become just another parent, who shares the same pleasures and problems of parenthood as his female friends.

Looking to the future

Your constant role

A parent's role as nurturer means respecting your child, and offering support without forgoing your own principles. It takes many forms.

Comforter

You can only help your child to cope with emotional or physical pain by acknowledging it, and offering comfort when it's needed.

Playmate

Play is a serious business for your child, and the best play is with other people, the most important of whom are his parents.

Limit-setter

The first limits you set for your baby will be to prevent him from hurting himself; later, these limits will prevent him from hurting others as well. Never be apologetic about consistently setting reasonable limits, but try not to do so in a punitive or accusatory manner. Rather than saying "no" all the time, help him to understand the reasons why you say "no".

Teacher or role model?

The role of teacher is crucial for any parent; but it isn't formal teaching: you do it by example. Your child learns about life from you, so you can't shrug off responsibility for an errant school child or a truculent teenager.

Authority figure

Don't confuse authority and power: power results from the use or threat of force; authority comes from a person who has influence over, and receives consent from, others without force. Your child will accept your authority if he also sees that you are fair, competent, loving, and, above all, reasonable.

Your baby has now completed his first year of life; he's beginning to communicate with language, he's mobile, he's feeding himself, and asserting his personality as a full member of the family. He's growing up, so your roles as parents will be changing too, and they'll continue to change as he progresses on to school and ultimately to adolescence and adulthood. Under your care, he'll become more and more independent, but he'll always need you both as his permanent bedrock of security, sympathy, friendship, and love.

Your baby grows up

The main change you'll see, and must be prepared to accept, is that your baby is becoming a person in his own right, with personality, preferences, and a will of his own. He will gradually acquire a sense of place in the family, a sense of independence, and, most importantly, a sense of self-worth. Not all these changes are straightforward for you. On the one hand, they are all signs of growing maturity and so should be welcomed. On the other hand, some aspects of his growing up may lead to clashes with you and could result in a battle of wills that needs careful handling. Then again, his frustration at wanting to out-perform his ability may express itself as tantrums that leave you bewildered, perplexed, and sometimes helpless (see p.182). Tantrums, though, are a crucial milestone; he can't become a reasonable, self-controlled child without experiencing them.

A hierarchy of needs

Keep in mind the basic needs that will help your child to grow and develop normally. Health, of course, is a pre-requisite, but you also have to try to provide the right sort of environment for him to reach his full potential –

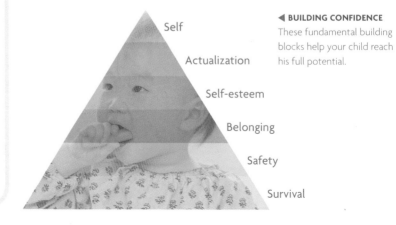

Self

Actualization

Self-esteem

Belonging

Safety

Survival

◀ BUILDING CONFIDENCE
These fundamental building blocks help your child reach his full potential.

physically, emotionally, socially, and intellectually. All children have a hierarchy of needs, starting from the very basic need for survival. You can think of your child's needs in terms of a pyramid (see opposite): the solid base is the provision of the food, drink, and shelter needed for survival; then comes safety – protection from harm; a sense of belonging – your child needs to feel wanted and secure; leading to self-esteem – no one can feel good about himself if he feels unloved. Near the top of the pyramid comes actualization, an understanding of his place in the world. Finally comes a fully developed sense of self, a pinnacle that can't be achieved without the other needs being met.

Becoming independent

Your child's burgeoning spirit of self-reliance is more important than you may think because so many good things can flow from it. Without a secure feeling of independence, a child can't relate to others. He can't share, be reasonable, outgoing, and friendly, have a sense of responsibility, and eventually respect others and their privacy.

Many other qualities stem from his belief in himself too – curiosity, adventurousness, being helpful, thoughtful, and generous. With such qualities people will relate well to him and he'll automatically get more out of life. What you pour in as love, expresses itself as self-worth and belief in himself. Love, of course, is not the only spur; you can encourage him practically as well.

GROWING UP Your baby is growing up. She's mobile and is beginning to know her own mind. As she gains independence, physically and emotionally, your role also changes.

Being reasonable

This heading disguises a few personal comments on discipline in young children. I have to disguise it because what I believe to be good discipline has little to do with the usual punitive interpretation of the word.

Re-defining discipline

Good discipline has nothing to do with a parent forcing a mode of behaviour on a child; it's about encouraging reasonable behaviour from a child. Your aim should be to create a desire to behave well most of the time, rather than to conform to an arbitrary adult code out of fear, weakness, or resignation.

Encouraging good behaviour

Praise good behaviour rather than penalizing poor behaviour.

Start from the beginning

It's easier if you start how you mean to finish; discipline doesn't just happen at, say, three years old. It's something that's been building from birth and is based on reasonable behaviour expressed by you.

Parental responsibility

All children are born with an overwhelming desire to please; if they lose that desire, my view is that we parents must take responsibility. If you think you're doing everything right, but still have a difficult child, you may be being too easy on yourself. Look at what you think of as "right", and ask yourself if it is right for your child.

Being consistent

Work out your joint attitude to discipline, and be consistent in your response. A child who gets different reactions from each parent will be confused about what her limits really are, and her behaviour will reflect this.

Helping independence develop

Helpfulness Ask her to fetch things for you, such as the shopping bag or the dustpan, so that she can help and she feels useful.

Decision-making Give her small decisions to make, like which toy to play with or which cup to use, so that she can use her judgment and rely on it. Let her choose what she wants to wear in the morning; dressing may take a bit longer, but it'll give her a real sense of achievement.

Sense of identity Ask questions about her preferences and solicit her opinion to give her a sense of identity and importance.

Physical independence Give her slightly more and more difficult tasks – like jumping up and down, throwing or kicking a ball, so that she can feel pleased with the strength and coordination of her body. Let her dress herself when she is able to. Choose clothes that are easy to put on, such as trousers with elastic waists. Don't intervene unless she asks you to, or she is very frustrated. Praise all her efforts at new tasks.

Emotional independence Show her that she can trust you: you always come back after leaving her, you always comfort her when she's hurt, you always help her when she's in difficulties.

Cooperation "We can do it together" is a motto that you should keep repeating – it breeds faith in your baby's own efforts. When she overcomes an obstacle or succeeds in a task on her own, she'll experience the thrill of achievement – especially if you heap praise on her.

Achieving control of her body

Many parents believe that they can set a clock for their baby to achieve bowel and bladder control. Those parents are doomed to frustration. Your baby's timetable has nothing to do with your expectations – only with her speed of development. Bowel and bladder control are undoubtedly important milestones between dependent baby and independent child, but they can't be reached until other areas of development have been achieved. Until the nerve connections or pathways between her brain and her bladder and bowel are in place, she can't control her actions. Likewise she can't control her bowel or bladder until her muscles are strong enough. This is why I dislike the label "potty training"; no child can do something until she's ready for it and, once ready, no child needs training.

When she'll be dry

At around 18 months and no earlier, your child might start to tell you that she can feel herself passing urine. She can't hold it, she can't wait, she has no control over it. She'll give you a sign; she'll point to the nappy and vocalize to draw your attention to it. Then, and only then, do you start a gentle programme of encouragement. The first step is to get her a potty of her own and put it in the bathroom. Let her sit on the potty when she wants to. If she does anything in it then praise her for it. You may also be able to encourage your child by giving her special pull-up nappies to wear during the day or night, so that when she does become more aware, you can take her nappy off quickly; she may even be able to do it herself.

Your daughter will probably have achieved bladder and bowel control by the age of two, and be dry at night by three; it may take your son longer. Being dry all night can take some children a long time – it's quite normal for a boy not to achieve full control until he is four or five. Never scold your child for wetting the bed, or having an accident during the day, especially if she's been "dry" for a while. It could be a sign of illness or emotional distress, so think about the underlying causes. Being angry with your child for something over which she hasn't much control will just upset her and make the problem worse.

Gender differences in development

Bladder and bowel control is one obvious area of development where there may be a marked difference between boys and girls (although there will always be exceptions to the rule). Many gender differences are actually imposed on boys and girls by adults' own prejudices about what boys or girls are expected to be like (see p.148), and so it's not always clear whether

Toilet tips

Here are a few tips that you might find helpful:

❋ Let your child develop at her own pace. There is no way you can speed up the process, just be there to help your child along.

❋ Never force your child to sit on the potty; let her decide.

❋ Praise your child and treat her control as an accomplishment. Always forgive and ignore any accidents.

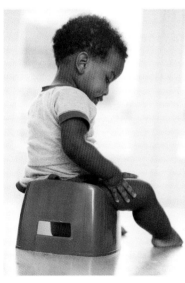

▲ **"POTTY TRAINING"** There's no need for "potty training". Let your baby develop at his own rate. He'll achieve bowel and bladder control as soon as he's ready and not a minute earlier.

▶ **GETTING DRESSED** By the age of about two-and-a-half, your child will find putting on her clothes (and taking them off) becomes easier. As her independence develops, she'll be increasingly eager to do this for herself.

Temper tantrums

By the time he's about two, your child's will is well developed, but his ambitions far outreach his capabilities. The resulting combination of stubbornness and frustration can be explosive – the classic temper tantrum. There are ways to cope:

✳ Accept temper tantrums as normal. Better still, see them as a cry for help. Having your child throw a fit of screaming, kicking, and crying is upsetting, but if you're firm, gentle, and have a steady nerve, you'll nurse him out of them; remember that he's not being wilfully naughty – he simply can't control himself.

✳ Don't shout, smack, or get angry. He needs you to help him regain control. A tantrum means he's saying, "Help me. Protect me from myself." Your very quietness should calm him down.

✳ A really upset child can frighten himself by the sheer strength of his emotions, so cuddle him close; be firm – he will struggle.

✳ Be businesslike; he's trying to elicit a dramatic response, but he'll calm down if you're cool.

✳ If this doesn't work, say you're going to leave the room. Go somewhere he can't see you, but you can see him. If you do as you promised, the screaming usually stops because he loses his audience.

✳ Try to stay where you can see him as much as possible, be ready to prevent him from hurting himself or others.

Caution

Some children develop breath-holding attacks that may be frightening to witness. Most are brought to an abrupt end by a firm tap between the shoulder blades.

the recognized differences are solely due to nature or nurture. However, differences in the rate of development of certain skills between boys and girls throughout childhood and into adolescence have been measured by researchers (see chart below). Being aware of the differences between the genders may help you to understand your children better, which can then enable them to move forward at an appropriate rate and also help overcome any difficulties before they become problems. It can also help to avoid the sort of gender stereotyping that doesn't allow girls to be adventurous or boys to show affection.

Widening horizons

As your child grows and develops, he'll become increasingly sociable and need contact with other people in order to develop natural curiosity and intellectual growth. He'll get these from the everyday interaction he has

✳ Some developmental differences

Girls	Boys
As toddlers, girls are better at hopping, rhythmic movement, and balance.	At school age, boys are usually better than girls at running, jumping, and throwing.
Girls are slightly faster than boys at some aspects of early language ability. They generally learn to read and write, and grasp grammar and spelling, earlier than boys.	Most boys talk later than girls, and take longer to make complicated sentences. They have more reading problems by adolescence, and are less adept at verbal reasoning.
Girls are more emotionally independent than boys and are also more sociable and form close friendships from an earlier age.	Boys are more emotionally dependent than girls, and tend to have more behavioural problems before and during adolescence.
There's little difference in strength and speed between girls and boys until puberty, but from that time fat-to-muscle ratio is greater in girls.	At adolescence, boys become stronger and faster than girls and have more muscle and bone, less fat, and larger hearts and lungs.
Physical growth is faster and more regular; girls mature at adolescence earlier than boys.	Physical growth tends to go in uneven spurts in boys; they reach puberty later than girls.
Girls may be slightly better at arithmetic than boys before they reach adolescence, after which the trend reverses.	At every age boys are better at spatial visualization and, from adolescence onwards, boys tend to be better than girls at mathematical reasoning.
In early childhood, girls generally appear to be more willing to obey adults' requests.	From toddlerhood, boys are more aggressive socially, and more competitive than girls.

with you, your friends, and their children, with grandparents and other relatives. But it's also a good idea to let him meet other children of his own age with you at a nursery or parent-and-toddler group, and later to think about playgroup as a way of preparing him for formal schooling in the future. Although your child may not start to form strong attachments – real friendships – until he's approaching three years old, he'll enjoy playing alongside other children. This will enable him to start finding out about giving and sharing, and to begin exploring the enormous potential for creativity in joint imaginative play.

Extending your family

Once you're settled as a family with one child, it's natural to think about whether or not you're going to extend your family and, if so, how long to wait. As with all family matters, there's no hard and fast rule about this. It suits some couples to wait until their first child is old enough to attend a nursery, or even until he's at full-time school. For others, a smaller gap seems better, but bear in mind that children have been found to benefit from a minimum gap of about two and a half years. You also need to take into account work commitments and financial considerations, as well as your own health; a mother who had a strenuous labour and birth, or perhaps a Caesarean section, would probably want to feel that her body is completely back to normal and has had time to become "hers" again, before embarking on another pregnancy. Age also has significance, although nowadays this doesn't have much bearing on the ability to bear and look after children. However, biology is against you: the older you are, the longer it will take you on average to conceive again (see p.18), so you may not want to wait too long before trying for another baby.

The impact on your child

Whatever the length of time between the two (or subsequent) births, it's important that you think carefully about the impact on the older child, and that you introduce the idea to him sensitively and in good time. Even a teenager can feel displaced by the arrival of a new baby, something that may well happen if you've entered a new relationship and one of you already has children (see p.142). Your decision to extend your family must always be inclusive: your first child is a fully paid-up member of your family unit and deserves to be treated as such, whatever his age.

A final word

Long after your child can cook himself a meal, iron his own clothes, and has set off on his own path in life, he'll still need both his parents to nurture him. True nurture caters not only for his material wants, but also offers continuing and unconditional love, and it's a lifelong commitment. If this unconditional love is combined with reasonable limits and guidelines, you'll both help him to mature into an individual who is sensitive to the needs of others, but remains independent of mind, confident, and open to all the possibilities that life can offer.

Sibling rivalry

Jealousy is a normal emotion for a small child to feel if his security appears threatened by the arrival of a new baby. Although you can't guarantee to avoid some jealousy, the best way to help him cope is to prepare him for the new arrival and to keep on showing him that his place in your affections is quite safe.

Before the birth

Talk to him about the new baby as soon as your tummy looks really swollen. Let him touch your tummy whenever he wants to, but especially to feel the baby kick. Refer to the baby as his baby, and ask if he'd like a brother or a sister to get him involved. If you know the sex in advance, tell him so he can start to identify with the new baby. Get him to show love and affection openly by reading parent and baby animal books together, by encouraging him to be gentle with other babies, and by exchanging lots of cuddles.

After the birth

When he visits you in hospital for the first time, make sure you aren't holding the baby – have your arms free for him and wait for him to ask to see the baby. Give him a present from the baby. Share bath and feeding times so that he can show you how helpful he is and be praised by you. It's important too to put aside at least half an hour every day when you give him your full attention. Keep telling him how much you love and treasure him.

The father's role

Reassure your elder child that you still love him. You're ideally placed to arrange special treats. With your attention and love, you'll enable your first-born to negotiate the choppy waters of sibling rivalry and you'll have cemented a lifelong friendship.

Useful information

This section provides information on the resources and benefits available to you. It also includes a summary of the healthcare procedures and recommended immunization schedule for your baby, and details of organisations that offer help and support.

Minimum rights

Regardless of how many hours you work or how long you've been employed, you're entitled to:

✳ Working conditions that are safe for your unborn child – any risk must be removed, or you removed from it, if necessary by moving you to a suitable alternative job or suspending you on full pay.

✳ Time off work without loss of pay to attend your antenatal appointments and classes.

✳ The right to keep your job – you cannot be dismissed as a result of your pregnancy – and the right to return to the same job after the birth.

✳ Minimum maternity leave and pay (see right).

Benefits

You may be eligible for benefits:

✳ If your income is low, enquire about the possibility of income-based Job-seeker's Allowance, Income Support, Housing and Council Tax Benefits, Tax Credits. You may also be entitled to a Sure Start Maternity Grant.

✳ Once your baby's birth is registered and you've got a birth certificate, you can claim for child benefit.

✳ The government provides a "Child Trust Fund" for every child born since 1 September 2002. The money goes into a savings account and will stay there until your child turns 18.

Finding out your maternity rights

Start making enquiries and getting help from the appropriate bodies early on in your pregnancy – don't leave it too late or you may find yourself losing out. There are two state benefits available – Statutory Maternity Pay and Maternity Allowance (see below and opposite) – and many women have additional maternity rights provided by their employer. It's a good idea to read your contract, especially if you work in a large company, to check your entitlements. If you're confused about anything, talk to your human resources officer. To qualify for maternity leave and pay, you will need to obtain the appropriate forms from your midwife, GP, local Social Security Office, or Citizens' Advice Bureau and apply by the deadlines (see opposite).

Maternity leave and pay

If you are an employee, you have the right to up to 52 weeks' maternity leave. This is made up of two parts – the first 26 weeks is Ordinary Maternity Leave (OML), and if you've worked for your current employer for 26 weeks continuously at the 15th week before your baby's estimated delivery date, you're entitled to a further 26 weeks' Additional Maternity Leave (AML). When you return to work you're entitled to return to the same job on the same terms and conditions. You need to write to your employer at least 15 weeks before your expected week of childbirth, stating that you are pregnant. Give details of your estimated delivery date, when you intend to start maternity leave, and whether or not you intend to return to work afterwards. You'll need to give your employer a copy of your maternity certificate (form MAT B1; in Northern Ireland, form MB1), which you can get from your midwife or doctor. You need to give your employer 28 days' notice of the date that you want to return to work.

Maternity pay

If you have worked for the same employer for at least 26 weeks by the end of the 15th week before your baby is due, you are entitled to Statutory Maternity Pay (SMP). This is paid for a maximum of 39 weeks starting when you leave work. You can decide how soon you want to stop work, but SMP can only start 11 weeks before your estimated due date. You can choose to work right up to the week of your baby's delivery. SMP is 90 per cent of your average pay for the first six weeks; after that it's paid at a set rate for up to 33 weeks. However, many companies offer better deals. SMP is subject to tax and National Insurance.

If you don't qualify for SMP

Any woman who isn't entitled to SMP, but who has paid her National Insurance contributions for 26 of the 66 weeks before the baby's estimated delivery date, can qualify for Maternity Allowance (MA). This is paid at a standard rate for up to 39 weeks starting any time between 11 weeks before the baby is due and the day after the baby is born and it's not liable to tax or National Insurance.

If you don't qualify for SMP or MA, but have paid some National Insurance contributions, you may be entitled to Incapacity Benefit, paid from six weeks before the birth until two weeks after.

Paternity rights

To qualify for paternity leave you should be the child's biological father, be responsible for his upbringing, or be the mother's husband or partner. You should have worked for the same employer for at least 26 weeks by the end of the 15th week before your baby's due. You can take either one week or two consecutive weeks' paternity leave (you can't have odd days). Most fathers are also entitled to Statutory Paternity Pay (SPP).

Registering the birth

You are legally required to register the birth within 42 days (21 days in Scotland) at your Registry Office. If you were married at the time of the birth, either parent may register. If not, the mother must attend, and if the father wants his details entered he must accompany her. You need to give the baby's names; your names, addresses, occupations, and dates of birth (and marriage if relevant). You'll be given a copy of the certificate, and a medical card for the baby.

Rights and benefits summary

When	What you need to do	Why you need to do it
As soon as pregnancy is confirmed	If you're working, inform your employer. If you're not entitled to Statutory Materniy Pay (SMP), find out about Maternity Allowance (MA).	To establish eligibility for SMP/MA and so that you can organise paid time off for your antenatal visits.
15 weeks before your baby is due	Confirm to your employer, in writing, when you intend to stop work and whether you intend to return after the birth.	By confirming your intentions to your employer, you protect your right to return to work and to get SMP.
15 weeks before your baby is due	Fathers: Inform your employer that you intend to take paternity leave, stating when the baby is due and when you expect to take leave.	To establish eligibility for paternity leave and for paternity pay.
	Mothers: Ask your doctor or your midwife for a maternity certificate (form MAT B1; in Northern Ireland, form MB1).	The maternity certificate must be given to your employer to confirm your right to maternity leave and pay.
11 weeks before your baby is due	This is the earliest date that you are allowed to finish work and start receiving SMP or MA.	You are entitled to claim your SMP or MA once you have stopped work.
After the birth to six weeks	You have to register the birth by the time your baby is aged six weeks (three weeks, in Scotland). Start to claim child benefit.	To get a birth certificate, and to be able to start claiming child benefit. After three months, child benefit won't be backdated.
28 days before returning to work	Let your employer know in writing the actual date that you intend to return to work. This also applies if you want to return before your maternity leave is due to end.	Again, writing to your employer with your return date protects your right to return to work.

Healthcare professionals

You'll be looked after by a series of professionals.

General practitioner (GP)

If you're not registered with a doctor (GP), sign up with one as soon as you find out you're pregnant. She'll confirm your pregnancy, if needed, and refer you to the hospital.

Midwife

The midwife is responsible for your antenatal care. She'll be with you during labour and delivery, and she'll monitor you and the baby for about two weeks after the birth.

Health visitor

A health visitor is a nurse with specific training in childcare. She advises on your baby's health and development and arranges any further help. She'll visit you at home about ten days after the birth to answer any questions you have and examine the baby. She is also available on the telephone or at the clinic if you need additional help.

Health benefits

During pregnancy and for the first year you will be eligible for health benefits, – more if you are on a low income:

✳ All women are entitled to free NHS dental care and free prescriptions while they are pregnant and for a year after the baby is born.

✳ If you are on a low income, you may be entitled to free eye tests, vouchers towards spectacles, assistance with travel to your hospital, as well as milk tokens and vitamins. Contact your Social Security Office for details.

Health information

Your baby's health will be closely monitored so that any problems can be picked up as early as possible. A record of your pregnancy, labour, and delivery is kept as well as anything from your medical history that could affect your child. Once the baby is registered, you will be given an NHS form to fill in so that you can register your baby with your doctor (see left). Details of your baby's growth and development are recorded and updated at the regular checks (see p.155).

To protect your baby from certain illnesses, you will be advised to take her for a series of immunizations. If you are anxious about the possible side effects, talk to your GP and health visitor about your concerns. The risk of complications is extremely small; the risk of harmful effects from the diseases themselves is far more serious. Your baby will not be immunized she has a fever. If she has had side effects from a previous vaccination, depending on the severity, your GP may delay or stop immunizations.

✳ First immunizations

Age due	Vaccination	How given	Possible side effects
Two months	✳ Pneumococcal infection	✳ One injection	✳ Redness and swelling at injection site, mild fever; irritability, headache
	✳ Diphtheria, tetanus, pertussis (whooping cough), polio, and Hib	✳ One injection	✳ A raised temperature; sickness and/or diarrhoea, a small lump at site that will disappear
Three months	✳ Meningitis C	✳ One injection	✳ As for peumococcus
	✳ Diphtheria, tetanus, pertussis (whooping cough), polio, and Hib	✳ One injection	✳ As for diphtheria etc., above
Four months	✳ Meningitis C	✳ One injection	✳ As above
	✳ Diphtheria, tetanus, pertussis (whooping cough), polio, and Hib	✳ One injection	✳ As for diphtheria etc., above
	✳ Pneumoccocal infection	✳ One injection	✳ As above
Around 12 months	✳ Hib	✳ One injection	✳ As above
	✳ Pneumococcal infection	✳ One injection	✳ As above
Around 13 months	✳ MMR (measles, mumps, rubella)	✳ One injection	✳ Fever; rash; slight risk of high fever and convulsions

Useful addresses

Labour and birth support

The Active Birth Centre
25 Bickerton Road
London N19 5JT
020 7281 6760
www.activebirthcentre.com

Independent Midwives Association
PO Box 539
Abingdon
OX14 9DF
08454 4600 105
www.independentmidwives.org.uk

National Childbirth Trust (NCT)
Alexandra House, Oldham Terrace
Acton, London W3 6NH
0870 770 3238
www.nctpregnancyand
babycare.com

Support for you as parents

Association of Breastfeeding Mothers
PO Box 207
Bridgwater, Somerset TA6 7YT
08444 122 949
www.abm.me.uk

Association for Postnatal Illness
145 Dawes Road
Fulham, London SW6 7EB
020 7386 0868
www.apni.org

BLISS
9 Holyrood Street,
London Bridge,
London SE1 2EL
020 7378 1122
www.bliss.org.uk

Cry-sis
BM Cry-sis
London WC1N 3XX
08451 228 669 (helpline)
www.cry-sis.org.uk

Gingerbread/One Parent Families
255 Kentish Town Road
London NW5 2LX
020 7428 5400
www.gingerbread.org.uk
Help and advice for one-parent families.

La Leche League (Great Britain)
PO Box 29, West Bridgford
Nottingham NG2 7NP
0845 456 1855
www.laleche.org.uk

Maternity Alliance
Third Floor West
2–6 Northburgh Street
London EC1V 0AY
020 8490 7638
www.maternityalliance.org.uk

Association for Improvements in the Maternity Services (AIMS)
5 Ann's Court, Grove Road
Surbiton, Surrey KT6 4BE
0870 765 1433 (helpline)
www.aims.org.uk

Meet A Mum Association (MAMA)
7 Southcourt Road, Linslade
Leighton Buzzard, Beds LU7 2QF
0845 120 6162
www.mama.co.uk

National Childminding Association
Royal Court,
81 Tweedy Road,
Bromley, Kent BR1 1TG
0845 880 0044
www.ncma.org.uk

Parentline Plus
520 Highgate Studios
53–79 Highgate Road
London NW5 1TL
020 7284 5500
www.parentlineplus.org.uk

Twins and Multiple Births Association
2 The Willows, Gardner Road
Guildford, Surrey GU1 4PG
01483 304 442
www.tamba.org.uk

First aid training

British Red Cross
44 Moorfields
London EC2Y 9AL
0844 871 11 11
www.redcross.org.uk

St. Andrew's Ambulance Association
Milton Street
Glasgow G4 0HR
0141 332 4031
www.firstaid.org.uk

St John Ambulance
27 St John's Lane
London EC1M 4BU
08700 10 40 65
www.sja.org.uk

Special needs

Association for Spina Bifida and Hydrocephalus (ASBAH)
42 Park Road
Peterborough PE1 2UQ
01733 555988
www.asbah.org

Contact a Family
209–211 City Road
London EC1V 1JN
020 7608 8700
www.cafamily.org.uk
For parents of children with special needs.

Cystic Fibrosis Trust
11 London Road
Bromley, Kent BR1 1BY
020 8464 7211
www.cftrust.org.uk

Down's Syndrome Association
Langdon Down Centre
2a Langdon Park
Teddington TW11 9PS
0845 230 0372
www.downs-syndrome.org.uk

MENCAP
123 Golden Lane
London EC1Y 0RT
020 7454 0454
www.mencap.org.uk

National Children's Bureau
8 Wakley Street
London EC1V 7QE
020 7843 6000
www.ncb.org.uk

National Deaf Children's Society
15 Dufferin Street
London EC1Y 8UR
020 7490 8656
www.ndcs.org.uk

Royal National Institute for the Blind (RNIB)
105 Judd Street
London WC1H 9NE
020 7388 1266
www.rnib.org.uk

Scope
PO Box 833
Milton Keynes MK12 5NY
020 7619 7100
www.scope.org.uk

Index

Acknowledgments

Medical consultant for this edition:
Dr Tim Wickham BSc (hons) MBBS MRCP FRCPCH

Picture library: Romaine Werblow
Proofreader: Alyson Silverwood

The publisher would like to thank the following for their kind
permission to reproduce their photographs:
(Key: a-above; b-below/bottom; c-centre; l-left; r-right; t-top)

Alamy Images: Bubbles Photolibrary 66; Janine Wiedel Photolibrary 150;
plainpicture 60; Peter Usbeck 63; Corbis: LWA-Dann Tardif 13, 19, 23, 33tr,
39tr, 45tr, 47, 49, 51tr, 57, 59tr, 73, 82tl, 95tr, 101tr, 129, 135, 137, 141, 149, 171,
175tr; Larry Williams 46; Carolyn Djanogly: 6; DK Images: Courtesy of
Simon Brown 112; Getty Images: George Doyle 16-17; Studio Tec / ailead

126-127; Mediscan: SHOUT 28; Mother & Baby Picture Library: 48, 52, 138,
146, 153; Photolibrary: Banana Stock 103; Brand X Pictures 128b; Stockbyte
59bl; Larry Williams 41; Science Photo Library: 32; Samuel Ashfield 29;
BSIP, Laurent 44; Ian Hooton 26

All other images © Dorling Kindersley
For further information see: www.dkimages.com

The publishers would also like to thank the following for modelling
in this new edition: Nicola Munn, Joe and Leo Hayward, Chloe and
Oscar Dunne, Mandeep and Ethan Kalsi, Louise and Ruth Izod,
Dharminder and Biba Kang, Chloe Webb, Nicole Bheenick-Coe and
Lily Coe, Sheela Lomax and Lorenzo Lapinid, Carrieann Austin and
Emily Collis, Daniel and Matilda Young, Roisin Donaghy, Elisa and Jolie
Margolin, Charlotte Seymour.